THE FORTIETH

A RECORD OF THE 40TH BATTALION, A.L.F.

BY

F. C. GREEN

WITH A FOREWORD BY SIR JOHN MONASH

The Naval & Military Press Ltd

Reproduced by kind permission of the Central Library,
Royal Military Academy, Sandhurst

Published by
The Naval & Military Press Ltd
Unit 10, Ridgewood Industrial Park,
Uckfield, East Sussex,
TN22 5QE England
Tel: +44 (0) 1825 749494
Fax: +44 (0) 1825 765701
www.naval-military-press.com
www.military-genealogy.com
© The Naval & Military Press Ltd 2007

In reprinting in facsimile from the original, any imperfections are inevitably reproduced and the quality may fall short of modern type and cartographic standards.

Printed and bound by Antony Rowe Ltd, Eastbourne

Contents.

			Page
Foreword			v
Chapter	I.	Formation—Training in Tasmania—Transported to England—Departure for France..	1
Chapter	II.	Disembarkation in France—A "Rest" Camp and Troop Train—Billets—Issue of Respirators—Armentières—In the Trenches..	6
Chapter	III.	Holding the Line for the First Time..	10
Chapter	IV.	An Infantryman's Day in the Front Line..	14
Chapter	V.	In the Line Again—A Quiet Day on the Western Front—An Enemy Raid on B Company—Attempt to Raid the Enemy Unsuccessful	21
Chapter	VI.	From Houplines to the Trenches at Bois Grenier—The 10th Brigade Raid at Houplines	27
Chapter	VII.	The Enemy Raid at Cowgate—Trench Warfare at Bois Grenier—Our Unsuccessful Raid—Out for a Rest	33
Chapter	VIII.	Resting and Training at Tatinghem—The New Offensive Tactics—Back to Houplines—The Enemy Tries to Raid Again at Hobbs' Farm	39
Chapter	IX.	Ploegsteert Wood—Enemy Raid at St. Yves—Our First Big Operation in Sight	44
Chapter	X.	In the Line at St. Yves—Great Activity on Both Sides—The Tunnels—Working Parties—Our Raid near the Douve River—Heavy Gas Shelling at Romarin—The Day Before the Attack at Messines	48
Chapter	XI.	The Plan of Attack at Messines—The Approach March—The Battle	56
Chapter	XII.	Working Parties—On the Messines Ridge in Support—Back to Reserve at Becourt—The New Plan of Attack—On the Road to Ypres	66
Chapter	XIII.	The Attack on the 4th October, 1917, in the 3rd Battle of Ypres	73
Chapter	XIV.	Phase 4 of the 3rd Battle of Ypres a Failure—The Attack on the 12th October	84
Chapter	XV.	Good-bye to Ypres—Back to Becourt—Musketry Competition—In the Trenches Again near Messines—The End of the First Year in France	94
Chapter	XVI.	Activity on Both Sides at Warneton—The 40th Battalion Raid at Warneton	100
Chapter	XVII.	In the Line at Warneton—Christmas Day at Neuve Eglise—Back in the Line Again—The "Chinese" Attack at Warneton—Attempted Enemy Raid Broken by a Patrol—Back to Reserve near Lumbres—Sports and Training—The German Offensive Opens..	104
Chapter	XVIII.	To the Somme—The British Retreat—Into the Gap between the Ancre and the Somme—The Attack by the 40th Battalion on the 28th March, 1918—Enemy Attacks and is Beaten Off—Into Reserve at Ribemont	113
Chapter	XIX.	More Enemy Attacks on the Divisional Front—Probability of a Further Enemy Offensive—"B" Echelon Established—Patrol Encounters—Our Successful Raid on Enemy Post on the Ancre—Back to Reserve at Frechencourt—To Blangy-Tronville—The Divisional Platoon Competition	124

			Page
Chapter	XX.	L'Abbé Wood—Messenger Dogs Tried at Villers-Bretonneux—The Trenches at Villers-Bretonneux—Our Raid on an Enemy Post—Back to Reserve at Querrieu—Sports and Races—Into the Trenches at Hamel..	138
Chapter	XXI.	The Battle of Amiens of 8th August, 1918—The 10th Brigade Reverse at La Flaque—The 10th Brigade Successful Attack at Proyart—Sergeant Statton Wins the V.C...	148
Chapter	XXII.	At Reginald Wood—Capture of Bray by the 40th Battalion—A Further Advance Towards Cappy and Suzanne	158
Chapter	XXIII.	A Further Advance towards Clery—Clery Captured by B Company	168
Chapter	XXIV.	D Company Attack at Clery Copse	173
Chapter	XXV.	A Further Attack East of Clery—Exciting Events on the Mt. St. Quentin-Bouchavesnes Road—Back to Reserve at Hem	178
Chapter	XXVI.	The Advance from Roisel towards Hesbecourt—Resting at Red Wood—Failure of the Enemy's Night Bombing	186
Chapter	XXVII.	The Attack on the Hindenburg Line, 29th September, 1918	190
Chapter XXVIII.		Conclusion	201
Epilogue		.. ..	204

Appendix A. Casualties and Other Statistics 212
Appendix B. Decorations and Other Honours 216
Appendix C. Roll of the 40th Battalion 219
Index to Names of Persons and Places mentioned in the Narrative 245

List of Maps.

No. 1. Houplines Sector, Armentières.
„ 2. Bois Grenier Sector, Armentières.
„ 3. 10th Brigade Raid, Pont Ballot, 28th January, 1917.
„ 4. 10th Brigade Objective, Battle of Messines, 6th June, 1917.
„ 5. Battle of Broodseinde Ridge, 4th October, 1917.
„ 6. Attack at Passchendaele, 12th October, 1917.
„ 7. The Somme, Morlancourt, 28th March, 1918.
„ 8. 10th Brigade Attack at Proyart, 12th August, 1918.
„ 9. Bray-sur-Somme, 22nd August, 1918.
„ 10. Clery Copse and Bouchavesnes Road (Battle of Mont S. Quentin).
„ 10A. Trenches at Clery Copse, 30th August, 1918.
„ 11. Hindenburg Line (Bony-Macquincourt), 29th September-1st October, 1918.

FOREWORD.

THE Australian soldier has won for himself a place in history. His reputation rests not merely upon his individual qualities of bravery in battle, steadfastness of purpose, resourcefulness, and adaptability, but also upon his remarkable capacity for well-ordered collective action, for " team work " in the broadest sense. This quality, born in the conditions under which he grew to manhood in his home land, was nurtured and fostered by the environment of war, and by the creation in the field of the collective spirit. The battalion was the schoolroom; its spirit the teacher and guide. Upon the fine comradeship and the sense of unity which were thus fashioned in the Australian battalions, the whole efficiency of the Australian Imperial Force did, in the last resort, truly depend. The battalion became much more than a tactical unit, a mere implement for achievement in the hands of the higher commanders. It was a psychological entity, a moral force, a sentient concourse, knit together by common impulses, common strivings, and common ideals. It became the physical embodiment of that fundamental principle of the art of war, that moral cohesion and spiritual solidarity which constitute the essential ingredients differentiating an efficient fighting force from a mere body of armed men.

Thus it was that the battalion became the nursery of the A.I.F. tradition, and it is because of this that the individual story of every A.I.F. battalion forms an indispensable part of the history of the A.I.F. Each one of the sixty infantry battalions, in spite of the very striking uniformity in their standards and achievements, had its separate individuality, its distinct characteristics. It is due to each one of them that its story should be recorded, from the time of its formation until the last shot was fired.

This book tells the tale of the Fortieth Battalion. It was a battalion which was in every way an embodiment of the best that was in the A.I.F. It had a notable career and a proud record of achievement. The fact that it was composed wholly of the men of a small island State, Tasmania, gave it a special stimulus to the highest emulation of all other units. In no other unit were the pride of origin, and the sense of responsibility to the people whom it represented, stronger than in the Fortieth. It enjoyed the almost unique experience of retaining the same commander and many of the same officers throughout its whole career. This gave to the Battalion the inestimable benefit of the continuity of a single leadership. And that leadership was of a kind which proved itself worthy of a quite special remembrance. In Lieut.-Col. J. E. C. Lord the Battalion found an officer of ripe experience, with a full knowledge of men, and one having a broad and sympathetic outlook, a man capable of setting and of enforcing a high example, and of forming and guiding the soul of his command. As a unit commander he enjoyed the implicit confidence of his Brigadier and Divisional General. I became accustomed never to need to look beyond him to those under his command. It was enough that he answered for his Battalion in all things, for their well-being, for their discipline, and for their readiness for and efficiency in battle. To set him the task was to find it as good as done; and it was always well done. The performance of the Battalion at the Battle of Messines, its first adventure on a full scale, set upon it the seal of efficiency which was its hall-mark throughout all the hard fighting that followed until the end.

In this uniformly high level of performance, and in the making of a record which was untarnished by any failure or shortcoming, this notable commander was supported by a devoted band of officers. Their names and their deeds are enshrined in these pages. Some of them gained a renown far beyond the limits of the Battalion. To know that an officer detached for other duties belonged to the Fortieth was always a guarantee of competence and efficiency. There is, however, one officer of this renowned unit of which next to nothing has been said in this book, and that because he is himself the chronicler. But the name of Frank Green became widely known throughout the A.I.F. for his soldierly qualities, his outstanding personality, and his capacity to do well everything that was worth doing. As Company Officer, and later as Adjutant, he laboured strenuously and sacrificed himself unflinchingly.

In spite of physical strain, the result of repeated serious exposures to shell-fire, from which he more than once escaped destruction by the narrowest of chances, Captain Green forewent the well-earned opportunity of an early return home after the Armistice, in order to yield to the unanimous wish of the whole Battalion that he should become its historian, thus giving until the end the fullest and most devoted service to his comrades in arms.

How well he has done his task, and how fully the glorious memory of the Fortieth Battalion has been perpetuated by his labours, this book bears witness.

JOHN MONASH,
6th June, 1922.
Lieut.-General

Explanatory and Apologetic.

THE material for this record was collected by Captain Green during the winter of 1918-19 in France, and the narrative nearly completed by the time he returned with the last quota of the Battalion in September, 1919. Arrangements were at once made for publication, but pressure of other work, combined with unexpected difficulties in connection with maps and the appendices, made progress very slow. When Captain Green left Tasmania in May, 1921, the drawing of the maps was still unfinished, and in the absence of anyone with leisure and ability to look after the work, delays became more protracted, and the book as it now at length appears is without the benefit of his final revision.

The sources of the work are, in the first place, the Battalion diaries and orders and other records, and Captain Green's own intimate and first-hand knowledge of nearly all the activities of the Battalion. But it soon appeared that the formal records, though on the whole carefully kept, were inadequate, and in many cases misleading. In the more confused and difficult operations it was only by collecting and comparing the individual narratives of those who had taken part in them that the story could be made clear. Luckily the Battalion was still together in the winter of 1918-19, and a sufficient number of survivors of all important operations was at hand. It was often by informal talks with half a dozen N.C.O.'s and men of one company or another, each contributing his bit and correcting the others, that the actual course of events was made plain. The Somme fighting of 1918 presented particular difficulties of detail, and a re-examination of the ground under peace conditions was desirable. This Captain Green was able to make early in 1918 from Amiens right up to the Hindenburg Line, accompanied by other officers and particularly by Lieut. B. J. Jackson, whose quick eye for country and tenacious memory for detail made his assistance of particular value.

There are no doubt here and there in the following narrative signs of need for more careful revision, for which indulgence may be asked under the circumstances. But there is one particularly misleading sentence on page 4, relative to the training on Salisbury Plain, to which particular reference is desirable. "Of all that we required to know for the trench-warfare which was before us, we learned practically nothing." This is partly contradicted by other sentences in the same paragraph, and is, in fact, ridiculously untrue. The only basis for it was the fact that we did not get instruction in the minor tactics of trench fighting as we evolved them for ourselves after three or four months' experience. Such instruction it was probably impossible to provide, and would have been equally impossible for us to profit by, except in actual trenches in the presence of the enemy.

Looking back at it coolly, we know that our training in England was good, and planned with particular care and thoroughness. But the sentence quoted above does to some extent—in an exaggerated way—indicate our feelings at the time. We were sick of training. We felt we were very late in getting to the war, and the other Australian divisions were in France and having rather a bad time. Under the circumstances a course of training planned by Julius Caesar and supervised in person by Joshua, Attila, Napoleon, and Jack Dempsey would have failed to touch our enthusiasm. We wanted to be in France.

Chapter I.

Formation—Training in Tasmania—Transported to England—Departure for France.

EFORE writing the history of the Battalion in France, it is necessary to give briefly the chief events in the story of the unit before its baptism of fire. To the reader this may appear of little interest, but it can be regarded as the prologue of the play. Moreover, to those of us who watched the Battalion grow from one thousand farmers, clerks, timber-workers, miners, &c., to an equal number of highly-trained soldiers who composed an efficient fighting force, it is doubly interesting.

In those days of preparation and training we learned the trade of war as well as it could be learned in a training camp, but more important still we learned to understand each other. It dawned on most of us that every man was distinguished by something more than a regimental number—a personality; and we knew those personalities in Tasmania, and we knew them in France. It was something like watching boys grow to manhood, and watching most of them make good, and just a few go wrong; and we watched some of them who seemed unfitted for that awful game come into their own. The writer remembers one man at Claremont Camp who dropped his rifle hopelessly, and his voice broke as he admitted that he would never be able to "slope arms." The fact that rifle exercises would always be beyond him was obvious, and he explained bitterly that he had earned his living with an axe since he was fourteen years old, and would never be able to use any other weapon. But one dirty night at La Flaque in August, 1918, this man lead his ammunition mule up a road where it seemed impossible to live, and he went on because his job was to help keep up the ammunition supply, and he would rather die than fail to get the ammunition where it would be wanted.

The 40th Battalion was Tasmania's contribution to the 3rd Division, which was formed in Australia early in 1916, while the 4th and 5th Divisions were being formed in Egypt. At first Tasmania was asked to provide two companies and Battalion Headquarters of the 40th Battalion, while Geelong district in Victoria was to find the two remaining companies. Lieut.-Colonel J. E. C. Lord was appointed to command the Battalion.

In Tasmania it was felt that it would be an encouragement to recruiting if the State were allowed to find a complete Battalion, and so representations were made by the District Commandant and Parliamentary representatives that Tasmania could find a thousand men, and would gladly do so for the honour of the island State. As a result, notification was received on the 18th March, 1916, that the 40th Battalion would be a Tasmanian unit, and by the 1st April, not only was the establishment complete, but the first reinforcement had also been raised.

The senior officers of the Battalion were mostly drawn from the militia, and the junior officers were generally men who had held commissions, but had enlisted in the ranks, and after a series of schools of training had been commissioned in the A.I.F. The rank and file were from every district in the State. Professional men, tradesmen and labourers from the larger towns, farmers and timber-workers from the North-West Coast, miners and farmers from the North-East, fruit-growers from the Huon, and miners from the West. Nearly every village in Tasmania was represented. The material was there, and all that was now required was training, and that commenced on entering camp.

It was laid down that every man before leaving Australia had to complete three months of systematic training, and this was carried out at Claremont with more thoroughness and hard work than enthusiasm. At that time the Lewis gun had not reached Australia, and the only bombs available were made from jam-tins and gelignite, so that without the two most interesting activities of the infantryman, the chief items on the syllabus were musketry and drill, and always more drill.

The formation of the Battalion and its preparation for departure were followed with great interest throughout the State. The whole unit was invited to Hobart and welcomed, and Launceston made us the guests of the town for two days, during which time the warm-hearted hospitality of that place was impressed on us in a manner not easily forgotten. All this was very gratifying, but there was a general suspicion that as we were hardly soldiers yet, we were being treated too enthusiastically, and this was rather resented by Tasmanians in France who read of our doings in the Tasmanian papers. We were also under a cloud from the circumstance that in spite of our protests and consciousness of the absurdity of it, we were christened "The Fighting Fortieth" before leaving Tasmania. His Majesty's Fortieth Regiment which had garrisoned Van Dieman's Land between the years 1824 and 1830 had been known as "The Fighting Fortieth," and the historical coincidence, with the lure of alliteration, was too much for the good sense of our countrymen. The title, however, was effectively left behind when we sailed from Hobart, and most of us never heard it again until we returned. Somewhat later we were further guilty (in common with all of the 3rd Division) of being kept training on Salisbury Plains when there was hard fighting on the Somme. This perhaps showed some lack of imagination on the part of our critics; but then the Somme fighting in 1916 was not exactly a training in sympathetic imagination. In the end, however—by 1918, let us say—we felt that these various sins had substantially been forgiven us.

On the 1st July, 1916, the Battalion, with its first reinforcement, marched out of Claremont Camp and entrained for Hobart, where we embarked on the transport "Berrima." Next morning, shortly after daylight, we slipped away from the Ocean Pier, and within a few hours had seen the last of Tasmania for some time. We reached Melbourne on the morning of the 4th July, where a reinforcement of the 29th Battalion and an artillery reinforcement embarked, and we left again the same day.

After getting outside Port Phillip we met with very rough weather, and for the first few days most of us were suffering from sea-sickness. As soon as we had got our sea-legs a regular syllabus of physical training, lectures, and other instruction possible on board ship, was begun. On the 27th July, after a very rough passage, we reached Cape Town, and found there several other transports carrying Australian and New Zealand troops.

We had two days ashore, and on the 1st August left Table Bay in company with the transports "Tahiti" and "Manganui," both carrying New Zealanders. We were convoyed up the African coast by H.M.S. "Kent," and on the 13th August we reached Dakar, the capital of Senegal, after a fine passage from Cape Town. We were not allowed ashore here, and on the following day left Dakar in company with the other two transports, and were convoyed by the auxiliary cruiser "Ophir."

After leaving Dakar the danger of enemy submarines increased, and in the Bay of Biscay we were picked up and convoyed by three destroyers to Plymouth, which was reached on the 22nd August. We disembarked the same evening, and after travelling by train all night reached Lark Hill, on Salisbury Plain, the following day.

The 40th Battalion was the last unit of the 3rd Division to reach England, and in consequence we were not so far advanced in training as the other battalions, some of whom had already been in England for several weeks.

We had hardly settled in camp when a thunderbolt fell in the shape of an order to detach 200 of our number to reinforce battalions that had recently had severe losses on the Somme; and the rumour ran that the whole Battalion was to be cut up for reinforcements. The two hundred going was a fact, and a very unpleasant one. Men were divided in mind between desire to get to the front at once and unwillingness to leave their mates, and the task of selection was an unenviable one. In the end most of these men, after various transfers from one camp to another, came back to us, but a considerable number we did not see again. Before we left Lark Hill we were given in compensation a batch of South Australians. These were not only a good lot in themselves, but they took the transfer in good spirit, and became as staunch to the Battalion as any original members of it.

We had worked hard in Tasmania, but soon realised that this work was child's play compared with the training of Salisbury Plain. From 6 a.m. to 5 p.m. daily we toiled, the only intervals being for meals. It was mostly hard work—musketry, Lewis gun work, bombing, drill, and route-marching—and everything done with the irksome discipline of a regular regiment. However, it had two advantages; firstly, it made us fit, and, secondly, it was an antidote for ever afterwards to any desire to adopt the Army as a profession.

As a practical preparation for War we did not think a great deal of our English training. Specialist schools, to which a number of officers and N.C.O.'s were sent, were generally good, and all the training we got in Lewis gun, bombs, and gas was useful and necessary, though inadequate. But such training occupied only a small part of the time, and there was not much profit in the remainder. Of all that we required to know for the trench-warfare which was before us, we learned practically nothing. One thing, however, we learned effectively—the great art of making military returns. For a time we were nearly snowed under by the avalanche of "States" and "Returns," and consequential "Please explains," and there was a prospect of numerous premature wrecks with snow-white hair and tottering legs being shipped back to Australia. Then we grasped the vital principles of the art. A return must be consistent with itself and other returns, and must be sent in to time. Within those limits, fill in details with a discreet imagination, and all will be well. This may be called one of the bed-rock principles of practical warfare.

With November came the news that the time for our departure for France was at hand, and never were men more eager to get to the front, not from any desire to taste the alleged sweets and glory of fighting, but to get away from training and all the many things so dear to the professional soldier of the Imperial Army pattern, and so galling to citizen soldiers born with the smell of the bush, and not the odour of the barrack-square, in their nostrils.

On the 23rd November we entrained and travelled to Southampton, where we embarked on a cross-channel transport the same evening. After a very rough trip across the English Channel, during which quite 95 per cent. of the Battalion were sea-sick, we reached Le Havre on the following morning.

Chapter II.

Disembarkation in France—A "Rest" Camp and Troop Train — Billets — Issue of Respirators — Armentieres — In the Trenches.

THE 40th Battalion disembarked at Havre on the morning of the 24th November, 1916, and marched to a camp about 7 miles from the town. This march was one of the worst in the history of the battalion. In addition to full marching order, we carried two blankets each, everybody had been seasick all night, and we were without food, whilst a number of men had just been released from the mumps hospital in time to embark with the battalion. Seven miles was a comparatively short distance, but the conditions made it an unpleasant experience. When we reached the camp (which was called a "rest camp"), it was with the idea on our part that it was to have a rest, but that idea was soon dispelled. The camp was of bare canvas, and we laid down in the dark, as there were no lights available. At 4 a.m. we were roused out in the dark in order to entrain at 7 a.m. We left the camp at 5 a.m., after a hasty meal, and reached the railway-station at Havre at 7 a.m. We stood in the rain at the station till 9 a.m., and then Battalion Headquarters, A, C, and D Companies entrained, and the train refused to move till 11 a.m. B Company came on by a later train. It always seemed part of an imperishable tradition in the army to arrive at a place three hours before it was necessary to arrive, and always to begin to move in the dark. No doubt there were excellent reasons sometimes, but on this occasion the reason was obscure.

A troop train in France was always slow and dreary, but this journey was one of the slowest on record, and took 41 hours from Havre to Bailleul. We had no knowledge of our destination, and when we were expected to arrive there. It might have been Marseilles or Verdun, for all we knew. The only stop notified was St. Omer, but the train often stopped, and nobody but the enginedriver knew when it would go on again, and perhaps he was not too sure about it. However, it stopped at St. Omer, and we got out with our dixies to get a meal which the quartermaster was arranging, but just as we were about to eat the train moved on, and we had to make a rush to catch it—we did not get the meal. We reached Bailleul at 4 a.m. on the 27th November, and outside the railway-station the battalion "embussed" (an apparently new war word, meaning to get aboard motor 'busses), and reached the village of Merris at 6 a.m., shortly after daylight. Here we were met by a guide, a Belgian interpreter, who was to guide us to our billets. He led us to our billets, and we started to make ourselves as comfortable as possible, and arrange for a long-delayed meal, when the interpreter came back and said he had made a mistake, and that we were in a billeting area belonging to some other unit. So we had to pack up again and move to another part of the village. That interpreter never in his life reached such a height of general unpopularity before.

At this village the battalion lived in billets in France for the first time. It was a novelty which soon wore off. Billets in France were much alike, and seldom varied in comfort or discomfort, but some were worse than others. Rural France is about half a century behind Australia in ordinary ideas of sanitation, for the smell of a Flanders farm would make the hair of an inspector under the Public Health Act stand on end in horror, even if he met it "outback" in Australia. The outstanding feature of every farm is the midden or cesspool at the front door, and the outstanding smell of every farm is the smell from the midden. The Sydney "Bulletin" once held a competition to decide what smell on earth hit the nose with most violence. The aboriginality column was full of entries for weeks, and the prize was finally awarded, after much argument, to a whale on which the inquest had been delayed for some time. But this was before the A.I.F. went to France, or the result of the competition would have been different, and there would not have been so much argument on the subject—there would have been no argument at all, but a unanimous resolution. The midden, which is always at the front door, is a sort of cesspool filled with stable refuse and all house refuse, and any animal that dies on the premises. Periodically it is cleaned out, and the contents used for manure, and then another collection is begun. It is never allowed to remain dormant, as there is always an old white sow prospecting in it, and stirring up the smell. Owing to the scarcity and high price of wood, the walls of buildings are generally made of a mixture of mud and straw, with a roof of thatch or tiles. These farm buildings were generally the billets, and, as stated before, some were worse than others.

At the billets we were introduced to coffee, as the chief beverage, for the first time. In every kitchen the coffee-pot stood on the stove, and for ten centimes (one penny) a thirsty soldier could always get a bowl full. At the time the inhabitants seemed very poor, but that opinion was chiefly arrived at by seeing the women working in the fields from the half light of dawn until dark. Afterwards we came to the conclusion that they were not really poor, but thrifty. In some dairying districts of Australia we have the "child slaves of the cow," and in Flanders there are the women slaves of the fields.

Whilst in Merris it was realised that the war was very close indeed—the front line was about 10 miles away, and artillery was heard all day and night. By day the chief attraction was watching the white puffs of shrapnel bursting round an occasional enemy aeroplane, and by night the Verey lights and other flares flickering in the sky were subjects of absorbing interest.

Until that time the use of protectors against poisonous gas was confined to a comparatively primitive arrangement called a P.H. helmet, which was a heavy flannel mask dipped in some chemical, and fitted up with a mouthpiece and eyepieces. On the 29th November an improved protector, called the small box respirator, was issued to all ranks and the method of using it explained. Its construction is so familiar that no description of it is necessary. Small box respirators were always used from that time, and in gas-saturated atmosphere were worn with perfect confidence. In addition to the small box respirator, the P.H. helmet was carried as a standby for nearly a year afterwards, in case of the small box respirator being perforated by a bullet or a piece of shrapnel at a critical moment.

On the 2nd December the battalion left Merris at 9 a.m., and marched about 14 miles to Armentieres, arriving there at 4 p.m. Before the war Armentieres was a big industrial town with a population of 36,000. In December, 1916, the population was about 6000 civilians. It was then, except for the suburb of Houplines, little damaged by shellfire, but individual buildings, such as the Town Hall, the churches, and large public buildings, had been wrecked. The hands of the clock on the Town Hall tower had stopped at half-past eleven, and the square in front of the Town Hall was renamed "Half-Past Eleven Square" by the troops. There was hardly a British unit on the Western front at that time which did not know that square. It was almost as familiar as the falling Virgin with the outstretched Babe on the church at Albert.

Several factories were still working at Armentieres, and estaminets and small shops were still open. The estaminets did good trade in indifferent beer and "eggs and chips," and the shops dealt mostly in souvenirs of the place, manufactured in Birmingham or the U.S.A. In December, 1917, the battalion was again near Armentieres, and it was then a dead town, and no civilians left except the dead. But when the 40th Battalion first arrived the trenches in front of Armentieres were comparatively quiet, and the town was referred to affectionately as a "home."

The 3rd Division had taken over the trenches immediately south of the River Lys, and of the 10th Brigade the 37th and 38th Battalions had gone into the front line, the 39th Battalion was in support, and the 40th Battalion in reserve in billets in factory buildings in Armentieres. From the 3rd to the 9th December the time was taken up with working parties, chiefly carrying ammunition and engineering material to the trenches. On the night of the 5th December practically the whole battalion was engaged in carrying gas cylinders into the front-line trenches. This was in the days before it was decided that the most effective means of throwing poison gas at the enemy was to fire it from artillery in a shell. These gas cylinders were very heavy and awkward to handle. Each cylinder weighed about 200 lb., and was fastened to a 6-foot pole, one man carrying at each end of the pole, and a relief of two men behind each cylinder; that is, it took four men to each cylinder.

It was always agreed that the worst kind of working party was carrying gas cylinders to the front line, for the weight and awkwardness of the cylinder, carried in the dark along a slippery duck walk in a narrow trench, or through mud and water in places, made it an exhausting job. These cylinders were placed in the parapet by the Royal Engineers, and remained there until the wind was favourable. When the gas had been released working parties had to go up and carry the cylinders out. It was on a gas cylinder job that the 40th Battalion first went into the trenches, and beyond a few machine-gun bursts sweeping the parapet, and an odd trench mortar shell bursting, the experience of being in the trenches did not seem very exciting at the time.

For the next few days the battalion was employed in carrying material and ammunition to the forward dumps, and officers spent most of the time reconnoitring the trenches held by the 38th Battalion, which the 40th Battalion would have to take over in a few days.

Chapter III.
Holding the Line for the First Time.

ON the afternoon of the 9th December, 1916, the battalion took over front-line trenches for the first time. The Quartermaster (Lieut. T. J. Horler) and his staff remained in Armentieres, and the Transport Officer (Lieut. B. T. Sadler) went to transport lines at L'Epinette, about 1½ miles west of Armentieres. A percentage of specialists (*i.e.*, Lewis gunners, bombers, scouts, signallers, and runners) had gone into the line 24 hours earlier, so as to make themselves familiar with their duties during the daylight, before the actual relief. The first few reliefs were made during daylight, but afterwards always by night.

The line taken over was the system of trenches immediately south of the River Lys, and directly east of the village of Houplines. The frontage was about 1500 yards, and extended from the Lys to a point about 250 yards south of a place marked on the map as Edmeads' Farm (**Map** 1). All companies were in the front line, with a proportion of each company in support and subsidiary lines. The disposition of companies from left to right was—D Company (Capt. L. F. Giblin), C Company (Capt. J. T. Tyrell), B Company (Major L. H. Payne), and A Company (Capt. J. D. W. Chisholm). The trenches on the whole were in a very bad state of repair, and the low-lying ground was responsible for several inches of mud and water everywhere in them. Long gumboots, which were a necessity, were issued to all ranks on going into the line. The sector of D Company, near the river, was very wet, and when the river rose it flooded part of the trenches, and several posts had to be temporarily evacuated until the water subsided. An example of the conditions was provided by one man, on an enemy aeroplane coming over. The trench officer ordered everybody to keep perfectly still, but he saw one man moving, and shouted a gentle reproof. The offender, who was very short in the legs, replied: "I can't help it; I'm swimming."

On the left of the battalion sector No Man's Land was about 100 yards wide, but on the right it widened to 500 yards. No Man's Land was very marshy, and this, combined with many ditches of water, made patrolling and scouting at night very unpleasant. There was generally a certain amount of sporting uncertainty about scouting. The prospect of meeting an enemy patrol, and the chance of getting in the way of a bullet or machine-gun burst made a man take an intelligent interest in the job; but here it meant crawling about in mud and water, wet through, and almost too cold to hold a rifle or revolver. These difficulties were not made easier by the fact that the enemy employed two searchlights on our front, with which he swept No Man's Land at intervals. He also had an advantage in the quality of his flares, which were always superior to ours, but he used them so lavishly that they were often quite useful to our scouts in finding their way about.

The enemy also patrolled No Man's Land, and probably knowing that new troops had moved in, tried to make the most of our inexperience by approaching our wire at night. Several parties of the enemy were dispersed by Lewis gun fire and bombs, and realising that the mastery of No Man's Land was a matter for dispute, our patrols were made more numerous and active, with the result that after a few nights the enemy did not venture far from his own wire. From that time the battalion adopted effectively the A.I.F. tradition that No Man's Land was Our Land, the enemy apparently contenting himself with lying up near his own wire, in the hope of cutting off one of our patrols. This he never succeeded in doing.

The enemy sniping was found to be very persistent for a time, and several casualties occurred during the first two tours in the line from this source. Probably there were two reasons for this, the first being that we were not familiar with the dangerous spots in our sector which were overlooked from the enemy trenches, and we were inclined to linger longer than was healthy in these places. The second reason was that our snipers had not been properly organised for counter-sniping, which gave the enemy the ascendency. An officer was according detailed to organise our sniping, and this was done so effectively that the enemy seemed to lose a lot of interest in what he must have once regarded as a very pleasant pastime. Our snipers daily " bagged " a few hits, and as their efficiency increased the enemy seemed to become less proficient. In addition to this, a number of his sniping posts were located, and knocked out by artillery or trench mortars.

At this time the enemy made little use of his artillery to "strafe" our trenches, but his use of rifle grenades, " pineapples " (granatenwerfer), and minenwerfer was lavish. The damage caused by minenwerfer was considerable, and all men who were not on duty were generally employed repairing broken parapets and smashed trenches. After every " strafe " a call would be sent from the front line for a working party to come up from the support line to make the trenches passable again. There was a very favoured spot (called Hobbs' Farm), on B Company's sector, into which minenwerfer fell intermittently. Every day and night the enemy gave it special attention, and made it a most unhealthy spot. The farm was almost in the front line, and had been reduced to a heap of bricks and stones, and every "minnie" that fell into it caused a shower of bricks for the next few moments. One man, after watching Hobbs' Farm going up for an hour or so, ventured the remark that "Old Hobbs will be wild if he comes back and sees this."

One feature of trench warfare was the superiority of the enemy wire to ours. Exactly why it was always so much stronger is doubtful, but the fact remains that while our wire was very thin and patchy, and would not offer serious resistance to the enemy, the enemy wire was always black and thick, and a formidable barrier. One reason is perhaps that the enemy wiring was done by parties of Pioneer Battalions or Engineers. At Warneton we killed a number of Saxon Pioneers who were repairing the wire and front-line trenches. Our Pioneer Battalions dealt only with the communication trenches and support lines; the front line was the province of the Engineers, and they provided only advice and supervision for any work there or in No Man's Land. The Engineers appeared to have general orders not to go into No Man's Land, and in the early days of the 3rd Division they observed them with some formality, and the infantry were inclined to slight their services. Later, with experience, they learned to adapt themselves, and orders, to the circumstances, and their popularity with the infantry went up 100 per cent. But at that time all repairs on and beyond the parapet had to be done by the infantry holding the line, consequently few men could be spared for the work, which was difficult and dangerous and took a long time. Moreover, as far as the men holding the line were concerned, if the enemy wanted to attack our trenches we did not want to stop him. If the wire had presented a difficulty to the enemy, and we knew it, we would have removed it. If he wanted to raid, the feeling in the trenches was that he was quite welcome at any time to try. It would have been a welcome change to being a passive target for minenwerfer.

Every new sector that we took over was always the same as far as wiring went. We looked over our parapet and saw a broad barrier in front of the enemy, and in front of us was just a scraggy broken line of wire. We improved it because we were ordered to improve it, and for no other reason. By the time we made it something like a barrier, we were ordered to another sector, and had to begin wiring again.

Wiring was always an unpleasant job. Parties were detailed and went out with screw pickets and coils of barbed wire. They worked among the muddy shell-holes till a flare illuminated them, and if the enemy did not then see them and drive them in with machine-gun fire, they carried on. When a flare went up everybody stood stock still, and trusted he was not observed. If the enemy did see them and opened fire they had to get down in the mud and flatten themselves in it until the fire stopped. And sometimes a stray bullet would get one of the party, and he would fall in a pathetic heap over his work.

During the whole of the time the battalion was in the trenches at Houplines the regimental transport brought the rations up to a point near the subsidiary line, from where they were taken forward by carrying parties. Food was cooked in the support and subsidiary lines, and sent forward to the front line. The trench rats were always persistent in getting at the rations. The wet trenches had driven them from below ground, and they foraged among the trenches and dugouts in great numbers. A few cats lived about the ruined buildings and trenches, but the job was too big for them, and a strict neutrality seemed to be observed between them and the rats. A biscuit left in a haversack meant a ruined haversack, as the rats gnawed through it, or if a man went to sleep with food in his pockets, he would wake to find his pocket eaten through. They would even gnaw a pair of well-greased boots.

The first tour of duty in the trenches finished on the 16th December, when the 38th Battalion took over from the 40th Battalion, and we went into support in buildings and cellars in Houplines. On the whole the trench conditions were indescribably miserable. There was no escape from the mud—from the mud in the merely splinter-proof dugouts to the mud in the front line in which the men stood sometimes knee-deep all night. We lived, slept, and ate in the mud, and each day can only be described as a day of misery and muck. The only thing that made it tolerable was a sense of humour that was boundless—the humour that made one man remonstrate with another for washing his gumboots in the water in which they had to sleep.

Chapter IV.

An Infantryman's Day in the Front Line.

HE ordinary trench life of a soldier is a dirty, dreary thing, and to be able to get an impression of trench warfare a description of a soldier's daily routine is necessary. It is given faithfully, for the benefit of soldiers who have forgotten their miseries, for soldiers who were never in trenches and imagine it to be a place of excitement and souvenir hunting, and for civilians whose ideas on the subject are somewhat hazy and imagine the life of an infantryman to be midway between that of D'Artagnan and Tom Sawyer. The day is from "stand-to," an hour before the dawn, to "stand-to" on the following day. "Come on, chaps, stand to"—the voice sounds miles away, but on half waking you find the post commander or another N.C.O. with his head in your dugout opening, inviting you to leave your bunk on the ground to stand-to in the front line with your rifle, for no other apparent reason than to watch the enemy's flares or listen to his machine-guns playing tunes over the parapet. The dugout in which you are is about 6 feet long, 5 feet wide, and 3 feet high, and is occupied by two others besides yourself. By this time you are awake, and when awake the dugout does not seem as comfortable as you thought it was when you were half awake, so you crawl out, put on your equipment, respirator, and steel helmet, grab your rifle, and wade through the foot of mud and water to your post about 20 yards away. From the dugout to this spot there are the usual shell-holes and broken duck-boards, and usually in the darkness, and sleepy as you are, you find the holes, and, with curses on everybody and everything and the scheme of things generally, you pull yourself out of them and face the day more miserable than ever.

You arrive at your post and find the other six or eight men there already, and you help them gaze into No Man's Land beyond which the enemy is going through the same routine. As you watch his flares and listen to his machine-gun bursts, you suddenly see out in front a dark object. You strain your eyes, and it seems to move—you tell the man alongside of you in a whisper. He laughs and says, "You are seeing things—that's a stump." Then you realise that your eyes are playing a game with you, and you remember that the stump was there yesterday. Presently someone behind you says, "Get your dixies."

If you have not got your dixie you have a cigarette tin or some other suitable drinking-vessel, and you hold it out while a hot drink is poured into it from a petrol tin or hot-box. Sometimes the hot drink is replaced by rum, and if it is you feel much better, and begin to take an interest in life and feel at peace with the world, when—whizz, bang, crash—your train of thought is upset, and you get down in your trench, with your back to the parapet and pretend to be thinking of something else, though "Ginger" there on the same post cannot bear to miss anything that is going on, and has his head over the parapet till the trench sergeant pulls him down as he passes. This lasts a few minutes and things become normal again—it is just the enemy's morning hate. It is now getting daylight, and you look along the trench and see something covered with a waterproof sheet, lying on a duck-board. You say, "Who stopped one?" Somebody tells you it is Bill ——. "'Minnie' fell on his post. Only got him, but wounded Digger —— and Darkie ——. Stiff luck! He was going on leave to-morrow." You swear about Bill's "stiff luck" to hide the emotion you feel at the death of a pal you went to school with, and you make a mental note to get one of the Pioneers to make a good cross to put over Bill's grave, which will be in Armentieres, because you know Bill's father, and you know it will hit the "old man" pretty hard, and you rather think Bill's mother would like a good cross put up. Then you ask if anything else has happened, and someone says one of the scouts were killed just in front of our wire—machine-gun got him. Somebody else says Ted —— was wounded out on a wiring party. You ask if he was badly knocked, and the sergeant says, "Well, I thought he was; but he borrowed 20 francs off me as they carried him out, so I reckon he wasn't too bad."

By this time it is quite daylight, and the trench officer comes along and says, "Stand down." Everybody goes to their dug-outs, except one whose turn it is to take the first two hours of sentry duty. It is not wise to put his head over the parapet in daylight. Fritz's snipers are pretty keen, and anyhow it gives the position of the post away. So he looks through the periscope fastened on to the parapet, which gives him a view of No Man's Land in front of him. You do not lie down and rest, as breakfast will be along presently. That is, if the communication with the cookhouse is fairly safe by daylight. If not, breakfast, dinner, and tea all come up together before daylight, and nothing more will occur till after dark. In that case you depend on "Tommy Cookers" to heat up your tea and stew during the day. Whilst waiting you spend ten minutes cleaning your rifle, running the barrel through with the pull-through, and scraping the mud off the outside of it. In trench warfare your rifle is a nuisance; it is always dirty, and you do not use it much, except to show it to an officer, when he wants to see if it is clean. You then hear heavy footsteps coming along the duck-walk, and a man appears, his figure bent double with the weight of a hot-box strapped to his back. He stops and gasps, "Tea." You help to take the hot-box off his back, and pour drinks into the dixie-lids. The hot-box is replaced on the carrier's back and he moves on to the next dug-out behind the next post, while you wait for the more substantial portion of the breakfast to arrive. A few minutes later another carrier arrives. You take the lid off the hot-box and stare at it, as if you expected poached eggs on toast or a grilled chop, but it is the same old inevitable bacon, very thick and very greasy and half-way between hot and cold. You get one piece and the carrier moves on. You put the bacon on bread or an army biscuit (generally known as an "Anzac wafer"), and have your breakfast. Then comes the indispensable cigarette, which even if it is only an "issue," gives a lot of satisfaction. After that you have to clean your dixie. The water in the shell-holes is too dirty for washing eating utensils, even if it is not frozen hard, but you have saved a drop of tea in the bottom of your dixie, and wash it out with that, with the help of a bit of sandbag or paper.

The next thing of importance is the daily wash—so far as a wash is practicable. If the shell-holes are frozen you cannot wash at all, but you generally can get water from a shell-hole or trench. A "Maconochie" tin or an old steel helmet is the best washing basin. You fill the helmet, get your pocket mirror, towel, and soap from your haversack, and carry on. If you are particularly energetic and the water is not too dirty, you have a shave. You then take your gumboots and socks off, and sit down in the mud on your gumboots and rub powder on your feet. The powder is issued by the quartermaster-sergeant, and you are ordered to use it to prevent the complaint known as "trench feet." You are doubtful of its virtue, but, anyhow, it is not much trouble, because you have to change your wet socks. In any case it is better to do it, as the officers inspect feet to see if orders are carried out, and if the platoon commander does not inspect he asks awkward questions which make you really wish you had done it, if only to ease your conscience. When the feet business is done, you remember something that worried you last night, so you take off your shirt and singlet, and have a hunt, putting your cardigan jacket and tunic on to keep you warm. You are just getting interested in the hunt, and have made a pretty good kill, when the sergeant appears and says, "I want you chaps to come and do a little job." Now these little jobs vary a good deal. It may be repairing a trench where a "crump" has landed, or building dugouts, or laying duck-boards, or pumping out water, or cleaning bombs. It may be filling sand-bags, or making wire "gooseberries," or "knife-rests," ready to use at night for building up the parapet or wiring in No Man's Land. It may be anything in the shape of work that appears to make us muddier than ever. Of course, we growl and curse at everything and everybody connected with the war, not because it does any good, nor because we are very annoyed, but it relieves our feelings. We would have been surprised if we had not been put on a job.

We work until about noon, when the dinner arrives. One of us goes and relieves the sentry at the periscope. The carriers come along and we get tea, and with our dry rations, consisting of bread and jam and cheese, which came the day before, get ready to have the midday meal. Just as we are going to have it, a salvo arrives from the enemy. Two or three "minnies" land very close, and the food is covered with mud and a lump of dirt falls into your tea while you are dodging falling debris. This time you curse harder than ever, and you start your meal wondering why all these short "strafes" always occur at meal-times. It seems as if everything is done by everybody for the purpose of making life just one continual misery to you. While you are having your after-meal cigarette the captain's batman comes along, with an air of one who speaks with authority, borrows a cigarette from you, and tells you the captain has told him that the battalion is going to the South of France to spend the rest of the winter. You are mildly interested, but not convinced, because a runner has already told you during the morning with equal authority that the Australians are going to capture Lille within a fortnight.

You are finishing your smoke when a drone is heard in the sky, and you look up and see a squadron of German aeroplanes sailing over you, with our old scout machines quietly making off as they advance. The "Iron Crosses" float over—no one moves for fear of attracting attention, and they pass on towards Armentieres, with feathery puffs of shrapnel around them. Then they turn round and come back. The "Archies" never hurt them, and they have probably seen all they wanted to see.

There is now probably a chance of some sleep, and you tackle the problem of converting yourself from a wet, muddy figure in the trench, with greatcoat and gumboots caked with mud, into an ordinary dry one, curled up with a blanket in a dugout. The floor of the dugout is probably a foot above the duck-walks (to give drainage), and the dugout is probably 2 feet high, so it is a matter of crawling. It is probably raining, and you take off your equipment and place it handy on the top of the dugout in the rain. Then you get your greatcoat off, and leave it at the entrance of the dugout, while you dive in. Having got your body in, you continue, with much wriggling in the narrow space to get your feet out of your gumboots, leaving them just outside your dugout, with the tops turned down, so that they will not fill with water from rain or drips. This is not as easy as it looks, because there is no room to sit up. Now you can roll up in your blanket and drag your greatcoat over you, keeping the muddy side on top, and you are now " set up " for the sleep you badly want, and will not move till you are roused for tea.

About an hour before dark the meal comes up, and consists of tea and stew. After tea you begin to get ready for the night, and when the twilight comes down so that you can barely see the enemy's line, the "stand-to" begins, and the whole trench garrison stands at its posts with their rifles and Lewis guns until it is quite dark, and the order to " stand-down " is given. Through the day there has been very little movement; everybody has been quiet, and moving about as little as possible, but now it is getting dark, and observation impossible, the trenches are alive with men. Working parties are doing all kinds of repairs, and carrying parties are going past with duck-boards and wire—the material for the night's work. The scouts are starting out, and a sergeant and five scouts come to your post wearing cap-comforters instead of steel helmets, and with the butts of revolvers poking out of their respirators. They throw their lighted cigarettes away, climb over the parapet, and disappear through the wire.

After " stand-down " it is your turn to take the first two hours on sentry duty; one man remains with you, and the other five are only a few yards away in the trench. They have put a couple of sheets of iron over the trench against a traverse, and fasten waterproof sheets at the side to keep the heat in and the draught out. The brasier is then lit, and in this temporary dugout they sit round the glowing coke, waiting for their turn to stand on the fire-step. You stand on the fire-step with your head over the parapet and look into No Man's Land, and the conversation from around the brasier

floats up the trench to you. You hear an argument as to what
won the Hobart Cup in 1906. Then the subject gets on to
dogs, and one man puts forward the claims of a dog he once
had that would catch "gummy" sharks, and another man
enters his sheep dog that knew the milking cows from the
"drys," and so it goes on. You see something moving in front
and consult your watch. You ask the corporal in charge of the
post what time the night patrol should be passing, and it
seems certain that this is our patrol. He comes and has a look
and verifies the fact. A machine-gun opens, and the crack-
crack-crack like a whip above your head makes you get your
head down till the burst passes further along, cutting the top
of the parapet in places. You become interested in watching
the enemy Verey lights falling round a ditch where one of your
patrols go every night, and you hear someone step up beside
you on the fire step, and a voice says, "Anything doing?" It
is one of the trench officers, or sometimes the commanding
officer himself. You hear a crack like a distant rifle report in
the enemy lines, but it is not a rifle; if it were you would
not be interested; you know what it is, and look towards the
sky and see a thin trail of sparks. You speculate as to who
is going to get it, and the next moment you hear the unmis-
takable crash of a "minnie" about 200 yards to your right.
It is your business as sentry to locate the gun that threw that
"minnie," so you keep a sharp eye to observe the flash of
discharge of the next one, and mark down the line of it with
a couple of pegs in the parapet. Perhaps it is a new position,
and in that case is duly reported on and observed more carefully by an officer. Or it may be an old friend, "Nellie" or
"Susan" on the official list, and in that case a message is
soon going over the wires from Company Headquarters to the
artillery, "Give my love to Nellie." Then you watch with
renewed interest to see what sort of shooting the artillery will
make. Everything is soon quiet again, and you are next dis-
turbed by someone coming into your post with a hot-box.
This is cocoa and milk, and a very popular contribution from
the Australian Comforts Fund. The trench officer comes
along with one of the scouts, who has just come in. The
scout reports seeing an enemy wiring party on the right
of Willow Ditch. They ask you if there are any enemy Verey
lights going up there; you say there are not, and point out
the places whence flares have been coming, but the vicinity
of Willow Ditch is not one of these places. The officer goes
off, and in a few minutes the rip of two of our Lewis guns
indicates that the enemy party is not being allowed a peace-
ful job. This annoys the enemy, and he has a shot at our
posts with his "minnies." More trails of sparks are seen

in the sky, and several "crumps" land in your vicinity
The coke brasier is forsaken, and your mates spread out
to avoid one "minnie" getting the lot. The "hate" lasts
for ten minutes, and you hear the trench sergeant tell someone to go to Company Headquarters for a stretcher. You
are then relieved and go and sit with the others round the
brasier. You decide to sleep for a couple of hours there,
and three of us go off to sleep with our backs against the
trench-wall, while the other two who are going on sentry duty
next silently gaze at the glow, and lose themselves in their
thoughts. At midnight it is your turn for sentry duty again,
and the same programme is gone through. You go back to
the fire at 2 o'clock, and are just getting off to sleep for a
while when suddenly our guns behind open with an intense
bombardment. We all turn out and watch the wonderful
sight. The whole country behind us is lit up with the flashes
from our guns, and over the enemy line is a succession of
crashes that almost becomes a rumble. We wonder what it
is till the trench sergeant comes along and tells us it is
another battalion raiding on another front a mile away. The
enemy opens fire, and our sector gets its quota of high
explosive shell and "minnies," and all along the front his
machine guns keep up a continuous rattle, while his many-
coloured flares continue to go up. This lasts for an hour,
and we get tired of the display and go back to our fire
speculating on the result of the raid. We are still talking
when we hear the call of "stand-to." We go into the trench
and stand waiting for the dawn.

Chapter V.
In the Line Again—A Quiet Day on the Western Front—An Enemy Raid on B Company—Attempt to Raid the Enemy Unsuccessful.

ROM the 17th to the 20th December the battalion remained in support at Houplines, chiefly engaged in working parties, carrying engineering material into the trenches, and improving and draining the trenches. On the evening of the 20th December the 40th Battalion relieved the 38th Battalion in the line.

During this tour, apart from the usual garrison duties, a great deal of work was done improving the trenches. Bomb and ammunition stores were constructed, new dugouts were built, and the wire in front of our line strengthened. For three days prior to Christmas Day the enemy, apparently with the intention of arranging an unofficial neutrality for festivities, waved white flags every day from his front line. No response was made from our side, and on the evening of Christmas Day his mind was disabused of any wild idea he may have had of our goodwill towards him when the 37th Battalion sent a raiding party over from our B Company sector. This raiding party entered his trenches, and although it did not secure any prisoners, captured some material and inflicted casualties.

Days in the trenches did not vary very much, and although there were a good many exciting moments, the British communiques continued to record " another quiet day on the Western Front." To give some idea of a quiet day on the Western Front, a daily intelligence report of the 40th Battalion is quoted :—

Intelligence Report.
From 6 a.m. 23.12.16 to 6 a.m. 24.12.16.
Reference Map—Sheet 36 N.W. 1/10,000.

Our Operations.
Artillery—
> 10.15 a.m.—10 high explosive rounds fell on enemy front line, opposite locality 13, doing considerable damage to his parapet.
> 2 p.m. to 3 p.m.—Our artillery fired on enemy front line, and support line, west of Les Quatre Hallots Farm

Trench Mortars—
> 1.30 p.m.—16 rounds from Stokes gun on the " Chicken Run."

Patrols—
(1) A patrol of 1 officer and 9 men left our trenches from M Gap at 1 a.m. Crossed stream at C 23 a 4525 and proceeded to a point about 25 yards from enemy wire at N.W. corner of the "Censor's Nose." Searchlight from support line disclosed our position, and patrol was fired on from "Censor's Nose" by several rifles. Moved to the left to get round enemy post, but encountered enemy patrol of about 10 men. Our patrol immediately withdrew back to the ford, where, under the searchlight, we were fired upon by machine gun from enemy front line. Enemy patrol still in sight, and following our patrol, so we withdrew across the ford to our own wire, being fired upon all the way from the "Censor's Nose," and enemy machine gun behind it. Entered our trench at 2.35 a.m.

Searchlight showed enemy wire around "Censor's Nose" very plainly. It is extremely thick and about 5 feet high. There is no doubt the position is strongly held.

(2) A patrol in locality 16 from 9 p.m. to 11.30 p.m. reported a good deal of rifle fire from that locality. During this time the enemy threw several bombs into his own wire.

(3) A patrol left the right of locality 16 at 11.30 p.m., and returned at 1.45 a.m., having located an enemy wiring party opposite locality 16. A Lewis gun was turned on to the party from our parapet.

Sniping—
Two shots fired at enemy snipers in C 23 c, and one hit (certain) claimed. Snipers' post discovered in Willow Tree in No Man's Land at C 17 c 9505, about 10 yards from enemy parapet. Artillery informed.

Artillery—   **Enemy Operations.**

3 p.m. to 4 p.m.—12 high explosive (4.2) between Edmeads' Farm and Cambridge Avenue.

Trench Mortars—
1 p.m.—6 minnenwerfer on Irish Avenue. One fell in old support trench, killing 3 men, wounding 1, and 1 unaccounted for.

3 p.m.—10 minnenwerfer fell in Hobbs' Farm.

3.30 p.m.—10 "pineapples" on C 17 c 3 8 (north of Hobbs' Farm).

7 p.m.—10 rifle grenades in P Gap.

8.30 p.m.—6 minnenwerfer on locality 16—no damage.

11 p.m.—14 minnenwerfer on locality 13—damage slight.

Machine Guns—
Enemy machine guns fairly active during the night. One man wounded by machine-gun fire whilst looking over the parapet.

Sniping—
Enemy snipers quiet, except for constant shooting at a gap in Irish Avenue. Probably from a fixed rifle.

Working Parties—
Water observed being pumped through enemy parapet at a point directly opposite Gap N, from 8 a.m. to noon. Enemy working party seen at C 17 c 7 8 at 2 p.m. Smoke also seen at this point.

On the 28th December the battalion was relieved by the 38th Battalion, and went into reserve in billets in Armentieres. While in reserve working parties were continued, and on the 3rd January we relieved the 38th Battalion in the same sector as before. The relief was completed by 4 p.m., during fairly heavy enemy shelling, which continued for some time, and at 4.35 p.m. retaliation was asked for from the battery behind us. The enemy continued his shelling with artillery until 5.35 p.m., when it increased to a heavy bombardment with minnenwerfer, high explosive, and shrapnel on B Company sector, and the left of A Company. There was then little doubt that the enemy was about to raid our trenches, and at 5.40 p.m. the S.O.S. rocket was fired by the O.C. B Company, Major L. H. Payne, and our protective barrage came down in No Man's Land. The enemy barrage continued on our front and support lines, and also on the main communication trench, until 6.10 p.m., when it lifted from the front line to allow the enemy to enter. The enemy immediately appeared in a large body, estimated at 80 strong, in front of our wire on the left of Hobbs' Farm. Unfortunately, all our Lewis guns, except one, on B Company's sector, had been put out of action by the bombardment, and when the enemy showed up in the moonlight, only this one gun, worked by No. 324, Pte. J. Ackroyd, opened fire. Its fire was supplemented by the riflemen who were not casualties, and our men also used hand grenades with good results. Some of the enemy got within a few yards of the parapet through our broken wire, but the resistance was so strong that they were unable to force an entry and retired. Our patrols at once went out, but a strong enemy covering party with a machine gun prevented them getting far in the bright moonlight, and the enemy was able to get his wounded away. The patrols brought in one dead German for identification, as well as a quantity of rifles, bombs, and equipment that the enemy had left behind in No Man's Land. This German was the first one brought in by the Division, and no later event of a similar nature created quite the same interest.

Our casualties during the preliminary bombardment and the raid were 8 killed and 23 wounded. This included one sergeant and two men who at the time could not be accounted for. Their bodies were found two nights later in No Man's Land. A minnenwerfer had fallen in their post and blown them at least 20 yards over the parapet.

Considerable damage had been done to our trenches, and that night at least 150 men were employed in clearing away the debris and making the trenches passable. Working parties continued during the following days to put the trenches in order, and wiring parties were out each night repairing the badly smashed wire.

On the 4th January a raiding party of the 40th Battalion were sent to the Ecole Professionale, Armentieres, to prepare for a raid on the enemy trenches.

On the 9th January the battalion was relieved by the 38th Battalion, and went into support at Houplines. Here our billets were subjected to considerable bombardment, and several casualties resulted, including the O.C. C Company, Capt. J. T. Tyrell (killed), and the Battalion Signalling Officer, Lieut. A. R. Allan (died of wounds). Capt. Tyrell had served with the 26th Battalion at Gallipoli. His experience, judgment, and fine initiative made him from the beginning one of the pillars of the battalion which through its history suffered no heavier individual loss than this.

On the 10th January another raiding party of two officers and 50 other ranks left the battalion and went to the Ecole Professionale, Armentieres, to form part of a brigade raiding party of 200, 50 from each battalion in the brigade.

On the 13th January our first raiding party were to make a raid on the enemy. The place selected for the operation was opposite D Company's sector, on the enemy trenches known as Cell Trench, at a point about 600 yards south-east of the River Lys.

The training had been carried out at the Ecole Professionale, and consisted of physical training, bayonet fighting, revolver shooting, bombing, and practice at entering trenches in the dark. The training was carried out under the direction of Capt. C. L. McVilly, who was officer commanding raid.

Preliminary reconnaissance had been carried out each night by the officers and scouts, in order to ascertain the daily effect of our preparatory bombardment of the enemy wire, and to accustom them to the ground between the enemy trench and ours. During this scouting very valuable work was done by No. 443, Corpl. J. E. Linnell.

The preparatory bombardment with trench mortars of the enemy front line and wire was continued each day for four days prior to the raid. This effectively cut a gap, but it also gave the enemy indication that a raid was contemplated. In this case succeeding events showed that he accepted the "tip."

On the afternoon of the 13th the raiding party left Armentieres, and arrived in our front line at 5.20 p.m. At 5.40 the Lewis gun covering parties were taken out into No Man's Land, and placed in position by Lieut. S. I. Suter, who was in charge of the assault. The party was divided into two storming parties, the right party commanded by Lieut. H. C. Barclay and the left party by 2nd Lieut. J. S. Cranswick.

At 5.55 the whole party was lying up in No Man's Land immediately in front of our wire, waiting for our artillery to open at 6 p.m. The artillery opened punctually, but several rounds fell very short and landed among our own men, causing six casualties. This short shooting (which appeared to be from one gun only) also caused casualties in our front line. The raiding party went forward at the double, and as they reached the enemy wire the enemy S.O.S. barrage came down behind them.

The party got through the gap in the enemy wire, but found that the enemy had apparently forecasted our raid from our wire-cutting programme by trench mortars, and had filled his front line at this point with wire, also the "borrow" ditch in front of his trench had been wired, but was not impassable. As the borrow ditch had been inspected the previous evening, his wiring must have been done in the early hours of the morning of the raid. It was quite impossible to get along his trench, even if the party had got into it, and previous enemy tactics had been to wire his trenches when a raid was expected and bomb his front line from the rear immediately the raiding party jumped into it.

The party withdrew into dead ground a few yards from his wire, and the men were sent back to our lines in small parties to avoid heavy casualties whilst returning through the enemy barrage.

Our total casualties were two killed and eight wounded. 2/Lieut. J. S. Cranswick, who was killed, had just received his commission. He had been wounded on Gallipoli wtih the 12th Battalion, and had been Company Sergt.-Major of D Company in the 40th from the beginning. His death was an irreparable loss to his company. His company commander, in writing of him afterwards, said, "Before the company saw fighting, some of the men had a grudge against him for hardness and severity as company sergt.-major. Directly we got into the line that was all forgotten, and within a week they thought nothing could be done right unless the sergt.-major had a hand in it. I never fell out with him but once, when he set out into No Man's Land at night in pursuit of a 'Fritz' without warning anyone, and was nearly killed by our own bombers, and then he was so penitent I could not say much. I think he was the finest soldier I struck during the war."

One of the features of all raids on the enemy was the number of coloured flares he used. The whole thing was most spectacular. He put up ordinary flares, showers of green and red stars, golden clusters in great numbers. There were many theories as to why he used such a variety during a raid. They seemed to be too varied and numerous to be separate signals, and at times it looked as if in his excitement he was firing off his whole collection of flares. As far as we could see they did not appear to be of much value, except to decorate a grim and dangerous undertaking with a tastefully arranged display of illuminations.

The weak point of all our raids on strong trenches seemed to be our preparatory wire-cutting, which gave the enemy an indication of our intentions. To cut wire with trench mortars and then to keep the gaps open with bursts of machine gun fire all night was too big an advertisement. The enemy in his raids had the advantage of his minnenwerfer, which combined accuracy with enormous explosive power. Before a raid he would register on our wire and front line all along the front. We might forecast a raid from this registration, but we never knew where he was going to make a gap, because he would not smash our wire with his minnenwerfer until his barrage was down on our trenches. On the other hand, we made a gap in his wire two or three days before the raid, and then advertised the fact that we meant to use it.

Still, the enemy often tried to raid our trenches, and never once succeeded in getting over our parapet. Though we suffered somewhat heavily in his preliminary bombardments, our casualties at the hands of his raiding parties themselves were negligible. We raided him at times, and on several occasions got into his trenches, took prisoners, and did considerable damage to men and material. So, although he had the advantage in preparation, the net profit must have been to us when it came to the final balance.

Chapter VI.

From Houplines to the Trenches at Bois Grenier— The 10th Brigade Raid at Houplines.

N the 14th January the 40th Battalion relieved the 38th Battalion, and on the following day a very heavy fall of snow made conditions a little more unpleasant than before. The River Lys had risen and flooded a great deal of D Company's sector. Patrolling work was impossible, except in white garments, which were not available at that time. Up till now the artillery covering our front had been New Zealand and English batteries, as our divisional artillery had been completing their training in England. During this time in the line our own artillery moved in. At that time they seemed to us to be inexperienced, compared with the New Zealanders. No doubt they were, as there were many things that could only be learned in the line—things that no training could teach. We said good-bye to the New Zealand artillery officers who were in the line with us, and told them that we were sorry that they were going. One of them said, "You won't be sorry for long. Some day you will be proud of your artillery." He was right.

On the 19th January the enemy registered the whole of D Company sector with minnenwerfer, and caused several casualties, and much damage. The damage included the complete disappearance of a new bomb store, that the bombing officer and his bombers had carried up in sections and put together, and filled up with a new collection of bombs and rifle grenades. On that day the 40th Battalion was relieved by the 36th Battalion, and two days later the D Company sector was bombarded and raided by the enemy. The Battalion had moved out to Armentieres, and the 10th Brigade was now Reserve Brigade of the Division. Training was begun, but at very short notice the 40th Battalion was ordered to relieve the 26th Northumberland Fusiliers at Bois Grenier, south of our previous sector. The relief took place on the night of the 26th January. It was rather a difficult relief, as there had been no opportunity to reconnoitre routes. The duck-walks were very slippery with ice and frost on them, and many bad falls resulted, including one broken leg. The dash of the Northumberland Fusiliers in getting out excited mixed feelings. As we moved in, they moved out, and we took over empty front-line trenches. Our officers were accustomed to having a lengthy and leisurely talk with the officers relieving us, and *vice versa*, concerning the different places in the sector, strong points, communications, dumps, stores, water points, &c.; and, in fact, our company commanders generally stayed in the line for 24 hours with the company commanders who relieved them. But on this occasion we heard a vanishing "good-bye" in the darkness, and realised our total ignorance of everything about the sector we wanted to know. Among Australian battalions a "relief" was a matter of great detail and courtesy. We always asked our opposite numbers after going over the sector with them if we could help or assist them any further. If they said they had all the information and assistance they required both parties adjourned and had a drink, and wished one another "good hunting." The only gratifying feature about this relief was that the relieved battalion were so elated at getting out that they left behind large stores of rum. In view of the intense cold, and the fact that up to that time the 3rd Australian Division had never been issued with a rum ration, this lot of rum was received with enthusiasm. Shortly after this, rum was issued sparingly, on the advice of medical officers. There was a small section of the Army and a large section of civilians who deplored the issue of rum to troops. But there were times when the mental and physical sufferings of the troops were so great that the use of anything to alleviate their sufferings was warranted. It was only issued to men as they came off duty in the early morning, and were about to go to sleep in their dugouts. At that hour the men were numbed and cold, and weary with the strain of standing for hours gazing into the blackness towards the enemy, or crawling about the shell-holes of No Man's Land. In the early morning a man's vitality was lowest, and he went to his wet dugout and slept, or lay shivering beneath his blanket, too cold and weary to sleep. With a ration of rum he went to sleep, with the pleasant sensation of feeling himself going to sleep, and he went to sleep with his ugly existence appearing to him just a little rose-coloured. In justifying the issue of rum to men in the trenches, it would be well to make it clear that on no occasion in the history of the Battalion was rum ever issued before an advance or attack, nor was the suggestion to do so ever made.

The sector taken over was known as the left subsector of the Bois Grenier sector (Map 2). The right subsector was taken over by the 39th Battalion. The left subsector had a frontage of about 1200 yards. It was, roughly, about 5000 yards south of the River Lys. Just beyond the enemy front line, and immediately north-east of the sector, was the village of Wez Macquart. The trenches were in better order than at Houplines, and the frost had eliminated the mud conditions. The only weak point about these trenches was that there was no front-line trench. The front line was a breastwork of earth about 6 feet high, which presented a better target to the enemy than a trench, and he often knocked it down in places, and blew gaps in it, which we painfully repaired the following night. There was also no parados behind the breastwork in places, which meant there was no protection against a shell bursting behind us. The dispositions of the companies from left to right was C Company (Capt. J. H. Dumaresq), D Company (Capt. L. F. Giblin), B Company (Major L. H. Payne), and A Company (Capt. J. D. Chisholm). A proportion of the strength of each Company was in posts in the second support line, the chief posts being Lille Post on the left, and Orchard Post on the right. Battalion Headquarters was in the second support line near the Farm Du Biez.

On the 28th January the 10th Brigade raiding party, of 7 officers and 224 other ranks, raided the enemy trenches opposite Pont Ballot, on the Houplines sector. The party consisted of 1 officer (Lieut. Parker) and 56 other ranks of the 37th Battalion, 1 officer (Lieut. C. H. Peters, and 56 other ranks of 38th Battalion, 2 officers (Lieut. L. Grondona and Lieut. E. Fleiter), and 56 other ranks of the 39th Battalion, and 2 officers (Lieut. S. I. Suter, and Lieut. H. L. Barclay) and 56 other ranks of the 40th Battalion; Capt. Lamden, of the 37th Battalion, was Officer Commanding raid.

The party had been training at the Ecole Professionale, Armentieres, since the 13th January, and also had carried out practice attacks on skeleton trenches dug at L'Hallobeau, similar to the German trenches to be attacked.

A rough plan of the trenches to be attacked is contained in Map 3. The approximate frontage was 400 yards, and the depth of the raid 200 yards. The raid was carried out with an artillery barrage for three minutes on the front line, lifting to the support lines, where it remained for five minutes, lifting to the reserve line, where it remained for seven minutes, and then lifting and forming a box round the trenches for 25 minutes. It then returned to the front line, and remained there for 20 minutes, while the raiding party were supposed to be withdrawing across No Man's Land.

The disposition of the whole party was as follows:—

(1) 37th Battalion party to leave our trenches at C, enter enemy trenches at R, and establish blocks at R, S, and T.

(2) 38th Battalion party to leave our trenches at A, enter enemy trenches at L, and establish blocks at L, M, and N.

(3) The 39th and 40th Battalion parties were formed into the Centre Assault Party, under Lieut. S. I. Suter; and the Centre Demolition and Searching Party, under Lieut. E. Fleiter. These parties were to leave our trenches at B, and enter the enemy trenches at O.

The Centre Assault Parties were divided up as follows:— (i) Strength, 12; enter at O; thence via L to M. (ii) Strength, 12; enter at O; thence via R to S. (iii) Strength 17; enter at O; thence via X, M, N, Y, and back to O. (iv) Strength, 17; enter at O; thence via X, S, T, Y, and back to O. (v) Strength, 22; enter at O; thence via X to Y, and establish a double block at Y, until (iii) and (iv) joined them, when they would withdraw to O. The demolition and searching parties were divided up as follows:—(vi) Strength, 8; search and demolish dugouts between O, L, and M. (vii) Strength, 8; search and demolish dugouts between O, R, and S. (vii) Strength, 8; search and demolish dugouts between O, X, M, N, Y. (ix) Strength, 8; Search and demolish dugouts between O, X, S, T, Y. These four parties each included four engineers, with several 10 lb. guncotton charges for demolition purposes.

(4) Lieut. L. Grondona with runners at O, establishing forward headquarters, and in communication with rear headquarters.

(5) Lieut. H. L. Barclay and 14 men at O to take charge of any prisoners.

The usual trench mortar shoots for wire-cutting preceded the raid for three or four days, but owing to the bright moonlight and thick coating of frozen snow on the ground, it was impossible to reconnoitre the enemy wire to ascertain if the gaps were properly cut. Two attempts by patrols were made prior to the raid, and on each occasion casualties resulted.

At 6 p.m. all parties left our trenches as the barrage opened. The 37th Battalion party, under Lieut. Parker, left our lines at C, and approached point R under cover of a road. As the head of the party passed through the gap in the outer belt of enemy wire, they were bombed from point R, and a machine gun opened at point-blank range. The second belt of wire was uncut and impassable, and the party suffered heavily before it could be extricated. Lieut. Parker was severely wounded, and died in enemy hands. The total casualties in this party were 7 killed and 20 wounded.

The 38th Battalion party, under Lieut. Peters, failed also to enter the enemy trenches, after several attempts. There was no opposition in the trench, but the wire was impassable. They suffered no casualties.

The 39th and 40th Battalion parties reached the point O at 6.4 p.m., and got through the partially cut wire, and entered the enemy front line amid a shower of bombs. Parties (i) and (ii) had a hard fight bombing their way along the front line, and they reached their points L and R respectively, but as the 37th and 38th Battalions had failed to get in, they remained there, keeping the enemy at bay with bombs until the signal for the withdrawal. Parties (iii) and (iv) also had to bomb their way against strong opposition, and succeeded in reaching their points N and T respectively, but were unable to continue owing to the absence of blocks, and enemy opposition from two directions. Party No. 5, under No. 253, Sergt. J. Pugh, 40th Battalion, successfully reached point Y, and had a bomb fight with the enemy at that point until withdrawal at 6.35 p.m. Sergt. Pugh was killed during the withdrawal across No Man's Land. The four demolition parties had a busy time demolishing dugouts, and destroyed eleven, as well as securing enemy equipment and material for identification.

A dugout between O and X contained two of the enemy who were firing up the trench. A phosphorus bomb was put in the dugout door. At 6.15 p.m. a party of about 40 of the enemy were seen about 100 yards away, coming over the top from the direction of point M. Lieuts. Suter and Fleiter collected as many men as possible near point X, and opened fire with rifles, while No. 6 demolition party and several other men in the front line also opened fire on them from the front line. Several of the enemy were killed, and the remainder withdrew towards point M. Identification was obtained from the dead. If this counter-attack had succeeded it would have cut off several of our parties.

At 6.35 p.m. the Verey light signal was given for all parties to withdraw. This was done, the parties carrying their wounded with them. No Man's Land was crossed under heavy machine-gun fire, the progress being slow owing to the difficulty in getting the wounded back. The casualties in the 39th and 40th Battalions amounted to 6 killed and 22 wounded. One enemy prisoner was taken back for identification.

The officers of the 39th and 40th Battalions collected several stretcher-bearers and went to the assistance of the 37th Battalion, carrying in a number of their dead and wounded. During the whole operation the work of Lieut. E. Fleiter, of the 39th Battalion, was very conspicuous, and the 40th Battalion party were very gratified to learn that he and Lieut. Suter received the Military Cross for gallantry during the raid.

As far as the 39th and 40th Battalions were concerned, their part of the raid was successful. The objective of cleaning up the whole area was not attained because of the failure of the 37th and 38th Battalions to enter the enemy trenches, but their failure to do so was no fault of theirs.

Chapter VII.

The Enemy Raid at Cowgate — Trench Warfare at Bois Grenier — Our Unsuccessful Raid — Out for a Rest.

N the 31st January, shortly after dark, the enemy put down a heavy artillery and minenwerfer barrage on our front and support lines in the Lille-road locality. On B. and C. Companys' sectors the barrage was particularly heavy, and after some time the S.O.S. signal was put up, when there was no doubt as to an intended raid. Casualties were very heavy, not only from pieces of shell, but from lumps of ice. Heavy shells, landing in frozen shell-holes and miniature lakes round the front line, caused large pieces of ice to fly round, and the absence of a parados was felt. The portion of the front line garrison who were not casualties were ready to deal with the enemy when he appeared, but only one post actually saw the raiding party, and this one post repelled them.

The enemy had thought out his plans well, and taken advantage of the ground being covered with frozen snow. His party, dressed in white, had crept up a deep ditch which ran from his trenches to ours. The ditch had several inches of ice at the bottom, which was also covered with snow. It was therefore imposible to see the enemy, except from a point in line with the ditch, and it was the enemy's bad luck that a post was at this point. This post was in charge of No. 370, Sergt. N. A. M. Findlay, who was badly wounded during the bombardment, but continued to direct his post as he lay on the ground. There were three men on the parapet of the post, and they saw the enemy for the first time when he was about 20 yards away. The enemy party seemed to muster about 50. Our men at once threw bombs into the ditch, and some of the enemy stood up and threw bombs at them, while four of the enemy rushed on to our parapet, where they were fired on with rifles from two of our men, while the third man, No. 1651, Pte. J. D. Jeffrey, met them with bombs. Finding that they were not followed by the remainder of the party, these four men ran back, and the attempted raid turned into a race back across No Man's Land.

An officer who was near at once took two scouts to try and get any of the enemy wounded who may have been left behind. Blood was found on the snow in the ditch, establishing the fact that casualties had been inflicted. The enemy had apparently come prepared to do some damage, as this party found a number of axes, coils of rope, and explosive charges, as well as some stretchers, bombs, rifles, and revolvers. A telephone cable had also been laid almost to our wire.

B. and C. Companys' front and support lines had been very badly smashed by the bombardment, some idea of the heaviness of which may be obtained from the fact that our casualties were 15 killed and 40 wounded. In one place in the front line the Medium Trench Mortar Battery had made a dump of their ammunition, and where a shell hit this dump the trenches and dugouts in the immediate vicinity had disappeared. In another place a gap 15 yards wide had been made in the breastwork.

The next few days were fairly quiet, which allowed us to do some necessary repairs. The enemy artillery was active, but contented itself with pounding clouds of brickdust out of the farm buildings round Lille Post, where there was a water point, about which the enemy apparently had suspicions.

Covering us was a 13-pounder battery of horse artillery, who used the Farm Du Biez as an observation post, and a favourite pastime was to get into the observation post and watch the effect of our artillery shoots. A good view was obtained from here of the village of Wez Macquart, behind the enemy lines, and parties of the enemy could often be seen about the village. Divisional Intelligence also noted this, and one daily report read: "At noon a party of about 60 of the enemy, carrying picks and shovels, were seen going through the village of Wez Macquart. They reached the estaminet at the cross-roads, and there disappeared." The obvious deduction to be drawn from this intelligence was that even the enemy had his pleasant moments.

A good deal of discussion and uneasiness arose at this time from the fact that almost daily homing-pigeons were seen crossing our lines and alighting at the same spot in the village of Wez Macquart. There was at that time a general feeling that there were a number of spies round Armentieres, and although on more than one occasion civilians were taken to the Military Police for committing suspicious acts, the results of investigations were never made known to the troops, except on one occasion, when the following evidence came to light:— "Lights were seen in an unoccupied house in the Rue Sadi Carnot. Invisible seals were placed on all doors and the cellar. The seals were examined next day, and those on the front door and cellar were broken. The cellar contained wine."

In the Houplines sector most of the enemy minenwerfer were small and medium ones, but at Bois Grenier we met with the big ones for the first time. The smallest "minnie" is not much larger than our 18-pounder shells. The biggest are about 3 feet 9 inches long and about a foot in diameter at the base. The medium ones are about 6 inches in diameter, but are only about half the length of the big ones.

On the 8th February the Battalion took over the right subsector from a composite battalion of the 37th, 38th, and 44th Battalions. This battalion was known as X Battalion, which was formed while 800 of the 37th and 38th Battalions were preparing for a raid.

This subsector had a frontage of about 1200 yards, and was not in such good repair as the left subsector. No Man's Land was from 300 to 500 yards wide, except at one point, known as the Rue du Bois salient, where the trenches were only about 40 yards apart. The disposition of the companies from left to right was D Company, C Company, and A Company, with B Company in the second support-line. Battalion headquarters was in dugouts near the junction of Wellington-avenue and the subsidiary line (Map 2).

The Rue du Bois salient was a most unhealthy spot. The enemy disliked its existence, and paid it a lot of attention. At all hours of the day and night he threw minenwerfer and other smaller trench-mortar shells into it. Minenwerfer shoots on this spot at night were always preceded by a flare which burst into several green stars, and immediately after this flare went up the "minnies" would begin to arrive. Most of these minenwerfer positions were located, and given code names, such as "Gertie," "Alice," "Mabel," &c. These names were known to the covering artillery, and on receipt of a message that "Gladys" and "Clara" were throwing things into our yard, the artillery would send some rounds in the required direction. But for this retaliation, which was often heavy, life in the salient would have been unbearable. The nerves of the garrison were naturally frayed at being in a state of constant expectation all night, and the artillery retaliation had the effect of giving the enemy something to think about, and was most soothing to the feelings of the "strafed" garrison.

Artillery retaliation up to that time had not been lavish. It was a popular theory in some quarters that retaliation did little good, and only encouraged the enemy, who would realise by the retaliation that he was hurting our feelings. So far, if we had asked for retaliation, we sometimes got as much as 10 rounds. At Bois Grenier we made different arrangements with the artillery. They were English batteries, and particularly helpful. Their forward observation officers saw some of the "strafes" on the Rue du Bois salient, and realised that something ought to be done about it. Consequently, on our call for retaliation, they sometimes gave as much as 200 rounds, including heavy stuff, on the minenwerfer positions.

The enemy used often to be heard walking along the duckwalks opposite the salient, and the battalion bombing officer often dealt out a little retaliation. About 10 of the bombers would wait for footsteps in the trench opposite, and fire a salvo of 10 Mills' rifle grenades in the proper direction. It seemed a feeble retaliation for minenwerfer, but showed the enemy that we took an interest in him. On this front the enemy made full use of his field guns, and took advantage of the high ground behind him, from which he overlooked our trenches, to snipe small parties and working parties with "whizz-bangs." Two particularly unhealthy places were the trenches round Dead Cow Farm and Burnt Farm. The enemy also paid a good deal of attention to the road up which the battalion transport came to deliver the rations and stores. At about the time the transport was due he sometimes put over 20 or 30 shrapnel and high explosive on to the road near Wellington Dump, where the limbers unloaded. But the shelling always arrived a few minutes too early or too late. Needless to say the transport never stayed there to indulge in social amenities any longer than was absolutely necessary, particularly as this spot was under indirect machine-gun fire also.

On the 11th February a big raid was made by English troops on the left subsector of the Bois Grenier sector. This raid appeared to be fairly successful, but their casualties were heavy. In withdrawing the raiders left a large number of their wounded in No Man's Land. Our regimental band, who were acting as stretcher-bearers, were in our front line to render assistance, if required. They heard the wounded calling out, and went into No Man's Land and brought back a number of wounded. Two men, No. 55, Pte. R. Garrett, and No. 57, Pte. E. Hilmer, went as far as the enemy wire, and brought wounded back from there.

On the 12th February a silent raid was attempted by a party of 50 men, under Lieuts. W. J. Culton, R. H. Smith, and T. J. O'Sullivan. The raid took place on the right subsector, opposite the Willow locality. Wire had been cut the previous day by the trench mortars, and had been kept open during the 12th by Lewis-gun and machine-gun fire. The enemy apparently realised the position, and managed to repair his wire shortly after dark, and placed a strong garrison at this point. The raid was attempted without artillery support, and on the raiding party getting to the enemy wire they were unable to get through, and came under heavy rifle-fire and a barrage of hand-grenades. Lieut. W. J. Culton, in attempting to force his way through the wire, was killed, and Lieut. T. J. O'Sullivan, in trying to assist him, was very severely wounded. Capt. A. D. McKinnon, who was observing from our parapet, was also severely wounded. Several casualties occurred in the remainder of the party, and, realising the impossibility of getting through the wire, the order was given for the party to withdraw. This was carried out. Our casualties were 1 officer and 3 other ranks killed, and 2 officers and 2 other ranks wounded.

On the 20th February the Battalion was relieved by the 39th Battalion, and went into support in billets at Chapelle D'Armentieres, and on the 25th February we relieved X Battalion in the left subsector of the Bois Grenier sector. The disposition of the companies from left to right was A Company, D Company, and B Company, with C Company in support at Lille Post, and platoons of D and B Companies in support at Orchard Post and Paradise Alley.

During the next few days the enemy artillery and trench mortar fire on the sector was fairly heavy. In one day, on the Chards' Farm locality (A Company), the enemy put 120 minenwerfer, which did considerable damage. The rear support-line was also heavily shelled, particularly the Farm du Biez and Lille Post. On the 26th February the enemy first used gas-shell on the sector, which was then an innovation. About the same time our heavy trench mortars were installed, and the first shoot created much interest. Those who witnessed it were much impressed by the quantity of earth displaced by these enormous shells, which were generally known as "flying pigs"; but later they were looked upon as a doubtful possession, owing to their inaccuracy. The front line had always to be cleared for about 200 yards in case the shells fell short. The mortar emplacements were near the second support-line, and on one occasion, which is worthy of mention, five "flying pigs" were sent towards the enemy. The first two fell near our support-line, and caused a stampede from the neighbourhood. The next fell on our parapet, and about 15 yards of perfectly good parapet went skywards. The next fell in No Man's Land, and made a nice crater there; and the last was a splendid shot, which fell in the enemy front line. It was a "dud."

On the 2nd March the Battalion was relieved by the 38th Battalion, and moved into billets at Chapelle D'Armentieres, remaining in support there until the 8th March, when relieved by a battalion of the 25th British Division.

This was the first time the Brigade had been really out of the line for 14 weeks. During the first half of that time the battalions worked about eight days in the line and an equal time in support; but since moving to the Bois Grenier sector we had worked double shifts—10 days in the line and only five in support, and the latter well occupied by working parties. It was a standing grievance that a battalion could not get one good sleep and a "clean-up" after coming out of the line before being called upon for working parties. So, on the whole, our first three months of active service had not been a holiday. Under the conditions of wet and cold the work was heavy, and though there were no big operations, it was mostly trench warfare of the more active kind.

Chapter VIII.

Resting and Training at Tatinghem — The New Offensive Tactics — Back to Houplines — The Enemy Tries to Raid Again at Hobbs' Farm — Into Belgium to Ploegsteert Wood.

FTER being relieved at Chapelle D'Armentieres, the Battalion marched to Erquinghem Baths, where the night of 8th March was spent, and from there proceeded by road to Steenje, 2 miles south of Bailleul, on the following day. This was the area allotted to the 10th Brigade for training. Specialist training, such as bombing and Lewis gun work, was carried out at Steenje, and on several occasions the Battalion went to the training area at Mont de Lille with the rest of the Brigade. The weather was now warmer, but the ground was still very wet and muddy.

While at Steenje an important change in battalion organisation took place. Until that time the Lewis gunners, scouts, and bombers of the Battalion were in separate specialist platoons attached to Battalion Headquarters under the Lewis gun, scouting, and bombing officers, who were responsible for all the specialist work. These platoons were now abolished, and the Lewis gunners, scouts, and bombers were attached to companies, and placed with platoons, each platoon being organised into 1 Lewis gun section, 1 rifle grenade section, 1 bombing section, and 1 section of riflemen. The previous organisation meant that each company was not an independent fighting unit, but dependent on Battalion Headquarters for nearly everything that mattered. The change was therefore very desirable.

On the 21st March the Brigade commenced to route-march to an area farther back from the line, and that day the Battalion reached the village of Petit Sec Bois, where the night was spent in billets. The following day we marched 14 miles to the village of Lynde, and billeted there.

On all occasions when on the road the Battalion moved in full marching order. Blankets were generally carried by motor transport, but sometimes we had to carry them fastened round the pack. The billeting officer, with representatives of each company and Battalion Headquarters, went ahead of the Battalion on bicycles, and allotted the billets, so that when the Battalion arrived at their resting-place for the night each company moved straight to its billets, which were generally the usual farm buildings; that is, if all went well with the billeting party. Sometimes they lost the Battalion, and sometimes other battalions were found in possession of the allotted billets. On this occasion the transport moved with the Battalion, and on arrival at billets each night a meal was issued. Generally most of the Battalion were too tired to wander about, and remained in billets; but there was also a number who patronised the local estaminets, and prevailed upon Madame to cook the inevitable eggs and chips.

The Army Medical Corps details attached to the Battalion were always busy at the end of each march. They visited each billet and inspected the feet of the footsore ones, pricking the blisters and decorating chafes and blisters with the army's great remedy for all things, from a shell-wound to a sore throat, the infallible iodine.

It was very seldom that anybody fell out on the march. It was a point of honour with everybody to keep going, and if a man felt that he would be unable to finish, he got permission from the medical officer to put his pack on the transport, while he marched with the rear party. If a man fell out to do this, his company looked upon it as a disgrace to them, so it seldom happened, except among the sick and in cases where old wounds troubled. And so we considered ourselves a good marching battalion. In the long three days' march to Ypres, during the end of September, 1917, we did nearly 60 miles in three days on the road, and did not lose a man. On the third day a horse-drawn ambulance vehicle was detailed by higher authority to drive behind us to pick up stragglers, but the men regarded it as an insult, and threatened to upset it if it remained, so it went off ahead and looked for a unit who might appreciate it.

On the 23rd March we marched from Lynde to Tatinghem, about 14 miles, and were inspected on the way by the Army Commander, Sir Herbert Plumer. At Tatinghem we were billeted in farms, and having commenced the new organisation, this necessitated a good deal of training; and after a course of Lewis gun and bombing training, we started platoon and company training. Later we got to working as a battalion, and later the Brigade carried out a trench to trench attack practice. Another day was set apart for a similar attack, but it was cancelled owing to a heavy snowstorm.

Before leaving Bois Grenier the Divisional Commander gave a lecture to officers of the Division on the new tactics laid down by the "Higher Command" for the offensive. One object of the new tactics was to get absolute uniformity of procedure in all units. Practically nothing was left to the initiative of officers lower than Brigade Commanders, and the result was a rigid, mechanical uniformity of movement, which required a similar level uniformity in ground and enemy dispositions and morale to be effective. In fact, the intended practice was badly punctured at our first offensive at Messines, and thereafter was amended at intervals, always in the direction of greater freedom of movement, until it died a natural death in the open fighting of August, 1918; but not before the Germans had taught us a better way in their offensive of March, 1918.

The lecture by General Monash was followed by a succession of pamphlets on the attack, and small-talk ran on "lines" and "waves" and "moppers-up," as a variation on the biggest "minnie" or the best tune played by "Parapet Joe" as he ran along our front line at night. However, the new tactics made a welcome change in the exercises available for training, and were practised with a great deal of zeal at Tatinghem, though before we left there was a general suspicion that you can have too much even of a good thing.

About this time the officer commanding B Company, Major L. H. Payne, proceeded to England for three months to attend a Senior Officers Course at Aldershot.

During this time several company football matches took place, and battalion sports were held. The town of St. Omer, about 2½ miles from Tatinghem, was out of bounds for a time, but later liberal leave was granted to go there, which was availed of. On the 2nd April a reinforcement of 40 arrived.

On the 5th April the Battalion left Tatinghem, and marched to Arques, billeting there for the night. The next morning we marched to St. Omer, and entrained for Steenwerck, from where the Battalion marched to Armentieres, and relieved the 34th Battalion in the Houplines sector on the 8th April.

The sector taken over was the one held by the 10th Brigade during the latter half of December, 1916, and January, 1917. In addition to holding the line we previously held, the 40th Battalion now had the sector of the right battalion also, the battalion sector now extending from the River Lys southwards to Australia-avenue, a frontage of about 2600 yards. The sector on the right was known as the L'Epinette sector, and was held by the 39th Battalion. The disposition of the companies from left to right was D Company (Capt. L. F. Giblin), C Company (Capt. H. J. Dumaresq), B Company (Capt. A. Cruickshank), and A Company (Capt. J. D. W. Chisholm). The trenches had been much knocked about since we last occupied them. The front-line breastwork in many places was subsiding on itself, and gum-boots were still necessary to cope with the mud and water in the communication trenches. The weather was still wet and cold, and snow fell as late as the 10th April.

With spring approaching, the artillery activity on both sides had increased, particularly on the left half of our sector, and on the 10th, 11th, and 12th April the enemy appeared to register with his artillery and heavy minenwerfer on all trenches from the River Lys to Edmeads-avenue. He also burst his heavy minenwerfer in the air over our front line, which was the biggest explosion, outside of an artillery ammunition dump, we had heard up to that time.

On the afternoon and evening of the 12th April this bombardment was very heavy, and finally at 10.15 p.m. developed into a barrage on the D and C Companys' sectors, embracing front and support lines, communication trenches, and the points where the communication trenches joined the subsidiary lines. This was preparatory to a most determined attempt to raid our trenches. The barrage lasted for nearly an hour, battered our front line out of recognition, blocked all communication and support trenches, and severed all telephone communications. At about 10.45 p.m. the barrage lifted off the front line at Hobbs' Farm, but continued on the front line to the left and right of the farm. As all passage along the trenches was blocked, nobody knew what was happening, except just round their own particular posts. Only two posts actually saw the enemy, the one being a Lewis gun post immediately on the left of Hobbs' Farm, and the other a Lewis gun post about 100 yards to the right of it. No. 599, Sgt. H. C. Long, on the latter post, saw the enemy, about 80 strong, in front of Hobbs' Farm. He put up a succession of Verey lights over them, which enabled the Lewis gunners to see them. These Lewis guns were worked by No. 734, Pte. E. W. Stevens, and No. 5752, Pte. D. L. Pitchford, who opened fire on the enemy as soon as the Verey lights from the right showed them up. This fire appeared to cause a number of casualties and much confusion. Some of the enemy ran and some took refuge in shell-holes, round which the Lewis guns continued to play. A Stoke's mortar of the 10th Australian Light Trench Mortar Battery, whose duty it was during an attack to put down a barrage in front of Hobbs' Farm, had put down an excellent barrage immediately behind the party, which also added to their troubles. Verey lights from Sgt. Long still continued, and between each light a few of the enemy could be seen making a run back to safety. Just behind where the raiding party appeared the ground in No Man's Land sloped away, and here the enemy was safe from frontal fire. Behind this the enemy was able to get his wounded away, as he was not interfered with during his withdrawal, owing to the fact that the trenches between posts had been blocked, and at the time only about six people knew what had happened. Two men were sent out as soon as possible, but owing to the very black night they were unable to find anything, but on the following afternoon an officer and non-commissioned officer crawled out among the shell-holes in daylight and brought in a dead German and a quantity of equipment. Further details of the raid were obtained from a prisoner captured on the south of the Lys a few nights later. He stated that this raiding party was part of a large storming party, who had been specially selected and trained for raiding near the River Lys. He also stated that their casualties on the night of the 12th were heavy. Our casualties during the raid were 19.

The two Lewis gunners, Ptes. Pitchford and Stevens, received the Military Medal for their part in repelling the raid, and Capt. H. J. Dumaresq, Lieut. F. C. Green, 2nd Lieut. T. T. Hoskins, No. 605 Sgt. R. K. Wilson, No. 773 Pte. J. Spellman, and No. 1911 Pte. L. F. Metcalfe were congratulated in Divisional orders for their work during the raid.

The damage done during the bombardment was very considerable, and in places it was impossible to repair it. The whole of the front line, from Cambridge-avenue to Irish-avenue, had been blotted out. A start was made at once to repair the trenches, but the work was considerably hampered by enemy shelling. On the two following days we had several casualties, including Capt. L. F. Giblin, Officer Commanding D Company, who was wounded by a shell. On the 15th April the enemy again heavily shelled the D Company's sector, and at 7.45 p.m. he put down another heavy barrage on that company's front and support lines. It looked as if the enemy was about to try another raid on us, when he suddenly switched his barrage across the river on to the trenches held by a British unit, and raided there, where he succeeded in entering their trenches and captured several prisoners. Our casualties during this bombardment amounted to 16.

On the 16th April the 38th Battalion relieved the 40th Battalion, and we moved into support in Armentieres. During the next fortnight 79 reinforcements turned up, and training and working parties were proceeded with until the 27th April, when we crossed the River Lys into Belgium for the first time, and moved up to Ploegsteert Wood, relieving the 44th Battalion in their support position in Ploegsteert Wood.

Chapter IX.

Ploegsteert Wood — Enemy Raid at St. Yves — Our First Big Operation in Sight.

HE support position in Ploegsteert Wood consisted of a system of trenches and wire, forming a series of strong points for the defence of the wood. Battalion Headquarters was at a log cabin known as Rifle House, in the centre of the wood. Companies were distributed in defensive positions, as follows:—

A Company at Ploegsteert Hall and Bunhill Row.
B Company in Hunter's Avenue and Eel Pie Forts.
C Company at Lancaster House and Bunhill Row.
D Company at Touquet Berthe.

The wood consisted of about 200 acres of heavily timbered, flat ground, and was in pre-war days a game preserve. In April, 1917, it was little damaged by shell fire, except on the northern edge, where constant shell-fire on the Ploegsteet-Messines-road had left a number of shattered tree-trunks. In odd places, where our batteries had drawn artillery fire, the wood was also damaged a little. The enemy used to put a few shells into the Wood, and machine-gun bullets flew about among the trees at night; but at that time the Wood was a "home." It was early spring, and the trees were turning to green. The Wood was full of birds, and they did not worry about shelling; in fact, they whistled louder during a "strafe" than at any other time. Even the cuckoo, who from his voice would appear to be a bird of sorrows, seemed to have a derisive note when a shell dropped near him. After living in the trenches, where the only animal was the loathsome rat, we took much interest in these birds; the same sort of childish interest as of a city youngster let loose in the bush. Even the little fish that appeared mysteriously, from Heaven-knows-where, in the shallow ditches in the wood were objects of absorbing interest.

With our entry into Ploegsteert Wood, the weather suddenly turned, and remained fine. Within three weeks it was full summer. The Battalion lived in shirt sleeves, and "shorts" became the popular wear, until the heavy hand of "Division" fell on this engaging fashion. A faith in the ultimate sanity even of "Division" led us to believe that this was not due to a blindness to the merits of "shorts," so much as to well-grounded fears that "shorts" would be obtained in general by mutilation of "Breeches cord, G.S." This touching belief was shattered, however, in the summer of 1918, when a battalion request to be allowed to appear in legitimate "shorts" purchased from regimental funds met with a chilly reception, and was ultimately lost in the recesses of "corps" pigeon-holes.

But to get on with the war. Through the Wood, and leading to the trenches north of it, were several duck-walk tracks named after London streets, such as The Strand, Regent-street, Picadilly, &c. On the north of the Wood, at the junction of Mud Lane Breastwork with the Ploegsteert-Messines-road, was one of the best and most unfavourably known places on the Western Front, known as Hyde Park Corner. A few yards from Hyde Park Corner was the beginning of Hill 63. It was only about 200 feet above sea-level, but in Belgium that is quite a mountain. From Hyde Park Corner were several tunnels capable of holding a battalion. These tunnels were lit up with electric light, and known as "The Catacombs."

The village of Ploegsteert, which was about 700 yards south of the Wood, was very badly knocked about, and was a very unhealthy spot on account of the numerous batteries round drawing the enemy fire. At that time the traffic of horse transport, ammunition mules, and motor lorries along the Ploegsteert-Messines-road was very heavy, and made a favourite target for the enemy artillery.

Around the Wood were several dumps, mostly off the Ploegsteert-Messines-road, and from these dumps light railways ran through the Wood, and were used for taking rations, ammunition, and engineering material forward by trucks, which were pushed up by working parties.

A party of about 60 men were detached from the Battalion for duty with a tunnelling Company, who were preparing the tunnels for mines under the enemy trenches at Messines. The Lewis gun teams were also attached to the 39th Battalion, who were holding the front line. Just before daybreak on the morning of the 30th April, the enemy put down a heavy barrage on the trenches in front of the Wood at St. Yves, apparently with the object of getting into the mine saps from our front line and blowing them in. A few of the enemy actually got into the 39th Battalion trenches, but the main attack was broken by a Lewis-gun team of the 40th Battalion, which was attached to the 39th Battalion for duty. No 89. Pte. S. H. Lawler, and No. 314, Pte. H. Evans, worked this

Lewis gun, and fired 16 magazines (752 rounds) into the enemy attacking party. with great effect. As the enemy withdrew there was sufficient light to follow him with fire to his own trenches, and these two men made the most of it, inflicting heavy casualties. Pte. Lawler continued to fire his gun, although his hands were badly burned by the gun running hot. Both of these men were commended by the Divisional Commander in Divisional Orders for their gallantry on that occasion.

While in Ploegsteert Wood, Captain J. H. Gard, Adjutant of the Battalion (and an officer of the A. and I. Staff in Australia) left the Battalion to take up staff work. His place as Adjutant was taken by Lieut. F. C. Green. Capt. Gard was afterwards killed while Acting Brigade Major of the 11th Brigade. He was on a visit to the 40th Battalion sector at Hamel in July, 1918, when he was mortally wounded by a German sniper, and was carried out past the Battalion Headquarters, of which he was for some time a valued member. He was, in fact, one of the first officers to be allotted to the Battalion, and materially assisted in its first organization and training.

About this time the Commanding Officer (Lieut.-Col. J. E. C. Lord) was informed that the 3rd Australian Division would take part in the intended attack on Messines Ridge, and that the 40th Battalion would attack on the right of the New Zealand Division, whose objective included Messines, and that our objective would probably include the trenches immediately north of the River Douve, known as Ulna Beak, Ulna Support, and Ulna Switch. We were also told that we would have to throw bridges across the River Douve, and get across them before we reached the enemy's front line. The commanding officer at once arranged for all officers to have every facility for reconnoitring approaches, and having a look at the enemy's trenches from a distance. A concrete observation post on the top of Hill 63 was therefore placed at our disposal during certain hours of the day. From Hill 63 one could get a fine view of the enemy lines, such points as La Petite Douve Farm, and La Douve Farm, and Schnitzel Farm become familiar. It was a favourite pastime to lie in the sun on the top of Hill 63 and watch our artillery sending the enemy trenches into the air, and hammering clouds of dust out of the defences of Messines. The only unpleasant sight on the landscape was what appeared to be wide brown stretches of dead ferns, from the enemy front line up the hill towards Messines, and along the valley of the Douve, but closer inspection through the field-glasses revealed the unpleasant fact that they were not harmless plants, but stretches of barbed wire entanglements of great strength. We also rather took an interest in the River Douve, and with the object of a closer inspection of it, visited the New Zealanders on the north of that stream, who gave us hospitality, information, and a good view of the river. It was the first time that Austrailans and New Zealanders were to attack together since Gallipoli, and the prospect was obviously pleasing to both parties. Right up to the day of the attack the New Zealanders said, "We must get Messines, or the Australians will get hell"; and we said, "We will have to get there, or the New Zealanders will fall in."

On the 6th May the 40th Battalion relieved the 39th Battalion in the Ploegsteert-St. Yves Sector.

Chapter X.

In the Line at St. Yves — Great Activity on Both Sides — The Tunnels — Working Parties — Our Raid near the Douve River — Heavy Gas Shelling at Romarin — The Day before the Attack at Messines.

HE sector taken over extended from a point known as Seaforth Farm, about 250 yards south of the River Douve, south-easterly to Lowndes-avenue. The disposition of companies from left to right was B. Company (Capt. C. L. McVilly), A Company (Capt. J. D. W. Chisholm), C. Company (Capt. H. J. Dumaresq), D Company (Capt. W. C. G. Ruddock).

On the 7th May, the day after taking over this sector, the enemy artillery was fairly heavy along our front, and he registered certain points with smoke-shell. At 7.15 p.m. that evening he opened a heavy bombardment with artillery and trench mortars on the C and D Company sectors. Artillery retaliation was obtained, and the bombardment continued until 9 p.m., when it ceased, but at 9.15 p.m. it opened again heavier than before on D Company's sector. The S.O.S. was called for on D Company's front at 9.20 p.m., and machine guns and Lewis guns also brought heavy fire to bear across our front. The barrage continued until 9.40 p.m., when it suddenly ceased. It was believed that the enemy had attempted a raid, but that he had been caught by our artillery and machine-gun fire in No Man's Land, and the raiding party broken up, as the answer to our S.O.S. call was particularly prompt and heavy. The damage to our trenches was considerable, and took our working parties some days to repair. Our casualties amounted to 16.

On the 8th May the largest reinforcement the Battalion ever received arrived. It numbered 105 other ranks, who were welcomed and inspected by the Commanding Officer in Ploegsteert Wood. This reinforcement had a cheerful introduction to the trenches. As a reply to the enemy activity on the previous day, a very special shoot had been arranged for 8 p.m., in which every gun on the corps front was to be let loose for 15 minutes. This caught the reinforcement in the 60-pounder zone, and gave them a high standard of normal artillery activity on the Western Front.

The next few days were full of incident. Our own artillery fire was particularly heavy, but the troops in the line were mostly concerned with the trench mortar shoots, which took place several times daily on every part of the front, and to which the enemy generally replied. Our medium trench mortars (known as "plum puddings," on account of the shape of the shell) were chiefly used, and hundreds were sent over every day into the enemy belts of wire, with great effect. It was here that we changed our opinion of the trench mortar batteries. Up to that time their custom was to fire off about 20 rounds and then clear out, leaving the infantry to get the retaliation from the enemy. But here they were always ready for a bout with the enemy, and did deliberate and correct shooting with proper observation. Having done their shoot, they then waited for the retaliation, and as soon as they saw the first "minnie" in the air some more Stoke's shells and "plum puddings" would be let go. The way the trench mortar people stood by their guns was greatly appreciated by the infantry, and we got much assistance from them, particularly through the efforts of Lieut. J. D. Oliver and Lieut. G. S. Brown, of the 10th Light Trench Mortar Battery. The artillery also fired on the wire with a new wire-cutting fuze, and the combined efforts of artillery and trench mortars soon showed that the enemy entanglements would not be a serious obstacle on the "Day of the Race."

Our patrols were also very busy exploring No Man's Land and making a reconnaissance of the River Douve. These patrols generally went to the enemy wire, and established the fact that the enemy was very busy on his defences, as his working parties could be heard all night.

Sniping was very active on both sides of No Man's Land, and often developed into a periscope-smashing contest, at which both sides became very proficient. It was rather thought that the enemy won this game, as our periscopes only measured 4 inches by 2 inches, while his were much bigger. Anyhow, if the game had kept going any longer, we should have had no more periscopes to play with.

One of the most interesting features of this sector was the tunnels from our front line under the enemy line, in which mines had been placed ready for exploding at the right moment. The entrance to the tunnels were carefully camouflaged, but inquisitive people found the occupants to be mostly Canadian tunnellers. These Canadians took little notice of anybody except the trench mortar personnel, who sometimes placed their trench mortars alongside the sap-heads and drew fire on to the entrances to the tunnels. Our sympathies were always with the tunnellers in this argument, as the trench mortar people had often alienated what affection we had for them by putting their contraptions alongside our Headquarters and dugouts and important parts of trenches. The disadvantage of having them alongside a cherished spot was that the enemy always threw his ironmongery at them when they fired, and damaged the landscape in the immediate vicinity. The tunnellers at Messines were men of mystery. They were silent as to what was under the enemy lines and what strange things happened there. Sometimes they came out of their burrows and stretched their limbs, and gazed at the sun with the eyes of a sun-worshipper who seldom sees his God. They drank our whisky and beer in fellowship, cursed the scheme of things that caused them to live underground, and crawled back into the darkness again.

On the 15th May the Battalion was relieved by the 37th Battalion, and proceeded to hutments at Oosthove Farm, near Nieppe. During this spell of 10 days in the line our casualties were six killed and 43 wounded. From this time until the 7th June working parties never ceased, and every available officer and non-commissioned officer and man was employed in constructing gun emplacements for the artillery, unloading artillery ammunition from trains and carrying it to dumps, carrying trench mortar ammunition up the line, and constructing dugouts and assembly trenches. Another frequent job was cable-burying, which meant that miles of trenches 7 feet deep had to be dug and filled in on top of the cable, so that communication during the battle could be kept up between artillery and infantry and the various infantry headquarters. Some of the regimental transport were also having a strenuous time in getting ammunition and material forward by horse-drawn trolleys along the tram-lines through Ploegsteert Wood. They were subjected to heavy shelling, and suffered many casualties in this work.

By this time preliminary orders for the attack had been issued by Brigade Headquarters, and a large model about 30 yards square of the country around Messines, showing the enemy trenches and defensive positions, as disclosed by aeroplane photographs, was constructed at Brune Gaye. Certain hours had been allotted to each battalion to visit the model, and when not on working parties all available men went there, and the country was studied and explained so fully that everybody knew what his objective was and what his job would be in the attack.

In addition to this, aeroplane photographs were received and circulated, showing the state of the enemy's defences from day to day. These necessarily altered daily, as the enemy dug trenches and our artillery blotted out trenches. The country around Oosthove Farm was the scene of much enemy counter-battery work. Our batteries were very numerous, and the enemy shelled them daily. He also searched the area with his artillery for ammunition dumps, and extra violent concussions frequently indicated that he sometimes found them. There was a 6-inch battery about 50 yards from the farm. This battery was shelled daily, and no greater tribute could be paid to the enemy's gunnery than the fact that the occupants of the farm, the 40th Battalion Headquarters Staff, never moved during the enemy's shelling. Even the officers' mess in the farm would carry on with the menu to the accompaniment of 200 5·9 shells landing from 50 to 100 yards away. It was felt that the enemy was a good gunner, and would not spoil his reputation by sending over a shell as much as 50 yards from his target. The philosophy of the regimental Omar was, "He's a good gunner, and 'twill all be well."

About this time the Commanding Officer was sent for by Division to act upon the Divisional Staff until after the attack on Messines. Major J. P. Clark therefore temporarily commanded the Battalion. At the same time a percentage of officers and 110 other ranks, who were not going into the attack, were sent off to the divisional concentration camp at Morbecque. This was in accordance with orders from General Headquarters. The 110 other ranks consisted of a percentage of non-commissioned officers, instructors, signallers, &c., from which the Battalion could be reorganised in the event of heavy casualties. At this time four officers per company was the maximum allowed to take part in an attack. At Ypres this number was cut down to three per company, and in the first four months of the Somme fighting in 1918 the system was extended to the somewhat intensive trench fighting, and 20 officers per battalion was the maximum allowance for a tour of duty in the line.

On the 27th May the Battalion left Oosthove Farm, and proceeded to a camp of hutments known as Regina Camp, near Romarin, where working parties were proceeded with as before. Here final preparations were made, such as sewing diamond-shaped pieces of coloured cloth on the backs of tunics to indicate the troops for different objectives; distributing different coloured arm-bands, indicating which men were signallers, runners, carrying-parties, stretcher-bearers, moppers-up, scouts, &c.; issuing bombs, rifle grenades, flares, iron rations, &c.; and also sharpening bayonets on a grindstone and blackening them so that they would not show up before the attack.

Regina Camp was surrounded by batteries, which were shelled heavily by the enemy. Dumps of ammunition grew in every field and under every hedge, and some of these were exploded daily by the enemy fire. The result of this was, that when a dump went up, heavy pieces of shell fell in our own camp. On one occasion Lieut. N. R. Meagher was reading a battalion order in his hut, when about half a 6-inch shell crashed through the roof, carried the order out of his hands, and buried itself and the order in the earth under the hut floor. The enemy also used incendiary shells in the vicinity of the batteries, and blazing huts, farms, camouflage, and dumps resulted. The Quartermaster's store was set alight in this manner.

We were practically free from air-bombing by the enemy, as at that time he confined most of it to the railways and towns further back. His aeroplanes were particularly active in "spotting" for their batteries, and occasionally an air fight took place above our heads, which was always a popular sight. Towards evening the enemy planes liked to make a sporting attack on our observation balloons, and despite the barrage of dozens of anti-aircraft guns, often brought one down in flames.

As the day of the attack drew nearer the necessity for obtaining prisoners daily became greater, in order to learn of any change in the enemy dispositions. No attempt had been made to conceal the fact that we were going to attack Messines, and we were told that it was part of the army plan to advertise the fact. Anyhow, the enemy could not have been in doubt as to our intentions.

With the object of securing prisoners, small parties raided the enemy lines on our divisional front almost every day. On the morning of the 31st May the 40th Battalion sent over a raiding party of three officers and 40 other ranks. Capt. C. L. McVilly was officer commanding raid, and Lieut. L. W. Barnett and Lieut R. C. Walters were in charge of the storming parties. The trenches to be raided were in that part of the enemy front line known as Ulrica Trench, at a point about 150 yards south of the River Douve. The raid was carried out without artillery assistance.

The raiding party arrived in our front line at Seaforth Farm, where raid headquarters was established, at about 11 p.m. on the 30th May, and two scouts at once went out and laid a tape from our front line to the enemy trench, at the proposed point of entry. The scouts reported back at 12.30 a.m., and the raiding party moved off across No Man's Land in three sections in single file.

Owing to the enemy putting up many Verey lights, progress was slow, and it took an hour to get to the enemy wire. The party got through the gap in the enemy wire safely, but were confronted with a deep ditch between the wire and the trench. Until that time the enemy had remained quiet, but it was believed that he had seen our party. At 2.5 a.m. it was beginning to get light, and Lieut. Barnett gave the signal to rush. As the party crossed the ditch they were met with a shower of bombs, which caused several casualties. The unwounded got on to the enemy parapet and found the trench full of Germans. A bomb fight took place, and our party suffered severely from bombs in front and also rifle fire from the flanks; but we inflicted heavy casualties with bombs on the enemy in the trench, and were making headway against big opposition when the signal was given by the officer commanding raid for the party to withdraw: it was getting quite light, and therefore dangerous for further delay. Our party therefore withdrew, and had great difficulty in getting across No Man's Land with the wounded, owing to the heavy machine-gun fire that had opened.

Our casualties amounted to two killed and 18 wounded. At that time there was also one man missing, No. 1008, Pte. W. Kelty. The manner in which he turned up would be incredible but for the number of reliable witnesses. During the raid Pte. Kelty jumped into the enemy trench, and proceeded to get busy with his bayonet, when a bomb burst behind him. He felt a blow on the head at the same time, and lost consciousness and any further interest in the proceedings. Some time about midday he woke up in the enemy trench, and took stock of his position. He was severely wounded, his arms and equipment had been taken, and he had apparently been left for dead by the enemy. The trench where he was lying was badly damaged, and was being bombarded by our medium trench mortars. He seemed unable to move to get away from the bombardment, and decided to remain there, when a trench mortar shell burst in the trench near him, and he again lost consciousness. At this moment a trench mortar officer and an officer of the 39th Battalion, who were watching the shoot from our front line, saw the body of a man blown into the air by a burst and fall into No Man's Land. They thought it must be one of the enemy, and drew the attention of several others to the incident. As they were looking at the body it was seen to move, stand up, and stagger towards our line. It was then seen that he was an Australian. After going about 20 yards he collapsed, and an officer of the 39th Battalion jumped over the parapet, ran into No Man's Land, picked him up, and carried him in. At any other time this would have been suicidal, but owing to our heavy continuous bombardment of the enemy trenches prior to the attack at Messines the enemy sought shelter in his concrete dugouts during the day, and seldom appeared.

Pte. Kelty was found to be severely wounded in several places, but gave a coherent account of what had happened. He recovered from his wounds, and rejoined the Battalion, but was wounded again at Morlancourt on the 28th March, 1918, and lost a leg. He was sent to Australia, but the hospital ship he was on was torpedoed and sunk. He was rescued from the ship, and finally reached Tasmania.

On the evening of the 4th June the enemy put a heavy gas shell bombardment on all the batteries round Romarin. It was a very still evening, and the gas hung round Regina Camp so thickly that box respirators had to be worn. A trial assembly march had been ordered for that evening. It was commenced, but C Company ran into thick gas, and sustained casualties, so the march was cancelled. Realising that to remain at Regina Camp meant that everybody would have to sit up all night wearing small box respirators, the Acting Commanding Officer took the whole Battalion to Brune Gaye, where the rest of the night was spent in the fields. One company selected a potato field, and slept in lines between the rows of potatoes. Next morning at 5 a.m. we went back by companies towards Romarin. The roads were blocked with horse transport unable to get forward on account of the gas, which hung there in an invisible cloud, and all movement forward was suspended until 8 a.m., when a light breeze dispersed the poisoned atmosphere. This was the first heavy "gassing" we had, and the casualties amounted to 36, some of which were serious, and took nearly six months to recover, while others came back in a few days.

There was a pleasant theory fostered by the Higher Command that there would be no working parties for a week before the attack, and that the last two days would be devoted to sleep and other religious exercises. As it happened, a particularly heavy piece of assembly-trench digging was our lot up to the last night, and final preparations had to take the place of sleep on the day before Zero Day.

During the afternoon of the 6th June a code message was received that Zero Hour would be 3.10 a.m. on the following morning. Working parties were hastily recalled, final preparations were begun. A hot meal was issued, and the men advised to snatch an hour's sleep, but everybody seemed too excited to rest. In later operations it was unnecessary to advise anybody to get all the rest and sleep they could, but Messines was our first big battle, and we had a lot to learn.

The popular idea seems to be that soldiers were always eager to get into battle. That idea was certainly promulgated by English war correspondents and other people—no doubt in the interests of recruiting. It is admitted that if most men were offered a chance to stay out of a fight they would refuse, because it is a fundamental principle of the code of "dinkum blokes" to stick to friends and go through hell with them if they have to go; so to stay out of a fight of your own free will is to forfeit self-respect. But to say that men are anxious to get into the horrors of a battle for sheer pleasure is an insult to the intelligence of an outsider, and not exactly complimentary to the mentality of the soldier who knows what it means. He knows that some ugly and untidy death will strike down some of his pals, and he knows that he himself is perhaps spending his last day on earth. He realises that the result of the day will be that in many more Australian homes will be despairing women—and perhaps in his own home. He does not mention these things. He hides his feelings behind a camouflage of cheerful optimism on his prospects of a nice clean wound. If he takes some letters and treasured things and hands them to a pal who is not going into the "stunt," he does it with careless detachment. And yet the "stunt" war correspondents talk glibly of the eagerness and lightheartedness of the troops at going into action. A man who says he went into battle with a light heart is either a liar or a mental pervert.

Chapter XI.

The Plan of Attack at Messines — The Approach March — The Battle.

EFORE giving a narrative of the part played by the 40th Battalion in the Battle of Messines, it would be well to explain what made the capture of the Messines-Wytschaete Ridge a vital necessity. It is necessary to go back to the fateful and historic month of October, 1914, when the German Army, fresh from the capture of Antwerp, tried to force a way through Ypres to the Channel Ports. The attempt was nearly successful, and after the second attempt, known as the second Battle of Ypres, our line was like a tightly-strung bow, with Ypres at the notch of the arrow, and the enemy held all the high ground, the most important part of which was the Messines-Wytschaete Ridge, from which the enemy had direct observation over the Ypres salient. In addition to the fact that this advantage made life unpleasant in the salient, it was obvious that no big offensive operation could be undertaken in the vicinity of Ypres until the commanding position of Messines-Wytschaete Ridge had been captured.

The attack was made by the Second Army, with nine divisions. The 3rd Australian Division was on the right flank of the attack, with the New Zealand Division on their immediate left, until the Black Line (Map No. 4) was reached, when the 4th Australian Division moved through the New Zealand Division to the furthest objective, known as the Green Line.

The 3rd Australian Division attacked, with the 10th Brigade on the left, and the 9th Brigade on the right, with the 11th Brigade in Divisional Reserve.

The 10th Brigade attacked with the 37th, 38th, 39th, and 40th Battalions, less one company of the 39th Battalion in Brigade Reserve. The brigade attacked with two battalions in line—the 39th Battalion south of the Douve, and the 40th Battalion north of the Douve. The following were the objectives of each battalion in the brigade. (Map No. 4).

40th Battalion (less 1½ Companies attached to 37th Battalion)—To capture the Beak, Ulna Support, and Ulna Switch, and clear the enemy territory within the following area:—

Douve River, brigade northern boundary, and the line shown on the map; also to bridge the River Douve, on the southern front of the Beak.

39th Battalion—To capture and clear enemy territory within the boundaries of the Douve River, Black Line, and the brigade southern boundary.

38th Battalion—To pass through the 40th Battalion and capture Ulna Avenue, Ulcer Reserve, Douve Switch, Schnitzel Farm, Ungodly Trench, Bethlehem Farm, and consolidate the Black Line.

37th Battalion (with 1½ Companies of the 40th Battalion)— To pass through the 38th Battalion and assemble in rear of the Black Line not later than 9¼ hours after Zero hour. At 10 hours after Zero hour to push forward, with the 47th Battalion on the left, to the capture of portion of Ungodly Avenue, and portion of the Uncanny and Undulating trench systems, finally consolidating the Green Line between the bridge over the Douve River and Huns' Walk.

The 1½ companies of the 40th Battalion (Capt. L. F. Giblin) attached to the 37th Battalion consisted of the whole of D Company, and 60 men made up from A and B Companies, under Lieutenant H. L. Foster. These 60 men were to act as a carrying party from our front line to the Green Line.

The objectives of the 40th Battalion were as follow:—

> A Company (Capt. J. D. W. Chisholm) to bridge the river, capture 200 yards of the enemy front line immediately north of the river, and capture Ulna Switch.
>
> B Company (Capt. C. L. McVilly) to bridge the river, capture the south side of the Beak (on the left of A Company), and advance and clear Ulna Avenue to the Battalion objective.
>
> C Company (Lieut. C. W. Baldwin) to capture the part of the Beak along the Messines-road, to clear Ulna Support from Ulna Avenue to the left of the Sector, and to join up with B Company on the objective.

Special parties of A and B Companies were detailed to carry bridges out at Zero hour, and throw them across the river. In addition to these tasks, A Company had to dig a communication trench from Ulcer Reserve to a point in the enemy front line, south of Ulna Avenue.

The assembly trenches of the 40th Battalion were near the front line, north and south of the River Douve, with Nos. 1 to 7 platoons immediately south of the river, between the river and Seaforth Farm, and Nos. 8 to 12 platoons immediately north of the river, in the New Zealand sector. D Company assembly trenches were in the subsidiary line, as they were not to attack until 10.10 a.m., which was the hour for the advance to the last objective. Battalion headquarters was in a dugout 200 yards behind the front line, between Seaforth Farm and Donnington Hall, and the R.A.P. (Capt. W. I. Clark) was in a dugout near where the Ploegsteert-Messines-road crossed our front line.

The River Douve ran diagonally across our front; from our front line to the enemy's. It was about 12 feet wide, and the banks were very steep. The enemy had wired both banks, so that the river presented a formidable obstacle, which would be a death-trap to troops who failed to get across, as they would be held up under the enemy fire at close range. Six light bridges had been carried up and placed near the front line, ready to be carried out and thrown across the stream as soon as the attack commenced. Not only did the first seven platoons of the 40th Battalion have to use these bridges to get across, but they were also vitally necessary for the 37th and 38th Battalions, who were leapfrogging through the 40th Battalion.

Two routes were used in the approach march. These routes which were marked out and reconnoitred beforehand, kept clear of the roads, which were likely to be shelled. One route was known as the "Brown Route," and was used by Battalion Headquarters, Nos. 8 to 12 platoons, and D Company with the 37th Battalion. This route was from Regina Camp up the Romarin-Ploegsteert-road to a point 400 yards west of Ploegsteert; from there, north-east, crossing the Messines-Ploegsteert-road; thence west of Creslow Farm, and crossing the road about 100 yards beyond Hyde Park Corner; thence over the western slope of Hill 63, and down the other side past Dead Cow Farm, Barossa Farm, and across the Douve into the Assembly trenches in the New Zealand sector. The second route was known as the "Green Route," and was used by Nos. 1 to 7 platoons. The starting point of this route was Oosthove Farm; from there crossing the Ploegsteert-Armentieres-road about 300 yards south of Ploegsteert, and passing midway between Ploegsteert and Touquet Berthe; thence to the west end of Regent-street, and then through Ploegsteert Wood, *via* the Strand and Bunhill Row; thence along Mud Lane to Poole's Cottages, and then by Ainscroft Avenue to the front line at Anton's Farm, and then along the front line to Seaforth Farm.

The experiences of the Battalion on both routes were very similar. We moved from the starting points at about 11 p.m. Before going half a mile the effects of the enemy's counter measures were felt, when gas shells began to arrive. He was saturating the country south of the Wood, and the Wood itself, with gas. Every German gun seemed to be pouring gas shells over, and the air was full of the whine peculiar to the aerial flight of a gas-shell. They burst all round the columns, and a number of men were killed or wounded by flying nose-caps. Occasionally the monotonous whine and pop of impact was relieved by a high explosive or an incendiary shell, and the casualties were fairly heavy. The remainder of the approach march was like a nightmare. The actual wearing of a small box-respirator is a physical discomfort at any time, but on a hot dark night for men loaded with ammunition, arms, and equipment, it is a severe strain. Wounded and gassed men were falling out, and officers and non-commissioned officers were continually removing their respirators to give orders and to keep their platoons together. A shell would burst in a platoon, the dead and wounded would fall, and the rest of the platoon would pull themselves together and move on, for above everything was the fixed determination to be in position at the Zero hour, and the realisation that this terrible gassing, if it prevented our arrival on time, might easily result in the failure of the whole operation. The columns of goggle-eyed men moved forward among the trees, and on both sides was the glare from burning dumps lit up by the incendiary shells. By the time we reached Hyde Park Corner and Mud Lane we were just about "all out," but beyond this point was comparative sanctuary. The enemy was not putting gas on to Hill 63, or the high ground between the Hill and Prowse Point, so we sank on the ground, pulled our respirators off, and breathed air as refreshing as cool beer on a hot Australian summer day. The Medical Officer provided the comic relief. He was in front with the Adjutant, and fell into a shell-hole. Being loaded up with medical stores, he decided that the best way out was to crawl out, so he started to crawl on his hands and knees, while the Headquarters Staff watched him with great interest and delight. He crawled up what he thought was the side of the shell-hole for some time, and came to the conclusion that it was "some" hole. So he cautiously removed his respirator and had a look round. He then realised that he had been crawling up the side of Hill 63.

After a brief rest and hasty reorganisation we pushed up to the trenches. Our casualties during the approach march numbered 90, and seriously affected the strength of some platoons. At 2.35 a.m. the Battalion was in the Assembly Trenches. Here was comparative quietness, as all the enemy artillery seemed to be throwing gas-shell into the back areas. Occasionally a high explosive crashed into the front line, and one of these caused several casualties in C Company. Zero hour had been fixed at 3.10 a.m. At 3 o'clock everything was quiet, just as if another ordinary day in the trenches was about to begin. A few minutes later the enemy opened with machine guns, as if he suspected some movement. Several flares went up, but at 3.6 a.m. all was quiet again, except for the gas-shelling away back. Officers looked anxiously at their watches, counting the seconds, but a signal—perhaps louder than any other in the history of war—was to mark the hour of 10 minutes past three o'clock on the 7th June, 1917. The machine guns, probably realising that perhaps their only chance of being heard was to "beat the pistol," started 15 seconds too soon. Their staccato notes swelled into a rip, only to be drowned a few seconds later, as the whole of our artillery barrage from hundreds of guns crashed down. Simultaneously with the artillery barrage came a deeper rumble from the 19 mines and their million pounds of high explosive. The trenches shook and rocked like a ship in a heavy sea, and in some places fell in, and at the same moment a mass of earth, thrown hundreds of feet high, was seen in front against the sky, like a black column capped with a dull red flame. The infantry climbed the parapet and walked quickly towards the enemy. The battle of Messines had begun.

The battle of Messines in its opening stages was as much a soldier's battle as Inkermann, which was fought in thick mist. The infantry plunged from the half light of dawn into a curtain of mist, dust, and smoke, which hung over the valley of the Douve. Platoons made straight to their objective, but saw nothing beyond what was going on round them. Visual signalling was impossible through the mist. The fact that the enemy artillery was busy throwing gas shell was, perhaps, responsible for the fact that we had few casualties in crossing No Man's Land. By the time his S.O.S. barrage came down our troops had thrown their bridges across the river, and crossed themselves. Some did not wait for the bridges, but plunged into the stream and climbed up the opposite bank. About 40 prisoners were taken from shell-holes in front of the enemy trenches, the enemy apparently thinking these shell-holes safer than their own trenches when the attack began. The only opposition from the front line was from a machine gun where the Messines-road crossed the south point of the Beak. This machine gun was firing on A Company, and Lieut. W. T. Crosby and No. 2156, Sergt. L. K. Swan, of C Company, moved behind it and disposed of the crew with bombs. After crossing the front line, machine-gun fire from the higher ground in front caused several casualties. One machine gun, firing from Ulna Switch, was rushed by a party from A Company, who disposed of the crew, and turning the gun round opened fire on numbers of the enemy who had jumped out of the trenches and were running towards Ulcer Reserve Trench. About 50 prisoners were captured in Ulna Avenue and Ulna Switch, with scarcely any resistance. They were evidently demoralised by the noise of the mines and the bombardment.

At 3.30 a.m. the 40th Battalion objective had been won, and we were in touch with the 39th Battalion on our right, and the New Zealanders on the left. A few minutes later the 38th Battalion leapfrogged through us on their way to the second objective—the "Black Line." As soon as the 38th Battalion passed through, B and C Companies began to dig in on our objective, while A Company started a communication trench from the south of Ulna Avenue towards Ulcer Reserve. This was intended to be joined up with a communication trench across No Man's Land, which was being constructed by the 3rd Pioneer Battalion. Shelling on the position was light and scattered till 10 a.m., when the mist cleared, and from that time our position was overlooked by enemy balloons, and the whole valley of the Douve was heavily shelled with 4.2 and 5.9 high explosive. Casualties were fairly heavy, and included the O.C. A Company, Capt. J. D. W. Chisholm (wounded). Lieut. N. R. Meagher then took command of the company. Work was proceeded with amid heavy shelling until 2 p.m., when most of our men were sent forward to assist the 37th Battalion in consolidating the Green Line.

Meanwhile D Company had remained in their assembly trenches until 10.15 a.m., when they moved forward in artillery formation on the right of the 37th Battalion. In this formation they crossed our old front line at Seaforth Farm, and moved across the bridges over the Douve, and then up the north side of that river, with the river as their right flank. This advance had been carried out under scattered shelling, which caused about seven casualties. They reached the Black Line at 11.30 a.m., and took up a position in shell-holes and old trenches immediately behind the Black Line, and waited for the hour to advance. They were timed to advance at 1 p.m., but this was postponed until 3 p.m. At

3 p.m. they moved forward across the Black Line, and at once came under heavy machine-gun fire, but pushed on with heavy casualties. When about 200 yards from the Green Line the Company Commander (Capt. L. F. Giblin) was wounded, and his place was taken by Lieut. A. A. Downie, but this officer soon afterwards collapsed, as a result of the gas on the approach march, and Lieut. W. A. Moon took command of the Company. The only enemy encountered between the Green and Black Lines were in a pill-box on the road from Messines to Ash Avenue (U 10 a 0370). Machine-gun fire was coming from this point, and caused several casualties. This pill-box was a combined machine-gun position, and an observation post, built of concrete, and with two storeys. It commanded the whole Douve Valley. As D Company commenced to work up to it the garrison of about 15 men left their guns and ran, but were nearly all picked off by our rifles and Lewis guns. From there the company pushed on to the Green Line, and arrived on their objective at 3.40 p.m. The machine-gun fire was heavy as we started to dig in, most of it coming from the direction of La Potterie Farm and the low ground among the trees on the north side of the river immediately in front of the Green Line. It was at once decided to deal with this low ground, and a platoon, under Sergt. T. G. Cranswick, pushed forward from the objective in small parties. A machine gun was located in a pill-box about 100 yards beyond the objective. A party, under the direction of Sergt. Cranswick, put a barrage of rifle grenades round it, while others got behind and rushed the position, killing several of the enemy, and capturing the gun. A covering party, consisting of a Lewis gun and crew, under No. 1649, Pte. T. S. Jones, remained there until night, doing valuable work. They silenced a machine gun across the river, and scattered several parties of the enemy around La Potterie Farm, inflicting heavy casualties. Another machine gun was rushed and captured by a party under No. 956, Cpl. S. J. Barrett. This gun was among the trees on the bank of the river (U 10 a. 4575). No. 818, Pte. J. Davidson, also captured another in a very gallant manner. He saw one in the sunken road about 200 yards beyond the objective (U 10 a 4090), and worked towards it. The enemy fired and wounded him in the face, but he got up and rushed into the sunken road, from where he shot the crew.

At 4 p.m. the enemy began to shell the Green Line with whizz-bangs, and Lieut. W. A. Moon was wounded, leaving the only officer now remaining, Lieut. R. J. D. Loane, in command of the company. They continued to consolidate, and by 7 p.m. had a continuous trench along their front from the river through Ungodly Avenue to U 4 c 2030. At 7.30 p.m. the enemy shelling became very heavy, but caused few casualties. D Company were well "dug-in." At the same time about 250 of the enemy were seen advancing in close order from Undulating Support through the row of trees on the south side of that trench (U 4 d central). The S.O.S. was put up by C.S.M. R. J. Goodyer, and our machine gun and artillery barrage opened. It was a magnificent reply to an S.O.S., and the 18-pounders came down in front of and among the advancing enemy. Clouds of dust from the bursting shells obscured them from view, and when it cleared about 15 minutes later only dead Germans could be seen. At 7.45 p.m. the 37th Battalion on the left were seen to be withdrawing. Lieut. Loane went across and interviewed the Company Commander on his left, who promised to keep his company there and "stick it," but apparently he was unable to do so, as a few minutes later the 37th Battalion were seen dribbling back towards the Black Line.

As D Company was under the orders of the 37th Battalion, Lieut. Loane sent a message back to the Officer Commanding the 37th Battalion in the Black Line to report what was happening.

Meanwhile A B and C Companies of the 40th Battalion had passed through the Black Line on their way to the Green Line, to assist the 37th Battalion in consolidating, in accordance with orders from Brigade. When half-way between the Green and Black Lines they were ordered to withdraw by the Officer Commanding the 37th Battalion in the Black Line, who also requested Capt. C. L. McVilly, the senior officer of the 40th Battalion there, to withdraw D Company. This Capt. McVilly declined to do, pointing out that such an order was the responsibility of the 37th Battalion, to whom D Company was attached. The Commanding Officer 37th Battalion then sent Lieut. Loane an order to withdraw his company. At 9 p.m. the withdrawal was begun, and D Company had to come back through our own protective barrage, which had been brought back between the Green and Black lines.

D Company spent the remainder of the night in carrying back their wounded from the Green Line, under heavy artillery fire, and at 3 a.m. a patrol under Sergeant T. G. Cranswick reported that the enemy had not occupied the Green Line, nor was it damaged by shell-fire. The whole of the 40th Battalion was now in or near the Black Line, and as this line was overcrowded, A, B, and C Companies were sent back to their original position near Ulna Switch. Before 5 a.m. the 37th Battalion moved forward to the Green Line, and D Company were sent to dig a communication trench from the black line back through Bethleem Farm. This work was commenced at 7.30 a.m., and was under direct observation of enemy observation balloons, in consequence of which an intense bombardment was put down on the position. This caused very heavy casualties in D Company, and continued intermittently until noon, when D Company were sent back to the rest of the 40th Battalion, and came under the orders of their own Commanding Officer again.

The problem of the supply of ammunition, water, and tools was a difficult one, and Lieut. H. L. Foster, with a party of 60 other ranks, had been detailed to carry supplies to the forward troops of the Brigade. This party carried through both days and nights of the operation, sometimes under very heavy shell-fire. Some indication of their very difficult task can be obtained by the fact that this party was reduced by casualties to a total of 11 men. All the supplies were brought up by our pack-transport as far as Seaforth Farm.

At about 8.30 a.m. on the morning of the 9th June the Battalion was relieved by the 42nd Battalion, and we moved out along the Ploegsteert-Messines-road to Ploegsteert, and from there to Nieppe. A good many were completely knocked out, but motor ambulances and lorries picked up the weary ones on the road and took them to their destination. As we got to Nieppe the Belgian newspaper boys were flourishing English papers with black head-lines, "Capture of Messines-Wytschaete Ridge. Great British Victory." But we were all too tired to read them. The only comfort one man could find in his weariness was, " Well, anyhow, we had a fine day for it."

A few words are necessary on the work of the regimental stretcher-bearers. Up to and including Messines the stretcher-bearers were the regimental bandsmen, under Sergt. H. Emms. Their first-aid work was as good as their music, and their stretcher-bearing at Messines was of the highest order. A glance at our casualties will give an indication of the magnitude of the work. They sustained nine casualties, which was a serious blow to the efficiency of the band, and it was decided by "Higher Authority" that in future the band would not go into action. This was adhered to, except on a few occasions when the military situation demanded it. The casualties of the Battalion during the battle were:—

	Officers.	N.C.O's.	Men.
Killed in action	—	3	38
Died of wounds	—	—	5
Wounded	6	23	274
Total	6	26	317

In addition to the names of several officers, N.C.O's., and men who were awarded decorations for gallant conduct during the battle of Messines, the gallantry of the following N.C.O.'s and men was placed on record in Divisional Orders:—No. 1674, L/Cpl. O. W. Sweeney; No. 501, Pte. C. E. Smith; No. 1117, Pte. J. T. Balmforth; No. 1914, Pte. N. Norquay; No. 85, Cpl. C. T. Flood; No. 360, Pte. W. C. Clements; No. 5677, L/Cpl. F. J. Cunningham No. 745, Sgt. H. S. Winburn; No. 651, Sgt. C. Hope; No. 2278, Cpl. J. Braid; No. 825, Pte. C. Ellis; and No. 945, Pte. W. Tapner.

The battle of Messines was undoubtedly a British victory. In one day the Second Army had advanced 2½ miles on a front of nearly 10 miles, wiping out the German salient and capturing the Messines-Wytschaete Ridge. Positions on the ridge had been stormed which the enemy regarded as impregnable, and 7000 prisoners and 70 guns had been captured. Everything had been elaborately prepared. Guns were concentrated, the enemy forward trenches mined; everything was rehearsed, and nothing was overlooked. It was a masterpiece of preparation, and stands as perhaps the best example of the successful capture of a limited objective.

Chapter XII.

Working Parties — On the Messines Ridge in Support — Back to Reserve at Becourt — The New Plan of Attack — A Rabbit, and a Matter of Discipline — On the Road to Ypres.

ON the 9th and 10th June the Battalion remained in billets at Nieppe, and rested. There were a good number of civilians in Nieppe then, most of them refugees from Armentieres, which was being constantly shelled. Nieppe was also being shelled a little, but mostly with gas. On the afternoon of the 11th June we left Nieppe, and moved across country to a point about 700 yards south-west of Wulverghem, where we bivouacked in the open fields. Some bivouac shelters were provided, and there were plenty of empty ammunition boxes about, which enabled us to make ourselves fairly comfortable. The days were very warm, and the whole Battalion was hard at work on the reconstruction of roads and tracks through our old trenches and the newly-captured area. The position was rather heavily shelled at times, particularly the Wulverghem-Messines road. At night our bivouac area was several times shelled, and casualties occurred.

One incident happened which is worthy of note. An ammunition dump near the Wulverghem-Messines road was hit by a shell and exploded, killing and wounding a number of English troops. Four badly-wounded men were carried to a building close by, in which was stored a quantity of ammunition. Shortly afterwards a shell set fire to this building, which was soon in a blaze, and the ammunition contained in it was likely to explode at any moment. Four men of the 40th Battalion— No. 2133, Pte. A. L. Rule; No. 2615, Pte. C. W. V. Matthews; No. 2542, Pte. W. R. Cooper; and No. 2158, Pte. A. J. Whitney—were passing, and heard an R.A.M.C. Sergeant asking for volunteers to go and bring out the wounded men. They at once went across, entered the burning building, and brought out the wounded, and had just got clear of the dump when it exploded. For their gallant action these four men were commended in Divisional Orders. The R.A.M.C. Sergeant received the D.C.M.

On the 18th June the Battalion left Wulverghem, and went to another bivouac area on the Connaught-road, between Neuve Eglise and Nieppe. Here one half of the Battalion was employed on salving material in the captured enemy territory around Messines, while the other half was in training. Hitherto we had had practically no leave to England or to Paris, but from this time leave allotments began and were continued. On the 23rd June the Battalion left Connaught-road and went to Waterloo-road, nearer Neuve Eglise. Battalion Headquarters and C Company were at Mahutonga Camp, and the rest of the Battalion at Vauxhall Camp. On the following day the whole of the 10th Brigade proceeded to a bivouac area on the banks of the Douve, near Kemmel Hill. Tents and bivouac-shelters were put up, and we settled down to recreation and training. The weather remained fine, and cricket matches and other sports made a large part of the programme. The military training culminated in a skill-at-arms competition among representative platoons of the four battalions of the Brigade. This competition embraced Lewis gun work, bombing, musketry, bayonet fighting, gas and tactical exercise. It was won by No. 13 Platoon of the 40th Battalion, under Lieut. A. R. Mills.

Battalion sports were also held, the chief event of which was an obstacle race, one of the obstacles being the River Douve. About 50 competitors plunged into the stream and stirred up the mud and smell of centuries, which raised a mild protest from the rest of the Brigade. Brigade sports were held among the four battalions, the 10th Field Ambulance, 10th Machine Gun Company, and 10th Field Company of Engineers. The highest number of points was gained by the 37th Battalion, with the 40th Battalion second.

On the 10th July the Battalion moved to another bivouac area within a few hundred yards of Neuve Eglise, becoming reserve battalion of the brigade. Tents were provided, and these were camouflaged with branches of trees. The whole Battalion were employed on working parties around Messines until the 20th July, when we relieved the 38th Battalion as support battalion, and occupied trenches on the ridge immediately north of Messines. The chief work here was cable-burying and improving and digging support and communication trenches. This support position, where we remained for 15 days, was constantly and heavily shelled. On the night of the 22nd July C Company were subjected to our first taste of mustard gas. Though all precautions were taken which were in use against ordinary gas, the shelling resulted in about 30 casualties, 18 of whom were evacuated to hospital. On the 31st July, amid heavy rain, which continued for five days, an attack was begun east of Ypres, and also south of Messines, where the New Zealand Division took La Basse Ville, and the 11th Brigade advanced towards Warneton. The first day was very successful, but the exploiting of it was made impossible owing to the ceaseless rain. In our support position we lived under most trying conditions, as trying as we have ever experienced. It rained incessantly till the shelters were flooded, and trenches became running streams of water. In addition to these discomforts the whole area was heavily and continuously shelled. During the 14 days on the ridge we suffered 65 casualties. At this time Major J. P. Clark, who had been second in command of the Battalion since its formation, was transferred to the 44th Battalion as Commanding Officer, and Major L. H. Payne became second in command of the 40th Battalion.

On the 4th August the 40th Battalion was relieved by the 13th Battalion, and moved to a bivouac area at Neuve Eglise amid heavy rain. The area was simply a wet field, but fortunately we only remained there one night, and moved the following day with the rest of the Brigade to a bivouac area known as "The Tankadrome," on the edge of the wood between Dranoutre and Neuve Eglise. Here we lived in tents. The weather remained unsettled, and the place was almost a bog. Here we had our first taste of continuous night-bombing, though probably the enemy planes intended their bombs for the railway-line which ran past the camp. We were also subjected to long-range high-velocity gun-shelling. These guns deserve some comment, as a lot of argument has been wasted on the reasons why we heard an explosion in the distance and the next moment a shell would arrive. The explosion could not have been from the firing of the gun, as the gun was probably 20 miles away. Still we argued about it, and the argument was never settled to the satisfaction of all parties.

On the 11th August the 10th Brigade marched towards Bailleul, and were inspected by the Army Commander, Sir Herbert Plummer. On the 14th August we marched to Bailleul, entrained there, and detrained at Wizernes. From Wizernes we marched 12 miles to Vaudringhem, arriving wet through and very tired. We stayed the night there in billets, and on the following day marched to our own rest area at Bécourt, near the town of Desvres, and 18 miles from Boulogne. This was part of the area allotted to the 3rd Division to train and organise for the next offensive. Battalion Headquarters and B Company were in billets in Bécourt, C and D Companies at Trois Marquets, and A Company at Dignopré. Hard training was at once begun. Rifle, Lewis gun, and bombing ranges were constructed, and platoons were reorganised and trained by sections. After this platoons were trained in tactical exercises, and later in company and battalion operations. A system of route-marches was also carried out, the distance of each march being increased until 18 miles a day in full marching order was reached.

We had lost a large number of valuable non-commissioned officers, and while there was plenty of good material in the unit, they had no training as N.C.O.'s. In order to supply this training, a brigade school was started at Blequin, to which we sent 32 selected privates. These men worked hard, under capable instructors from the brigade, and the results were very good. In many cases the school brought out in men qualities of leadership which, until then, they had never had a chance of showing. Many of them turned out excellent N.C.O.'s and some afterwards gained commissions. A similar school for prospective N.C.O.'s was afterwards organised whenever an opportunity offered, and results were always equally good, and added to the efficiency of the brigade.

Leave was granted after parade hours to the town of Desvres, and bathing parades were also sent there to use the hot baths at the local cement factory.

Nearly every evening the regimental band gave a programme in the village of Bécourt. Officers and men stood round listening, while the village children played; somewhat reminiscent of Franklin Square, Hobart, or the City Park, Launceston, on a summer evening.

Company inspections by the commanding officer were also frequent, till arms, clothing, and equipment were almost faultless in cleanliness and completeness. The battalion was also inspected by the G.O.C. 10th Brigade (Brig.-Gen. W. Ramsay McNicol, D.S.O.), who, in addressing the battalion after the inspection, assured us that it was the best battalion inspection he had held in France.

On the 11th September the 10th Brigade carried out a route march with the four battalions of the brigade, 10th Australian Light Trench Mortar Battery, 10th Field Ambulance, 10th Machine Gun Company, and all 1st and 2nd line transport. The brigade was inspected during the march by the Divisional Commander (Major-General John Monash).

About this time a German document was captured which gave details of the new method of defence laid down for the 4th German Army in Flanders. This was promulgated among units, and gave us food for thought and discussion. It was realised that a new plan of attack would be necessary to meet the new German defence, and we naturally turned our minds to ponder over it. Not that our opinions would matter. The plan would be worked out by "Higher Authority," and we would simply have to follow it. Officers were lectured on the subject by the G.S.O. 1 of Division, who, after going into the "pros" and "cons" of several plans, told us that the policy must be, in his own words, "On the day of the race, back a favourite." On the day of the race we backed a favourite—"Limited Objective," by "Unoriginality," out of "Previous Success," and even though it was a narrow-minded policy to back it, it was not the first favourite to lose on a sodden course.

In Flanders the sodden nature of the ground prevented the enemy making another Hindenburg Line, and its place was taken by the "Pill Box." These were small forts of reinforced concrete, as low as possible above the ground, and containing one or more machine guns each. They were easy to make, and the enemy supply of cement seemed inexhaustible. They were difficult targets to hit, and were proof against anything but heavy artillery.

The enemy plan was to allow us to waste our strength in making small gains of little strategic value. He held his front line with few men, who would withdraw before an attack. His guns were well back ready to put down a barrage in front of his pill-box zone. His reserves were in the second line, behind his pill-box zone, ready to counter-attack before we could consolidate. Any attack could advance a short distance, but the advance could only be temporary and costly. Instead of the solid defence of the Hindenburg Line, the Flanders defence was designed to be elastic, and to rebound into position after being hurled back. On the 20th September a brigade tactical scheme was carried out, which was designed to experiment with the new method of overcoming the German defensive system. The exercise was carried out in the presence of the Corps Commander (Sir A. Godley) and staff, and the Divisional Commander (Major-General John Monash) and staff. The practice attack was made by the brigade on a front of 800 yards, with troops on both flanks. The depth of the attack was 2100 yards. Horsemen represented the creeping barrage. The whole territory to be captured was divided into three areas, each being captured and mopped up by one battalion, the remaining battalion being in reserve. In this case the nearest area to our front line was captured by the 38th Battalion, the second by the 39th Battalion, and the third by the 40th Battalion. The 39th and 40th Battalion leapfrogged the 38th Battalion, and the 40th Battalion leapfrogged the 39th Battalion. Each battalion attacked with two companies in line, one company "mopping up," and one company in reserve.

Therefore, as the enemy defended in depth, we attacked in depth. Each unit as it reached its objective automatically consolidated a line of defence, through which the next attacking unit leapfrogged. So that across the captured ground were successive lines of defence to prevent the enemy's elastic defence springing back.

The actual attack on the 4th October at Ypres was carried out in accordance with this attack practice, except for a few minor details. The practice itself was criticised by the Brigadier and the Divisional Commander. They both commented severely and unfavourably on the noise during the attack's early stages. The noise was caused by the sudden appearance of a rabbit just as the attack was developing. The rabbit dodged through the battalions advancing in artillery formation, and this was too much for Australian sporting instinct. After eluding the two leading battalions the rabbit was finally captured by the 40th Battalion, amid cheers from the whole Brigade. This incident was probably not a good advertisement for the discipline of the Australian Army, but it is quite typical. There was no excuse for it, and we deserved all the unpleasant things said as a result of it. We have often been told that we were wonderful soldiers, but that our discipline was hopeless; in fact, this has been so often impressed on us that a reply to the libel is necessary. The Australian is unconventional, and surrounded by others, whose "josses" are tradition and convention, he is proud of it. He realises the value of true discipline, but does not regard saluting, heel-clicking, and other frills as a necessary part of discipline. He knows he is regarded as undisciplined, and in a "leg-pulling" way encourages the idea. Hence, some staff officer on his way to his job at the War Office of a morning fails to receive salutes from the casual Australians on leave from the firing-line. He therefore calls his friends to witness the fact that the Australians are undisciplined. A few Australians get into touch with a town major of a town well back from the line. They omit to call him "Sir," and forget to remove the cigarettes from their lips while addressing him. He is horror-struck. They do not intend it offensively, and they are paying him a delicate compliment by suspecting that he is a reasonable "bloke," and anyhow, they do not come from a country where the labourer touches his hat to the squire, and it requires much training and concentration of thought always to remember these points of etiquette. But the Australian discipline, when he is near the enemy, is a different thing, and that is the discipline he is proud of—the discipline that matters. In action it has stood the greatest test scores of times—the discipline which, under fire and against heavy odds, keeps a battalion still a fighting force. The theory that the Australian Army is undisciplined has been put forward so often that it is generally believed; but only by those who have never seen them in the line or in action. It is a libel on the Australian Army which is bitterly resented.

On the 22nd September the whole of the 3rd Australian Division was inspected on a divisional parade by the Commander-in-Chief (Sir Douglas Haig), and this was regarded as a sure indication that we would be in another offensive within the near future; so nobody was surprised when orders arrived the following day that the whole division would move immediately towards Ypres. Accordingly, on the 25th September we left Bécourt and route-marched to Remilly-Werquin, where the night was spent, and the following day, after a 20-miles march, reached Sercus, and billeted there for the night. Next day the battalion was again on the road, and reached a camp between Terdeghem and Steenvoorde. During this long march (which lasted three days) the Battalion did not lose a man.

At this camp we were quite close to the other Tasmanian battalion (the 12th), and much visiting took place between the two units. The 12th Battalion had just come out of the Polygon Wood Battle, and conversation was chiefly on Tasmanian affairs and Polygon Wood.

On the 28th September we marched another 6 miles to a camp near Winnezeele. Here we received the preliminary orders for the attack, and 10 officers and 103 other ranks, who were not to take part in the attack were at once sent to the concentration camp at Morbecque. A proportion of officers who were going into the attack went daily by motor lorry to Ypres, and made a reconnaissance of the ground from which the attack was to be made. On the 1st October the Battalion embussed from Winnezeele to a camp at Vlamertinghe, approximately 8 miles from where the attack was to commence.

On the 2nd October we supplied large parties to assist in cable-burying in the forward area. This party made part of a brigade working party, which was heavily shelled just as the work was completed, and our casualties numbered five killed and six wounded.

Chapter XIII.

The Attack on the 4th October, 1917, in the 3rd Battle of Ypres.

HE object of the Ypres offensive, known as the Third Battle of Ypres, was to clear the Belgian Coast, and turn the northern flank of the enemy's defence on the Western Front. It was an ambitious scheme, which would, if successful, have big results. It would get rid of the German submarine bases at Zeebrugge and Ostend, capture a large part of Belgium, and cut the enemy's main communications with the lower Rhineland.

The Battle of Messines had been a preliminary offensive to get suitable ground from which to attack, and smaller attacks were also made, with varying success, on July 31, August 15, and August 22. The month of August was one of almost continuous rain, and greatly handicapped the attack through the mud. In September the weather improved, but the whole of the Ypres battlefields were such a morass that it took three weeks to dry sufficiently to resume the attack. The main attack in which Australian Divisions took part began on September 20, and was known as Phase 1. Phase 2 began on September 26; Australian troops took part in this also, and captured Polygon Wood. Phase 3 commenced on October 4, and it was in this phase (known as the Battle of Broodseinde) that we took a hand.

The attack was made by Australian, New Zealand, and English Divisions. The 3rd Australian Division attacked with the 10th Brigade on the left and the 11th Brigade on the right. The New Zealand Division was on our left, and the 2nd Australian Division on our right. The 10th Brigade attacked with the 37th Battalion, taking the first objective, the 38th Battalion the second, the 39th Battalion the third, and the 40th Battalion the final objective on Broodseinde Ridge. The 40th Battalion attacked with B Company (Capt. C. L. McVilly, M.C.) on the right, and D Company (Capt. W. C. G. Ruddock) on the left. These two companies formed the leading waves. A Company (Lieut. N. R. Meagher) was the mopping-up company, and C Company (Capt. H. J. Dumaresq) was in reserve. The objectives of the Battalion are shown on Map No. 5.

At 6.30 p.m. the Battalion moved out from Vlamertinghe, and proceeded up the main-road towards Ypres. That skeleton of a city was reached just about dark, and we filed round the northern edge through the town, across the canal, and halted in a shell-pitted field midway between Ypres and Potijze. Here everybody tried, more or less successfully, to get a couple of hours' sleep in shell-holes and among piles of ammunition-boxes, but the night was bitterly cold and there was very little shelter, so most of us sat and shivered, watching the flash of our own guns round us and the enemy's flares and incendiary shells in front.

At 11.30 p.m. we moved on behind the rest of the Brigade. Our place on the assembly position was to be in rear of the other three battalions, as we were to take the last objective. We moved along a track which conformed to the line of the Ypres-Zonnebeke road. The first part of this track was duck-walk, but most of it was simply a track marked out with white tape. From Bremen Redoubt the ground in front was being shelled persistently, and although there were no casualties in the 40th Battalion, we passed quite a number of dead and wounded from the battalions in front of us. The march up the track was carried out in single file, and took a long time, owing to halts in front, chiefly caused by the shelling. The assembly position was at least reached at 4 a.m., and we moved in behind the other battalions, between the Zonnebeke Creek and the Zonnebeke-Langemarck road, immediately south of Van Isacker's Farm. While getting into position the enemy shelling caused several casualties, particularly in A Company, but finally we settled in shell-holes, where a good many went to sleep. About 5 a.m. rain set in, and made conditions more unpleasant than ever.

At 5.30 a.m. the enemy put down a heavy barrage on our assembly positions. Fortunately most of the shelling went just beyond us. If it had been right on us the result would probably have been disastrous. As it was, we had over 20 casualties in the Battalion from this bombardment. At that time it was thought that the enemy must have been aware of our intended attack, but it was afterwards discovered that the enemy was preparing to attack on our front, and that his attacking troops had actually formed up about 200 yards in front of us. Our zero hour was 6 a.m., and his was fixed for 10 minutes later, which placed him in the position of a man administering a pill to his horse by blowing it down its throat through a tube; everything would have been all right, but the horse blew first.

Our barrage when it opened came right down on the enemy's assaulting divisions, and, before he could recover, the bayonets of the leading waves were upon him. At 6 a.m. our barrage opened from the biggest mass of artillery collected on the Western Front up till that time, and the Brigade went forward behind it. The leading waves were surprised to meet the enemy in No Man's Land in such numbers, and the fight began there, but our infantry simply went through them, killing a great number, while others surrendered and went towards our lines until they met troops who were not too busy to take them prisoners. The first objective was taken without much trouble and with few casualties, and while the 37th Battalion started to dig in the rest of the Brigade moved through them towards the next objective. In getting to the next objective a good deal of confusion was caused on account of the creeks and ditches between Bordeaux and Springfield being impassable. The battalions were forced right on their flanks to get round, and the sodden mass in front was cleared by a few moppers-up. Beyond the 38th Battalion objective the barrage halted for an hour, while the 38th Battalion consolidated their line, and the enemy artillery, which up to that time had been very badly directed, got on to our troops, and a large number of casualties resulted. Machine-gun fire was also considerable, and B Company, which had suffered heavily, was reinforced by two platoons of C Company.

After the 39th and 40th Battalions had leap-frogged through the 38th Battalion, very heavy machine-gun fire was encountered, coming from the defensive systems on the Broodseinde Ridge and the Gravenstafel Switch. The 39th Battalion in front was having a heavy encounter with the enemy in the Gravenstafel Switch, and were fighting with great gallantry and determination. On the left the New Zealanders had heavy odds against them, and had not yet come up to us. This was handicapping the 39th Battalion, who were being enfiladed from the left. Seeing this, a platoon of D Company went out to the flank of the 38th Battalion into the New Zealand sector, and cleared the opposition in the left of the Gravenstafel Switch, capturing several pill-boxes and disposing of a large number of the enemy. It was here also that a lance-corporal of the 10th Australian Light Trench Mortar Battery, No. 2033, L/Cpl. W. R. Langdon, brought his mortar into action most effectively on several of the enemy machine guns, demonstrating that the light trench mortar in the hands of an efficient gunner is a valuable weapon of opportunity.

After the 39th Battalion reached their objective, the 40th Battalion moved through without halt, as the barrage had gone on. Owing to the heavy opposition and the mud conditions we had been unable to follow it closely. From the 39th Battalion objective a stiff fight against the heaviest opposition began. On the top of the ridge the trench system and line of pill-boxes along it seemed alive with men and machine guns, and heavy fire was also coming from Bellevue Spur on the front of the New Zealanders. The only possible way to advance was from shell-hole to shell-hole by short rushes. To add to our difficulties, there was a thick belt of wire immediately in front of us, which had very few gaps in it. On these gaps the enemy had trained machine guns, and we dribbled through in ones and twos, but dead and wounded remained in each gap. Casualties were very heavy, and when B Company swung to the left to avoid an impassable bog a big gap opened. This was filled by the prompt action of Lieut. J. J. Gatenby, who signalled to A Company, and two platoons of A Company, under Lieut. N. R. Meagher, filled the gap. On the right was a bigger gap, and the remaining two platoons of C Company, under Capt. H. J. Dumaresq, rushed forward from reserve on to our right flank. The machine gun fire had become very heavy, and B Company were singularly unfortunate in the way of casualties. In front of his company the tall figure of Capt. McVilly stood out, calling his company to follow him, but before going far this gallant officer was seriously wounded. Lieut. J. J. Gatenby was also badly wounded whilst leading what appeared to be a forlorn hope, and Lieut. E. Boyes was the only officer left with the company. The situation looked critical. All companies were making slow progress under a perfect tornado of machine-gun fire, but D Company rose to the occasion. Captain Ruddock worked his company through the New Zealand sector along partly dead ground till he got on to the left of Hamburg Redoubt, where he was able to bring fire on to the redoubt and the enemy's line of pill-boxes on top of the ridge. The ridge appeared to be held by about 500 of the enemy, and D Company's fire, sweeping across the position, appeared to demoralise those of the enemy who were not safe in their pill-boxes. This gave the other companies their chance for a frontal attack, and Sergt. Lewis McGee, of B Company, made a start on a pill-box immediately in front of Hamburg Redoubt. This pill-box contained a number of the enemy, who had their machine gun in a recess on the top of the fort, and were firing straight at B Company, the machine gun bullets cutting the tops of the shell-holes where our men were taking cover. Sergt. McGee rushed straight at the pill-box in the face of what looked like certain death, but he got across that 50 yards of open ground and shot the crew with his revolver. Hamburg Redoubt was the next point of resistance, and Lieut. N. R. Meagher rushed this with a platoon of A Company, but the machine guns there got them, and Lieut. Meagher fell in that gallant rush. The assault was at once taken up by another platoon of a A Company under Lieut. A. R. Grant, who rushed with his platoon and captured the redoubt, with 4 machine guns and 25 prisoners. Hamburg Redoubt consisted of a double pill-box partly surrounded by a moat. It had originally been the site of a farm, and among the ruins of the farm was a sniper's nest that was overlooked by A Company, who moved on after capturing the redoubt. As they moved on they were shot at from behind by the snipers, which was a most unfortunate occurrence for the snipers captured there. Meanwhile D Company had worked forward in sections on to the objective, and there had a short hand-to-hand fight among the wire, pill-boxes, and trenches on the objective. Dab Trench and Dagger Trench were taken by a rush by D, A, and B Companies, while two platoons of C Company arrived on the right of the objective about the same time. C Company had worked forward under heavy fire to the shelter of the winding road which ran across our front about 150 yards from the objective, and were under cover from the heavy machine-gun fire from the objective. From here they worked forward from shell-hole to shell-hole. A Lewis gun team, under No. 665, Pte. J. A. Freestone, got out on the right flank and opened fire on the enemy among the pill-boxes in front, and under cover of this fire the right of the objective was gained by small parties rushing forward. The honour of getting on to the objective first in C Company was won by Cpl. E. D. Weston, who beat everybody else over 100 yards of open ground. He was wounded during the race, but that did not stop his offensive spirit, for he captured the first pill-box single-handed, and was then reinforced by his section. Capt. H. J. Dumaresq also successfully led a similar party, and after a short fight the enemy surrendered. Too much credit cannot be given to Capt. H. J. Dumaresq for the admirable manner in which he handled his company. Although in reserve, he personally kept in touch with the leading companies, and at the right moment and in the right place threw his company into the fight with telling effect, clearing up the unsatisfactory position between the 40th Battalion and the 11th Brigade.

The capture of the final objective on the Broodseinde Ridge was probably one of the hardest fights the battalion ever had. The line of pill-boxes with the wire and trenches along the front made a very strong defensive position. It was gained by sheer determination. It was impossible to take it by a frontal attack, and the action of D Company in taking advantage of the dead ground and working round the flank from where they gave covering fire, was probably the action which turned the scales in our favour. Approximately 300 prisoners were captured there with 17 machine guns.

When the objective was finally won at 9.15 a.m., two incidents happened in front. Immediately in front of D Company was a concrete building, from which came a party of about 12 of the enemy, who fired with rifles and revolvers. One of our Lewis guns opened and wiped the party out. A couple of men went across to attend to any of them who might be wounded, and found that eight of them were officers. Another big pill-box was seen about 100 yards on our left in front of the New Zealanders, and C.S.M. H. Boden and No. 956, Sergt. S. J. Barrett, went out to see what was in it. A shot was fired at them from a loophole, and Sergt.-Major Boden had a flying shot at the rifleman in the loophole with his revolver. The rifleman withdrew hastily, and a stick with a piece of white rag was waved vigorously from the loophole. They went to the door and invited the occupants to come out. A battalion commander and 70 men came out, and were sent towards our line. The New Zealanders who were coming up on our left saw this large body of men, and apparently thought it was an attack coming, and a Lewis gun opened fire. The enemy prisoners ran for the shelter of our line, which increased the Lewis gun fire of the New Zealanders considerably, and hurried explanations had to be made to the New Zealanders before they would renounce such an attractive target.

Our casualties had been heavy during the attack, and we were reinforced by two platoons of the 39th Battalion shortly after arriving at the objective. This party remained with us until the following day. There was at the time a serious shortage of ammunition, but the situation was a good deal relieved by the efforts of the 39th Battalion behind us, who sent up all they could spare, and continued to assist us throughout the whole operation by foraging for ammunition, the supply of which seemed to have been cut off for some unknown reason. For the efforts of the 39th Battalion we were more than grateful.

Covering parties with Lewis guns were sent out about 100 yards in front of the objective. These Lewis gunners had a busy time firing on parties of the enemy making back towards Passchendaele, and dodging about among the shell-holes around Augustus Wood. Our snipers were also engaged in sniping the enemy in front. Three "Whizz-bang" guns were also located about 1000 yards in front, near Friesland Copse. An enemy machine gun was mounted, and did some useful sniping at the crews as they moved out of the gun-pits for ammunition. These "whizz-bangs" were firing at point blank range, and seriously interfered with the work of consolidation, till our own artillery had a shoot at their position and silenced them.

The captured pill-boxes along the objective, were very strong. Most of them were machine-gun positions, but there was one Brigade headquarters, two Quartermasters' stores, and various other places interesting to the many "souvenir" hunters. At the captured Brigade headquarters our forward signal-station was set up, where the signallers on duty smoked large cigars and drank good bottled beer at the enemy's expense. A feature of all German dugouts was the smell, which was peculiar to all things German. Every German dugout in France had the same unpleasant aroma, and all were lousy. The question was often asked as to the reason for it, and it was never satisfactorily explained, though one man ventured the remark "They all smell alike. I'd bet 10 francs old Hindenburg would smell the same if we got close enough to him."

By 11 a.m. we had a continuous trench right along our front, and connected up with the 41st Battalion on our right, on the other side of the railway. We were also in touch with the New Zealanders on our left. Our defensive line was particularly strong. A section of engineers had constructed strong-points for machine-gun positions, and machine-guns from the 10th Machine-gun Company moved up, and occupied them. The 10th Trench Mortar Battery also moved up and put their guns in emplacements, from where they were able to fire on small parties of the enemy near Augustus Wood. Battalion Headquarters was established in a shell-hole near Beecham Farm. During the afternoon small parties of the enemy were seen collecting in trenches and shell-holes on the right of Augustus Wood. This was apparently an attempt to counter-attack with local reserves, but they were dispersed by the light trench mortars, who fired still the parties started to run, when our Lewis gunners, who were waiting, opened fire, and caught them. The enemy appeared to have many wounded in front of us, and stretcher-bearers were working in conjunction with motor-ambulance vehicles on the road. These were not fired on, but on one occasion a motor-ambulance was seen surrounded by wounded men trying to get into it; unfortunately our artillery fire was heavy at the time, and a shell fell on the road under the ambulance.

The afternoon was spent in sniping and improving the defensive position. The enemy shelling was not heavy, and was chiefly directed at the roads and tracks behind us. Towards morning the S.O.S. was put up somewhere along the front on three occasions, and this seemed to be repeated along the whole front, except on our part of it. The S.O.S. was the last thing we wanted, as several of the 18-pounders were firing short, and although the short shooting was continually reported, it did not improve. We could not blame the artillery, as it was realised that some of their guns must be firing at extreme range, and the mud conditions made it impossible for them to get forward. The machine-gun S.O.S. barrage was very fine, and developed into a continuous rattle whenever the S.O.S. went up.

The morning of the 5th October was very quiet, and enemy activity seemed to be limited to the air. His 'planes came over at daylight and hovered over our positions. One of our own contact 'planes also came over calling for flares to see our position. As he was not marked as a contact 'plane we refused to have anything to do with him for some time, but he flew up and down, making such plaintive noises with his Klaxon horn, that we finally took pity on him, and obliged with some illuminations. This was probably the aeroplane that took the photograph of our consolidated line, which showed the line of the 40th and 41st Battalions (the first-line battalions of the division), to be exactly where it had been planned on the map. The Army Commander afterwards stated that this consolidated line was the best done by any division in any offensive in his experience.

The enemy artillery fired hardly a round all the morning; probably he was getting his artillery back, in view of the possibility of an immediate attack, which, had he known, our "limited objective" policy prevented. It seemed a pity that we were not able to exploit our successes, for, as far as we could see, it was possible to walk into Passchendaele. Eight different counter-attacks were reported between the Menin-road and Reutel, but on the front of the 40th Battalion they were slow in developing, and none was made until the evening of the 5th October.

About 2 p.m. the enemy began to shell our position, and continued during the whole afternoon. About 3 p.m. the S.O.S. went up some distance away on our left, and the barrage came down on our front, causing several casualties, and burying two English officers of the 66th Division, who were reconnoitring the position with a view to a relief that night. Our S.O.S. barrage was getting shorter, and we were not at all happy about it. About 5 p.m. the enemy bombardment became much heavier on our position, and also on all approaches behind us. This made everybody realise that the long-awaited counter-attack was likely to develop at any moment, and at about 6 p.m. it began. Two columns of infantry were seen advancing about 1000 yards in front of the New Zealanders on our left. It was estimated that there were 500 in each column. On our left front a column of about 500 were advancing from the direction of Haarlem, about 1000 yards away. The New Zealanders put up the S.O.S., and our artillery and machine-guns caught the enemy as he was deploying into close waves. It was magnificent gunnery, and the targets had probably been picked up by artillery officers, as it was the only S.O.S. barrage that day that was not short. The enemy came on about 100 yards under it, and then scattered into cover, and when it got too dark to see their position the artillery was still pouring its fire on to them. No more was seen of this counter attack.

At about 8.30 p.m. English troops of the 66th Division began to move into our sector to relieve us, but shortly afterwards the S.O.S. was put up by units on the flanks, and this, combined with the enemy bombardment, held up the relief some time, as we did not feel disposed to hand over till the situation was quiet. Our own barrage was very short, and quite a number of 18 pounders were firing on to our front line. This caused a number of casualties, including Capt. H. J. Dumaresq and Lieut. W. T. Crosby, who were both severely wounded. The work of the artillery, but for this, had been admirable. Their barrage during the attack had been a moving wall, but our position on the ridge was no doubt the extreme range for some guns, so that some allowance must be made for short shooting. But it is hard to understand why it continued after being reported at least eight times. The 3rd Australian Division was not covered by Australian artillery.

At 10 p.m. all was fairly quiet again, and the relief was continued and completed by 11 p.m., when we began to move out by companies. The journey out was very laborious through the mud, and before the 8-mile march back to Vlamertinghe was completed a number of men dropped exhausted by the road. We were nearly all enthusiastic collectors of souvenirs, and a great number of helmets, revolvers, &c., had been "souvenired," and carefully kept. But in extreme weariness there is no desire for anything—only a dull longing for sleep and warmth—and most of the souvenirs were thrown away on the tramp back. Men were too tired to carry anything but themselves and their arms.

At Messines the medical arrangements had been splendid. At Ypres the A.M.C. organisation broke down completely. There was a very grave shortage of stretcher-bearers and stretchers in forward areas. Regimental stretcher-bearers are supposed to carry wounded from the firing-line to the Regimental Aid Post, and Field Ambulance bearers carry from the Regimental Aid Post to the Amubulance Dressing Station. Our Regimental Aid Post was in a pill-box about 1500 yards behind our objective, which, under the circumstances, was a very suitable place. The Field Ambulance bearers did not come to the Regimental Aid Post, and consequently the Regimental Medical Officer (Capt. W. I. Clark) had to keep the regimental stretcher-bearers to carry from his aid post back to the Field Ambulance. The result was that wounded men who were unable to walk had to lie in shell-holes, and trust to somebody seeing them, and detailing German prisoners or carrying parties to take them out on improvised stretchers. At one time on the day of the attack no wounded were evacuated from the Regimental Aid' Post for over 12 hours, in spite of urgent messages to the field ambulance for stretcher-bearers and stretchers.

The casualties of the Battalion were:—Officers—killed, 1; wounded, 6; total, 7. Other ranks—killed, 49; wounded, 198; total 247.

The battle of Broodseinde was, no doubt, a great victory, and had the weather remained fine the results might have been far-reaching. At the time it was described by the Army Commander as the biggest defeat inflicted on the enemy since the Marne. Not only had his attacking divisions been shattered, but his elastic defence was broken in a decisive manner, which indicated that it could be broken again. When the objective of the 3rd Division was taken, the main pillbox zone was penetrated, and what was even more important, the enemy was in that thoroughly beaten state which would have prevented for some time any effective organisation of his rear defences. Had our success been followed up immediately on the 4th October, the strong enemy positions opposite the New Zealanders would have been turned, and Passchendaele taken; but what was revealed clearly to the units in the Front Line on that day was hidden from General Headquarters, who still hugged the "limited objective." Plans for semi-open warfare were a few days later foreshadowed as a possible development of our next advance, but the opportunity of the 4th October had been lost, and never came again.

Chapter XIV.

Phase 4 of the 3rd Battle of Ypres a Failure — The Attack on the 12th October.

N the 6th October the Battalion slept at Vlamertinge, and on the following day preliminary orders were received for a further attack during the next few days. Winter had set in unmistakably, and the 7th, 8th, and 9th October were continuously wet. Our own Camp at Vlamertinghe was a hopeless bog, and we had no delusion that the Ypres battlefield was anything else but a sea of mud and water. The Commander-in-Chief, in his 4th Despatch, when concluding his remarks on the result of the Battle of Broodseinde, says: "I determined to deliver the next combined French and British attack on the 9th October." This determination must have been a rigid one, and not likely to be affected by weather conditions or *terrain*.

Reorganisation was begun on the 7th October. A small draft of men arrived back from hospital, and the surplus personnel of 10 officers and 103 other ranks who had been sent to Morbecque, came up. The usual nucleus could not be sent to take their place, as practically all hands were required to make up the minimum strength of 24 per platoon. The scanty surplus and a few cripples were left at the wagon lines, when the Battalion moved up to the next attack.

The plan of the further operations was explained. On the 9th October, Phase 4 of the battle would take place, and the attack would be renewed from the east of Zonnebeke to our junction with the French north-west of Langemarck. Phase 5 of the battle would begin on the 12th October, when we, with other divisions, would continue the attack from the objective gained in Phase 4.

Phase 4 opened amid heavy rain on the morning of the 9th October from the objective gained on the 4th October. Practically no advance was made by the 66th Division on the late 3rd Divisional fronts. They met heavy opposition, and were held up by the mud. Small parties of English troops did get forward a few hundred yards, but they had not mopped up the area, and no line was established. They were found there, some dead and some alive, when we advanced three days later. On the left of the whole operation some advance was made, but in front of Passchendaele the attack was a ghastly failure.

At 7.15 a.m. on the morning of the 10th October we left Vlamertinghe and moved through Ypres with the rest of the brigade to a bivouac area east of Ypres, among some shell-holes between Dragoon and Hussar Farms, close to the Zonnebeke-road at Potijze. It was a sodden place pitted with shell-holes three years old, over which long grass had grown. And it still rained. Something had to be done to make the place habitable, and within an hour shelters of timber, iron, and ammunition-boxes were going up everywhere, while distracted engineers rushed about looking for armed guards to put over their dumps. During that afternoon a large party from the Battalion (including the Regimental Band) went forward and worked on the new approach route, afterwards known as "K" track. The men who used K track are no more likely to forget it than Picadilly or Horseferry-road, but the recollections will be less pleasant.

On the night of the 10th October all instructions had been issued for the attack to take place on the 12th October. The only thing that was not clear was the line from which the attack by the 10th Brigade would be launched. This obscurity was the result of the failure of the attack by the 66th Division. The position was not made clear, and very little information could be obtained. The proposed jumping-off line for the 12th October was changed repeatedly as the information varied. Finally, on the night of the 10th October, our 11th Brigade was sent in to relieve the English division, and clear up the situation. In consequence of their report, on the afternoon of the 11th October the jumping-off line was brought back to the line reached in our advance of the 4th October. Our front was side-slipped to the left, so as to coincide, roughly, with the right brigade objective of the New Zealand Division on the 4th October; while the 9th Brigade started from the line which the 10th Brigade reached on the 4th October. This change disposed of some of the advantage of familiarity with the ground, which we would have had if we had kept our previous front; and there was no opportunity under the circumstances for the usual reconnaissance of the ground, nor even of the jumping-off line. On the front of the New Zealanders the 47th British Division had much the same misfortune on October 9 as the 66th Division had on their right. An unkind story from our Divisional Staff was that on the evening of the 9th the 66th Division reported "All objectives gained. Position of the 47th Division obscure." While at the same time the 47th Division reported "All objectives gained. Position of the 66th Division obscure." As a matter of fact, they were both obscure, and remained obscure until we attacked. That part of the report was accurate, but the "Objectives gained" part of it was hopeful imagination.

The 3rd Australian Division was to attack with the 9th Brigade on the right, and the 10th Brigade on the left. The 10th Brigade dispositions were as follows:—The 37th Battalion to take the first objective, known as the Red Line. The 40th Battalion to take the second objective, known as the Blue Line. The 38th Battalion to take Passchendaele, and advance to the final objective, known as the Green Line (Map No. 6). The 39th Battalion was in reserve. The left boundary of the area allotted to the 10th Brigade was the Ravebeck Creek, and the right boundary was a line through the south edge of Augustus Wood to a point 300 yards south of Passchendaele Church.

The dispositions laid down by the Commanding Officer of the Battalion were similar to those adopted on the 4th October, with two companies forming the leading waves, one company mopping-up, and one company in reserve. The Officers Commanding companies were Capt. J. D. W. Chisholm (A), Lieut. W. L. Garrard (B), Lieut. C. W. Baldwin (C), and Major L. F. Giblin, M.C. (D). The dispositions were not followed in any particular, as once the attack commenced the three attacking battalions were merged inevitably into one body of men struggling through mud and under heavy fire to get to their objective.

At 9 p.m. the battalion left the bivouac area in rear of the 37th Battalion, in the following order:—Battalion Headquarters, two platoons of A Company and two platoons of C Company (first wave); D Company (mopping-up company); two platoons of A Company and two platoons of C Company (second wave); B Company (reserve company). The route followed was up the Zonnebeke-road as far as Bremen Redoubt; thence north-east along "K" track, which ran past Van Isacker's Farm, Bordeaux Farm, Beecham Farm, to the jumping-off place near Dab Trench. The journey up the road was very slow, owing to the congestion chiefly of pack transport carrying artillery ammunition. Just after getting on to "K" track a few gas-shells fell near the track, but this was practically all the shelling during the approach march. The passage along "K" track was also slow, due to the many halts of troops in front. The troops in front evidently thought it necessary to stand stock still when an enemy Verey light went up. As there were hundreds of Verey lights going up in front, and thousands of deep collective curses going up from behind, the units in front at last decided to push on, and the march up "K" track was continued without unreasonable delay. "K" track was a good track, and the men who constructed it deserved every credit, but to step off it meant stepping into from 1 foot to 4 feet of mud and water, and it was difficult to keep to the track in the dark; still, it had one bright spot of humour, in the shape of a solitary digger crawling along the track on his hands and knees, and wearing a small box-respirator. An officer ordered him to get up and remove his respirator. He did so cautiously, and stood in the mud gasping for breath. "What, ain't there no gas?" he said. The officer assured him emphatically that there was no gas. "Billjim" gave expression to his feelings with great indignation. "Well, show me the ———— wot said there was."

At 3.30 a.m. we reached the assembly position. The wire along the road parallel to Dab Trench gave us very little room, and we finally bunched up on the road to the left of Dab Trench (D 10 d 45 45), with the intention of spreading out into position as we advanced. Battalion Headquarters was established at Berlin Wood.

Zero hour had been fixed at 5.25 a.m. This would appear to be 35 minutes earlier than the attack on the 4th October, but it was really 25 minutes later, as "Winter Time" had just come into operation. About 4.30 a.m. the enemy began to shell the assembly position, and although this did not cause many casualties it was unpleasant to the men who had to lie under it in the mud and rain. This bombardment continued until the attack, and the reason for it is explained by the fact that the enemy knew we were coming. A man had deserted from a British unit during the early part of the night, and given details of the attack. This fact was ascertained from German prisoners captured during the day, and also from captured enemy orders.

At 5.25 a.m. the barrage opened, and we went forward. The barrage was so thin that it could not be distinguished as a barrage, and we made no attempt to conform to it; there was really nothing to conform to. The artillery had been unable to do the impossible and get their guns forward. Simultaneously with our attack the enemy machine-gun and artillery barrage opened, and came down on the brigade. The result was heavy casualties. The 37th Battalion pushed on 100 yards under devastating fire, and were held up, with the result that the 40th and 38th Battalions telescoped into the 37th Battalion, and the three battalions together pushed forward toward the first objective, in the hope of being able to reorganise there. On the right front of the Brigade the ground was passable, and in spite of heavy fire, B and D Companies reached Augustus Wood, where they cleared the Wood and the pill-boxes in it, capturing about 50 of the enemy and killing a similar number. The fight in the Wood was fierce, the enemy resisting with great determination.

In the first 200 yards each company suffered severely, a whole platoon of A Company under No. 651, Sergt. C. Hope, being wiped completely out. Captain J. D. W. Chisholm, Officer Commanding A Company, was severely wounded; so also was the Officer Commanding C Company (Lieut. C. W. Baldwin). Lieut. C. F. Sharland was killed, and Lieut. M. H. O. Whitaker and Lieut. R. C. Walters were both badly wounded; while the Battalion lost three gallant non-commissioned officers in Sergt. Lewis McGee (posthumously awarded the Victoria Cross), Company Sergt.-Major R. K. Wilson, of C Company, and Sergt. Hugh Black, of D Company—the three of whom were killed. In that 200 yards were also great numbers of dead and wounded of the 66th Division, the result of the attack three days before.

On the left the position was very bad. At daylight the New Zealanders were seen coming up on our left in two magnificent waves. They were seen all that day still in two waves, lying dead in the mud in front of the uncut wire at Dab trench. That was as far as they got. The enemy had great numbers of machine guns on Bellevue Spur, and he wiped the New Zealanders out with concentrated fire, which played on them like a hose. Those who got through the machine-gun fire were hanging on the wire, at which they had rushed with their usual gallantry. Seeing this, A Company sent a party of 30 men, under Lieuts. A. R. Grant and H. Chamberlain, across the Ravebeck. They rushed up the road that passes Waterfields Farm (the only point where the Ravebeck could be crossed) and attacked the enemy pill-boxes in front of the New Zealanders. They captured two of these strong-points, but in rushing for the third, machine-gun fire caught them, killing Lieut. Grant, and killing or wounding the whole party except Lieut. Chamberlain, who came back alone.

The failure of the New Zealanders brought enfilade fire to bear on the 10th Brigade from Bellevue Spur. The Ravebeck Creek was in flood, and had been diverted in places by shell-fire, with the result that it had overflowed, and filled up all the neighbouring shell-holes. This made the creek an

expanse of shell-holes filled with water. In places it was like
a series of lakes, sometimes 100 yards wide, and quite impassable. On the right of this flooded area, it was difficult
to get forward from shell-hole to shell-hole, as every shell-hole, except the brand new ones, contained at least 2 feet of
mud and water. It was impossible to get right into one without danger of not being able to get out, but it was possible
to perch on the side of one. Several cases were seen of men
who had jumped into shell-holes being unable to get out.
They had to be packed up with timber and rifles and pulled
out. Some were not seen by their comrades, and remained fast
in the mud until next day, when stretcher-bearers got them
out.

All this time we were under heavy enfilade fire from the
left of the Ravebeck, and casualties were very heavy. The
enemy snipers, with their telescopic-sighted rifles, took a big
toll, and in one place near Waterfields Farm it was estimated
that no less than 50 men were brought down by snipers,
mostly shot through the head. It was impossible to retaliate,
as rifles and Lewis guns were choked with mud. The Lewis
gun officer (Lieut. R. B. Penny), although badly wounded,
managed to clean a Lewis gun in a shell-hole, and opened on
the enemy across the creek, but showers of mud flying from
shell explosions soon clogged it again.

Across our front, running into the Ravebeck, was another
creek, about 200 yards beyond Augustus Wood. This creek
was in much the same state as the Ravebeck, and was only
passable at two points, on to which some enemy machine guns
were trained, and at these points our dead and wounded lay
in heaps.

At about 7 a.m. the first objective was reached by the remnants of the Brigade. They arrived in twos and threes, and
by 8 a.m. numbered nearly 200 of the three battalions. The
position that we were in was that our left flank was in the
air, and there did not appear to be any hope of the New Zealanders coming up. On our right flank we were in touch
with the 9th Brigade, who had advanced beyond us towards
their second objective. We were under fire from the front,
left flank, and left rear, and were almost entirely without
artillery support. Under these circumstances it was decided
to dig a line of posts and remain on the Red Line. We therefore commenced to dig in, which was no easy job in consequence of the enemy machine-guns and snipers, and the
fact that the mud oozed back into the trenches as fast as it
was shovelled out. The line consolidated was about 100 yards
in rear of the Red Line (D 11 d 5575 to D 11 a 8050). The

enemy could be seen in Haalem Wood, and fire was coming from that Wood and from Crest Farm.

At 9.30 a.m. enemy 'planes came over, and shortly afterwards our position was subjected to heavy shelling. On the right near the trench was a prominent tree, which was such a good directing mark for the enemy that a new line had to be dug 50 yards in rear of it. At 10 a.m. parties of the enemy could be seen working down from the direction of Friesland Copse. These parties disappeared in the trenches behind Laambeek, round our left flank. This continued for some time, and it was realised that there was a possibility of being surrounded. About this time the 9th Brigade was seen coming back, reporting that their right flank was in the air, and that they were enfiladed in their position from both flanks. It was thought that they were coming to join up with our right flank, but through some mistake they were sent back too far, and took up a position in rear of us.

Our position was serious, and at noon a conference was held of all officers of the brigade. It was decided to withdraw and take up a defensive position, in touch with the units on our flanks. Why a conference was held instead of waiting for orders was because communication was so bad that operations passed out of brigade and even battalion control. The signallers carried on as best they could with their usual efficiency and bravery, and several of them were sniped while carrying messages, and never reached their destination. One runner (No. 257, Pte. L. Rogers) was seen running the gauntlet from shell-hole to shell-hole through a hail of bullets with a most important message. He got through, but he was about the only runner who did. In consequence of the impossibility of communication the initiative had to be taken by the senior officer of the brigade on the spot, Major L. F. Giblin, M.C.

The withdrawal commenced at 1.45 p.m. by sending back parties of two and three at a time, carrying any wounded they could find. The withdrawal was spread over an hour and a half, but it was observed by the enemy, and parties were followed by artillery fire as they moved back. Several cases were seen of small parties, carrying wounded, being knocked out by a direct hit. By 3.30 p.m. the withdrawal was completed with the exception of two posts of about 30 men. These men had been collected by the Commanding Officer (Lieut.-Col. J. E. C. Lord, D.S.O.), and placed in defensive positions by him immediately east of Waterfields Farm to protect our left flank. These posts were under the control of No. 832, Sergt. H. Gillam, and No. 834, Sergt. W. N. Grey. Movement in their position was impossible owing to the enemy's snipers across the creek, and they remained there until 10 p.m. that night, when they were withdrawn.

The Battalion forward signal station, under Lieut. B. Jackson, was also at Waterfields Farm, and the signallers and runners had collected about 50 of our wounded and placed them in the farm ruins. They were also withdrawn that night, with the exception of those of the wounded who were unable to walk. It took the party two hours to drag themselves through the mud from their station to Battalion Headquarters, a distance of 600 yards.

The defensive position taken up by the remnants of the brigade was from Augustus Wood to the road on the left of Dab Trench (D 11 c 5510 to D 10 d 4545). The rest of the afternoon was spent in consolidating this position for defence. The bad weather continued. All night squalls of rain came in quick succession from the east, and men huddled in their waterproof sheets in the mud-holes, so that they became numbed, and staggered like drunken men when they tried to move.

Early in the morning of the 13th October the Battalion Signal Officer (Lieut. B. Jackson) took a party of men forward to bring in any wounded who had been left behind. The party was fired on at once, but when the enemy saw they were carrying wounded he ceased firing, and sent out a party of stretcher bearers with a Red Cross flag. Our bearers moved about with the Germans, and we showed them any of their wounded, and they pointed out ours. The condition of the wounded was very bad, lying in shell-holes of mud and water, and some hopelessly stuck in the mud. The whole area was searched, and by dark all the wounded were carried back, including some of English units. These had been there for four days, and their wounds were rotting. Only one man was left. He was unwounded, but stuck in the mud near the Ravebeck. He was not seen by the stretcher-bearers, but was found that night by the enemy, who dug him out, and made him a prisoner.

During the day the company quartermaster-sergeants appeared with a carrying party with stew in hot boxes. It was a gallant attempt to provide a hot meal, but owing to the incredibly slow rate of movement it was only by faith that we knew it had once been hot. Still, it cheered us, as a link with a better world.

While the wounded were being brought in, the enemy put down a heavy bombardment on our position, and also on the pill-boxes along Dab Trench. One of these pill-boxes was being used as an aid-post, and was full of wounded. It was smashed to pieces, and a number of wounded in the vicinity were killed. Practically every man who could be spared was either looking for wounded or carrying wounded back towards the dressing-stations. There was not a man in the Battalion who was not on this job during the 13th October, and every one of them was completely exhausted by carrying through the mud, where every step was an effort.

During the afternoon, Lieut. B. Jackson, with No. 92, Pte. F. Teniswood, and No. 257, Pte. L. Rogers, crossed the Ravebeck by the road, and went into enemy territory behind Dab Trench in search of any wounded of Lieut. Grant's party, who had crossed the creek to help the New Zealanders. They went over Dab Trench, which was occupied by the enemy, but he took no notice of them, except to wave encouragingly for them to carry on. They found there several New Zealanders, English, and three of our wounded. These were brought out. As the last man was being carried through Waterfields a wounded German followed the two runners carrying the stretcher. As they were unable to take him they tried to induce him to go back, but he was badly wounded, and only seemed to realise that it was a stretcher, and a stretcher—German or otherwise—meant help. He tried to follow them on his hands and knees. His progress became slower and slower till he stopped, and his head sank forward and buried in the sea of mud.

At about 10 p.m., as parties of the 11th Brigade moved in to relieve the 10th Brigade, parties of the 40th Battalion were sent out, carrying wounded men with them. At 11 p.m. the brigade relief was complete, and the remains of the battalion, about 100 in number, began their weary march out. "K" track had been a wonderfully good track (under the circumstances) when we came in, but two days of miscellaneous traffic (including mules) had left little to distinguish it from the surrounding shell-holes. Half the men had not strength enough left to get out of a bad place without help, and would not have heart to plug on without company. Every 100 yards the word came along "Halt in front," and the leaders halted until the bogged men were extricated, and the column closed up again. It took three hours to reach the Zonnebeke-road, where going was comparatively good, but only one man gave up, and was left behind at a dressing-station, suffering from exhaustion. An hour later we were trickling into Hussar Farm Camp, where the Quartermaster and his staff had hot food and drink, blankets, and dry clothes for us.

Our casualties during the whole operation were:—

	Officers.	Other Ranks.
Killed	2	77
Wounded	5	163
Prisoners	—	1
	7	241

The killed included 34 N.C.O.'s and men who at the time were shown as "Missing." A court of enquiry afterwards took evidence and found that they were all killed in action except one, who was taken prisoner, as mentioned before.

The attack on October 12 was a severe defeat. It failed on account of wet weather, and the consequent mud, which made it impossible to get artillery forward after Phase 3 of the battle. It was owing to insufficient artillery preparation that Phase 4 failed, and although Phase 5 was a repetition of Phase 4, with a further objective, there was no information as to the cause of the failure of Phase 4. When the New Zealanders attacked they were faced with uncut belts of wire across their front, with strong machine-gun positions behind it, untouched by artillery fire. They did not get past this wire, and in justice to the New Zealanders it is admitted that no troops could possibly have got through under the circumstances.

Had the New Zealanders been successful and captured Bellevue Spur, there was every possibility of the 10th Brigade overcoming the resistance in front of them and taking Passchendaele. As it was, the fire from the left flank and rear held up our advance, and caused the majority of the casualties. We had to advance 2000 yards to get Passchendaele, and though after the 12th October several attacks were made by the Canadians, Passchendaele was not captured until 6th November, after three weeks of constant fighting.

The conditions made the last stages of the third battle of Ypres one of the most terrible conflicts in the history of war. Mud was the enemy's real defence, and under heavy fire we had struggled through it. It was under terrible conditions which made the fighting men reach the lowest possible depth of human misery. Belgium should no longer be called "the cockpit of Europe," for after the third battle of Ypres it became one of the biggest graveyards of the Anglo-Saxon race. Strategically the battle was a failure, for we were never within measurable distance of the great objective aimed at, and it cost the British and Overseas Armies 260,000 casualties.

Chapter XV.

Good-bye to Ypres — Back to Becourt — Musketry Competition — In the Trenches Again near Messines — The end of the First Year in France.

THE 14th October was spent in resting as much as possible in bivouac. Nearly everybody had slight "trench feet," which kept the A.M.C. details busy attending to cases. The clothing of everybody coming out of the attack was unfit for anything but salvage, but changes were obtained from the packs of our 500 casualties. At 1 a.m. on the 15th, during fairly heavy gas-shelling of the area, orders came to move at 7 a.m. back through Ypres to an embussing point at Kruistraathoek. The transport moved off earlier by rail from Vlamertinghe.

At 7 a.m. we moved on to the Zonnebeke Road and proceeded towards Ypres. The city had not been shelled for some days, but now that our attack had failed the enemy artillery had moved up within range, and he was shelling the city and the Menin Road with heavy high explosive. We crossed the canal by the Menin Gate, and at the Cloth Hall turned south to pass out of the Lille Gate. We were only about 200 strong, and were moving in four parties in file at 50 yards interval between parties. Just before the Lille Gate was reached it was seen that four heavy shells were landing every two minutes on or near the road we had to pass. The battalion was too tired to hurry, and did not quicken its pace. A platoon of the 38th Battalion in front of us got the next salvo among them, killing or wounding most of them. The pace of the 40th Battalion never changed, and we dragged past the danger spot as the next salvo fell 50 yards short. The pavé under our feet was dry and shells did not matter. The next salvo just missed the tail of the column, and we passed safely through the Lille Gate and across the canal, destined never to see Ypres again. We do not want to see Ypres again, yet it has an interest for the whole world. It has been described as a "dead city" but it is more than that, it is the skeleton of one. Its outline still remains, and points a mute finger in protest against the scheme of things that made its destruction possible. And beyond it is the waste which is as much desert as the sands of the Sahara. At that time it was a vast expanse of mud and watery shell-holes, the mud-lined prison of the living, the mud-covered tombs of the dead. So thick were the shell-holes of water that in places where they had overflowed and joined small lakes existed, and where the artillery fire had churned it up was nothing but morass. Places marked on the map had disappeared in the mud; some bare bones of Zonnebeke church still emerged, but almost the only other landmarks were the dozens of concrete "pill-boxes." Where the fight had been thickest the bodies of the dead protruded, their clothes so covered with mud that dead friend and dead foe were indistinguishable one from another. The popular conception of Hell was once Fire, but Dante's "Inferno" describes part of the lower regions as a sea of ice where enemies frozen in the ice gnaw furiously at one another's skulls. And to us who fought at Ypres Dante's awful picture is reduced to a dull monochrome compared with the sight of two armies of the white race fighting furiously amid a sea of mud in a struggle of extermination.

Kruistraathoek was reached at 11 a.m., and we left there by motor 'busses at 1 p.m., arriving at Becourt, our previous training area, at 11 p.m. The news that we had arrived soon got round among the villagers, who soon realised that only the remnants of the battalion had returned. The French peasantry are not demonstrative as a rule, and although courteous do not generally go out of their way to do a kindness to soldiers; this is natural enough as they must have been sick of armies marching through and living in their villages. But at Becourt that night they treated us as if we were the sons of the village. Billets were thrown open, meals were cooked, bottles of wine were brought out and opened, and the hospitality of the village was offered to us. It was spontaneous and surprising. The writer sat by the kitchen fire of a farm while Madame filled his cup from time to time with coffee and cognac. Madame and Papa and the two children sat round and watched him, till Madame at last asked the inevitable question, "And where are the others?" They were told where the others were and the tears rolled down Madame's cheeks, and Papa wept, and Georgette and Marcelle wept, and probably the writer had a lump in his throat.

From the 16th to the 21st October the time was spent in reorganising and re-equipping. Reinforcements, and men who had been evacuated sick and wounded, began to arrive from base camps, and companies were able to reorganise two complete platoons per company. On 22nd October training commenced, chiefly musketry and Lewis gun work. A battalion musketry competition was held and medals presented to the winners of the different events, which resulted as follows:—

Inter-Company Competition

Winner.	Best Shot in Coy.	Score of Best Shot.
1st—C Coy.	578 Sgt. L. T. Partridge	45
2nd—D Coy.	2311 Cpl. C. S. Cosson	45
3rd—A Coy.	Lieut. R. J. Goodyer	42
4th—B Coy.	351 Sgt. A. P. Brown	44

Inter-Platoon Competition—

Winner.	Best Shot in Platoon.	Score of Best Shot.
1st—No. 10 (C Coy.)	5775 Pte. A. A. Stott ...	42
2nd—No. 11 (C Coy.)	2026 Sgt. J. A. Lincey...	40
3rd—No. 9 (C Coy.)	559 Cpl. L. G. Garth...	44
4th—No. 8 (B Coy.)	2782 Pte. J. R. Barker	40

Best Shot in the Battalion, N.C.O's.—

Winner.	Score.
1st—No. 578 Sgt. L. T. Partridge (C Coy.) ...	45
2nd—No. 2311 Cpl. C. S. Cosson (D Coy.)	44

Best Shot in the Battalion, Privates—

Winner.	Score.
1st—No. 2105 Pte. R. W. Gill (D Coy.)	45
2nd—No. 5775 Pte. A. A. Stott (C Coy.)	45

Sniping Competition—

Winner.	Score.
1st—No. 2105 Pte. R. W. Gill (D Coy.)...	50
2nd—No. 3039 Pte. A. E. Flint (B Coy.)...	40

Patrol Shooting Competition—

Winner.
1st—No. 11 Platoon (C Coy.).
2nd—No. 10 Platoon (C Coy.).

On the 5th November the 2nd Anzac Corps ceased to exist, and the New Zealand Division went to a corps with British Divisions, and we went to the 1st Anzac Corps, which now became the Australian Corps. We regretted being parted from the New Zealanders, but we went to where we always wanted to be, with the rest of the Australians.

The popular belief at this time, based always on the highest authority, was that the Australian Corps was to rest for the winter. It struck us as a very reasonable arrangement, especially as we were still only about 50 per cent. strong. But somehow, no one was greatly surprised, when after three weeks of rustic peace, orders came for the 3rd Division to move into the line again.

On the 10th November the battalion left Becourt by motor 'busses and travelled to La Motte, near Hazebrouck, arriving there shortly after dark. After waiting for two hours in heavy rain, guides and instructions turned up, and we marched to Le Tir Anglais, where the night was spent in billets. On the following day we marched through Vieux Berquin to billets in Le Verrier. On the 12th November we moved on and relieved the 1st Royal Irish Rifles at Waterlands Camp in the Steenwerck area, being now part of the reserve brigade of the division. On the following day the battalion took over Romarin Camp from part of the 8th British Division, and now became reserve battalion of the 10th Brigade, which had taken over the sector immediately south of the River Douve, in front of Warneton.

For the next few days the battalion was employed on working parties, and was engaged in taking engineering material to the dump at Prowse Point. The work was facilitated by a light railway (managed by a Canadian unit) which ran past Romarin to Hyde Park Corner, on which all working parties and other troops travelled to and from the trenches.

On the night of the 20th November an advance party of the 40th Battalion, consisting of Lewis gunners, scouts, snipers, and signallers, went into the front line, and on the following night we relieved the 38th Battalion in the front-line trenches. At the same time a raiding party of 4 officers and 70 other ranks was left at Romarin to prepare for the raid.

The battalion sector taken over was part of the Warneton sector, and extended south from the River Douve to a point about 500 yards north of La Basse Ville. C Company occupied the left front, and A Company the right, with B Company in support, and D Company in reserve near Grey Farm. Battalion Headquarters was in a pill-box about 50 yards from Grey Farm. The right of this sector was very wet and had no front-line trench that could be occupied. No garrison was kept there during the day, and it was protected by patrols during the night. The centre and left of the sector were dry enough to use, but required a lot of improvement, as the trenches were neither traversed nor revetted. There was also very little wire on the front. One of the chief disadvantages of the sector was that it was overlooked from the Warneton Tower, which the enemy had probably constructed when he saw the possibility of losing the high ground at Messines. The tower was a concrete observation post which rose out of the ruins of Warneton like a chimney stack. Our observers could see the enemy entering it and could see the big periscope at the top swing round. It was as valuable to the enemy as a high ridge would have been, and it resisted all attempts of our artillery to demolish it. The field guns often had a shot at it, but their shells either flew off it or exploded on it without much visible effect. Shortly after we left the sector a 15-inch toy was brought in and knocked it down with the third round.

During September, October, and the first half of November, the Warneton sector had been fairly quiet, but when the Australian Corps took it over the enemy apparently suspected us of the worst possible intentions. We had been used solely as storm troops during the summer, and our move to Warneton rather suggested to the enemy that we were going to wind up the season with an attack. His artillery increased daily, and the daily registration of new enemy batteries suggested to "Higher Command" that the enemy might be considering an attack to capture Messines. Fresh units were arriving from Russia which considerably increased the German strength on the Western front, and there was every possibility of an attack, so our artillery on this part of the front was increased. It may have been an erroneous impression, but the infantry in the line had the idea that both sides had the "wind up" about each other's intentions, and were both dragging in all available artillery. On the other hand, it might have been that "Higher Command" were pulling the enemy's leg with a view to operations elsewhere. But, in any case, we had a bad time and sometimes wished that the enemy knew we were there for a rest.

The 21st November was a day of rain; the trenches began to subside as a result, and the following day all available men were employed on repairs. That evening the enemy put over about 170 rounds of high explosive and gas, mostly along the only track into the sector. This was a duck-walk track known as "Douve Walk," which ran along the south side of the river. Next day he shelled the same place heavily several times, putting over a total of 350 rounds of high explosive, and also about 100 minenwerfer on the front line. The following day

(November 24) our artillery began a policy of retaliation, and put down several heavy shoots on his trenches and rear communications. That day was the end of our first year in France, and we took out a few statistics which are interesting:—

Strength on Landing in France—
32 officers, 980 other ranks.

Present Strength—
41 officers, 647 other ranks.

Original Members of Unit still Serving with Battalion on 24.11.17—
27 officers, 280 other ranks.

Casualties—	Officers.	Other ranks.	Total.
Killed in action, including died of wounds	9	233	242
Wounded	25	1067	1092
Prisoners	—	1	1
Total	34	1301	1335

Reinforcements—
12 officers, 618 other ranks.

Promotions to Commissioned Rank—

From warrant officer	12
From sergeant	14
From corporal	3
From cadet battalions	7
Total	36

Chapter XVI.

Activity on Both Sides at Warneton — The 40th Battalion Raid at Warneton.

EFORE daylight on the 26th November 300 gas bombs were thrown into the enemy lines by Levin Projectors. The enemy retaliated with 500 rounds of high explosive on our front and support lines, and during the evening he shelled the reserve line near Grey Farm very heavily, blowing up the details'* cook-house near Battalion Headquarters.

On the 27th November the enemy was fairly quiet, and our observers could see a relief apparently in progress, as parties with packs on their backs could be seen going out of a trench through Warneton. This was pointed out to the artillery officers, and at an appropriate moment when a large party of the enemy could be seen, the artillery let loose its full weight on the trench and the village, with good results. Next day our front and support lines were heavily shelled by 4·2, 77, and 5·9 high explosive, and Sunken Farm was shelled all day with 5·9 high explosive.

On the 29th November the whole sector was again heavily shelled, and about every half-hour the enemy put down a shoot on Douve Walk, blowing the duck-walk up in several places. That evening the shelling was heavier than ever, and included 200 rounds of 5·9 on Battalion Headquarters. We were relieved that evening by the 38th Battalion, who suffered about 30 casualties during the relief. On relief we went back into support to dugouts at Red Lodge, on the south side of Hill 63. While here the battalion was kept busy, sending daily working parties to the trenches we had just left.

We were fortunate while in the sector at Warneton in having good artillery support. The Australian artillery officers in the line with us were full of energy, and lived in our observation posts all day. They were always ready to retaliate or fire on any good target picked up by our observers. In trench warfare this meant a good deal and helped us considerably in putting up with the abnormal enemy activity.

It was decided by the brigadier that the 39th and 40th Battalions raiding parties would raid the enemy trenches on the night of the 30th November-1st December. The objective was

---

* Details.—Battalion Headquarters Details, *i.e.*, signallers, runners, &c.

the enemy trenches immediately north of the railway from
Warneton to La Basse Ville. The plan was for the 39th Battalion to raid at 5.15 p.m. on the 30th November, and that
7½ hours later the 40th Battalion party would raid the same
place, hoping to find the enemy somewhat disorganised and
repairing his trenches. This was carried out with remarkable
success. At 5.15 p.m. the 39th Battalion party went over,
following a heavy bombardment of the trenches to be raided.
They were completely successful in spite of strong opposition.
They killed a number of the enemy, brought back prisoners,
and sustained about 20 casualties. The enemy shelling as a
result of this raid was very heavy, but a special overland track
had been built the night before the raid from Prowse Point
to the support lines, which allowed both raiding parties to get
away from our lines without casualties. This track was afterwards brought into general use, and was known as the Warneton Track.

The 40th Battalion party consisted of 4 officers and 72 other
ranks. The O.C. raid was Lieut. H. L. Foster, and the other
officers were Lieuts. E. Moon, A. P. Brown, and R. A. Swan.
The frontage of the attack was about 200 yards, and the
average depth about 100 yards. The party was divided as follows:—Lieut. H. L. Foster, with signallers, at raid headquarters, in our front line; Lieut. E. Moon, with signallers, in
front of enemy wire with telephone communication to Lieut.
Foster; Lieut. A. P. Brown, with 32 other ranks, as left
storming party; and Lieut. R. A. Swan, with 32 other ranks,
as right storming party. Both storming parties had to obtain
possession of the enemy front line and establish blocks to prevent interference from the flanks. When the blocks were made
the left party was to attack down a communication trench on
the left, while the right party worked down a similar trench on
the right. A support line joined these two trenches, and both
parties were to meet in this support line. It was estimated
that the work of clearing up dugouts and overcoming opposition would take 20 minutes, and this was the time fixed during
which the raiding party would remain in the enemy trenches.

The whole party moved up the Warneton Track without incident, and went into No Man's Land at 12.55 a.m., where they
remained while the scouts went forward. All the officers and
scouts had been to the enemy wire at the points to be raided
on previous nights, and they were quite familiar with the
ground in front. The scouts could see a party of the enemy on
his parapet mending the wire that had been smashed during

the previous raid earlier in the evening. At 1.15 a.m. the barrage opened on the enemy front line, and remained there for three minutes, when it lifted and formed a box round the area to be raided. Immediately the barrage lifted the party who had moved across No Man's Land while the barrage was on the front line, entered the trenches.

The right storming party (Lieut. R. A. Swan) met with no resistance before getting into the trench, but on jumping in they found the line full of bewildered Germans. Bombs were thrown among these, and they offered no resistance, but ran in all directions into dugouts and over the parapet. Several of these were shot before going far. The party then made their way along the front line and into the communication trench, bombing several occupied dugouts on the way. In the communication trench they met with organised resistance in the shape of a bombing party, and a short fight resulted, the enemy being ultimately driven back, leaving many dead. Sergt. Hector C. Long, who was remarkably expert with bombs, did brilliant work in overcoming this resistance by dropping bomb after bomb among the enemy. On reaching the support line most of the party remained " doggo," waiting for the enemy to be driven towards them by the left storming party, while a few men who had been detailed for demolition and searching dugouts went on with their work.

Meanwhile the left storming party were having a strenuous few minutes. On attempting to enter the enemy front line they were met with a shower of bombs from the enemy immediately in front. Lieut. Brown at once moved his party to the right, and, followed by a few men, jumped the front line where there were no enemy, moved back to the left, and attacked the enemy from the rear. Lieut. Brown did great execution with his revolver while the men with him bayoneted the enemy from the parados. They then jumped in and called upon the rest of the party to do likewise. After clearing the front line and establishing a block, the rest of the party, minus those detailed for protecting the flanks and clearing dugouts, moved along the communication trench without opposition. In this communication trench they came to four occupied dugouts, and disposed of the occupants. On arriving at the support line the enemy was met in great force, but a sudden bomb and bayonet attack demoralised them, and they offered practically no resistance. Some scrambled out of the trench and tried to escape by running back overland, while our men fired on them as they were running about in the moonlight. Others sought refuge in dugouts, but were bombed out and bayoneted. The left party then moved on and got into touch with the right party, who had accounted for some more of the enemy driven back by the left party's attack.

The 20 minutes having passed, the party leaders withdrew their men, making sure that nobody was left behind. On getting out of the trenches a machine gun opened on them from the right flank, and the coming back was carried out with great skill under the circumstances. Advantage was taken of the fact that the machine gun was firing in bursts, with about 10 seconds between each burst. While the machine gun was firing the men hugged mother earth, but as soon as it ceased they rushed forward a few yards till the gun opening fire gave the signal to drop again. This was continued all the way back across No Man's Land. Our total casualties during the raid were one missing and one wounded. The missing man subsequently turned up as a prisoner of war. He got out of the trench with the rest of the party, but while on the ground waiting for the machine gun to cease fire, he was shot through the legs and was unable to move. His comrades did not notice that he did not move forward in the next rush, and he was found later by an enemy patrol.

Two prisoners were brought back for identification and for the purpose of information. From them it was ascertained that the majority of the men in the trenches we attacked belonged to a regiment of Saxon Pioneers, who had been brought up to repair the damage caused by the first raiding party. The reason why we met such poor opposition was that a new trench garrison had just moved in to replace the garrison who had been badly mauled by the 39th Battalion, and they were not properly organised into posts when our party appeared. The enemy casualties (exclusive of those caused by the artillery) were estimated at about 100 killed.

This was the most successful raid ever carried out by the battalion. The whole plan was well thought out and carried out. Generally in a raid one of the many details goes wrong, but on this occasion everything worked smoothly, and the raiding party made the most of it at very little cost. The idea of sending two raiding parties over in the same place on the same night was a new one, and emanated from the Commanding Officer of the 40th Battalion (Lieut.-Col. J. E. C. Lord, D.S.O.), who profited by our experience that, after an enemy raid, our trenches were necessarily more or less disorganised and easy to attack. But while such disorganisation existed we took the necessary precaution of protecting our front with patrols.

Chapter XVII.

In the Line at Warneton—Christmas Day at Neuve Eglise—Back in the Line Again—The "Chinese Attack" at Warneton—Attempted Enemy Raid Broken by a Patrol—Back to Reserve near Lumbres—Sports and Training—The German Offensive Opens.

N the 6th December the battalion again relieved the 38th Battalion on the Warneton sector, the disposition being: D Company (Lieut. H. L. Foster) on the left, B Company (Capt. G. L. McIntyre) on the right, with A Company (Capt. G. S. Bisdee) in support, and C Company (Capt. W. C. G. Ruddock) in reserve. Our own artillery and the enemy's were both still very active, and our trenches were several times subjected to concentrated area shoots. About midday on the 7th December the enemy shelled our front and support lines with 200 rounds of high explosive, and repeated this programme on the following day. During the evening of the 10th December about 400 rounds of 4·2 and 77 high explosive fell on the sector, as well as 80 minenwerfer on the front line. These shoots appeared to be observed closely from observation balloons, there being about seven as a rule opposite the brigade front.

During this period in the line our patrol operations were altered in view of the possibility of the enemy replying to our raid. The usual patrols were withdrawn and remained stationary, acting as listening posts in front of our wire, and a fighting patrol of an officer and 12 other ranks, with a Lewis gun, went out every night as close to the enemy wire as possible, in order to meet any raiding party. The experience on other parts of the front had recently been that the enemy confined his raids to isolated posts, and as we had such posts on our right flank the idea was to protect them in this manner. To defend an isolated post when attacked on all sides is difficult. In the gap between our extreme right post and the battalion on our right a patrol moved backwards and forwards at intervals all night. The work was generally carried out by Lieut. H. Chamberlain, and proved a very unpleasant job on account of the waterlogged ground that in places was waist deep in water and mud. Between our left flank and the 5th

Division, north of the Douve, there was also a gap of 200
yards. This was also patrolled alternately by our patrols and
those of the unit on the other side of the river. The river had
to be crossed by a plank, and on one occasion an enemy patrol
waited under the bank of the stream and caught two men of
another unit by grabbing their ankles as they crossed by the
plank.

During this tour in the line we were visited by the Corps
Commander (Lieut.-General Sir William Birdwood), who was
inspecting the divisional front. The official war correspondent
(Capt. C. E. W. Bean) also came up one day, and found absorbing interest in trying to get a successful photograph of a bursting 5·9 among other things, to the great danger of his camera
and himself. Our opinion of the work of a war correspondent
generally was not high; in fact the descriptions of some
"stunts" written by correspondents of the English Press were
so ludicrous that they were a source of constant joy to us.
Their information seemed concocted of the yarns of the early
wounded and stragglers who had judiciously left the fighting
at an early stage, and the joyous romances of the professional
leg-pullers, dished up with the sentiment of a coloured Christmas number. But the Australian correspondent was an exception. He was a persistent and careful narrator, and it was
impossible to "pull his leg" with a hair-raising episode,
because he knew as much about the whole operation as we did,
and possibly more. And he followed every detail closely. Incidentally, he was regarded as a "dinkum bloke," and nobody
wanted to mislead him for pure fun.

On the 15th December we were relieved by the 26th Battalion, and moved out to hutments known as Shankhill Camp,
at Neuve Eglise, where a few civilians still remained. For the
next few days most of the battalion was employed on working
parties, which consisted largely of loading stone for road-
making. The weather, after a heavy fall of snow, was fairly
fine, but a frost set in, the ground being covered with several
inches of snow, and the trees white with frost. Fuel was very
scarce, and a few ruined houses in Neuve Eglise mysteriously
disappeared. The result was that claims by French civilians
for heavy damages were sent in against all battalions of the
brigade, and it looked as if we were going to pay for about
half the town. However, some four months later, when the
file of papers on the subject had reached an abnormal size, and
we were just about to put our hands in our pockets and find
the amount of the claims, the enemy attacked and captured
Neuve Eglise. So everybody concerned breathed sighs of relief,

and sent their files of documents on the subject to paper salvage. Incidentally, there were pious reflections that it is an ill-wind that blows nobody any good.*

On the 19th December the 3rd Australian Division took over the line south of the Lys in front of Armentieres. The 10th Brigade was in reserve, and the 40th Battalion remained at Neuve Eglise, while all officers reconnoitred routes, examined communications, and inspected the defences of the town. Armentieres was a much-changed town since we had last seen it. In February, 1917, about 5000 civilians still lived there, and small shops and estaminets were open. But in December the civilians had all gone, and the wreckage of houses blocked the streets. It was afternoon when we passed through the town, and not a living thing was seen among the ruins. The atmosphere of loneliness was over everything. The streets preserved their contours, but on either side the houses stood shattered and roofless, fronts knocked out, walls hanging in pieces, furniture fallen through broken walls, and household treasures a forlorn heap of rubbish.

Christmas Day was a holiday for everyone. The day was fine except for a few light falls of snow, and a football match was played in a snow-covered field. The sum of £76 had been received from the women workers of the 40th Battalion Comforts Fund, and this had been spent in " good cheer " for the battalion. This, supplemented by boxes of comforts from the Australian Comforts Fund and the expenditure of about £25 from regimental funds, provided an excellent Christmas dinner for everybody. The only item on the menu not appreciated was the beer. It was always believed that beer was never out of place anywhere and at any time. But it is quite uninspiring when the barometer is at zero, although there is a well-known saying on the West Coast of Tasmania that " it is a poor belly that cannot warm its own beer."

On the 26th December working parties were again commenced and carried on through extremely cold weather. New Year's Day was spent in recreation, including a pierrot entertainment at Neuve Eglise, the battalion hiring the show for the afternoon. On the whole the day was not a success, as nobody could get interested in anything but trying to keep warm.

On the 3rd January we handed over our Armentieres sector to the 57th British Division, and became support division on the Australian Corps front.

---

* Since the above was written it was discovered that unfortunately, owing to the carelessness of the Adjutant, the Neuve Eglise file was not lost during the exciting events of 1918 : and in 1919 Regimental Funds were depleted (after we had no further use for them) to make good our alleged depredations.

Lewis gun and signalling schools were commenced under the direction of the Lewis gun and signalling officers, and the battalion scouts and observers also received training from the intelligence officer. A brigade school for junior officers was also organised, and Army and Corps schools also took a large number of N.C.O.'s and men from the battalion. At the Army schools the following won special distinction during the month of January:—(i) No. 930, Pte. H. A. H. Smith (D Company); scored highest aggregate in rifle shooting at the 2nd Army sniping school, among 200 competitors. (ii) No. 630, Cpl. H. L Grimmond (D Company); received a medal for being the best shot in the 4th Army musketry school, consisting of 96 officers and 96 N.C.O.'s.

On the 12th January the battalion lost the services of Capt. C. L. McVilly, M.C., and No. 2146, Sergt. H. J. Smith, M.M., who were detailed to proceed on some mysterious mission with a number of other selected officers and N.C.O.'s. They turned up again in England in February, 1919, looking very thin and worn out, after various adventures. They had been sent to Mesopotamia, and thence to Persia, on what was afterwards known as the "Baku Expedition," which is now history. They formed part of the 70 officers and 140 N.C.O.'s who organised the Armenians, and led them in constant fighting against the Turks for several weeks, until the treachery of the Armenians forced them to retire from Baku. As a result of his work in this expedition Capt. McVilly was mentioned in despatches.

On the 27th January the 40th Battalion relieved the 27th Battalion at Red Lodge (Hill 63), and became reserve battalion to the 10th Brigade, who had taken over the Warneton sector. While in reserve every available man was employed on working on the trench systems behind the front-line system. It was realised that the enemy would be able to take the initiative in the spring owing to the collapse of Russia, and to be able to meet him strong points and lines of defence were constructed behind the front trench system round Messines, Hill 63, St. Yves, and Ploegsteert Wood. The defences built by the Australian Corps in the Ploegsteert-Messines sector were enormously strong, and it was then thought impossible for the enemy to break through them. But within three months he did break through, but that is a story which does not directly concern the Australian Corps.

On the 4th February the battalion relieved the 38th Battalion in the Warneton sector. The dispositions were different from those when we held the sector previously. The dugouts in River Lane were flooded, and the support line was also uninhabitable. A new support line had been dug, called Wally Support. D Company (Major L. F. Giblin, M.C.), was on the right of the front line, and A Company (Capt. G. S. Bisdee) on the left. C Company (Capt. W. C. G. Ruddock) was in the subsidiary line near Grey Farm, and B Company (Lieut. G. L. McIntyre) was in reserve in the Catacombs at Hyde Park Corner. In addition to B Company, about 120 men were sent to the Catacombs from the three companies in the line, as all companies were now up to strength again, and only a limited number of men could be accommodated in the line. The personnel at the Catacombs were employed on working parties, and also carrying rations, engineering material, &c., up to the front-line system. A great deal of engineering material was required, as the Division had started adequate defences for La Basse Ville.

The enemy artillery was not so active as it had been during December, and our artillery had increased, while the enemy seemed to limit his artillery fire to retaliation for our daily "strafes." On the other hand, his minenwerfer were very active on the front line, and did a lot of damage. No less than 18 minenwerfer emplacements had been located opposite the battalion sector, and were given code names, such as Alice, Clara, &c., so if the artillery received a message requesting them to "box Maggie's ears," they knew what to do. These minenwerfer shoots were like a nagging toothache, for we got no rest from them. About every hour through the night one or more would start, and the trench officers would take bearings on the flash of the guns, and decide which ones were responsible. He would then go to the telephone at Company Headquarters and tell the adjutant that Florrie and Gwen had just tossed fifteen over, and were continuing to throw more. The adjutant would ring up the covering battery, and tell the artillery officer on duty the names of the ladies. Within two minutes afterwards barks from a couple of guns behind proclaimed that we were hitting back. This went on all night with few variations.

On the 10th February, at 10.45 p.m., a raid was made by the 37th and 38th Battalions from the sector on our right, the trenches raided being immediately south of the Warneton-La Basse Ville Railway. On the 40th Battalion front, a diversion was provided, called a "Chinese attack," in the shape of dummy figures in No Man's Land, lit up well with flares, the idea being to divert the enemy fire from the real raiding party. The ruse was quite successful, as the dummies were fired at vigorously during the whole raid by machine guns and trench mortars. The raid was a success, and the 37th and 38th Battalions parties inflicted heavy casualties on the enemy and brought back 38 prisoners. The enemy shelled our sector heavily during the raid, killing four men and wounding one. The casualties among the enemy appeared to be very heavy, and all next day our observers could see parties of enemy stretcher-bearers carrying dead and wounded out of the trenches.

On the 12th February we were relieved by the 38th Battalion, and went into support at the Catacombs, where working parties on the rear defences were continued. While at the Catacombs a good deal of time was given over to preparation for an enemy attack, and the defence scheme of the brigade was closely studied. In the event of an attack the *role* of the 40th Battalion was to move to Ploegsteert Wood, and remain there in artillery formation ready to counter-attack or occupy a defensive position, as required.

On the 12th February we again relieved the 38th Battalion in the front line, with B Company on the left, C Company on the right, D Company in support, and A Company in reserve at Hyde Park Corner. The 21st February was marked by heavy enemy artillery fire, which several times concentrated on our sector during the day and night. This bombardment caused several casualties, including two very gallant non-commissioned officers, No. 2418, Sgt. W. G. E. Woolley, D.C.M., and No. 587, Cpl. J. Saddington, M.M., who were both killed. At about 2.30 a.m. a particularly heavy bombardment was put down on our right front. This action appeared to indicate an intended raid, and at 3 a.m. a fighting patrol of 1 officer (Lieut. T. G. Cranswick, D.C.M.) and 14 other ranks, with a Lewis gun, went out from the right of our sector and "laid up" about 50 yards in front of the enemy's wire. At 4 a.m. a party of 15 of the enemy came through his wire in front of our patrol, and worked to the left of it. Immediately afterwards a second party of 15 came through the wire at the same place, and moved straight towards our patrol. When about 15 yards away our Lewis gun opened fire on them, and either killed or wounded the whole party. Rifle fire was at once opened on our party by a party of the enemy who had worked out from another point unobserved, and were now on our right rear. Our patrol then withdrew, under fire from both the enemy parties, to the middle of No Man's Land, where they took up a position covering our right isolated post, but no more was seen of the enemy parties. There is no doubt that Lieut. Cranswick and his party frustrated an enemy attempt to raid one of our posts. They met and wiped out one of his parties, and caused the remainder to give up the idea. At that time his raiding programme was confined to mopping up isolated posts, and we knew that on other parts of the front he had been fairly successful. His plan was generally to attack in three parties, one taking the front and the other two the flanks. In this case it is believed that his objective was our right post, which had always been a source of uneasiness to us. When General Birdwood visited the sector he noticed it, and pointed out the obvious helplessness of the garrison in the event of a determined raid.

During the night of the 25th February the battalion was relieved by the 34th Battalion, and moved out to Hyde Park Corner, from where we were taken to Romarin by the Canadian light railway. At Romarin Camp we were now part of the reserve brigade of the division, and were employed in working on the Corps defence line.

While at Romarin Major J. T. McColl, M.C., was posted to the 40th Battalion. This officer belonged to the Australian A. & I. Staff and had seen much service early in the campaign in France, and later in Gallipoli and Salonica with British units. On the 4th March the battalion was relieved by the 20th Battalion, and moved out from Romarin to Steenwerck, where we entrained at 1.35 p.m. for Lumbres. We detrained at Lumbres, and from there route-marched to Seninghem, which was reached in a heavy storm at 6.15 p.m. This was the area allotted to us for training, and during the next few days the whole division was relieved and came back into reserve. The Commanding Officer (Lieut.-Col. J. E. C. Lord, D.S.O.) proceeded to England for a month's rest before the spring campaign, and Major L. H. Payne, D.S.O., temporarily commanded the battalion in his absence

Company inspections were carried out during the next few days, as well as a training syllabus consisting of musketry, Lewis gun work, bombing, sniping, scouting, and signalling. The brigade school for prospective N.C.O.'s was established. Sport was not neglected, and the football competition created much enthusiasm. At football A Company beat C Company; Battalion Headquarters beat D Company; and B Company beat A Company. The premiership now rested betwen Battalion Headquarters and B Company, but before the final match was played the German offensive began, and the issue was never decided. On the 17th March a very successful sports meeting was held by the battalion in very fine weather. The weather, combined with athletics and training, put new life into everybody, and within a fortnight the change was remarkable. After a long stretch of fighting or trench warfare everybody became very haggard, worn, and war-weary. The only remedy was to be in reserve with fine weather and plenty of sport and amusement.

During the training at Seninghem every platoon in the battalion was working hard to win the platoon competition. This was a competition in every division in the army to decide ultimately the best platoon in every division. Medals were provided for the winners of brigade and divisional competitions by the Army Rifle Association. This competition created great interest. Eliminating competitions were held to decide the best platoon in each company and in each battalion. On the 19th March the whole battalion route-marched to Lumbres, and every platoon did the attack practice laid down, which included musketry, bayonet fighting, Lewis gun firing, and general efficiency, while advancing as in an attack. The result of the battalion competition left four platoons to represent the battalion in the brigade competition. The four platoons were No. 10 (Lieut. M. H. O. Whitaker), No. 11 (Lieut. W. E. K. Grubb), No. 7 (Lieut. A. P. Brown, M.C.), and No. 4 (No. 999, Sgt. F. A. Fletcher). The next eliminating contest was between the four leading platoons of each battalion in the brigade. This contest was held on the 21st March, and the first four platoons selected from the brigade to take part in the final competition were:—No. 7 Platoon, 40th Battalion (Lieut. A. P. Brown, M.C.), 1st; a platoon of the 39th Battalion and No. 4 Platoon, 40th Battalion (No. 999, Sgt. F. A. Fletcher), equal 2nd; No. 10 Platoon, 40th Battalion (Lieut. M. H. O. Whitaker), 3rd. This gave the 40th Battalion three platoons in the final competition between four platoons from each brigade in the division. The competition was to have taken place on the 23rd March, but on the evening of the 21st March official notification was received that the German offensive had begun on the front of the 3rd and 5th British Armies, and we were ordered to be ready to move at six hours' notice. So the result of the platoon competition was held up while every platoon in the division was thrown into the gap east of Amiens. The final round was in the end held on the Somme during the following May, and was won by No. 7 Platoon, 40th Battalion. The same competition in the First Division was also won by Tasmanians with a platoon of the 12th Battalion.

On the morning of the 22nd March orders were received to entrain at Lumbres the following day and proceed towards Ypres to Winnezeele. The reason for this was that the enemy, in addition to his southern attack, was expected to make another attack in the north, with a view to breaking through to the Channel ports. So far the news from the south was good, but unfortunately incorrect. We were told that the German offensive had been held up in the second zone of resistance with enormous losses to the enemy. On 23rd March we received no information whatever. The battalion left Seninghem at 7 a.m. on the 23rd March, and reached Lumbres at 8 a.m., with the rest of the 10th Brigade, but, owing to the general dislocation of traffic, no trains arrived till about 1.30 p.m., and we got away from Lumbres at 3.30 p.m. instead of 9.30 a.m., as ordered. Part of the division had moved off the previous day, and were getting towards Ypres, but meanwhile orders had been received that the Division would go south, and the train was stopped by the G.S.O.1 Division (Colonel C. H. Jess) at Eblinghem, where we got out of the train and marched to Campagne, near Arques, arriving there at 9 p.m. The battalion remained there the next day waiting for orders to move, and on the morning of the 25th March all officers of the brigade were ordered to assemble at a point near Campagne. There we met the Brigadier (Brig.-Gen. W. Ramsay McNicol). He stood in the centre of the road with the officers of the brigade around him, and, with his map before him, he put the position plainly. He told us that the 5th Army had been driven back, and were retreating everywhere, and that the British front was broken and the British and French armies were in danger of separation; that the German divisions were pushing forward with great rapidity; and he added the surprising information that a long-range gun was shelling Paris. He finished by saying that we would entrain the following morning, and would go straight into action, and that we would have the fight of our lives, as the result of the war now hung in the balance.

Chapter XVIII.

To the Somme — The British Retreat — Into the Gap between the Ancre and the Somme — The Attack by the 40th Battalion on 28th March — The Enemy Attacks Again and is Beaten Off — Into Reserve in Ribemont.

N the morning of the 26th March we left Campagne and marched to St. Omer, entraining there at 3 p.m. At St. Omer we saw several Red Cross trains full of wounded going through, and interviewed several people who had come from the front of the retreat. There was a most depressing atmosphere of hopelessness about them all, but we saw some New Zealanders, who told us that their division had gone down, and that the 4th Australian Division was also on the way, so we bucked up considerably and had a drink, and ventured the opinion that it was not all over yet. We left St. Omer at 3 p.m., and after a long journey in cattle-trucks reached the vicinity of Mondicourt at about 1.30 a.m. on the morning of the 27th March; but the train had to wait some distance outside the station till 3 a.m., owing to congestion in front. We finally pulled into the station at Mondicourt, and detrained in the dark at 3.40 a.m. Orders were waiting for us to issue 24 hours' rations to each man, and get ready to move forward into action at once. We got ready, and by 5 a.m. were in a field awaiting orders. In the meantime we searched for information from an authoritative source. We found an English staff officer, who told us the enemy was about 10 miles away, and that his advance guard, cavalry and armoured cars, had been in villages 8 miles away the previous afternoon, and that the only troops between us and the enemy were totally disorganised and in full retreat. This information, with the exception of the armoured motor-cars, was fairly correct. When daylight came the village seemed full of English troops and civilians, all moving back as fast as possible. Some civilians were on foot, carrying bundles of their belongings, while others were driving carts loaded with their valuables, and in some cases towing livestock behind the vehicles. The troops in retreat seemed worn out, and were mostly straggling back, though some were marching back under their officers, and in some cases officers were collecting stragglers and trying to reorganise them.

We had detrained at Mondicourt, because it was intended to throw the division into the gap between Bucquoy and Beaumont-sur-Ancre. Undoubtedly a gap existed there, and the enemy cavalry had got through to Auchonvillers on the morning of 26th March, but that part of the line was restored by the New Zealand Division on the same afternoon, and the 3rd Australian Division was moved farther south to stop the enemy getting through between the Somme and the Ancre.

Some idea of the conditions north of the Ancre may be gathered from the experiences of Lieut. E. J. Bertram and four sergeants of the 40th Battalion, who had gone ahead with Brigade Headquarters, and arrived at Mondicourt about 10 a.m. on the morning of the 26th March. There it was reported that the enemy was in Pas, about 2 miles away; but on this information being found to be incorrect, the Brigadier sent Lieut. Bertram and his four sergeants out on bicycles to find out where the enemy was. At this time disorganised English troops were streaming back through Mondicourt in hundreds, reporting that the enemy were just behind them. The Brigadier and his staff officers stopped a number of them and reorganised them for a stand, and placed the 10th Machine-gun Company with their guns in a defensive position east of Mondicourt.

Lieut. Bertram and his party found a hopeless condition of affairs. The roads were full of transport and vehicles of all kinds, and troops were coming back everywhere. They seemed absolutely demoralised, and advised our party to come back with them, as "Jerry" was just behind. A number of men had thrown away their rifles, and arms and equipment littered the sides of the roads. Bertram's party went as far as Coigneux, and ascertained there that the enemy cavalry had reached Heburterne that morning. They reported back to Brigade Headquarters at Mondicourt, and at 6 p.m. went out as far as Auchonvillers, where they got in touch with the officers of the New Zealand Division, and ascertained from them that the line had been restored that afternoon by the New Zealanders, who had moved up from the south. The restored line was now, roughly, through Beaumont-sur-Ancre, Serie, Puisieux-au-Mont, and Bucquoy. The line from Bucquoy to Basseux had apparently not been broken. The retreating troops had been quite certain that armoured cars were behind them, and this information was persistently repeated; but the armoured cars had probably been French plough tractors, which were making back to safety as fast as they could, quite oblivious of the panic they were creating.

From daylight on the 27th March we awaited orders at Mondicourt, as Brigade Headquarters had moved on with the rest of the brigade before we arrived there, and at 11.30 a.m. the G.S.O.1, Division, came along and ordered us to move to an embussing point midway between Thieves and Marieux. We were going in between the Ancre and the Somme. As usual, someone had blundered. An English division had been successfully holding the line between the Ancre and the Somme, and had been ordered to withdraw. The Divisional Commander protested, but had to carry out his orders. The division withdrew during the night of the 26th March, and when every unit was moving back it was discovered that the order to withdraw was a mistake. It was impossible to rectify it, as the troops were moving on in the darkness, and came right back. The enemy followed up the withdrawal, and the 3rd Australian Division was ordered to fill the gap.

We moved from Mondicourt at 12.15 p.m., and arrived at the embussing point, where we got aboard the busses, and arrived at Franvillers at 5 p.m., where we debussed. At Franvillers we received orders to proceed to Heilly at once, and moved off in that direction. After crossing the Albert-Amiens road, the proximity of the enemy was beyond all doubt, as he began to shell the valley through which the Heilly-Franvillers road runs. We opened out and moved by platoons through the dangerous area, though most of the shells burst from 50 to 100 yards beyond the road. We moved through Heilly, and crossed the Ancre to some open ground among the trees near the railway-station, where we bivouacked for the night as reserve battalion of the brigade. Everybody was made comfortable shortly after dark, while officers went forward to reconnoitre the line now held by the 37th and 38th Battalions, who had moved in and occupied the Amiens Defence Line during the day. (See Map 7.)

The defence line between the Somme and the Ancre was now held by the 10th Brigade on the left and the 11th Brigade on the right. The line was an old defence system constructed by the French army for the defence of Amiens. The part held by the 10th Brigade was across the high ground from the junction of the Mericourt l'Abbe-Sailly-le-Sec road with the Bray-Corbie road to a point on the Ancre about 1000 yards east of the village of Mericourt l'Abbe. The boundary between the 10th and 11th Brigades was the Bray-Corbie road. The distance from our bivouac area to the line was about 3000 yards. The enemy was supposed to be a mile east of this line on the afternoon of the 27th March, and between this line and the enemy were supposed to be cavalry patrols in touch with the enemy advance guard. It is believed that these patrols crossed the Somme and moved south as we moved in.

The night of the 27th March was fairly quiet, but it was realised that the following day would be a day of events.

On the morning of the 28th March information was received that a company of the 38th Battalion had pushed forward to a distance of about 800 yards and occupied the wood known as Marett Wood, about 700 yards south of the village of Treux, accounting for about 30 of the enemy who were found in the wood. It was also ascertained that columns of the enemy, estimated at two brigades, were advancing towards Morlancourt from the direction of Bray. At 11.30 a.m. the Acting Commanding Officer (Major L. H. Payne, D.S.O.) was sent for by the Brigadier, and received verbal orders that the 40th Battalion would attack that afternoon at 4 p.m., in conjunction with the 41st Battalion at the same hour. We were to advance through the brigade line with our right flank on the Bray-Corbie road for a distance of about 1700 yards, and at 7 p.m. the 39th Battalion were to come up on our left flank and go forward with us for another 1000 yards, and establish a line 1000 yards west of Morlancourt. It was anticipated that very little resistance would be met with as the ground between us was probably held by the enemy advance guard only. The object of the advance was to seize the high ground west of Morlancourt before the main body of the enemy came up. At that time we had no artillery behind us, as the divisional artillery was still on the way, but there was an artillery brigade north of the Ancre, who were supposed to be able to assist if required.

At 3.40 p.m. the 40th Battalion crossed the railway-line at Heilly Station, and moved up the low ground towards our line by platoons in fours at 50 yards interval. The disposition of the battalion was—B Company (Capt. G. S. Bisdee) on the right and C Company (Lieut. M. H. O. Whitaker) on the left, with A Company (Capt. J. D. W. Chisholm) in support of B Company, and D Company (Lieut. C. H. Cane) in support of C Company. When the crest of the hill behind the Amiens Line was reached, we opened out into sections in file, and a few minutes later we came under well-directed artillery fire from guns that could be seen on the ridge east of Morlancourt. No sign was seen of the 41st Battalion coming forward on our right, and the Adjutant, who was on the right flank, got into touch with the 43rd Battalion on the south side of the Bray-Corbie road, and learned for the first time that the 41st Battalion were not advancing until after dark. Evidently there was a misunderstanding or bad liaison between the staffs of the 10th and 11th Brigades. However, our instructions were clear, and we pushed on, with A Company protecting the right flank if necessary. As each wave crossed the Sailly-le-Sec-Mericourt l'Abbe road each section extended into line, as we came under heavy machine-gun fire, and we continued on with heavy casualties through the 10th Brigade front line. The advance was quite a parade-ground movement, the automatic precision of which was probably due to recent training for platoon competitions, and also possibly to the fact that we were advancing under fire over open grassy country for the first time. There were few old trenches and practically no shell-holes. The ground over which we were attacking would have been a pleasure to plough; as a golf-links or football ground it was ideal; but as a place to advance over under heavy machine-gun fire it was a failure. But still the wonderful fact stood out that the advance was carried out like a parade-ground movement, and in such a way that it was hard to believe that the little huddled heaps of men that remained as we pushed on were anything else than men put out of action by an umpire on a field-day in peace training. Sections went forward in short rushes, and gave covering fire with Lewis guns and rifles as the other sections and platoons advanced. Fire orders could be heard above the rattle of Lewis guns and the enemy machine-guns, and drill-book orders were shouted by platoon commanders which had never before been heard, except on a training ground. Parties of the enemy could be seen running back towards Morlancourt, and in a depression on the left about 100 men were seen, who appeared to have been digging machine-gun positions when our attack surprised them. With cold fury at not being able to get among the enemy, our Lewis gunners dropped down and opened fire at the running Germans, till the order "to fire only at machine-guns" went along the advancing line. The machine-gun fire was hotter than ever as we crossed the Treux-Sailly-le-Sec road, but it could not be kept down, as it was mostly coming from more than 1000 yards in front. Our casualties continued, and by this time included the Acting Commanding Officer (Major L. H. Payne, D.S.O.), who was wounded, but continued on. Lieut. W. E. K. Grubb was also wounded early in the advance by a machine-gun, but refused to go back, and was killed by a shell while leading his platoon with great skill and coolness. Lieut. C. W. Marshall, Lieut. R. A. Swan, Lieut. A. Bertram, and Lieut. H. Chamberlain were also badly wounded, and the latter died shortly afterwards.

Shortly after crossing the Treux-Sailly-le-Sec road we met with a surprise. The enemy were seen advancing in several columns, about 2500 yards in front, as he came over the ridge immediately south of Morlancourt. We continued on, wondering what sort of a mix-up it would be when we met, and the enemy halted for a few minutes. He hesitated, deployed, came on a hundred yards, hesitated again, and then went to ground, presumably to dig in. His machine-guns were pushed out in front, and the enemy fire became heavier than ever. After an advance of 1200 yards beyond the original line held by the 10th Brigade, in face of the heaviest machine-gun fire and scattered artillery shelling, it was impossible to advance any farther, and we dug in on a line about 400 yards west of the Treux-Sailly-Laurette road, to wait for the further advance at 7 p.m. The ground was dead flat between us and the enemy, an ideal field for machine-gun fire, and every inch of cover had to be dug. A solitary chalk bank about 200 yards in rear provided useful shelter for Battalion Headquarters and the reserve platoons. We got down and used entrenching tools as well as possible, while Lewis gunners in the open did what they could to keep down the enemy machine-gun fire. Some machine-guns, which had been doing considerable damage, had been located in a copse at the junction of the Bray-Corbie road with the Ville-sur-Ancre-Sailly-le-Sec road. These machine-guns were silenced for the time by our Lewis guns. Our right flank was about 300 yards west of the copse, and it was obvious that we could not advance beyond it until the machine-guns there were dealt with. As we had no artillery behind, an application was made for the 10th Light Trench Mortar Battery to come up and deal with it; but the trench mortar battery had no ammunition. It is not quite correct to say we had no artillery. The English battery north of the Ancre was "assisting" by firing about 400 yards in rear of our position, and as they were using instantaneous fuse, we did not want to encourage them to further efforts.

At 6 p.m. our ammunition was delivered in a spectacular and gallant manner by the regimental transport. While the machine-gun fire was still heavy, three limbers, driven by No. 1706, Dvr. J. A. Robinson; No. 207, Dvr. C. Hearps; and No. 883, Dvr. C. McIntosh galloped across the open, and delivered their ammunition within 300 yards of our foremost position, and then drove out again with several bullet-holes in their limbers.

At 7 p.m. the 39th Battalion advanced in the dusk. They were subjected to heavy machine-gun fire, but came up to us without many casualties. Shortly afterwards the enemy machine-gun fire suddenly ceased, as he also was apparently consolidating a position for defence. This enabled us to move about freely, and patrols tried to get in touch with the 41st Battalion, whom we expected to come up on our right flank. We failed to get in touch with them, and at 8 p.m. received orders to dig in on our present position and try to dislodge the enemy guns in the copse during the night.

At dusk a cold rain began to fall, and continued intermittently throughout the night. The half-dug trenches churned into mud, in which our men stood and shivered with such poor shelter as a waterproof-sheet afforded.

At 8.30 p.m. the 41st Battalion came up on our right, and proposed to advance; but acting under the instructions of our brigade, we were unable to comply, and eventually the 41st Battalion established an outpost line in continuation of our line, which we had now begun to dig. Arrangements were made with the 41st Battalion to assist us in capturing the copse which had caused so much trouble, and during the night a platoon of that battalion worked out to the right of the copse and opened fire on it, while No. 7 Platoon (Lieut. A. P. Brown) rushed it from the left flank. This was unsuccessful, as the copse was alive with machine-guns, and after making two attempts Lieut. Brown had to withdraw, when his platoon was reduced to a strength of five. The position was too strong to take without an artillery or trench mortar bombardment. The remainder of the night, which was wet and cold, passed without incident, as both sides were busy consolidating their defence in expectation of another attack the following day. The casualties in the battalion during the day amounted to 160, and all the wounded were carried out. After previous experience among mud and shell-holes, the stretcher-bearers found the job comparatively easy to work among green fields. They were also assisted by some of the regimental band, who, under the leadership of No. 55, Pte. R. R. Garrett, who had !"souvenired" a civilian cart and two mules, followed up close behind the infantry. The cart conveyed the wounded to the Regimental Aid Post (Capt. W. I. Clark, M.C.), which was about 800 yards behind our new position, and from the aid post took them to Heilly Station, where they were picked up by motor ambulances.

The result of the day was that we had advanced 1200 yards, and the enemy was at least 1200 yards further from Amiens than he would otherwise have been. It does not seem much, but that distance was of tremendous importance, as that piece of ground overlooked the whole valley of the Somme towards Amiens. Our unexpected attack had also held up the attack which the enemy was making in strength. He sat down and waited for 40 hours, wondering if the whole of the Australian corps were behind it, and every minute of the 40 hours was precious. It enabled us to get forward more machine-guns, to improve our defensive position, and, most important of all, it gave our artillery time to arrive. It is probable that had his attack developed at 5 p.m. on the evening of the 28th March, he would have pushed us back, as ours was a thinly-held line without artillery or trench mortars, and no support or reserve troops behind us; and if he had pushed us back there was practically nothing to stop him reaching his great objective, Amiens. Before daylight the following day two machine-guns came up and established posts on our front, and two were established on the front of the 39th Battalion, while eight were put in behind us, to provide an S.O.S. barrage when required. These machine-guns played an important part when the time came.

After daylight very little movement was possible, as no communication-trenches had been dug, and the enemy snipers and machine-guns were very active. The enemy artillery also shelled our position intermittently during the day, as well as all roads behind us. The Acting Commanding Officer (Major L. H. Payne, D.S.O.), who had been wounded the previous day, was forced to leave, and Major L. F. Giblin, M.C., took command, with Major J. T. McColl, M.C., as second in command. During the morning some of our artillery moved in, and their first registration rounds gave a most comforting feeling to the troops holding the line. They had some very fine targets. Enemy transports and bodies of troops were seen on the roads near Morlancourt, and the artillery put up some fine shooting. In the afternoon the artillery put down a registration shoot on the copse that had given so much trouble, and two platoons of the 37th Battalion and one platoon of the 41st Battalion were detailed to capture the copse that evening. At 9 p.m., after a short artillery bombardment, these platoons rushed the copse, but found that the enemy had departed, leaving several machine-gun positions and piles of empty cartridge-shells. Our right flank was then pushed forward about 600 yards, and new posts were established on the advanced line. Apparently the machine-gun crews in the copse had cleared out as soon as our bombardment began, and omitted to tell their friends that the place was getting too hot for them; consequently, several unsuspecting Germans walked into our lines that night on their way to the copse.

The morning of the 30th March was crowded with happenings that pointed to one thing—an attack. Immediately after daylight several enemy observation balloons went up in front of us, and his artillery began to shell our positions. About 9 a.m. the enemy attacked the 9th Brigade, south of the Somme. Our observers climbed up trees on the Bray-Corbie road and had a good view of the operation; but our turn was soon to come. Two British aeroplanes with enemy crews came over at about 10 a.m. and bombed and machine-gunned our posts before we realised that they were not friends. There were dozens of enemy aeroplanes flying low, and at 11.30 a.m. one was brought down by our anti-aircraft Lewis gun at Battalion Headquarters, and fell behind us into the village of Ribemont. The crew who brought it down were killed a few minutes later by a shell. At about 11.45 a.m. about 10 horsemen appeared on the hill south of Morlancourt, on the Bray-Corbie road. At the time they looked like cavalry, but they were probably the mounted officers of the brigade about to attack us. At 11.45 a.m. the enemy bombardment, which had been intermittent all the morning, increased into a barrage of great intensity, particularly on our support line and also the chalk bank about 300 yards behind our advanced posts, where Battalion Headquarters and the reserve company were situated. His machine-gun barrage was also very heavy, and swept our positions, so that everybody had to take cover. The observers (under Capt. Alan Cruickshank) who were above ground, reporting what was going on, were not to be beaten by machine-gun bullets, and climbed up trees, from where they shouted valuable information as to what the enemy was doing. During the bombardment the enemy could be seen coming across the Bray-Corbie road in K 21a in three columns, and advancing towards Morlancourt. When the head of his column was about midway between Morlancourt and the Bray-Corbie road, he changed direction towards us, opened out into waves, and came down the hill astride the Bray-Corbie road, moving diagonally across our front on to the 11th Brigade sector south of the road. He was then about 1700 yards away, and a nice range for our machine-guns, which opened as he advanced in waves. Every Lewis gun opened also; and although the range would have been too far in an ordinary case for effective shooting, here the target was too big to miss. At the same time that the machine-guns opened the artillery barrage also came down, shells bursting in the advancing waves, and the casualties among the enemy were enormous. The hill down which the enemy were advancing had hardly any cover, and every wave was practically wiped out. The enemy dead and wounded were lying in hundreds on the slope of the hill, and the rear waves broke and ran back to safety. By noon the attack had definitely failed. During the afternoon his stretcher-bearers came out under the Red Cross flag and collected the wounded on the slopes of the hill, and no further attack was made on our front, although on another occasion he seemed to be making an attempt on our right, which was easily broken by the 11th Brigade.

During the afternoon heavy rain fell, which made our posts and trenches very wet and muddy. Orders were received that we would be relieved that night by a battalion from the 11th Brigade, and here again there seemed to be lack of cohesion between the Brigade Staffs, for which battalions have to suffer. We got into touch with the battalion supposed to be relieving us, and they knew nothing about it; in fact, they were relieving somebody else. After referring the matter to our brigade and the 11th Brigade, we were at last relieved by a company of a battalion of the 11th Brigade at 4 a.m. in the morning of the 31st March, and we moved into Ribemont, about 2500 yards behind our front line, and became reserve battalion. All civilians had left this village, and the last troops to leave it had barricaded the streets with vehicles and farm implements. No doubt their action in doing so was in accordance with Field Service Regulations, but it looked as if they had made up their minds that the enemy would get through. At any rate, we felt better when we had run the carts and machines into the nearest yard and opened up the streets for traffic. A few shells were falling in the village, so we billeted ourselves in houses containing cellars, so that we could shelter in the event of a bombardment. In the event of a gas bombardment, open fields near the village were selected for assembly points.

Our casualties during the three days (28th, 29th, and 30th March) were:—

	Officers.	Other Ranks.
Killed	2	44
Wounded	10	169
Prisoners	—	1
	12	214

Ribemont, like Heilly and other villages of the neighbourhood, was in a deplorable state. The inhabitants had left at short notice, leaving everything standing. Shell-fire had not yet done much harm, but each house had been ransacked, cupboards rifled, drawers emptied, mattresses split open in the search for loot, and all the household treasures tumbled in a dirty heap on the floor with empty bottles and broken glass and china. The wantonness of the destruction was sickening; and this was the work, not of the " Unspeakable Hun," but of the drunken stragglers of the 5th Army. Some of these were still in Ribemont when we entered it, and, reinforced by a few Australians, were still carrying on a brisk offensive on the wine cellars.

During the morning we established a guard-room, threw all drunken soldiers into it, and notified their units to collect them, except in cases of British soldiers whose units were Heaven-knows-where. We placed guards over the cellars containing wine, and put guards over all entrances to the village, to prevent unauthorised persons entering. All wine was, later on, handed over to the French Mission, as well as the contents of a woollen-mill and a flour-mill. All livestock, with the exception of poultry, was also collected and handed over.

Chapter XIX.

More Enemy Attacks on the Divisional Front — Probability of a Further Enemy Offensive — "B" Echelon Established — Patrol Encounters — Our Successful Raid on an Enemy Post on the Ancre — An Unsuccessful Attempt to Capture Ville-Sur-Ancre — Back to Reserve at Frechencourt — To Blangy-Tronville — The Divisional Platoon Competition.

THE 1st April was spent in resting and reorganising. The 10th Brigade had now moved about 800 yards further north, to bring the brigade astride the Ancre; while the 11th Brigade moved 800 yards further to the left, taking over 800 yards of front from the 10th Brigade. The 4th Australian Division was now holding the line north of the Ancre on our left, after holding up the enemy's attacks at Dernancourt and Albert by hard fighting. The brigade sector was held by two battalions in front, one in support in the old Amiens Defence Line, which was our front line on the morning of the 28th March, and the other battalion in reserve at Ribemont.

On the 2nd April the approaches to the front line from Ribemont were reconnoitred, and after dark a strong working party went out to improve the brigade support line by digging a number of posts east of Mericourt. That day the Commanding Officer returned from England, and took over command of the battalion again.

In the evening of the 3rd April we took over the right half of the brigade front line, with our left flank at the northern corner of Marett Wood. We held the sector with three companies in the front posts and one company in support. D Company (Lieut. C. H. Cane) were on the right; A Company (Lieut. H. L. Foster, M.C.) in the centre; and C Company (Capt. W. C. G. Ruddock) on the left, with B Company (Capt. G. S. Bisdee) in support in a hollow about 400 yards behind the front posts. It was at once decided to hold the position in greater depth, and posts were dug and garrisoned in rear of the front posts. This also relieved the congestion in the forward posts. As no movement overland was possible during the day, owing to the absence of a communication trench, the support company was employed every night in carrying forward ammunition, rations, and food during the hours of darkness. It was impossible to do any cooking near the line, so the company cooks remained at the Quartermaster's store at Heilly, where they cooked the meals, which were carried forward by the regimental transport, and taken into the line by the support company. The enemy shelled all roads and approaches every night, and the regimental transport did very fine work in getting their limbers up to the rear of Marett Wood. Battalion Headquarters and the Regimental Aid Post consisted of holes dug into a chalk bank in rear of Marett Wood, which were improved daily under the supervision of Major J. T. McColl, M.C., as "engineer-in-chief," and the Medical Officer (Capt. W. I. Clark, M.C.) as "architect." The Battalion Headquarters "hole" was officially known as the "Chateau McColl."

The 4th of April was an anxious day, while the 9th Brigade were holding off a determined attack south of the Somme. The 9th Brigade fought all day against tremendous odds, and with both flanks in the air at times. Several times the situation was very critical, and had the enemy succeeded the 10th and 11th Brigades would have been forced to fall back. On the following day the enemy attacked on the front of the 39th Battalion on our left and the 4th Division north of the Ancre. It was difficult to see what was going on, as a heavy mist hung in the Ancre Valley, but the information that reached us was that the enemy had attacked the 39th Battalion at Treux and had been driven back. All day we were expecting an attack on our battalion front. At 7 a.m. the enemy bombarded our sector heavily, and paid a great deal of attention to Marett Wood. The shelling of Marett Wood lasted all day, with short intervals, and was at times very intense, causing 23 casualties, including Lieut. A. C. Thurstans (killed) and Capt. W. C. G. Ruddock (wounded). There was a peculiar feature about the bombardment of Marett Wood, in the fact that the enemy shrapnel was bursting beautifully just above the tops of the trees. The enemy seldom used shrapnel, and when he did he either burst it too high or too low; but on this occasion it was wonderfully good, and gave us the impression that he was using our ammunition captured during the retreat.

The mist lasted all the morning, and it was impossible to see how the Fourth Division were faring. Our observers several times crawled forward for information, and about 10 a.m. one of them reported that about 60 of the enemy were behind a big haystack, about 800 yards east of Treux, in front of the 39th Battalion. In the words of the observer, it looked like a "two-up" school or a massing for an attack, and artillery were communicated with. Their first shot hit the top of the haystack, and the enemy scattered in all directions, which gave our waiting machine-guns a target, which they made good use of. The attack on our left failed.

The following day (April 6) was wet, but fairly quiet, and in the evening we were relieved by the 37th Battalion, and moved back to the support line east of Mericourt l'Abbé, the dispositions being three companies in the support line and one company in the village of Mericourt l'Abbé. This spell of three days in the line, like the preceding one, was very exhausting. Officers and men lived for the three days almost without sleep and exposed to the persistent rain. The weather was bitterly cold. The trenches consisted of isolated narrow slits in the wet soil, with deep mud or water under foot. No movement was possible in the daytime; men dozed standing in the mud, and woke as shells burst near them. Night was the busy time. Food, water, ammunition, wire, &c., were brought in; officers went their rounds and counted their casualties; all available men were hard at work improving and extending their trenches, or more often digging new ones to conform to some improvement in the system of defence. After the relief on 6th April the men reached Mericourt fairly dropping with fatigue. While in the support line the time was spent in improving the support position and putting belts of wire out in front of it. New posts were dug to give local command of ground, and the position was prepared to meet the enemy in case he broke through the front line. Three tanks, which had managed to get back during the retreat, were attached to the brigade, and camouflaged themselves in a chalk-pit in rear of the support position, with a view to assisting in a counter-attack on Marett Wood in the event of the enemy capturing it.

On the 9th April, about 5 a.m., the enemy began to shell Mericourt and Ribemont with gas and high explosive at the rate of from three to nine shells per minute. This lasted till 6.30 a.m., and then recurred at intervals throughout the day, causing four killed and 10 wounded in D Company in Mericourt. One shell came through the roof of the regimental canteen, but failed to explode. That evening the 40th Battalion relieved the 38th Battalion in the left battalion sector of the brigade, about 500 yards east of the villages of Treux and Buire. The disposition of companies was A Company (Lieut. H. L. Foster) on the right, D Company (Lieut. C. H. Cane) in the centre, B Company (Capt. G. S. Bisdee) on the left, and C Company (Lieut. A. R. Mills) in support in Buire.

The position of the left and centre companies was a matter for great competition, as the River Ancre flowed through the sector, and fish were very numerous. There were many ways of catching them, and the most legitimate methods were with improvised lines of telephone cable and bent wire. Another method was to wait in the shallows with a stick, and hit them as they passed, but the true sportsman "tickled" them under the banks of the river in the approved Scotch fashion. All methods were productive, and it seemed a cheerful occupation with the enemy only a few hundred yards away; but cheerfulness was in the air, as spring had now come with a rush.

While we were in this sector we were again covered by our old friends of the 17th Battery, who had previously been behind us in the Messines attack and at Warneton. The 17th Battery was a Tasmanian unit, with whom we were particularly friendly, and they often went out of their way to do us a good turn; which proves that Scotchmen are not the only clannish people in the world.

At this time all intelligence reports pointed to the possibility of another enemy attack on our front. This affected artillery operations considerably, and heavy shoots were carried out every morning on possible enemy assembly positions and communications. These shoots were generally put down at intervals from midnight to daylight, and were very heavy, causing a good deal of retaliation. Our patrol work was also affected, and the policy was adopted of keeping as close to the enemy posts as possible during the night, in order to detect any assembly or preparations for attack. The enemy bombing-planes were very active, particularly on villages immediately behind the front line.

At this time, although the onrush of the German armies had been stopped for the time, the situation on the Western Front was still critical. It is described by the Commander-in-Chief in his despatch as follows:—

"The immense weight of the enemy's onslaughts in March and early in April, and the unprecedented masses of men and material employed by him, had practically called for the whole strength of our armies to withstand them, and had left our forces greatly weakened. The American army, though rapidly increasing in numbers and efficiency, was not yet ready to take the field in sufficient strength to affect the situation. In short, the German attacks, though they had failed to break the Allied Line, had stretched the resources of the Allies to the uttermost. Under these circumstances the possibility of the enemy's offensive could not but be viewed with grave anxiety."

Even these words were putting the situation mildly, when the total number of German divisions in reserve available for an offensive was 75, while the British and Overseas divisions on the whole front had been reduced in number to 45, and most of these were below establishment. Three-fourths of them had been heavily engaged in one or other of the enemy offensives, if not in both, and all were urgently in need of a rest. The French had also been compelled to employ a substantial proportion of their reserves in the fighting south of the Somme and north of the Lys.

With regard to the attack believed to be coming on our front, the Commander-in-Chief says:—

"The Allied High Command repeatedly expressed the opinion that the enemy would renew his attack on a large scale on the front Arras-Amiens-Montdidier. The strategic results to be obtained by the capture of Amiens, the separation of the French and British armies, and an advance towards the sea along the valley of the Somme were great, and might well prove decisive. The enemy's opening offensive had already brought him within a measurable distance of success, and had carried his armies through practically the whole of our organised lines of defence. Since the conclusion of his attacks on our front in the first week of April, the enemy had time to re-establish communications through this devastated area and make his preparations for a fresh advance. This period of delay had also afforded us some opportunity, of which full use was being made, to lay out new trench lines and defences."

Early in April the principle of keeping a percentage of each battalion out of a battle was extended to trench warfare, and about one-fifth of the officers and other ranks of each battalion formed what was known as "B" echelon. This had the advantage of providing each brigade with an extra reserve battalion, and gave everybody a rest from the trying summer fighting of 1918. Every officer and man had his turn to go to

"B" echelon, and commanding officers and seconds-in-command of battalions took their turns in commanding it. Definite days were allotted for "B" echelon reliefs, each relief taking place after a tour of duty in the line. It was formed into a reserve battalion with battalion organisation, engaged in training and having its own signalling, Lewis gun, and bombing schools. It even had its own newspaper at times, and organised its own sports and swimming races. This practice was continued to some extent through the rest of the campaign, but later during our advance units were so reduced in strength that only very small numbers could be spared at one time. It proved particularly useful in training men for the largely increased number of Lewis guns (36) now allotted to a battalion, and for the new and important branch of anti-aircraft defence with Lewis guns.

On the evening of the 12th April the 38th Battalion relieved the 40th Battalion, who moved into Ribemont as reserve battalion of the brigade. While in reserve we were employed on improving the defensive position east of Ribemont, by digging trenches, making strong points, and putting up belts of wire. On the 16th April we relieved the 38th Battalion in the front line east of Treux and Buire, with D Company on the right, B Company in the centre, A Company on the left, and C Company in support in cellars in Buire. Battalion Headquarters was established in an old building among the trees about 400 yards west of Buire.

On the 18th April we were ordered to obtain identification of the unit in front, and several officers' patrols went out to locate an enemy post with a view to raiding it. One of these patrols, consisting of one officer (Lieut. S. G. Stebbins) and eight other ranks, pushed out about 1000 yards from our line, and located a post on the right of Ville-sur-Ancre (K 1 a 5 1). Their job was to locate the post, and raid it the following night, but, realising that they would have to go out and do the work the next night, the patrol decided to obtain the identification then and there. Just as they were about to rush the post they saw an enemy patrol moving past, which took up a position in shell-holes about 30 yards away, between our patrol and our line. Lieut. Stebbins then decided to attack the patrol instead, and our party rushed them from the rear. Lieut. Stebbins and No. 1964, Sgt. A. H. Richards, who were in front, were called upon in English to "Hands up." The officer replied by shooting one of the enemy, and Sergt. Richards shot another, while No. 7438, Pte. J. D. Brilliant, accounted for two with his bayonet. Three of the enemy were killed and two badly wounded, and one of the enemy dead was carried back to our line for identification, which proved the unit in front to be the 231st R.I.R.

At 2 a.m. on the morning of the 22nd April we were relieved by the 38th Battalion, and moved into reserve at Ribemont, where we carried on improving the defences east of that village. On the 24th and 25th April the enemy shelled Ribemont very consistently, putting over 1000 rounds of high explosive and gas in and around the village. On the night of the 26th April we relieved the 38th Battalion, who had previously taken over part of the sector of the 2nd Australian Division on our left. Our battalion sector now extended from Buire to a point about 1200 yards due west of Dernancourt. The disposition of companies was C Company on the right, B company in the centre, A Company on the left, and D Company in support in Buire.

Information was again required concerning the enemy in front of us, and a raiding party was detailed to attack an enemy post which had been located in a ruined building on the right bank of the Ancre, about 500 yards north of Ville-sur-Ancre (E 25 b 0 4). The raiding party consisted of 2 officers and 34 other ranks. It was divided into two sections, one under Lieut. T. G. Cranswick, D.C.M., and the other under Lieut. A. P. Brown, M.C. Each section consisted of two Lewis gunners with a gun, 10 rifle bombers, and 5 bayonet men. Both parties moved from our line at 9 p.m., and worked along the left bank of the Ancre, Lieut. Cranswick and his party taking up a position about 40 yards on the right of the post, while Lieut. Brown and his party took up a similar positon on the left of it. At a signal from Lieut. Cranswick, 20 rifle grenades were fired on to the post, and at the same time the Lewis guns each fired a magazine into it. This was followed by a rush on the post. On arriving there our men found that the enemy, numbering about 30, had taken refuge in eight small dugouts in the trench in rear of the building. The dugouts were conveniently lit up by candles. Bombs were thrown into the dugouts, killing or wounding most of the occupants, while a few got out and ran, but were pursued, and most of them disposed of. An enemy machine-gun opened on our party from the opposite side of the river, but it was silenced by our two Lewis guns. Practically everybody in the post was accounted for, and one man was taken back as a prisoner. The whole of the raiding party got back without a casualty. The prisoner was asked by our intelligence linguist why he did not run. He replied with great dignity that he was on duty, and therefore could not leave his post. As a matter of fact, he was discovered trying to do the "ostrich" act, and was half-way into an empty sack when he was pulled out. The raid was excellently carried out, and the two officers in charge of the party and No. 915, L/Cpl. R. J. Ratcliffe, and No. 92, Pte. G. Parsissons, were congratulated by the Divisional Commander in Divisional Orders for their work.

The following night our patrols again visited the post, but the enemy saw the patrol coming and made off. The next night a patrol went out again, and cautiously approached the post. They saw lights in the dugouts, but the enemy had the "drop" on us this time. A shower of rifle grenades burst on the post and machine-guns opened, and our patrol got back with two casualties.

Our scouts were now very active, fighting patrols were out all night and every night. Enemy patrols were often seen, but always made off without a fight; but on the night of the 30th April one of our patrols captured a sergeant and a private of the 247th R.I.R., who were moving from one enemy post to another. The sergeant was a particularly fine type of man, from whom no information could be obtained. Very little information could be obtained from any prisoners captured on the divisional front at that time. They showed good training and morale, and generally said that they had just come from a school or hospital, and knew nothing of their dispositions or intentions.

During this tour in the line a rather humorous incident happened to our artillery friends. An enemy post had been located near Ville-sur-Ancre, about 600 yards in front of our line, and the artillery were invited to have a shot at it with a 4·5 howitzer. The artillery liaison officer took his telephone to the front line one quiet afternoon to do the shoot. The first shot was wonderfully accurate, and fell on the edge of the post. One German was seen in the air, and about 10 others got out of the post and ran. The next shot arrived, and fell just in front of the enemy rush to cover. They turned and ran to a tree, behind which they scuffled with one another, trying to get cover. The tree was rather a failure for 10 men to get behind, and the artillery officer grabbed his telephone to direct the next shot at the tree, but at the critical moment he was cut off by the signallers to let somebody else use the line. He rushed back to the parapet, on to which he jumped, and called upon someone or any one to give him what he termed a "hand-gun." No "hand-gun" being available at the moment, he pulled out his revolver and opened fire with it on the enemy behind the tree at 450 yards range. At that moment another shell fell near the tree, and the collective "Fritz" made for the river, into which they jumped and swam across to the shelter of some reeds on the opposite bank. The artillery officer was very annoyed. There were not many sounds in the front line that afternoon, but one striking sound was an indignant artilleryman pouring out torrents of profane abuse on the signal service in general and the signallers who had cut him off in particular. But after all the joke was against us, for our Lewis gunners should have been ready for the occurrence, although most of us were much more pleased at seeing the enemy getting a ducking than we would have been if we had shot them.

During the early morning of the 1st May we were relieved by the 38th Battalion, and went into reserve at Ribemont, where four days were spent in improving the support position and digging a communication-trench east of Buire. On the night of the 5th May we relieved the 38th Battalion again in the same sector. The work of making shelters and dugouts in the trenches was begun, as until that time practically no dugouts had been constructed, defensive positions being of first importance. One of our chief troubles was a herd of dead cows near Buire. They had been killed by enemy shelling, and, with the warmer weather began to make their presence felt.

On the 8th May the enemy shelled our sector very consistently with high explosive shells and trench mortars. That afternoon orders were received from brigade that a strong reconnaissance would be made of the village of Ville-sur-Ancre by parties of the 39th and 40th Battalions. If not held in strength it was to be mopped up and a new line formed clear of the village to the east. It had been reported that the enemy were shelling Ville-sur-Ancre, and it seemed probable that he had evacuated it, except perhaps for a post or two. The battalion thought otherwise, but orders are orders.

A party of 30 other ranks under Lieut. S. S. McMillan was detailed from the 40th Battalion for the work, and a similar party of the 39th Battalion were to operate on our right. Both parties were to push through the village and establish a line east of it. At 7.30 p.m. the 40th Battalion party assembled in Buire; rifle grenades, bombs, &c., were issued, and the details of the operation hurriedly explained to them. They left our front line at 9 p.m., and by 9.30 p.m. had crossed the bridge across the Ancre on the Buire-Ville-sur-Ancre-road,

and were in position. The party was split into two sections,
Lieut. McMillan taking one half on the right of the road,
and No. 999, Sgt. F. Fletcher, took the other on the left of
the road. It was intended that they should advance well clear
of the road, but owing to the marshy nature of the ground
they had to stick to the sides of the road and move forward
from tree to tree. They had gone forward about 200 yards
beyond the bridge, and were 250 yards from the church in the
village, when the leading men saw one of the enemy a few
yards in front. He crossed the road, but nobody fired, as they
wanted to see where his post was, and they saw him enter a
post about 60 yards away on the right of the road. Shortly
afterward they heard the enemy getting their gun ready on
this post, and the rifle grenadiers were ordered to get ready
to fire their grenades. A salvo of grenades was fired at this
post, and both parties crawled forward to attack it from both
flanks. They were within 30 yards of it when a Verey light
was fired and fell among the right party, and machine-guns
opened on them from both flanks. Lieut. McMillan moved his
party to the road, down which machine-gun fire was sweeping
from the village. The left party was on the other side of the
road, and he called to them to move forward straight to the
village, trusting that the 39th Battalion would get through
and assist him. Both parties crawled forward, still under
heavy machine-gun fire, and when about 150 yards from the
village the telephonist with them received a message that the
39th Battalion were held up and had withdrawn. This
message had come through, thanks to the efforts of the Battalion Signalling Officer (Lieut. B. Jackson, M.C.), who was
sitting in our front line in telephone communication with the
40th Battalion Headquarters, the 39th Battalion attacking
party, and our own attacking party. If this had not been
done our party would have undoubtedly been sacrificed. By
this time the enemy realised that an attack was being made,
and his machine-guns in the village and behind it opened, firing
down the road towards our lines. The withdrawal then began,
and it was carried out with great skill and coolness. Anybody
losing his head and getting up to run would have committed a
pleasant form of suicide, as the stream of bullets was passing
a few inches above the heads of our men lying flat in the
swamp on both sides of the road. Eventually our party
reached the bridge across the Ancre, with one dead man and
four wounded. The job of getting across the bridge was difficult, as the enemy fire was concentrated on it, and the party
had to crawl across one by one. The job of getting the dead

and wounded across looked an impossibility, but it was accomplished with much resource. It took 25 minutes for the whole party to cross the bridge, and as soon as they got clear the enemy artillery came down on it, killing the two men holding the post behind it. The whole party had a very trying time, and came out of a critical situation with comparatively few losses. Lieut. McMillan, a Scotchman by birth and an Australian by adoption, had no less than three bullet-holes in his breeches, but was still unwounded. After reporting the whole of the circumstances to his Commanding Officer, he looked at his perforated garment, and remarked: "It's a guid thing I didna hae ma best breeks on."

As was afterwards demonstrated, the taking of Ville-sur-Ancre was a brigade and not a platoon job. Behind the village was a deep cutting, alive with machine-guns, and the village itself was well fortified. A few days later it was attacked and captured by the 6th Australian Infantry Brigade, who took several hundred prisoners there and numerous machine-guns after a hard fight; but how Lieut. McMillan and his 30 men attacked the village of Ville-sur-Ancre, assisted by the 2nd Australian Division, was for a long time one of the battalion jokes.

On the 9th May, soon after dark, the battalion was relieved by the 24th Battalion, and moved out to the sugar refinery north of Ribemont, where we rested and had a meal, and then marched back 9 miles to Frechencourt into the Divisional Rest Area. The weather at this time was very fine, and for the first two days the time was spent in bathing in the lagoons near the Hallue River, cleaning up uniforms and equipment, and re-equipping. An attack on our front was still expected, and around Frechencourt were defences and gun-positions, and the area was full of reserve troops, including Strathcona's Horse. On the 13th May training was commenced, which included a good deal of recreational training, particularly swimming and football. Football was enjoyed keenly, because it made a swim more pleasant, and a few days of the combined exercise soon had us all in good health and spirits.

While at Frechencourt the Second-in-Command (Major L. H. Payne, D.S.O.), who had been wounded on the 28th March, returned from hospital.

On the 22nd May the battalion and transport moved by road to Blangy-Tronville, on the south side of the Somme, becoming reserve battalion of the reserve brigade, with one company billeted in Blangy-Tronville, two companies in dugouts in the steep bank of the Somme Valley about 500 yards east of the village, and one company in the Aubigny Line in l'Abbé Wood.

The village of Blangy-Tronville was practically untouched by shell-fire, as it was right in a hollow and screened from observation, but the civilians had all deserted it. The steep bank, east of the village, in which two companies lived, was like an ant-hill. The engineers and pioneers had terraced the bank, and on each terrace had constructed huts, in which hundreds of men lived. The pioneers had also erected spring-boards and showers on the river bank, and hundreds of men swam there daily. On a fine day Blangy-Tronville was a remarkable sight. In the river were dozens of laughing Australians, on the bank were hundreds of naked ones lying on the grass and enjoying the sun till they felt like plunging into the cool water again, and in the back-ground were the partly-dressed ones sitting about, reading, smoking, or yarning, while the battalion dogs lazily played and the regimental cow (supernumerary to establishment), tethered to a tree, grazed placidly on the lawn.

Meanwhile D Company, in l'Abbé Wood, were having a less cheerful experience. They found a virgin wood, and had just finished digging themselves in with some satisfaction when the enemy adopted the plan of keeping the wood drenched with gas—mustard and phosgene. In a heavy bombardment on the 25th May the casualties in the wood numbered some hundreds, chiefly of the 11th Brigade, and D Company had 23. Moreover, in the wood the mustard gas stayed, tainting for days afterwards the neighbourhood of a fallen shell. The nightingales were undismayed, and sang lustily through the bombardment itself; but every man in the company lost his voice, and shortly afterwards they were relieved by C Company.

On the 23rd May all officers reconnoitred the 9th Brigade sector immediately north of Villers-Bretonneux, and on the following day visited the 11th Brigade sector south of Villers-Bretonneux. The sector held by the 11th Brigade was the extreme right of the British line, joining up with the French army. Round l'Abbé Wood were a number of French 75 batteries, and the French gunners were very keen to show us their wonderful field-gun, which corresponds with our 18-pounder. We were equally keen on having a look at them, and were sometimes allowed to fire a few rounds. In return for these good services the Australians taught the French the way to play the great Australian game of "two up." The French gunners were very enthusiastic about it, and were of the opinion that under war conditions it beat their roulette to a frazzle.

On the 25th May working parties were commenced, chiefly engaged in burying cable along the north edge of l'Abbé Wood to forward headquarters near Villers-Bretonneux—a sure sign of large operations in view. These cable-burying parties were usually from 600 to 800 strong, and worked entirely at night. Each man had his task, 4 feet 6 inches long and 7 feet deep, sometimes in hard chalk, sometimes in clay, and there were 6 or 7 miles to march to and fro. The enemy played his artillery at intervals along the edge of the wood. Under these circumstances no time was lost, and in the dim light you saw a man sink out of sight like a porcupine in sandy soil. There was no doubt the "Diggers" deserved their name.

At that time the battalion lost the services of Major J. T. McColl, M.C., who now became a member of the Divisional Staff, and was later promoted to the rank of Lieut.-Colonel, and became G.S.O.1 of the 5th Australian Division. At the end of May there were many staff changes. Lieut.-General Birdwood went to command the 5th Army, and our Divisional Commander, Major-General Monash, took command of the Australian Corps, while Major-General J. Gellibrand took over the 3rd Australian Division. At this time we also lost the Regimental Medical Officer (Capt. W. I. Clark, M.C.), who had been with the battalion since its formation. He was now taken away for a rest from the line, where he had many trying experiences, and was sent to the 10th Field Ambulance. His place was taken by Capt. J. S. Reed, who, in addition to his medical duties, filled the role of conductor of the headquarters jazz band, which produced much noise and a little music of a peculiar haunting quality.

Owing to the heavy casualties in all battalions of the division during the months of March and April, the platoon competition to decide the best platoon in the brigade was carried out again. It had previously been held at Lumbres on the 21st March, but the final competition for the divisional championship had been postponed owing to the enemy offensive. The brigade competition at the end of May resulted very much the same as before, as follows:—

    1st—No. 7 Platoon, 40th Battalion (Lieut. E. Boyes, M.C.).
    2nd—No. 10 Platoon, 40th Battalion (Lieut. M. H. O. Whitaker, M.C.).
    3rd—No. 4 Platoon, 40th Battalion (Sgt. Fletcher).
    4th—A platoon of the 39th Battalion.

The competition was carried out about 1200 yards north of Daours. On the 31st May the last stage was carried out to decide the best platoon in the division. Only two platoons competed—No. 7 Platoon of the 40th Battalion, representing the 10th Brigade; and a platoon of the 41st Battalion, under Lieut. J. J. Moriarty, M.M., representing the 11th Brigade. The 9th Brigade did not compete, as their casualties had been so heavy that they would have had to carry out eliminating contests. The two competing platoons were the same two that attacked the copse on the Bray-Corbie road on the night of the 28th March. The result of the competition was a win for the 40th Battalion, the following being the scores:—

	Bayonet Work.				Musketry and Lewis Gun Work.			
	Discs Hit.	Points for Discs.	Deductions for Style.	Net. B.E.	Hits on Target.	Deductions.	Musketry. Net.	GRAND TOTAL.
40th ...	60	120	14	106	218	4	214	320
41st ...	53	106	18	88	186	6	180	268

The following are the names of the members of the winning platoon:—

Lieut. E. Boyes, M.C.

438	Sgt.	Koppleman, W.	3500	Sgt. Traynor, M. J.
695	T/Cpl.	Shalless, C. W.	1034	Cpl. Thompson, C. T.
97	Pte.	Parsissons, J.	7475	Pte. Belbin, L. J.
2728	,,	Binns, L. J.	7808	,, Thompson, H. L.
1902	,,	McCoy, J.	1662	,, Newman, H.
367	,,	Downs, H. A.	432	,, Imlach, J.
7550	,,	Spinks, T.	3603	,, Williams, H. A.
1941	,,	Sutcliffe, W. H.	3529	,, Fenton, C. H.
1710	,,	Smith, J. H.	3554	,, Pregnall, J.
7478	,,	Dent, C. E.	7793	,, Ransley, V. J.
7521	,,	Pilkington, J. T.	2782	,, Barker, J.
7565	,,	Whittle, E. A.	7496	,, Goldsworthy, C. T.
473	,,	Parry, R. O.	7508	,, Johnson, A. H.
2604	,,	Lambert, H.	101	,, Walker, A. E.

Chapter XX.

L'Abbé Wood — Messenger Dogs Tried at Villers-Bretonneux — The Trenches at Villers-Bretonneux — Our Raid on an Enemy Post — Back to Reserve at Querrieu — Sports and Races — Into the Trenches at Hamel.

HE 1st and 2nd June were spent in constructing dugouts round Divisional Headquarters at Glisy, and burying cable from l'Abbé Wood to Villers-Bretonneux. On the 4th June we relieved the 44th Battalion as reserve battalion, west of Villers-Bretonneux the 10th Brigade having taken over the front from the 11th Brigade. The disposition of companies was as follows:—

A Company (Capt. J. D. W. Chisholm) in Cachy Trench, about 1000 yards west of Villers-Bretonneux, and south of the main-road. Cachy Trench was the defensive position, and the company lived in the railway embankment.

C Company (Capt. W. K. Finlay), in trenches north of the railway line, about 400 yards west of Villers-Bretonneux.

D Company (Major L. F. Giblin, D.S.O., M.C.), in trenches near the railway line, about 2200 yards west of Villers-Bretonneux.

B Company (Capt. G. L. McIntyre), in four "keeps" in Villers-Bretonneux, where they were relieved by D Company on the 8th. The "keeps" at Villers-Bretonneux were strong-points at four different cross streets, one in the centre of the town and the other three on the outskirts. They consisted of fortified cellars, with trenches and wire round them, and each contained three Lewis guns, with a good field of fire up the principal streets. They also controlled the "button" of road-mines laid in the streets of the town.

At this time an enemy attack was expected, and the enemy shelled the town very heavily every night. Instructions to the troops occupying the "keeps" were that when the enemy stopped shelling they were to come out of their cellars and man the "keeps" ready for an attack. Villers-Bretonneux was of considerable strategical importance, as it was on high ground on the same plateau as l'Abbé Wood, the possession of which would have given the enemy our main defence of Amiens south of the Somme. In 1871, during the Franco-Prussian War, it was the capture of Villers-Bretonneux by the German troops under Manteuffel that gave them the city of Amiens, and if the enemy had got possession of Villers-Bretonneux and l'Abbé Wood in June, 1918, history would have repeated itself.

All available *personnel* were engaged in working on the support positions during the day and in the front system during the night. Except for shelling Villers-Bretonneux and the wood the enemy artillery fire was not very heavy until the morning of the 9th June, when the whole area was bombarded in conjunction with an attack on the French at Mondidier.

At Villers-Bretonneux we first used dogs as messengers. They were brought up to Company and Battalion Headquarters by signallers, and were sent back to Brigade with messages. But they recognised Brigade Headquarters as their home, and nothing would induce them to go to Battalion Headquarters with a message. On the whole they were a failure, though there were extreme cases where they could have got through a barrage where a runner could not, and might have been useful. Their failure at Villers-Bretonneux was due to the fact that their personal friendliness with other dogs could not be subdued, and there were a lot of dogs about the town left by civilians, and the battalion had several dogs belonging to companies and headquarters details. The dog is a warm-hearted chap, who wears his heart on his paw, and whose tail moves with violent emotion whenever he sees another dog. He will play with you, mourn for you, or die for you, but you cannot prevent him carrying out his social obligations to all other dogs. Consequently, if a messenger dog met another dog on the way, he would stop for a game, or an interchange of views on bully-beef and army biscuits, or if the other dog was a nasty sort of chap he would stop and fight him, and deliver his message after the demands of honour and etiquette had been satisfied. Such demands often took a long time to satisfy.

On the night of 11th June the 40th Battalion relieved the 38th Battalion in the front line east of Villers-Bretonneux. The disposition of companies was—A Company (Capt. H. L. Foster, M.C.) on the right, C Company (Capt. W. C. G. Ruddock) on the left, B Company (Capt. G. L. McIntyre) in the right support line, and D Company (Major L. F. Giblin, D.S.O., M.C.) in the left support line. Battalion Headquarters was in a quarry 200 yards west of Villers-Bretonneux, into the face of which dugouts had been built. The line held by us was astride the Amiens-St. Quentin-road, about 500 yards east of Villers-Bretonneux. The front line consisted of a shallow trench about 80 yards in front of which we dug posts

which were occupied by night. The work of linking the posts up
into a continuous trench and digging communication trenches
proceeded nightly under considerable handicap, for the country
was dead flat and machine guns active. The support line was
a continuous trench about 500 yards behind the front posts.
Dugouts in the support line were very poor, and if the weather
had been bad would have been uninhabitable. Many of them
were only burrows into the wall of the trench, liable to fall
in and block the trench in wet weather. At this time the
"Higher Command" was jumping on this lazy practice with
both feet, and corrugated iron had to be salvaged from
Villers-Bretonneux, and new trench shelters dug and roofed.
Two communication trenches ran back from the front line
through the outskirts of the town. These trenches were shallow, but the wheat crop screened us from view as we went
along. No Man's Land was all ripening wheat crop, which
made daylight patrolling possible, but the enemy posts were
very hard to find. Concerning the wheat, there was a good
deal of discussion as to which way the wind would be blowing
when the crop was ripe enough to put a fire into it. At that
time Verey lights falling in the wheat simply crackled for a
while and eventually went out.

The ground in front was perfectly flat for miles, and the
enemy line was very obscure. In some places he seemed quite
close and in others far away. The only places where his
trenches could be seen were on the extreme right and left of
the sector.

On the afternoon of the 13th June identification of the
enemy was asked for by "Higher Command," and a mixed
platoon of C and D were detailed to bring in a German dead
or alive. The O.C. D Company dealt out two poker hands to
his subalterns, and Lieut. T. T. Hoskins, having drawn a pair
against Lieut. Crosby's ace high, set off to make his dispositions and his will.

After collecting the Scout Officer, Lieut. Hoskins took him
up the front line, where the Scout Officer showed him where
he had approximately located an enemy machine-gun post
about 100 yards from our front line. This post was believed
to be behind the framework of an old aeroplane hangar in
No Mans' Land at P 25 b 9 3. It was decided to use the
platoon as follows:—

(i) Lieut. Hoskins, with 2 N.C.O.'s and 8 men, to go out
and locate the post and lay up behind it.

(ii) One corporal and 4 men, with a Lewis gun, to go about
30 yards from our line and act as a covering party.

(iii) One N.C.O. and 5 men to go out to the right and make a noise in the wheat to attract attention and induce the enemy post to disclose its position by firing.

(iv) The rest of the platoon to remain in the front line posts, and on receipt of word from the platoon commander that he had located the post, to fire a salvo of rifle grenades on to it. The rifle grenades were to be the signal to rush the post from the rear.

At 8.30 p.m. the platoon assembled in the front line, and the "decoy party" and the assaulting party went out. The decoy party made their way to a point about 30 yards to the right of the hangar, and in a most sporting manner proceeded to make the crop rustle in a way to excite suspicion. Meanwhile the assaulting party had got into position about 20 yards in rear of the hangar, losing one man on the way who was hit by a stray bullet. By this time the enemy had heard the rustling crop and opened with two machine-guns, one from each rear corner of the hangar. The platoon commander at once sent a man crawling back to tell the party in the front posts to fire their grenades into the back of the hangar.

For about an hour the assaulting party waited, and then, as a shower of rifle grenades burst in and around the hangar, they rushed the post. Lieut. Hoskins and several men jumped into a trench and found themselves among a number of the enemy. The officer emptied his revolver into them, while the men used their bombs. Any idea the party had of capturing the remainder of the garrison was dispelled by the fact that the enemy had cut dugouts from the trench underneath the hangar, and that these dugouts, about eight in number, were full of Germans. The enemy in the trench got into one end of it, while our men threw bombs into the dugouts, which caused a pandemonium. As one man afterwards remarked, he threw his bombs into a place where he could see nothing but heads and eyes. By this time the enemy who were not killed or wounded began to make a fight for it. They threw bombs at our party and among their own men, and Lieut. Hoskins, who was badly wounded by a bomb, ordered his party out of the trench, as they had no bombs left, and it was too great a mix-up to use bayonets. They all got out except one man, who was underneath two Germans and fighting for his life. It looked as if he would be taken prisoner, when a German threw a bomb which burst behind the struggling trio. The two Germans jumped up and ran to a dugout, leaving our man, who jumped out of the trench unhurt except for a bruised throat and "wind vertical."

The party then made their way back to our trenches by a long detour, under very heavy machine-gun fire, and some of them did not get back for two hours. Our casualties out of the nine who attacked were 1 killed and 4 wounded. The casualties inflicted on the enemy were certainly heavy, probably 30 at least. Several men were seen dead in the bottom of the trench, and at least 12 bombs were thrown into the crowded dugouts, which no doubt accounted for a number.

No identification was obtained, but the result of the raid disclosed the existence of an enemy strong-point 100 yards from our lines, holding a garrison of about 80 men, and steps were taken by artillery to smash it effectively.

On the 14th June, from 9.30 p.m. till midnight, the enemy heavily shelled the whole sector with about 600 rounds of high explosive. On the following day the hangar which Lieut. Hoskins and his party had found occupied was fired on by our howitzers and 6-inch Stokes mortars, which demolished the hangar, and apparently destroyed the trenches and dugouts behind it. The following night Lieut. W. T. Crosby took out a fighting patrol, and found the strong-point still occupied by the enemy, as they were bombed and machine-gunned from it. Consequently the howitzers and trench mortars had another shoot on it the following day, and this time completely destroyed it.

On the night of the 18th June the 40th Battalion was relieved by the 38th Battalion, and moved back into support west of Villers-Bretonneux, the companies being disposed as follows:—

A Company in trenches near the railway line about 2200 yards west of Villers-Bretonneux.

B Company in Cachy Trench and the railway embankment near it.

C Company in trenches north of the railway line, and 400 yards west of Villers-Bretonneux.

D Company in the "keeps" in Villers-Bretonneux.

On the night of the 19th June C and D Companies changed places. While in support all companies were employed on working parties in the front trenches and constructing dugouts in l'Abbé Wood. On the night of 23rd June the 10th Brigade was relieved by the 11th Brigade, the former becoming reserve brigade, and the 40th Battalion moved back near Blangy-Tronville, occupying part of the Glisy-Blangy Switch Trench, where we lived in shelters. In this position we were surrounded by a great number of English and French batteries One gun that created a lot of interest was a 13·5 French naval

gun that was firing on the railway junction at Chaulnes, over
28 miles away. The concussion when this gun fired was considerable, and it was discovered by enterprising people that
if they held their fingers three inches from the wall of a
building, the wall would touch their fingers when the gun
fired. A row of people could often be seen standing against
a wall with hands extended, to experience the sensation of
being hit by a house when the gun fired.

For the next few days the battalion alternately rested and
buried cable between Villers-Bretonneux and Aubigny, and on
the 26th June we were relieved by a battalion of the 7th
Brigade, and assembled among the trees on the banks of the
Somme near Glisy. At 1.30 p.m. we commenced to march to
Frechencourt, arrived there at 5.30 p.m., and occupied the
trenches of Frechencourt Switch, part of one of successive
zones of trench systems which now criss-crossed the country
for 20 miles behind the front line. That night the enemy
dropped bombs on our position, but did no damage. On the
28th June we left Frechencourt and marched about 2 miles to
Querrieu, taking over from the 21st Battalion. Headquarters
had billets in the village, A and B Companies were allotted
shelters very desirably situated close to the bathing pools of
the river, while C and D Companies found a virgin sylvan
retreat in the Bois de Mai, where they dug in with great
content.

It was perfect June and very good to be alive. For ten
days, we played cricket and bathed and lay in the sun, and
rambled in the cool depths of the wood, and loved all mankind except the Fritz aeroplane bombers. There was a judiciously small amount of training, and we managed to make
a game of it more successfully than ever before.

On the 1st July, battalion sports were held, and the first
half of the programme carried through. In the evening the
second anniversary of our departure from Tasmania was celebrated in a fitting manner. On the following day the second
half of the athletic programme was held, which was also a
great success. On the 4th July the Americans in the vicinity
celebrated the "Glorious Fourth" with a baseball match, and
we did honour to their day of independence by holding a hack
race at the conclusion of their programme. This race was
called "The Somme Cup," and was a six-furlong gallop over
a fairly good course, on which the only blemish was a shellhole 8 feet deep. A totalisator for betting purposes was run
by the battalion, and this was well patronised, particularly by
the American visitors, who seemed to have received some
unreliable stable information. It was the first time that any-

thing of the kind had been attempted in the way of horse-racing, and the result proved the Australian to be a great lover of the sport even if the field is composed of hacks, but the chance of having five francs on a horse was irresistible. The race was won by Lieut. L. W. Barnett's "Dolly," with Major L. F. Giblin's "Gumboots" second.

On the 5th July a tactical scheme was carried out by the battalion. The enemy were reported (for the purposes of the scheme only) to have broken through on the Albert sector and crossed the Hallue River. We marched out and took up a position in the St. Gratien-Frechencourt line. On the same day a competition for the best regimental transport in the brigade was held. This created much rivalry among the four transport sections of the brigade, who had put a lot of work into the cleaning of animals, equipment, and vehicles. The competition was won by the 40th Battalion, with the 38th Battalion second.

On the 6th July the 10th Brigade sports meeting was held. A feature of the sports was the fancy dress display of the 40th Battalion. In one of the abandoned villages a set of theatrical garments had been "souvenired," and one man appearing at the sports as a fowl, 9 feet high, which laid red and white eggs at unexpected moments, and another as an elephant, with an independent spirit and a set of parlour tricks, created a sensation. The fowl flapped its wings and crowed near the waggon-lines of an artillery brigade, and caused a stampede of mules and horses, and a horse bolted with an English colonel on the appearance of the regimental elephant. The horse stopped at the river, but the colonel did not.

On the 8th July the Hamel Sector was reconnoitred by officers, as we were warned that we would shortly have to take over that sector. That afternoon the battalion swimming carnival was held in the Hallue River. This was the first sports of its kind held in the brigade, and much interest and amusement resulted. The programme included novelty events, such as riding the barrel and the greasy pole. That evening a concert was given by the 10th Brigade pierrot troupe, known as "The Bandicoots," but unfortunately the programme was not finished, as the battalion was ordered to "stand to" and take up battle positions in connection with a practice alarm.

While at Querrieu the battalion lost the valued services of the bandmaster, Sergt. H. Emms, who was badly wounded by a bomb falling among the band while in billets during an enemy bombing expedition. The bandmaster had been with the battalion since its formation, and had materially assisted in building up a good regimental band.

On the 9th July the battalion changed areas with the 34th Battalion, and proceeded to a bivouac area near Rivery in order to carry out a practice attack with tanks. The practice was carried out the next day, with the following objects:—

(a) To demonstrate the use of tanks as a substitute for an artillery barrage.
(b) To accustom the infantry to work with tanks.
(c) To practice signalling between infantry and tanks.

On the 11th July we moved from Rivery and proceeded to Aubigny, where we rested on the banks of the Somme till 9 p.m., and then moved forward and relieved the 50th Battalion in the front line at Hamel. No casualties occurred during the relief, though the enemy shelling was fairly heavy.

The sector taken over was roughly 1000 yards east of Hamel. The disposition of companies was—D Company (Lieut. C. H. Cane) on the right, A Company (Capt. H. L. Foster, M.C.) in the centre, and C Company (Capt. W. K. Finlay) on the left, with B Company (Capt. G. S. Bisdee) in support in trenches about 400 yards north of Hamel. Next morning a company of the 33rd Battalion relieved C Company, 40th Battalion, and our B and C Companies relieved the 37th Battalion on our right. We now held the sector with four companies in the front line, our sector being from P 16 c 17 to P 11 a 44. The sector was fairly quiet, and the enemy artillery was mostly on the back areas and approaches, and the hill east of Hamel. On the night of 14th July our dispositions were again altered, and A Company was relieved by a company of the 3rd Pioneer Battalion, and D Company took over C Company's sector, while C Company moved into support, and A Company went back to reserve in the old German front line immediately west of Hamel.

In the Hamel sector about 5 officers and 80 other ranks of an American division were attached to us for experience, and a proportion was allotted to each company. At the same time 2 officers and 6 N.C.O.'s of the 40th Battalion were sent back to Querrieu and attached to an American unit there, who were occupying trenches in this reserve position, and carrying out routine work as if they were occupying front-line positions. Lieut. Cranswick, D.C.M., was also detached from the battalion and attached to a British brigade occupying the front line, in order to teach them Australian methods of scouting and patrolling. At that time, in all Australian divisions, we were getting prisoners whenever identification was asked for, and other divisions were finding it a difficulty. During April and May, for example, not a night passed without at least one prisoner being captured by the 3rd Division. So a number of officers and N.C.O.'s were detached from Australian divisions for the purpose of initiating British troops into our methods. Lieut. Cranswick personally took charge of the patrols he was teaching, and carried out practical work on the enemy positions, in which he was very successful.

On the evening of the 17th July the enemy put down a very heavy bombardment on the whole brigade sector, causing 21 casualties in the battalion. That day enemy identification was asked for, and Lieut. R. S. Mackenzie took out a patrol of 7 other ranks to procure it. They moved from our line at 10 p.m., and went about 800 yards down the Hamel-Lamotte-en-Santerre-road, north of Acquaire Wood, where they located an enemy post. Lieut. Mackenzie left his party about 30 yards from ths post at P 17 a 8 3, and crawled forward with No. 1964, Sgt. A. H. Richards, towards it. They got within 10 yards of it, threw bombs in, and rushed. They found two men in the post, and Lieut. Mackenzie shot one of them and secured the other as prisoner. Bombs were at once thrown at them from another post in rear, and Lieut. Mackenzie was wounded. He sent the sergeant off with the prisoner, while he made his way back more slowly to join up with his patrol. Just as he reached his patrol they were attacked by an enemy patrol, who threw bombs among them, fired a few shots, and ran, severely wounding Sgt. Richards and one of the men. Rifle grenades were by this time bursting on the road where the patrol was, and our party moved off with their prisoner, carrying two of the wounded, both of whom died later. Lieut. Mackenzie was able to walk back slowly without assistance.

On the 17th July the commanding officer left the unit to command temporarily the 15th Brigade; on 4th August he went to the 9th Brigade and commanded that brigade during the Battle of Amiens, returning in time to command the 40th Battalion in the capture of Bray on August 23.

On the night of the 18th July the battalion was relieved by the 37th Battalion, and moved into reserve in the old German front line about 2200 yards west of Hamel. There we were employed on working in the support and communication trenches until 26th July, when we relieved the 37th Battalion in the front line, our dispositions being—A Company and C Company in the front line, B Company in support, and D Company in reserve. During this period in the line there was a marked decrease in the enemy artillery and an increase in our own, which gave us a fairly quiet time in the trenches. During the month of July our casualties were 3 officers and 40 other ranks, while the sick evacuated to hospital amounted to 1 officer and 78 other ranks. The reason for the high sick rate was the prevalence of acute diarrhœa, which was giving the Medical Officer (Capt. J. S. Reed) a good deal of worry. In the first week in August the Medical Officer evacuated all such cases in order to prevent an epidemic of dysentery. Forty six cases were sent to the hospital during this week, and several of them were diagnosed as dysentery.

On the night of the 2nd August we were relieved by the 37th Battalion, and moved back into reserve again, west of Hamel. We rested there until the night of the 4th, when the 10th Brigade took over the 11th Brigade sector on the right, and held the whole of the divisional front in order to let the 9th and 11th Brigades prepare for the attack in a few days' time. We took over the same sector as before, with D and C Companies in the front line, A Company in support, and B Company in reserve.

On the 6th August our artillery fired continuously on the enemy back areas and communications. The enemy remained very quiet, but about 2 p.m. two of the enemy were seen in No Man's Land in front of C Company, and were fired on. One of them disappeared but the other put his hands up and came over to our lines. They turned out to be artillerymen who had lost their way and wandered through their own outpost line.

The day before the big attack was very quiet, on our sector, except for our artillery, which continued to fire on the enemy's back areas and communications. North of the Somme fighting took place all day, during which an English division was driven back between the Somme and the Ancre, but counter-attacked later and recaptured part of the lost ground.

The sector between the Ancre and the Somme had been held by Australians since the 27th March. Since then our line had been pushed forward bit by bit, about 2 miles, until it threatened Morlancourt. On the 6th August the Australians were relieved by an English corps, and on the 7th, half the ground, so painfully won, was lost.

Chapter XXI.

The Battle of Amiens of 8th August, 1918 — The 10th Brigade's Reverse at La Flaque — The 10th Brigade's Successful Attack at Proyart — Sergeant Statton wins the V.C.

THE military situation on the Western Front at the end of July, 1918, is described by the Commander-in-Chief (Sir Douglas Haig) as follows:—

"The definite collapse of the ambitious offensive launched by the enemy on the 15th July on the front of the French Army, and the striking success of the Allied counter-offensive south of the Aisne, effected a complete change in the military situation. The German Army had made its effort and failed. The period of its maximum strength had been passed, and the bulk of his reserves had been used up. On the other hand, the position of the Allies in regard to reserves had greatly improved. The fresh troops made available during the early summer had been incorporated and trained, while the American Army was rapidly growing. The Allied armies were now ready to take the offensive."

The first offensive action was the Battle of Amiens on a front of 11 miles, from just south of the Amiens-Roye-road to Morlancourt. The troops employed were the Canadian Corps on the right, the Australian Corps in the centre, and on the left north of the Somme, the 3rd British Corps. The left boundary of the Australian attack was the River Somme, and the right boundary was the Amiens-Chaulnes Railway. During the battle the left boundary of the Australian front was extended north of the Somme, owing to the failure of a British division at Chipilly.

The 2nd and 3rd Divisions opened the attack on the Australian front, with the 3rd Division from the Somme to the Amiens-St. Quentin-road, and took the first objective. The 4th and 5th Divisions passed through them to the next objective. The 3rd Division attacked with the 9th and 11th Brigades, with the 10th Brigade in reserve. This meant that prior to zero hour the 10th Brigade held the divisional front and the 9th and 11th Brigades went through us to the attack.

On the 7th of August it was known that the attack would be made next day, and at 1 a.m. on the morning of the 8th August we moved out of the front line to allow the assaulting troops to assemble there. Even at the most serious moments something humorous is bound to happen, and it happened then Zero hour had not been definitely fixed on the night of the 7th August, as it depended a good deal on whether the morning of the 8th would be misty or not. The acting commanding officer had arranged with company commanders that when word came of the hour of the attack he would notify them in a pre-arranged code, because of enemy listening sets. The agreement was that a number of rations of jam should mean that zero hour was at so many minutes after 4 a.m., and a number of rations of butter so many minutes before 4 a.m. However, zero hour was fixed at 4.20 a.m., and accordingly a telephone message went to companies: "Send 20 rations of jam to Battalion Headquarters at once. Acknowledge." Now the O.C. B Company happened to be away from his headquarters when the message arrived, and another officer was present who naturally thought that there were 20 men at Battalion Headquarters in urgent need of jam. So he set the Company Quartermaster-Sergeant to work, and the Company Quartermaster-Sergeant went round posts and dugouts and begged or borrowed small portions of jam from protesting men. A few minutes before zero hour a breathless runner dashed into Battalion Headquarters with a large tin containing a small quantity of hopeless-looking mixture of several kinds of jam which he put in front of the Adjutant, "With Capt. Bisdee's compliments, sir; he can't get 20 rations, but here's enough for 12:"

At 4.20 a.m. our barrage opened, and the infantry and tanks went forward. Very little impression could be obtained of the opening stages of the battle, on account of the heavy mist, which obscured nearly everything in front. The mist was so thick that some of the attacking troops lost their direction, and were guided by our men who were familiar with the ground. The tanks on our front seemed to have trouble in crossing our trenches, and no less than four in our vicinity stuck there. Beyond the front line nothing could be seen, and the crash and roar of the artillery drowned all other noises. There was no doubt as to the success of the initial stages of the attack, for out of the mist were coming batches of hundreds of prisoners and very few of our wounded. .About 8 a.m. the 4th and 12th Brigades passed through us on their way to the second objective. After the capture of the first objective the 10th Brigade became part of the corps reserve. At 8.30 a.m. the 40th Battalion moved forward about 750 yards into the newly-captured enemy trenches on the south side of Accroche Wood. Our men were very tired after two sleepless nights, and as soon as they got to the wood took the opportunity to sleep, lying about anywhere in shell-holes. Up to this time the enemy artillery fire on our front had been light, as probably a good number of his batteries were smothered by our artillery when the attack opened. At 5.25 p.m. we moved forward another 4500 yards in artillery formation to Reginald Wood, while the battalion transport moved to a position in the valley north-east of Warfusé-Abancourt. During this move the enemy artillery fire was heavy in places, but these places were easily avoided. In advancing over this recently captured ground the fact that struck us most was the very small number of our dead. The unexpectedness and "dash" of the attack, combined with the mistiness of the morning, had resulted in the enemy in the front line of defence surrendering to our infantry as they appeared, or at any rate putting up a very poor fight. This was the experience on the Australian front during the first day, but north of the Somme the 3rd British Corps had been held up at one point, and an Australian brigade was sent across the river later to their assistance. The enemy's defences were not strong, and the ground generally was very little cut up by shell-fire, except in limited areas, such as small woods and around villages which had been thoroughly destroyed by our shell-fire.

The night of the 8th August was spent in shell-holes at Reginald Wood, and the following day we still remained there. Officers reconnoitred the position reached by the 12th Brigade, while the men rested and improved their bivouac area. The enemy shelled our position lightly, and that night his 'planes bombed the wood, but caused no casualties in the battalion.

On the 10th August the Acting C.O. attended a conference at Brigade Headquarters, and received verbal orders that the 40th Battalion would take part in an attack by the 10th Brigade on the spur west of Chuignolles, and east of Proyart, from the Amiens-St. Quentin-road to the Somme. (See Map 8.)

At this time the enemy was holding the line Germaine Wood-Proyart-La Flaque, and the plan of attack laid down for the 10th Brigade was to advance by night with tanks up the Amiens-St. Quentin-road, through the enemy outpost line to a point about 1200 yards east of La Flaque and then turn due north to the Somme, thus getting behind the enemy position and cutting him off. This ambitious scheme was termed a "silent operation," but neither before nor since has a tank noise-silencer been patented. A tank is a noisy, smelly thing at its best, but on a hard road it makes a noise like a traction engine. As a matter of fact the operation was as silent as if the brigade had dispensed with the tanks and marched up the road with the four battalions' bands playing their hardest. There was every justification for a proper flank attack, because the advance along the Somme was lagging behind the advance south of the Amiens-St. Quentin-road. This was because the Somme Valley was more difficult ground, broke by cross-valleys, exposed to fire from across the river, and difficult to take by direct frontal assault.

At 7.30 p.m. on August 10 the battalion moved from Reginald Wood, and marched in artillery formation across country about 3500 yards to the hospital near Richmond Wood, on the Amiens-St. Quentin-road. The plan laid down for the advance up the road was for the battalion to move up the road with one tank on each flank at 50 to 100 yards distance. We had no opportunity of talking the scheme over with the tank officers beforehand, and when we picked them up at the hospital near Richmond Wood, we found they could not move off the road, and had great difficulty in even keeping to the road at night. This meant that both tanks and men had to move up the road, which made the chances of success very slender.

At the hospital platoons closed up, and we moved by companies in file along the side of the road with the rest of the brigade. In front was the 37th Battalion, preceded by two tanks; then came the 38th Battalion, followed by two more tanks and the 40th Battalion; while the 39th Battalion came in the rear. Each battalion had part of its regimental transport carrying ammunition and tools. The transport with the 40th Battalion consisted of four limbered wagons in rear of the battalion, and two pack mules with ammunition in rear of each company.

Before going more than 500 yards past the hospital several enemy aeroplanes were heard overhead. They dropped flares over the road, and by their light dropped bombs on the column and machine-gunned the road, causing a large number of casualties and a certain amount of confusion. Shelter was taken in the ditches and shell-holes by the roadside until the aeroplanes had dropped all their bombs. Nearly everyone took shelter but the transport men, and here again was one of the many examples of their simple heroism. They could not take shelter without leaving their animals, for to leave them would mean a stampede of horses and mules, and the ammunition with them—ammunition that would be a vital necessity if we reached our objective. One mule did get away when the man leading it was killed. It got tangled in the wire, and with two boxes of ammunition that had slipped under its belly, kicked and squealed till somebody shot it. The transport men stood by their animals on the road among the bursting bombs and machine-gun bullets. They were heroic, because at a time like that they had to be heroic or let the attacking troops down badly. The same thing happened the same night later, when the road was swept with machine-gun fire and artillery. In addition to the men who were killed or wounded with their animals, the bravery of two men was most conspicuous to the rest of the battalion. These men, No. 5690, Pte. James Doherty, and No. 5691, Pte. W. J. Dolting, kept their animals quiet and led them along the road with the ammunition, when it was apparently impossible for anything to live there. The casualties in the transport were two killed and three wounded, out of a total of nine men. Ten animals were killed and several wounded.

After about 10 minutes' delay the battalion again moved on, and when about 1000 yards west of La Flaque, alongside a very large ammunition and engineers' dump of the enemy's, the enemy put down a heavy barrage on the column with high explosive, shrapnel, and gas, causing us to take shelter again on the sides of the road, and to put on respirators. After a few minutes there we pushed through the enemy shelling, and got through the village of La Flaque to a point about 400 yards east of the village, where we came under very heavy machine-gun fire, which enfiladed us from the left flank. The battalions in front stopped, and parties of the leading battalion began to come back. On investigation it was found that the tanks in front of the 37th Battalion were held up. Every man of their crews was a casualty from the splash of machine-gun bullets through the joints of the shutters, and their officers walking ahead to guide them were killed. The Commanding Officer of the 37th Battalion had been killed, and casualties in that battalion were very heavy. By this time all the battalions were off the road taking cover, as the road was swept with the heaviest machine-gun fire. The machine-gun bullets produced a very creditable fireworks show of sparks, as they played a ceaseless tattoo on the tanks. The silent operation had failed, and it now remained to make the best use we could of our position with a view to another try.

The Acting Commanding Officer halted the parties of the 37th Battalion who were coming back, and ordered them to re-organise in shell-holes near. He then arranged with the 38th Battalion that they should occupy a line from the furthest point reached by them, while we made a flank on each side of the road, and connected up with the 39th Battalion in rear. This was done while Major Giblin went back to Brigade Headquarters near Richmond Wood and reported the situation. The 38th and 40th Battalions continued to occupy the positions they had taken up under heavy fire until about 3 a.m., when Major Giblin returned with orders for the 37th and 39th

Battalions to withdraw to support positions, while the 38th and 40th Battalions dug and occupied a line from a point on the Amiens-St. Quentin road about 500 yards east of La Flaque to a point on the Proyart-Harbonnieres railway, 350 yards north of the Amiens-St. Quentin road. This line was suitable as a position from which to attack Proyart, and also covered the left flank of the 2nd Australian Division on our right. Digging was very difficult, owing to the shortage of tools, and by daylight the line was not completed, but the thick mist which hung for about two hours after daylight enabled us to finish, by using shell-holes and old trenches. The line was not continuous, and consisted of a series of posts, of which the 38th Battalion occupied the right and the 40th Battalion the left (see map). Our B Company (Capt. Bisdee) and C Company (Capt. Ruddock) occupied our front posts, with A Company (Lieut. Game) and D Company (Lieut. Cane) in support just west of La Flaque. Lieut. Cane was wounded in the early morning, and Capt. Ruddock later in the day, and their commands were taken over by Lieut. W. T. Crosby and Lieut. C. W. Rock. With daylight the enemy put down a heavy and persistent bombardment on the whole position, and particularly on the little group of houses in La Flaque; so that Battalion Headquarters was practically isolated, and in the evening was moved to an old dugout about 500 yards to the west.

While the mist was still over our position in the early morning, our aeroplanes came over to see the position, and had to come down within 100 feet of the ground in order to see our flares through the fog. During the morning parties of the 38th Battalion on our right, by good individual work, got forward beyond this position in the mist, and captured several machine-guns and their crews. During the whole of August 11th the enemy kept up heavy artillery fire on La Flaque and all roads near it, and any movement near our posts brought machine-gun fire from the ridge in front, causing several casualties among signallers and runners, who were always forced to expose themselves in carrying messages and laying and mending telephone-lines. Their work at La Flaque was particularly good. Lieut. A. R. Mills, who was acting as a brigade liason officer between Brigade Headquarters and the forward battalions, also found La Flaque an unhealthy place, and had a very strenuous day, having to make several trips to the 38th and 40th Battalions over the open ground. He several times ran the gauntlet with his runners, sniped all the way by enemy machine-guns, and all his runners were wounded before the day was over. The sight of this officer breaking all previous records across the open with machine-gun bullets flicking up the dirt under his heels became quite a familiar sight on the landscape, and on each appearance the odds were called and bets made in our posts as to whether he would arrive. Odds were about 12 to 1 against. During that night the dispositions of companies were altered, and C and A Companies occupied the front posts, while D Company went into support and B Company into reserve. We also moved about 200 yards further to the north-west, taking over that amount of ground from the 9th Brigade, while the 38th Battalion took over a similar amount from us on our right. A hot meal, tools, ammunition, &c., were brought up the road by the transport under great difficulties from shell-fire, and carried forward by B Company. Our patrols pushed forward during the night, and reported that the enemy was apparently holding his outpost line very weakly with men, but was relying upon numerous machine-guns to hold up our advance. This was reported to Brigade Headquarters, and shortly after daylight orders were received for us to push forward with patrols in front in conjunction with the 37th Battalion on our left and the 38th Battalion on our right, swinging from a pivot on the main-road. Accordingly, a patrol of A Company, consisting of Lieut. L. Parry and 12 other ranks, went forward on the left, and a similar patrol of C Company under Lieut. C. W. Rock went out on the right. The object of this was to avoid the necessity of sacrificing men in a bold frontal attack over open ground against machine-guns. The patrols were to work forward till they got into a position where they could locate the enemy machine-guns, and the attack would be made by platoons moving up to suitable positions behind the patrols in a series of bounds. As a patrol worked forward 100 yards, the platoon behind it would do the same, taking advantage of all suitable cover. The plan was completely successful, and undoubtedly saved very heavy casualties, for time after time it has been demonstrated that an attack across open ground against machine-guns will nearly always fail. And if it does not fail the price is always too heavy. The other method, to be successful, demands determination and resource, two commodities in which the Australian soldier has never been lacking.

The objective of the 40th Battalion was the valley south of the Proyart-Chuignes road, while the 37th Battalion were to advance through Proyart to a line north of the Proyart-Chuignes road, beyond the light railway line. To get to their objective the 40th Battalion had to advance over open ground for about 1300 yards under direct observation and machine-gun fire from high ground east of Proyart.

The C Company patrol moved out about 7.30 a.m., and by 8.30 a.m. had got forward 800 yards into some old trenches on the Proyart-Rainecourt-road (R 27 a 38). This position had been gained under heavy artillery and machine-gun fire and the two Lewis guns with the patrol were both knocked out by shell-fire, and most of the patrol were casualties. Lieut. Rock left his patrol there, and went back to arrange a plan with the platoon in rear. The enemy seemed to expect a big attack to be developing from this point, and put down a heavy bombardment on the position, which made a further advance there for the time inadvisable.

The A Company patrol worked up the road towards Proyart, and reached the centre of the town by 9.30 a.m. The town was not occupied by the enemy, but he could be seen retreating from it, along the Proyart-Chuignes-road. No. 128, Sgt. E. W. Billing, went forward alone to the eastern edge of the town, and saw that the enemy trenches north of Chuignes-Proyart-road, just behind the railway-line, were held in force by the enemy. He went back and reported this to the patrol leader, and the patrol moved to the railway embankment about 400 yards south-east of the village. Here they were fired on by machine-guns from Robert Wood, but were supported by No. 3 Platoon of A Company, under Lieut. S. S. McMillan, who replied to the machine-guns with his Lewis guns. From there, under cover of the fire of their Lewis guns, the platoon and patrol moved, by short rushes, across the open ground under heavy machine-gun fire to their objective. It was decided that the remainder of A Company would do the same. To enable this to be done, No. 506, Sgt. P. C. Statton, M.M., had two Lewis guns firing on the enemy machine-guns from behind the road embankment on the Proyart-Chuignes-road, a few yards east of the railway-line. From this point Sgt. Statton could see that the 37th Battalion had reached the railway-line east of Proyart, but were held up by several machine-guns firing from posts about 150 yards behind the railway-line immediately in front of the 37th Battalion. Lieut. McMillan sent word to the 37th Battalion that as they moved forward our Lewis guns would assist them by concentrating on the enemy machine-guns. A party of the 37th Battalion therefore rushed forward, but the enemy fire was too strong, in spite of this assistance, and the 37th Battalion party was wiped out in their gallant rush. Seeing this, Sgt. Statton called on three men to follow him, and, under cover of the road embankment, got to a point 80 yards to the right of the four enemy machine-guns. Armed only with his revolver, he got over the bank, and followed by No 957, Cpl. W. J. Upchurch, No. 262, Pte. L. Styles, and No. 3275, Pte. N. T. Beard, rushed across the 80 yards of open ground to the nearest enemy machine-guns, which were still firing at the 37th Battalion and did not see him coming. He shot two of the enemy on the first gun, the remainder of the crew being killed by the three men with him. He then rushed at the next gun and shot the crew, with the exception of one man, for whom he had no cartridge left. This man attacked him with his bayonet, but Sgt. Statton seized the rifle, wrenched it out of the German's hands, and killed him with his own bayonet. He then rushed for the next posts, but the two machine-gun crews had left their guns and ran. As they ran back they were all killed by our Lewis gunners, who were waiting where Sgt. Statton had left them. The enemy machine-guns at Robert Wood had opened on Sgt. Statton and his party of three, and Pte. Styles was killed and Cpl. Upchurch badly wounded. Sgt. Statton and Pte. Beard crawled back to the shelter of the railway embankment. Later in the day Sgt. Statton went out and carried in Cpl. Upchurch and the body of Pte. Styles. For this very gallant action this non-commissioned officer was awarded the Victoria Cross. His action on that occasion was in keeping with the reputation he had won and maintained for soldierly skill and determination.

Meanwhile part of the patrol from C Company had pushed on and reached their objective, but owing to the heavy machine-gun and artillery fire which continued, it was not thought advisable for the remainder of the company to follow them, so C Company moved to the north towards Proyart, and followed the same route as A Company in a similar manner.

Enemy machine-guns and snipers were active in front of our objective, while C Company was working towards the valley, and some of A Company's scouts went forward to locate the enemy posts. One of these posts was found by No. 128, Sgt. E. W. Billing, at a point 300 yards beyond the valley. This N.C.O. crawled out with his rifle, and camouflaged himself in a heap of rubbish about 200 yards from the post, from where he picked off three of the enemy, and the remainder ran. It was not until 8 p.m. that the whole of C and A Companies were in the valley, as the progress of dribbling parties forward was slow, in order to avoid casualties from the heavy machine-gun fire which continued. During the day a very heavy bombardment was kept up, with little intermission, until late in the afternoon on Proyart and La Flaque and the roads between. This just passed over our advanced troops, but worried our reserve company and Battalion Headquarters considerably, particularly the signallers and runners at their work.

A platoon of D Company was brought up into close support, and the remainder of D Company moved up just behind them into old trenches on the high ground behind the valley which formed our front line, while B Company were in reserve about 400 yards north of La Flaque.

The battalion objective gained consisted of a valley, on the eastern side of which was a row of solid dugouts. Beyond the valley was level ground towards Matto and St. Martin Woods. An outpost line about 200 yards beyond the objective was formed immediately after dark, and at 2 a.m. on the morning of August 13 we were relieved by a battalion of the 17th British Division, who suffered heavily from bombing as they moved up the road to relieve us. We went back without incident to our previous bivouac area at Reginald Wood, where a hot meal and blankets were waiting for the tired troops.

The casualties since August 8 amounted to 12 killed and 60 wounded, including the commanders of C and D Companies.

This was the comparatively minor part taken by the 40th Battalion in the battle of Amiens, which lasted from the 8th to the 13th August. The result of this battle, in which the Australians and Canadians were predominant, was that within five days the city of Amiens and all its important railways had been disengaged. Nearly 22,000 prisoners and 400 guns had been captured, and our line had been pushed forward 12 miles in a vital sector. Further, this advance, combined with the advance of the French in the south, had caused the enemy to evacuate a wide extent of territory. It is doubtful whether the enemy ever recovered from the blow, and looking back over events that followed, it must be realised that the battle of Amiens was the beginning of the end of the war. The blow to the enemy morale was considerable, and when the battle of Bapaume opened 10 days later, the difference in his fighting spirit was very apparent. He was in the position of a boxer who has hit the ground, and comes up again a good deal shaken, and with his confidence gone. Ludendoeff has put it on record that his hope of victory vanished after 8th August, 1918.

Chapter XXII.

At Reginald Wood—Capture of Bray by the 40th Battalion—A Further Advance towards Cappy and Suzanne.

HE next few days were spent at Reginald Wood, as the whole division was now in reserve. Most of the time was spent in equipping and re-organising, and any spare time was mostly given over to hunting "chats." Generally, during the summer months everybody was more or less lousy, but during those few days at Reginald Wood the chats were remarkably numerous and well nourished. Even the medical officer, who, by reason of his knowledge and supply of various disinfectants, was generally immune, joined in the hunt and devoted much time, energy, and profanity to overhauling his shirt and dragging the nimble "chat" therefrom.

There was very little shell-fire at Reginald Wood, but enemy aeroplanes were fairly attentive. These were not welcomed by anybody, except the battalion runners, who had found a German machine-gun, rather the worse for wear, but with great ingenuity had repaired it and started target practice on various objects. The heavy arm of authority at once fell on them, and pointed out the heavy punishment on persons, other than authorised persons, who discharged firearms behind the front line at anything but the enemy. The runners pondered for a long time, and solved the difficulty. They mounted their gun with its nose pointing to heaven, searched the country, and brought back plenty of enemy machine-gun belts, and then sat down and prayed for enemy aeroplanes to come. They came, and the enemy machine-gun played its tune at intervals during the day, and there was much joy among the runners. At night the runners went to sleep, feeling like the village blacksmith, with "something attempted, something done," and the good work was taken up by Pte. H. A. H. Smith of D Company, a cheerful and indefatigable youth, who was never really happy unless he was firing at something. He spent the first half of every night plugging at enemy aeroplanes as they showed up in the numerous searchlight beams that criss-crossed overhead. Unfortunately he had set up his machine-gun within a few yards of the place where two companies were sleeping in shallow holes, and each burst of fire from the zealous machine-gunner was followed by a *feu de joie* of curses from the sleepy diggers. "That little —— Smithy, I'll screw his —— neck in the morning."

We were subjected to a little long-distance shelling from a gun trying to knock out the wagon to which an observation balloon overhead was attached. The balloon kept on moving round Reginald Wood, and the gun kept following it, while we got the shells in our area. But the balloon won, though the personnel in charge of it had some anxious moments.

On the 18th August the Commanding Officer, who had been temporarily commanding the 9th Brigade, returned to the unit and resumed command of the battalion. About this time Major Payne went from the 40th Battalion to command temporarily the 39th Battalion, but he was wounded a few days later and went to hospital.

Preparations were made for a move to Harbonnieres, with a view to continuing the push on the southern edge of our sector near Chaulnes. However, this area had been thoroughly devastated in the earlier Somme battles; roads had been wiped out, and the conditions for an advance were very difficult. It was therefore decided, on the initiative of the Canadians, not to continue the push there, which would be needlessly expensive, and the alternative was adopted of keeping pressure on that front while the position was turned from the left flank north of the Somme, by way of Mt. St. Quentin and Peronne. It was this latter operation that was ging to keep us very busy in the next 10 days.

At 5 p.m. on the afternoon of August 21 orders were received for the battalion to cross the Somme to Sailly Laurette. We moved an hour later and marched through a cloud of dust, which hung permanently over all the roads as thick as a London fog, and made figures invisible at 10 yards distance even in the light of a full moon. We arrived at 9.30 p.m., and bivouacked behind banks and in old trenches east of the village. The following day bombs and other fighting equipment were issued, and we remained under orders to move at an hour's notice. As the day was very hot permission was obtained for small armed parties in fighting order to go to the river for a bathe. During the afternoon of August 23 the commanding officer was sent for by the Brigadier, and received verbal orders that the 40th Battalion was to capture the town of Bray on the following morning. Orders for the attack had been withheld on account of the division on the left of the 3rd Australian Division having fallen back some distance before an enemy attack, and the Bray operations were in doubt. The left flank of our division was held by the 9th Brigade and the 3rd Machine Gun Battalion, and word came from the 9th Brigade that they would hold on if we would carry on with the capture of Bray. They did so, and instead of refusing their exposed flank actually pushed their front farther to the left to occupy some strong positions and made a flank back from these positions.

August 23 was the opening of the main attack of the Battle of Bapaume. Preliminary operations preparatory to the main attack had been carried out on August 21 and 22, but the main attack began on August 23 and 24, lasting nearly ten days, and resulted in driving the German Army from one side of the old Somme battlefield to the other, and turning the line of the Somme. The battle opened on a 33-mile front from the junction with the French, north of Lihons to Mercatel, and the first 24 hours of the battle consisted of a series of strong assaults along the whole front on selected points. One of these points was the town of Bray.

At 8 p.m. on August 23 we commenced the approach march of about 7½ miles. After leaving Sailly Laurette we proceeded by companies in single file to a valley just west of Gressaire Wood, and rested there for an hour. From there the road, which was rather steep, was blocked with transport, causing our own transport, which was carrying the Lewis guns and magazines, to stop. It was impossible to get them further, so the Lewis guns and magazines were taken off the limbers and issued to companies, and the battalion moved on in a direct route towards Bray. (See Map 9.)

The enemy outpost line was about 100 yards west of the edge of the town, and companies moved into their assembly positions near the Crucifix about 300 yards from the town, which they reached at 12.45 a.m., only 15 minutes before zero hour. As nobody had seen the ground before, and we had no guides, the last half-hour before finding our jumping-off place had some anxious moments, when it appeared an arguable point whether or not we were lost. C Company was on the right of the Bray-Corbie-road, and extended south from it for 200 yards; D Company was on the left of the road, and extended north from it for 200 yards. Two platoons of A Company were immediately behind C Company, and one platoon behind D Company. One platoon of B Company was also on the left of the road. Battalion Headquarters was about 1500 yards west of Bray, under a bank. Owing to the casualties of the past few weeks, and the non-arrival of reinforcements, the companies were all unable to form four platoons, and had merged their strength into three. The following were the tasks and objectives of companies: —

D Company (Major L. F. Giblin, D.S.O., M.C.) had to move past the northern side of the town and consolidate three posts at a distance of about 500 yards beyond it.

C Company (Lieut. M. H. O. Whitaker, M.C.) had to move past the southern side of the town and consolidate two posts on the right of those consolidated by D Company, and to effect a junction with the 3rd Pioneer Battalion at a bridge over the Somme 500 yards east of La Neuville. The Pioneer Battalion had crossed the river on 23rd August, due east of Etinehem, by means of boats, and had worked their patrols forward through Neuville-les-Bray.

A Company (Lieut. C. W. Game) was to attack the town and clear it of the enemy, and support D and C Companies beyond the town by consolidating a support position. A portion of the 10th A.L.T.M. Battery was attached to A Company to deal with machine-guns and strong-points.

B Company (Capt. G. L. McIntyre), with the exception of one platoon, was detailed to carry ammunition, tools, &c., from the battalion dump, about 1000 yards west of Bray, to the front line after the objective had been gained. The remaining platoon of B Company, which was behind D Company on the assembly position, was to advance behind D Company and keep in touch with the 37th Battalion, north of Bray. The 37th Battalion, who were holding the line on our left, northwest of Bray, were to push their right flank forward in conformity with our advance.

While in the assembly positions a machine gun from close in front of D Company began to play at random just over our heads. There was just time to send a scout (Corpl. T. A. Cook) to locate it, and to assign it to the sure attention of Lieut. Cranswick, when the barrage opened.

At 1 a.m. the artillery opened, and we went forward into the darkness behind the barrage. The action of each company must be dealt with separately, because of the fact that owing to the dark night and the plan of the attack, it was impossible for companies to work with any definite co-ordination of movement.

D Company captured three machine guns and prisoners in the post that had been located while on the assembly position, almost before the surprised gun crews knew what had happened. Machine-gun fire from the north of the town was fairly heavy, and several casualties occurred before the town was reached, including the officer commanding the company (Major Giblin), who was severely wounded. Lieut. T. G. Cranswick, D.C.M., immediately took command, and moved on. The enemy barrage had now come down, and D Company ran into a heavy fire of high explosive and gas on the north edge of the town. This caused a delay while respirators were put on, and the company moved on for a short distance, when it was decided to take off respirators and chance the gas. To have to fight while wearing a respirator is a serious handicap, but in the darkness it reduces men to a state of helplessness. The artillery and machine gun fire continued, but the company pushed on past the town and reached the cemetery on the western side of the Bray-Albert-road. In the cemetery two machine guns were located firing, and were dealt with. At this time several casualties occurred from a machine gun firing from behind in the town. In getting forward under these difficult conditions a non-commissioned officer whose work stood out was No. 979, Sgt. V. H. Buchanan, who had taken charge of two platoons when Lieut. Cranswick took command of the company. His voice could be heard above the noise directing and urging his men on in the dark, and he played a big part in leading the company under heavy fire to their objective. When about 200 yards beyond the town D Company were held up by a machine gun directly in front. No. 267, Sgt. A. H. Purton, with five men, crept forward, located the gun, and rushed it successfully. At the same time a party of the 37th Battalion captured a machine gun on the left of this post that was firing on D Company. From this point to the objective the advance was continued under heavy machine-gun and rifle fire from the vicinity of the objective, and the company got forward under cover of the fire from our Lewis guns. It was still very dark at 2.50 a.m., when D Company reached their objective. Their casualties had been very heavy, and they were soon afterwards reinforced by two platoons of A Company, while A Company were reinforced by a platoon from the 37th Battalion.

C Company had a much happier time than D Company, and reached their objective with very few casualties and little opposition. They moved as fast as the barrage would permit along the south edge of the town, and saw the enemy getting back through the town. After passing the town they met plenty of machine-gun fire, but it was mostly overhead, and they appeared to miss most of the enemy artillery fire, which was chiefly directed north of the town, and in the low ground near Battalion Headquarters. A light machine gun opened immediately in front of them near the railway line, but after firing a few rounds it stopped, and C Company found the crew waiting to surrender. They then pushed on to the objective, which was reached by 2.10 a.m. The objective here consisted of a trench with a garrison of 12 of the enemy and two machine guns. They surrendered without any resistance. It was then decided to exploit success, and Lieut. N. E. Lakin, with No. 12 platoon, pushed over to an enemy strong-point on his left front. After a short bomb fight the enemy surrendered, and pushed four light machine guns over the parapet as a sign of good faith. In addition to the machine-guns, 22 prisoners were captured at this point. No. 11 Platoon, under Lieut. C. W. Rock, also went forward and dispersed a number of the enemy, who were collecting in front, by opening fire with the Lewis guns. On the right flank it was impossible to get touch with the 3rd Pioneer Battalion, as the bridge across the Somme had been blown up by the enemy. To fill the gap between C Company and the river a carrying platoon of B Company, under Lieut. R. C. Walters, was placed there. One of the signallers, No. 2271, Pte. H. Pepper, had gone through with C Company, and got on to a bank near the objective, from where his lamp was soon winking messages back to the command post. A party of seven of the enemy, who were somewhere between him and the town, saw the lamp, and, thinking it was theirs, made towards it to enquire the reason for the disturbance. They found the reason when they got to the lamp, and surrendered to the signaller.

A Company advanced behind C and D Companies, and entered the town at three points in small parties detailed to clean up various portions of the town. At the north-west corner one party ran into thick gas, but were able to get their masks on before any damage was done. At the cross roads on the north-east edge, the machine-gun, firing on D Company, was located and rushed, but the crew left their gun and ran. Most of the enemy seemed to have cleared out of the town as soon as the barrage opened, for many of the cellars contained burning candles and warm food on the tables. Near the church, on the eastern side, a cellar was found to contain a number of the enemy, who were invited to come out. Two rifle shots from the entrance was the reply, so a phosphorus bomb was thrown in as a more pressing invitation. Immediately about ten of the enemy rushed out, some with their clothes alight. Our men rolled them on the ground and put out the burning phosphorus on all but one man, who made off down the street towards the river with the phosphorus illuminating his trail. He was found during the day near the river, quite naked, and rather badly burnt.

Lieut. McMillan and a party of men also took 15 prisoners out of a cellar in the south of the town, and small parties of prisoners were captured by various sections after practically no resistance. All the enemy seemed to have run or gone into cellars for safety, and those in the cellars realised their helplessness when invited to come out or be bombed out. After clearing the town A Company moved forward beyond it, and located a machine gun firing from the railway station towards the town. A Stokes gun was brought up and the machine gun knocked out; one of the crew was killed, and the rest made off. Immediately afterwards a small minenwerfer began to shoot from the left of the orchard, about 150 yards east of the town. A Lewis gun got out on the flank and disposed of the crew, leaving two mortars in our hands. No 126, Sgt. E. W. Billing, who had pushed forward as a scout, with his usual initiative, located a party of the enemy in the orchard, and went back and brought up a Lewis gun team, which did effective shooting. A horse, saddled and bridled, was tied to a tree in the orchard. One of our wounded was hoisted on to it, and started off to the dressing station, where he arrived in due course, and impressed the medical staff by the manner of his arrival. A Company obtained touch with C and D Companies, and dug a support position 200 yards behind them.*

As soon as it became daylight the enemy apparently took in the situation, and was seen making back over the hill towards Suzanne in great numbers. Immediately afterwards a great number of enemy 'planes came over, and for the rest of the day he shelled the town and the ground west of it very heavily, with all sizes of high explosive shells. Some of his heavier artillery was badly directed, and a great number of his shells fell in the Somme, making quite an interesting and harmless display. The shelling of the town made communication very difficult, and carrying parties had a strenuous and exciting time. The enemy also set fire to the town in three places, and one of them continued to burn for two days. The fire was very convenient next morning while attacking, as it made a good directing mark.

The remainder of August 24 was spent in consolidating the position and making dumps in preparation for a further advance. It was realised that the enemy was now badly shaken on the whole front, and an offensive programme would keep him on the move across the ridges north of the Somme, where, if allowed the time, he would be able to make a good defensive position. The old Somme battlefield now faced us,

---

*In the capture of Bray we took in all 200 prisoners. Our casualties were 43.

seared by old trenches, pitted with shellholes, and crossed in all directions by tangled belts of wire, the whole covered with the vegetation of two years. This derelict battle-ground presented great opportunities for machine-gun defence. During that afternoon Battalion Headquarters moved forward to within 500 yards west of Bray, the command post was moved to the railway station, east of the town, and telephone lines were laid to companies. Later in the afternoon orders were received for a further advance before daylight the following morning (August 25) to clean up the triangular-shaped piece of ground with Bray, Cappy, and Suzanne as the points. This meant a maximum advance of 3000 yards. The 40th Battalion were to be on the right of the brigade front, the 37th Battalion in the centre, the 39th Battalion on the left, and the 38th Battalion in support to the 39th Battalion. The task of the 40th Battalion was to move south-east and to capture the ground astride the Bray-Cappy-road, from our present line to the Somme. It was not expected that the 40th Battalion would meet with much resistance, as the enemy would not be likely to risk a large force in the bend of the Somme, but fairly strong resistance was expected on our left.

At 9 p.m. on August 25 company commanders reported to Battalion Headquarters for instructions for the attack. At that time the enemy was still pouring gas and high explosive into Bray and the ground west of it, in consequence of which the conference was carried out with all officers attending the conference in small box respirators, so that nobody made a long speech. In future wars, in order to meet a similar case, it would be advisable for everyone to have a knowledge of the deaf and dumb alphabet. It would certainly cramp the style of Henry V. if he had to splutter his remarks beginning with "Once more into the breach, dear friends, once more," through a rubber tube by the light of a sickly candle in a dirty hole in a bank.

It was decided that before zero hour the 40th Battalion would withdraw about 300 yards behind their outpost line, in order to give the 37th Battalion a clear field to follow the barrage. Our assembly positions overlapped, and to avoid confusion the 40th Battalion were not going forward until 15 minutes after zero hour. This withdrawal from the outpost line was carried out under most uncomfortable circumstances, as the gas was so thick that respirators had to be worn, and the night was very dark. The burning building in Bray was quite useful.

At 2.30 a.m. the barrage opened. This barrage was not one of the best that has been given us, and casualties resulted from short shooting as we waited for the 37th Battalion to get their 15 minutes' start. At 2.45 a.m. we hurried forward, with A Company on the right, taking the area between the Bray-Cappy-road and the river, B Company immediately north of the Bray-Cappy-road, C Company on the left of B Company, and D Company in support ready to render assistance when and where required.

A Company met with practically no resistance, and had an interesting time looking through an enormous enemy ammunition dump south of the road. They would probably have kept farther away from it had they known it was mined, and that the pulling of a cord would blow the whole dump up. It contained every conceivable kind of ammunition from heavy "Minnies" to S.O.S. rockets.

B Company were at one time held up by a machine gun immediately north of the Bray-Cappy-road. This gun was easily outflanked in the darkness, and a bomb at the dugout door was sufficient inducement for the officer and two men with the gun to surrender. A little further on, at Yakko Copse, a few prisoners were captured, and No. 7565, Pvte. E. A. Whittle, distinguished himself by capturing a machine-gun and crew of five men single-handed.

C Company came under heavy machine-gun fire at close range from a trench along the side of the road from Suzanne which joins the Bray-Cappy-road (L 24 c 2.7). This trench was near the junction of B and C Companies, and Lieut. R. C. Walters, with a few men from B Company, came across from the flank and rushed one of the posts in the trench, capturing the machine-gun and crew. They then bombed their way along the trench, capturing a total of four machine-guns and 22 prisoners. One enemy gun crew left their gun and escaped in the darkness.

The objective was reached at 4 a.m. B Company consolidated posts at the bridgehead opposite Cappy, and C Company dug in on their left. A and D Companies took up a support position at Yakko Copse. Our casualties during the operation numbered 22, and we captured 29 prisoners and eight machine-guns.

After daylight the enemy was seen retreating from Cappy, which was being attacked by the 1st Australian Division. During the remainder of the day the enemy shelled our position intermittently, but did not do much damage. A hot meal was brought up during the morning by the regimental transport as far as Bray, and carried from Bray to our position near Cappy. The night of 25th-26th August was fairly quiet, which enabled us to get our first sleep for over 48 hours.

At 4 a.m. on the morning of the 26th August instructions were received from brigade for D Company to move into the wood east of Bray, as support to the 37th Battalion, who were attacking in the direction of Vaux Wood. D Company moved at once, as ordered, and established communication with the 37th Battalion. A Company of the 37th Battalion were brilliantly successful during the day. They fought their way up a communication-trench, and after hard fighting reached the top of the hill east of Suzanne, which was strongly held by the enemy. After some hand-to-hand fighting, the enemy, who numbered about 500, broke and ran towards Vaux Wood, and were mown down by the 37th Battalion, who turned the German machine-guns as well as their own Lewis guns on to them, killing about 150 of the enemy. A 77 German field-gun was being galloped out of action round the west of Vaux Wood, and the drivers and horses were killed by the 37th Battalion, and the gun was afterwards captured.

The 26th August was fairly quiet in our position near Cappy, and was spent by the men in resting while officers reconnoitred the forward positions of the brigade. The Quartermaster's store was established at Bray, and blankets were issued. The field kitchens also came up to Bray during the afternoon, and the regimental canteen arrived at Yakko Copse with a good supply of biscuits, tinned meats, cake, fruit, cigarettes, and tobacco. The canteen corporal (Cpl. G. Ellis) always displayed great energy and resource in getting supplies when they were most required, and on this occasion excelled all the other battalion optimists by bringing along a supply of boot-polish. But nobody was optimistic enough to ask for any.

During the early morning of August 27 D Company returned to Yakko Copse, as the Brigade had been relieved. We therefore settled down with a pleasant idea of a few days' rest while somebody else continued on, but on the morning of the 28th we came to earth again when we were ordered forward, and at 1.30 p.m. moved to Suzanne, and from there to Vaux Wood, in support of the 38th Battalion, who were to attack Curlu.

Chapter XXIII.

A Further Advance towards Clery—Clery Captured by B Company—A Fine Exploit by an Officer and Non-Commissioned Officer.

AT Vaux Wood we took over the 38th Battalion position, in the valley 500 yards west of Vaux, and established Battalion Headquarters in a dugout 200 yards west of the wood, while the 38th Battalion pushed along the river road to Spur Wood, and then east to Fargny Mill. The 38th Battalion was held up for a time at Cemetery Wood, as the assaulting companies were under heavy machine-gun fire from the village of Curlu. "A" Company of the 40th Battalion was therefore sent forward to keep in touch with the 38th Battalion, and took up a support position at Fargny Mill. The journey of A Company from Vaux Wood to Fargny Mill was particularly unpleasant. The route was south of Vaux Wood, down the cliff into the river road, and this route was very heavily shelled for some time, as it was the only way round the bend in the river, the causeways across the river having been blown in by enemy shelling at several points. At the same time Vaux Wood was shelled, and the regimental transport, which had moved up the valley south-west of the wood, had five animals killed and three wounded.

That evening, at 7 p.m., a party under Lieut. O. E. Lawrence was sent forward to examine and report upon the causeways crossing the Somme. They crossed the one at Vaux with difficulty, as there was more than one gap in it, and proceeded to the causeway south of Curlu. They were unable to get on to it, as it was being swept by machine-gun fire from the bridgehead across the river. It was not until the 38th Battalion had fought their way into Curlu that our party was able to effect a crossing, and reported that with a few long planks the two causeways would permit of foot traffic.

Telephone communication to the forward battalions was very hard to maintain, for the country between Spur Wood and Fargny Mill was constantly and heavily shelled, and the linesmen had a busy time mending broken cables under fire. A fairly quiet night was passed in our support position, but intermittent shelling caused a few casualties. At 9.40 a.m. on the following morning (August 29th) we were ordered by

Brigade to move forward into close support behind the 38th Battalion, who were pushing forward to a line east of the village of Hem, with their right flank on the Somme at Monacu. The battalion moved off at 9.45 a.m., and made use of the causeways reconnoitred during the night before, crossing the river north of Vaux, and recrossing it south of Curlu. We took up a support positon north of Hem, with Battalion Headquarters in a quarry 500 yards north of Hem, A Company on the left in Observation Wood, C and D Companies in the centre in Deconfiture Trench, and B Company on the right in Debandage Trench. At 1 p.m. information was received that a squadron of the 13th Australian Light Horse had gone out on our left front to fill the gap between the 10th and 9th Brigades, the 9th Brigade being somewhere near Maurepas. The 38th Battalion were ordered to move due east, covering the 10th Brigade front, the southern boundary of which was the Somme and the northern boundary a line due east from Curlu. A and C Companies were ordered to move forward on the left of the 38th Battalion and act as a flank guard, and also to establish connection with the 9th Brigade on the left. B and D Companies moved off soon afterwards as support to the 38th Battalion, B Company being south and D Company north of the Curlu-Clery road. Battalion Headquarters was moved to Hem Wood, and word was received from the companies supporting the 38th Battalion that they were in touch with that battalion, who were occupying trenches 800 yards west of Clery. Battalion Headquarters was then moved forward 500 yards east of Howitzer Wood, and telephone communication was established with the companies in front, which enabled a battery that had pulled in near Hem to have its registration observed, and later to carry out a very effective shoot on Clery and the high ground north-east of that village. This shoot was observed for the battery by our battalion observers, who went forward for that purpose.

The first news from companies who were acting as a flank guard was received at 4.20 p.m., stating that they were well forward on the flank of the 38th Battalion, but could not get touch with the 9th Brigade. Machine-guns had been located at Junction Wood, and had been engaged by our artillery. At 4.50 p.m. a further message was received stating that they had made touch with the 9th Brigade (34th Battalion). As everything was now ready for the advance to continue and the assaulting battalions had been in position since 1.30 p.m., an officer of the 40th Battalion was sent forward to enquire the reason for the delay. On account of the explanation he brought back from the battalion in front, the Commanding Officer decided to take the initiative, and push his two remaining companies through the 38th Battalion. This was done, and our patrols, under Lieut. T. Mahoney, who had worked forward to the outskirts of Clery, reported that the enemy was apparently evacuating the village. This information was sent back to the assaulting battalions, who then moved forward to the western outskirts of the town.

At 9 p.m. A and C Companies were in Glands Alley, 1000 yards north-west of Clery, in support to the 38th Battalion, while B and D Companies were west of Clery, also in support to the 38th Battalion. Our positions were fairly heavily shelled during the night.

The next day (August 30) the 37th Battalion were to take over the line from the 38th Battalion and advance to the high ground north of Clery, in conjunction with the 9th Brigade on our left. As A Company of the 37th Battalion had met with heavy resistance north of Clery the previous day, the Brigadier ordered B Company to come under the orders of the 37th Battalion, and this company was given the task of clearing the village of Clery, where there were still many active machine-guns. (See Map 10.)

At 9.30 a.m. an Australian mail was brought up with the rations and distributed, and at 10.45 a.m., when everybody was forgetting the war and buried in the news from home, a message was received from Brigade that a strong counter-attack was developing from the direction of Clery Copse, and that the 40th Battalion would move forward immediately to the valley 500 yards north-east of Clery, and take up a defensive position there in some old trenches. Battalion Headquarters was also established in the valley.

At 11 a.m. B Company (Capt. McIntyre) started to clear up the village of Clery. The village was very badly knocked about, and not a house remained standing. Heaps of bricks showed where houses had once been. The company had been organised into two platoons, one taking the northern half and the other the southern half. Before going far through the heaps of bricks the machine-gun and rifle fire from the east end of the village became very heavy, and the company took cover while the scouts crept forward to find the exact location of the opposition. Two of the scouts, No. 7535, L/Cpl. E. V. Reardon, and No. 2125, Pte. D. R. Oates, crawled right through the village and located an enemy strong point, consisting of a trench about 50 yards long, containing dugouts and machine-guns, on the eastern side of the village, on the western side of the road that crosses the Somme at that point. This was reported to the Company Commander, and, under cover of a bombardment obtained from an English battery who had a forward observing officer with B Company, the two platoons moved forward. This English officer rendered very valuable assistance, and his bravery during the advance was conspicuous. Unfortunately he was killed shortly after we captured the village.

Immediately the bombardment opened the enemy put up the S.O.S., and their barrage came down in front of B Company. B Company worked through it, but the right platoon, under Lieut. R. C. Walters, was held up by heavy machine-gun fire, and the platoon commander severely wounded. The left platoon, under Lieut. Rattray, continued on by taking advantage of all available cover, and got within 100 yards of the strong-point. A Lewis gun was pushed out on each flank, and under cover of the fire of these guns the place was rushed. The fight with bombs lasted about a minute, and the enemy surrendered with 3 machine-guns and 59 prisoners, which was more than the total strength of our company. Among the prisoners was an officer who stated that he was Commandant of Clery. He seemed very depressed, and remarked several times in French that his reputation would now be quite gone. He seemed so crestfallen that someone assured him that he had put up a great fight, at which he brightened visibly and wore a "beaten-but-not-disgraced" air.

Immediately beyond the road at the captured strong-point were several communication trenches, in which were numbers of the enemy. They were at once fired on, and very heavy casualties inflicted, as our fire swept right down these trenches. About 20 yards beyond the strong-point the ground sloped away, and over this bank appeared a party of about 80 of the enemy advancing to attack. They were dispersed in an unusual and gallant manner by No. 2067, L/Cpl. J. Cox. Unable to get a good field of fire for his gun on the parapet of the strong-point, this man stood on the parapet with his Lewis gun to his shoulder. Being a man of great physical proportions and corresponding strength, he was able to use the Lewis gun like a rifle, and pump lead into the enemy advancing. Those who were able broke and ran back. The ground to the south-east of the village was crossed with old trenches, which seemed to be all occupied by the enemy, and B Company continued sniping actively with good results.

The objective had been gained at about 2 p.m., and at 3 p.m. B Company (whose strength was now under 40) were reinforced by A Company (Lieut. C. W. Game), in order to meet any counter-attack in force. As soon as they arrived Lieut S. S. McMillan and No. 2079, Cpl. S. E. Dale, went forward to reconnoitre the ground with a view to pushing on a little further, and in so doing provided one of the many examples of initiative, resource, and bravery which played so big a part in driving the enemy back with a few men, and at comparatively little cost in valuable lives. This officer and N.C.O. crawled out among the shell-holes to the road junction 400 yards east of the village. About 100 yards away on the right they saw a machine-gun in a shell-hole which was firing at Clery. The machine-gunners also saw them, and swung their gun round to fire at them, but they jumped into a trench which led towards the machine-gun. They got on the flank of it, about 20 yards away, and waited till it opened fire again on Clery, when Cpl. Dale threw a bomb into the post, and Lieut. McMillan rushed it. He shot two of the crew with his revolver, and the remaining eight surrendered with their gun, and were sent back to Clery. After looking about for a time Lieut. McMillan saw another post with a machine-gun about 150 yards further to the left, and crawled from shell-hole to shell-hole towards it. Both officer and N.C.O. stood up and fired a shot each, and two of the enemy dropped, while the remaining three ran for the nearest trench. In taking this gun they were fired on by another gun about 50 yards on their left. They worked towards it, and at the same time another of A Company's scouts, who was watching the proceedings from a distance, decided to take a hand, and made towards it from the opposite direction. This was getting on the nerves of the enemy machine-gunners, who left their gun and bolted. As there did not appear to be any more machine-guns in the vicinity they went back, and A Company came forward and established posts 300 yards east of the village, from where with their own and captured guns, they harassed the enemy on the higher ground towards the Canal du Nord.

Chapter XXIV.

D Company Attack at Clery Copse.

MEANWHILE D Company and a company of the 37th Battalion had been ordered to take Clery Copse. The hour fixed was 2 p.m., and each company had to advance from the valley and move up a different communication trench to the top of the hill on which was Clery Copse. The plan was to reach Mahoney Trench, which ran from north to south along the top of the ridge, and from this trench they could reach the copse. It was expected that heavy resistance would be met with, as the enemy had been collecting near Clery Copse during the morning, apparently in preparation for a counter-attack. Very strong resistance was met with by D Company, and although they got on to the ridge, any hope of holding it was broken by the fact that the company of the 37th Battalion did not attack with them. At the last moment, at 1.50 p.m., instructions were received from Brigade that D Company of the 40th Battalion would attack alone, while the company of the 37th Battalion protected D Company's left flank. There was no time to pass on the information and during operations a large part of D Company, and some at least of the 37th believed that the original plan was being carried out. (See Map 10.)

At 2 p.m. D Company (Lieut. T. G. Cranswick, D.C.M.) advanced up the trench marked on the map as Cranswick Trench. Lieuts. T. Mahoney and O. E. Lawrence went ahead of the company and reconnoitred within 50 yards of Mahoney Trench, where they met several of the enemy and exchanged shots with them. They returned and reported, and the company moved on. This trench was very shallow, and the company was soon fired on from the trenches on the top of the hill. Sniping was also very active from the shell-holes on both sides of Cranswick Trench. These shell-holes were two years old, and among them was a fine crop of weeds about two feet high, which afforded good cover for the enemy. Several of our men who put their rifles or Lewis guns over the trench to return the fire were either killed or wounded before firing a shot. After heavy opposition and several casualties the company at last reached Mahoney Trench. Here a Lewis gun team was sent a few yards along to the left of Mahoney Trench to point B, to cover the rear until the expected arrival of the company of the 37th Battalion. Lieut. O. E. Lawrence went back into the valley to see what had happened to this company, and was informed by the officer commanding that they were unable to advance. D Company pushed up Mahoney Trench towards Clery Copse, under very heavy fire from all sides. A party of the enemy came out of shell-holes from near point D with their hands up, and advanced towards the trench. A few yards from it they dropped down as a machine gun opened fire from behind them into the back of D Company as they were going up Mahoney Trench. This party of the enemy may have intended to surrender, and dropped from force of habit when the machine-gun opened. On the other hand, it may have been a dirty plan, and this is believed, because the enemy machine gun had got into a singularly favourable position, and because it is hardly likely that anybody would want to surrender to D Company seeing that they were almost surrounded, and fighting against big odds. However, the machine gun was put out of action by the prompt action of No. 2144, Pte. A. J. Sutton, who turned his Lewis gun on to it at close range. There were several gaps in Mahoney Trench, and into these gaps the enemy fired as our men passed through them. Lieut. T. Mahoney, while trying to get past one of these gaps, was killed by a machine gun bullet, and Lieut. Cranswick was very badly wounded while firing at an enemy sniper close to the trench. Our casualties were very heavy, and the position of the company precarious. The enemy were closing in on all sides, and the only remaining officer, Lieut. O. E. Lawrence, decided to try to withdraw. The withdrawal was carried out with great skill and coolness. The unwounded carried out the wounded. No. 857, Sgt. E. A. Hutchinson, organised the evacuation of the wounded, while the enemy was kept back under the direction of Lieut. Lawrence, by No. 834, Sgt. W. N. Grey, No. 955, Cpl. L. R. Turner, No. 979, Sgt. H. V. Buchanan, and No. 2315, Pte. C. W. Connors, who kept up heavy Lewis gun fire and inflicted severe casualties on the enemy, who realised that we had our backs against the wall, and was pushing up to cut us off. As the covering party got a safe distance down Cranswick Trench the enemy was seen to rush the top of this trench and Mahoney Trench. Two men had been left behind and were captured, as they had become detached from the rest of the company just before the withdrawal, and were overlooked. These men were No. 3608, Cpl. K. C. Masterman, who had gone back to try to get the body of Lieut. Mahoney, and No. 850, L.-Cpl. F. J. Heron, who also went back thinking a wounded comrade was there.

These two prisoners, after repatriation from Germany, gave interesting details of the fight from their point of view. L.-Cpl. Heron was interrogated by a German officer, who said to him, "You belong to the 40th Battalion. Colonel Lord is your commanding officer. The 37th Battalion is on your left. What is the strength of your company?" Being a good soldier, and not wishing to disclose the true position as regards our strength, L.-Cpl. Heron told him the strength was 120, to which the officer replied, "That's a lie. It is only 30." As a matter of fact it was under 40. As we had lost no prisoners for over six months, this information could not have been obtained from anyone in the 40th Battalion. The statement of Cpl. Masterman was as follows:—" At 2 p.m. D Company was waiting in the communication trench, Lieut. Cranswick in front, with Lieut. Mahoney, myself, and two bayonet men. We soon came to a side trench on the left, and as this flank was not covered Lieut. Cranswick left me to detach the rear Lewis gun team, and hold this corner, keeping watch for attempts to surround us from the left (corner marked A). By this time machine-gun fire from the flank and left front was sweeping the flat ground, through which our trench ran, machine-gun bullets passing just above ground level. There were dead Germans between A and B and a German abandoned machine-gun post at B. This post had retired with their gun, and were firing towards B from the north-east. The main party near E were having sharp fighting, and from B I could see wounded passing back through A, among them Lieut. Cranswick. We were trying to locate and silence a machine gun in front, when a message came back to say the main party wanted help, and I was to join them with the Lewis gun *via* B and D, a shallow piece of roughly-made trench. I brought my team to D, and found they were holding that point with only about 12 men, and the trench contained several of our killed and wounded. They were almost out of Lewis gun ammunition. Pte. J. E. Rhodes was shot while firing his Lewis gun as I arrived. I got my team into action, and gave magazines to the other guns, and they went on firing. Sgt. Grey pointed out the body of Lieut. Mahoney, who was lying at E, where he had gone forward and been hit in the head. We went forward and picked the body up. Sgt. Grey went first with the body, and at F the mess-tin on my back was riddled with bullets from our gun at D. I looked up to call to them to fire higher, and saw that they were firing at some Germans running towards us. I called Sgt. Grey's attention to them, and we put the body down and ran for rifles. Sgt. Grey joined the rest near D, and I seized a rifle I saw and began firing from where I was. I put several rounds into the enemy, then tried to reload, but the rifle jambed, so I dropped it and ran towards D for another, when several stick grenades fell in front of me, so I jumped out of the trench before they went off and ran to a big shell-hole I saw near the trench. As I got into it another grenade fell on the side of it, and I ducked down to the bottom, expecting to be smashed up thoroughly. It went off, and all I got was a piece in the arm. I looked up into the barrel of a revolver held by an officer of apparently high rank. I got an impression of junior officers behind him, and there were some men who ran up to bayonet me, but the officer shouted angrily at them, and kept them back, detailing two of them to take me to headquarters. Crossing a stretch of open field we went down a slope to a row of dugouts, and my captors pointed out a "Kamarad," who was L.-Cpl. Heron. . . . . . They asked for our papers, letters, &c., but did not search us. We were sent further back to some more officers, who tried in rather inadequate English to ask questions. The points they wanted to know were—(i) Did we know they were going to attack? (ii) Were there Americans in the line, and how many? (iii) Whether England was really starving as a result of the submarine campaign? I had not realised till then that it was a definitely planned counter-attack we had met. I heard somebody say something about withdrawing, but was too busy firing to take much notice of what was said, and that is how I, being round a corner, came to be left. . . . . We went straight on to Villers Faucon *via* Aizecourt, and saw nothing behind the front line for 15 kilometres, except desolate fields, and the villages we passed seemed deserted. At Villers Faucon an interpreter examined us, and employed rather obvious devices to try and get information. The great point that they were after was the whereabouts of the 38th Battalion during our advance on the 28th and 29th August. Was it on our left or right? We left them none the wiser." . . . . .

Though we failed to get the copse and the ridge on that day, owing to the superiority of the enemy's numbers, there is no doubt that our attack upset his planned counter-attack by meeting it. The enemy was holding the hill very strongly, and was massing his troops there for an attack which did not develop. The following day, when the 10th Brigade took the ridge, fully 300 German packs were found round Clery Copse, and 200 prisoners were taken in the vicinity. During the night 30th-31st August C and D Companies remained in the valley north of Clery, while A and B continued to hold their posts east of Clery until relieved by the 5th Brigade during that night. The casualties in D Company were so heavy that the commanding officer decided to amalgamate C and D Companies for further offensive action.

During the reorganisation that night for a further attack the following morning, a good supply of ammunition, bombs, filled Lewis gun magazines, flares, &c., were brought forward by the battalion supply officer (Lieut. V. C. Smith), who had worked under difficult conditions during those days of fighting, in co-operation with the regimental transport. In spite of the fact that we had advanced so far beyond our dumps and supplies, he always had a plentiful supply close behind on wheels. The value of this work can never be over-estimated. The battalion transport had a very strenuous time getting forward with ammunition, hot food, and rations, and that night did not reach Clery without several casualties among men and horses from shell-fire. The way our transport used to get forward behind the battalion excited the envy of other units, particularly when we were having hot stew and they were eating their iron rations. It seemed to be a point of honour with the transport officers, N.C.O.'s, and men, never to leave us short of food and supplies while human endurance could deliver it over the shell-swept roads behind us.

Chapter XXV.

A Further Attack East of Clery—Exciting Events on the Mt. St. Quentin-Bouchavesnes Road—Back to Reserve at Hem.

HE following day (31st August) was one of the most momentous of our offensive. On it began the successful attack on the last hold the enemy had on the old Somme defences, which resulted in a retreat while fighting a rearguard action to his last hope, the Hindenburg line. That day the 2nd Australian Division attacked Mt. St. Quentin, and after a battle which swayed for 24 hours captured Mt. St. Quentin the following day. The 3rd Australian Division attacked on the left of the 2nd Australian Division, with the 9th Brigade on the left and the 10th Brigade on the right. The boundary between the 10th Brigade and the 5th Brigade was a line due east of Clery to the junction of the Mt. St. Quentin-Bouchavesnes-road with the uncompleted Canal du Nord at Feuillaucourt. The 10th Brigade attacked with the 38th Battalion on the right, supported by the 40th Battalion, and the 39th Battalion on the left, supported by the 37th Battalion. The dispositions of the 40th Battalion were—the amalgamated C and D Company (Lieut. M. H. O. Whitaker) in front, and A Company (Lieut. C. W. Game) and B Company (Lieut. J. S. Rattray) behind.

At 5 a.m. the brigade went forward behind the artillery barrage. Clery Copse was taken by the 38th Battalion in the first objective, and after passing beyond it, it was seen that the 38th Battalion was making too far to the south, so the commanding officer directed C-D Company to fill the gap between the 38th and 39th Battalions and take Berlin Wood. C-D Company took the wood, with 1 machine gun and 45 prisoners, who did not offer much resistance, and just beyond the wood a small party under No. 834, Sgt. W. N. Grey, captured two minenwerfer with the two crews of 12 men. There was by this time a gap of about 800 yards between the 38th and 39th Battalions, and C-D Company advanced on the left of the 38th Battalion to their objective, and occupied part of Perkly Trench and Inferno Trench, about 800 yards west of the Mt. St. Quentin-Bouchavesnes-road. From here the enemy could be seen beyond the road moving forward in great numbers, and on our left flank, where the gap of several hundred yards existed he was heard bombing down Zombo Trench towards us. No. 3016, Pte. F. D. Brock, was on the left flank of the company and collected a large supply of bombs in readiness. As a large party of the enemy appeared he dropped several bombs among them and caused some casualties. They retaliated with stick bombs, and he threw some more of his, and followed it up by rushing the enemy party, who by this time were badly shaken. The enemy ran back up the trench, and a few minutes later were seen making for the road, and our Lewis gunners and riflemen had some busy moments.

At 9 a.m. the Commanding Officer, who was at the battalion command post on the ridge about 300 yards north-east of Clery Copse, saw the enemy moving forward in great numbers across the road about 300 yards west of Bouchavesnes. This gave the impression of a counter-attack, and he directed A and B Companies, who were still in support west of Berlin Wood behind the 38th Battalion, to move to the left and occupy part of the gap between the 38th and 39th Battalions. B Company were then placed on the left of Gassave Alley in Maoet Trench, while A Company took up a position in the same trench on the right of Gassave Alley. Communication was obtained with the 38th and 39th Battalions, and to fill the gap which still existed on our left flank, the support company of the 39th Battalion was brought forward. Later in the morning C-D Company was withdrawn to a support position east of Berlin Wood.

The Commanding Officer and his staff moved forward 800 yards in spite of hostile sniping and artillery fire. With him were also two forward observing officers of the Australian Artillery, Major H. Glover, D.S.O., 26th Battery, and Capt. B. L. Davies, M.C., 25th Battery. They established a command post on top of the ridge at Maoet Trench. This position commanded a good view of the ground between us and the Mt. St. Quentin-Bouchavesnes-road and the ground beyond the road. On the eastern side of the road great numbers of the enemy could be seen moving about and bringing machine guns forward. About 100 yards east of the road the ground slopes away into a steep valley, which was an ideal place for the concentration of counter-attack troops. Thanks to good telephone communication, which had been laid by the signallers as we advanced, the artillery officers at the command post were able to put down a destructive shoot on and beyond the Mt. St. Quentin-Bouchavesnes-road. The artillery officers also enjoyed themselves, in what was new for them, the novel experience of sniping the enemy with rifles, as he moved about

the road 700 yards away. During this bombardment A and
B Companies were dribbled forward into Zombo Trench, as a
better place from which to advance. In getting there it was
necessary to go over 150 yards of open ground. This was accomplished under very heavy machine-gun fire from the road, by
working forward in small parties.

At 12.30 p.m. the brigade was apparently ready to go forward again, but Capt. McIntyre, who was acting as liason
officer between us and the 38th Battalion, whom we were supposed to be supporting, reported that the 38th Battalion were
not prepared to go forward, so the C.O. decided to push A
and B Companies on to the Mt. St. Quentin-Bouchavesnes-
road, and to dislodge the enemy from his favourable position
there. (See Map 10.)

At 1.30 p.m. the Acting O.C. of B Company (Lieut J. S.
Rattray) moved his company down the trench marked as
Jackson Trench into the valley. The enemy was watching
this trench closely, and had machine-guns trained on to
the gaps in it, which he swept at any sign of movement
there. At the same time A Company (Lieut. C. W. Game)
moved down the remains of an old trench on the right of B
Company, and reached the valley. This journey had taken A
Company some time, and by the time they reached the valley
B Company had advanced beyond it. The movement forward
had been observed, and Zombo Trench was heavily shelled by
the enemy. The valley which B Company had now reached
was dead ground, and B Company waited there for A Company
to move up on their flank. Here they were joined by the
battalion signalling officer (Lieut. B. Jackson). This officer,
being a man of much enterprise and many parts, decided that
signalling was a dreary occupation, and his soul yearned for
higher things; and B Company being short of officers, he
decided to take a hand. Accordingly B Company, whose
strength was 1 officer and 30 other ranks, was split up into
two equal parties, one under Lieut. Jackson and the other
under Lieut. Rattray. The ground in front was crossed with
trenches, and it was decided not to wait for A Company, but
to push up different trenches towards the road. Accordingly
Lieut. Rattray took his party across to Rattray Trench, and
moved up it, while Lieut. Jackson moved along the trench
that bears his name. Both parties were surprised at running
into each other a few minutes later at point A, but they pushed
up the same trench in two separate parties. Shortly afterwards A Company came up the valley into Jackson Trench,
and advanced towards the road by McMillan Trench. In doing

so they crossed the trench that B Company had just passed, without knowing it, and got on to the left of B Company instead of being, as they thought, on the right. Throughout the rest of the operation each company thought that the other was lost, and that they were operating alone.

The two parties of B Company got forward within 50 yards of the road, and the officers made a cautious survey of the ground in front. At the point where Jackson Trench joined the road, and extending about 50 yards to the left of that point, was a high bank on the western side of the road. This bank appeared to be occupied by the enemy, as voices could be heard behind it, and the muzzle of a machine gun could be seen in an emplacement on the right end of it. It was decided that Lieut. Jackson and his party would rush the left end of the bank, and Lieut. Rattray and his party would take the right end of the bank. Both parties moved up the trench a few yards, and Lieut. Jackson, who was in front, saw a German in the trench about 15 yards ahead. He fired, and the German dropped. At the sound of the shot a row of heads appeared above the bank in the road, and some of the owners paid the price of not being on the look out. One of our Lewis guns swept the top of the bank, and all the heads disappeared, some undoubtedly damaged. The machine gunner, who had also looked up, was shot through the head by one of our riflemen, and fell forward over his gun. The enemy scattered behind the bank and threw showers of bombs towards Jackson Trench. Lieut. Jackson got out of the trench and crawled for some distance to the left, he then signalled to his party to follow him, and as they got out of the trench and rushed towards the left edge of the bank, Lieut. Rattray rushed to the right edge, thus attacking the enemy strong-point from both sides. A sharp bomb and bayonet fight took place on the road, during which we inflicted severe casualties, as our men fought with great determination and dash against superior numbers of the enemy, some of whom eventually ran, while the remainder surrendered. About 30 of the enemy were killed and 1 officer and 33 other ranks of the Prussian Guard were sent back. A large percentage of the prisoners wore the ribbon of the Iron Cross.

The bank on the road contained several dugouts and a machine-gun position. One of the dugouts was connected up by telephone, and apparently at the sign of our attack the enemy had communicated with his artillery, and he put a barrage down about 100 yards west of the road. A Company, on the left, who had not yet reached the road, suffered heavily from this shelling. While the dugouts were being cleared the Lewis guns had been placed on the opposite bank, ready to deal with any local counter-attack. At the sound of the bombing most of the enemy beyond the road had gone back about 100 yards to the safety of the valley, and suddenly a row of about 20 of them appeared at a point 40 yards in front where the ground dropped away into the valley. Immediately they appeared our two Lewis guns opened, and swept the line of the enemy, who fell killed or wounded over the bank into the valley.

B Company then crossed the road and got into the trench, which is a continuation of Jackson Trench on the eastern side of the road. By this time the enemy probably thought that the whole of the A.I.F. was coming, and much agitation could be seen in the trenches on the far side of the valley. Our Lewis guns continued to fire at the enemy in the distance, and after waiting there a quarter of an hour the enemy could be seen working forward along the trench on our flanks, having apparently realised the extent of our impudence. His artillery was firing at point-blank range on to the road, and his machine-guns were sweeping our position, which made it almost impossible for our Lewis gunners and riflemen to get their heads up to fire. The enemy could also be seen crossing the road at Feuillaucourt towards our line, where the 5th Brigade had been held up for a time. Lieut. Rattray therefore decided to withdraw, and take up a defensive position west of the road. At 4 p.m. this was done, and B Company occupied a shell-hole position about 80 yards from the road, where they were reinforced by a platoon of A Company.

It was unfortunate that A and B Companies were unable to see each other and realise what they were both doing, but the reason why there was no co-operation in their separate efforts was that a small ridge ran between the trenches up which they advanced. The whole operation could be seen from the battalion command post, and the tremendous odds against each company was realised better by the people there than by the companies themselves. It was considered that the positions could be maintained if the other battalions in the brigade would move forward in accordance with the orders as we understood them, and every assistance was given us by the artillery officers at the command post by turning their batteries on to the enemy in the valley beyond the road and the ground beyond the valley.

A Company had pushed up McMillan Trench about 20 minutes after B Company had moved up their trench. They were fired on by machine guns from the direction of Bouchavesnes, and when about 100 yards from the road the enemy put down a fairly heavy bombardment west of the road, and caused several casualties and a good deal of delay. As they could not see B Company, and both flanks appeared to be in the air, it was decided not to risk the whole company in making a reconnaissance, but that one platoon would remain in a defensive position about 150 yards west of the road, while Lieut. S. S. S. McMillan and his platoon would push forward and test the enemy's strength. Lieut. McMillan and his party then moved on to within 20 yards of the road, but by this time B Company had withdrawn to the west of the road and the enemy had come forward again. So when the platoon of A Company reached that point they were met by a shower of bombs from the opposite side of the road. These bombs were particularly well directed, and our casualties were fairly heavy. The Lewis gunners and riflemen got out of the trench and opened fire on the enemy across the road about 25 yards away. This fire had the effect of clearing the enemy off the bank on the opposite side of the road, but they got behind the bank and continued to throw bombs at our party, while enemy machine guns opened from our left flank towards Bouchavesnes. This forced our party to put aside their Lewis guns and rifles and resort to bombs, which drove the enemy back from behind the bank opposite. By this time the party was reduced to a total strength of six, and Lieut. McMillan and No. 254, Cpl. A. Rooney, crawled across the road to see the position with a view to bringing up the rest of the company. The sight they saw made it quite evident that the job was a brigade and not a platoon affair, for in the trenches beyond the road were hundreds of the enemy, and in the hollow on the left, about 200 yards away, were several groups with German officers addressing them, as if explaining the details of an intended operation. Lieut. McMillan and Cpl. Rooney got back across the road and joined the rest of A Company, who by this time had established communication with B Company. B Company had already sent back a message to the battalion command post reporting the enemy concentration east of the road, and at 5.30 p.m. the two companies were withdrawn back to Zombo Trench, while a heavy artillery bombardment was put down on the enemy concentration. This bombardment, which was intense, lasted for over an hour, and no doubt prevented the development of the counter-attack. At about 7.30 p.m. we received orders that the whole brigade would advance to the road, and the 40th Battalion again went forward and occupied the position which we had reached during the afternoon.

During the remainder of the night our position was shelled intermittently, but everybody was past caring. For four days the battalion had had neither rest nor sleep, and had almost reached the stage of complete exhaustion. When the excitement of the day had worn off, absolute physical weariness prevailed, which almost amounted to collapse. Some did collapse, and fell forward asleep half out of their trenches and shell-holes, with their rifles still in their hands, while others whose mental vigour was sufficient for them to hold out against physical exhaustion stood beside the sleeping ones, and with eyes red and sore from lack of sleep looked towards the enemy. During the night several enemy parties came out into the road and threw bombs towards our position, and on one occasion rushed towards our posts, but a burst of fire from a Lewis gun was sufficient to send them back at the double. The enemy appeared to be badly rattled, and his moral was poor.

About 4 a.m. on the morning of the 1st September we moved back as the 11th Brigade, who were to continue the advance at daylight, moved into our position, and we went back over the ground won during the last few days to Hem.

As we passed the valley north of Clery the noise from our artillery was deafening. Batteries with guns of all calibres had pulled into the valley, and were providing a barrage for the advance by the 11th Brigade and part of the 2nd Australian Division.

At Hem the Quartermaster had everything ready to make up a good reception. A hot meal was waiting and blankets were laid out under bivouac shelters and in dugouts. A change of underclothing was issued to everybody, and all ranks turned in and slept the round of the clock.

Our casualties during the battle of Bapaume, from August 24th to August 31st, were 1 officer and 29 other ranks killed, and 6 officers and 123 other ranks wounded.

The Commander-in-Chief sums up the result of the Battle of Baupaume as follows :—

" The 1st September marks the close of the second stage in the British offensive. Having in the first stage freed Amiens by our brilliant success east of that town, in the second stage the troops of the 3rd and 4th Armies, comprising 23 divisions, by skilful leading, hard fighting, and relentless and unremitting pursuit, in ten days had driven 35 German divisions from one side of the old Somme battlefield to the other, thereby turning the line of the River Somme. In so doing they had inflicted upon the enemy the heaviest losses in killed and wounded, and had taken from him over 34,000 prisoners and 270 guns."

As far as the 40th Battalion is concerned, and the same probably applies to all battalions of the Australian Corps, the only addition that might be made to "skilful leading, hard fighting, and relentless and unremitting pursuit" is the factor of "colossal impudence." The manner in which we continued pushing back superior forces of the enemy day after day was remarkable. The last two days' heavy fighting by the 40th Battalion was with companies reduced to a strength of below 40, and four companies were reduced to three, and four platoons to two. We were meeting fresh troops, who were being thrown in to stop us, and still we kept on advancing. But even our impudence would not have availed much without our magnificent artillery, who followed up behind us, engaging the enemy as he appeared, and backing the infantry up in every possible way.

NOTE.—The fighting of these two days (pp. 170-185) is a good example of the operations which miss official record. They are carried out largely on the initiative of battalion and company commanders, and possibly the battalion is too occupied or too tired to report to brigade at the time more than the bare results. Corps and army records are consequently likely to overlook or misrepresent them. The battalion itself would look back at its work on these two days with perhaps more satisfaction than at any others in its history. But Mr. F. M. Cutlack, the Australian war correspondent, writing from information supplied by "brigade and divisional staff officers," dismisses the narrative of the last fifteen pages in a couple of lines, though he devotes a page elsewhere to a small outpost affair of the 40th, which happened to be undertaken by direction of brigade, and was accordingly reported in great detail. Further, he does not allow that the battalion on the 31st at any time reached its objective—the Bouchavesnes-road. ("The Australians," 1918, p. 282.)

The Fourth Army official narrative of the "hundred days" is still worse, for on the elaborate map illustrating the fighting of 31st August, it leaves the 40th Battalion stationary all day back at Clery, and in the text records the unqualified failure of the 10th Brigade even to get near its objective. ("Story of the 4th Army," Map 6, and p. 100.)

Chapter XXVI.

The Advance from Roisel towards Hesbecourt — Resting at Redwood — Failure of the Enemy's Night Bombing.

N September 2nd everybody took the opportunity of a bathe in the Somme. The weather was fine, and the most was made of it for bathing and recreation, which, combined with sunshine, is a fine cure for nerves frayed to a raw edge by successive days of stiff fighting. That day the Commanding Officer left the battalion to take command of the 10th Brigade, during the absence of the Brigadier, and Major Robertson of the 37th Battalion took over the 40th Battalion temporarily in the absence of Major Payne (wounded) and Major Giblin (wounded).

On September 3rd we moved across the Somme, between the river and the canal, to La Grenouillere where there was better accommodation in the shape of a camp of German hutments. On the 5th September orders were received to prepare to move forward to the vicinity of Berlin Wood. At 6.30 p.m. we moved off through a very heavy thunderstorm, and arrived at Berlin Wood at 9 p.m., where the night was spent. This bivouac area was very desolate, and there was not a stick of wood or material to help make it comfortable. Next day we remained there under orders to move at short notice, while officers went forward and reconnoitred the position of the 11th Brigade, who had reached Tincourt, and were still pushing the enemy rearguard back. The following day, September 7th, we still rested, and that evening orders were received that we would move forward to Buire Wood next day. At 6 a.m. on the 8th we left Berlin Wood, and arrived at Buire Wood, about 1500 yards north-west of Tincourt. At 9.30 a.m. reconnoitring parties went on to the position held by the 37th and 38th Battalions, which was an outpost line 1200 yards east of Roisel, where they were in touch with the enemy. At 4 p.m. orders were received that the 40th Battalion would move through the 38th Battalion in conjunction with the 39th Battalion on our right, who would move through the 37th Battalion, and would take up a position with a frontage of 1500 yards in the German trenches immediately east of the line of Haut Woods and Hesbecourt (L 7 c and d and L 13

a and c), and at right angles to the trench known as the
Hargicourt Switch (right boundary at L 13 c 9 1 and left
boundary the grid line east and west through L 7 central).

At 6.30 p.m. we left Buire Wood and moved across country
in artillery formation to the factory on the eastern outskirts
of Roisel, arriving there at 9 p.m., where we were met by the
Lewis gun limbers which had come by road. After getting our
Lewis guns and magazines we moved to some banks 600 yards
north-east of Roisel (K 11 c), where we rested till 1 a.m.,
when we again moved forward in artillery formation with
patrols in front. We passed through the outpost line of the
38th Battalion, and from there were subjected to light shelling,
but reached our objective shortly before daylight without any
opposition.

Companies took up positions in the trench system, with A
Company on the right, C in the centre, and D Company on
the left, with B Company in support in a cutting 700 yards
west of Haut Woods. Touch was obtained with the 39th Battalion, whose left post was about 700 yards south of Hesbecourt, and also with the 16th Devons, whose right post was
800 yards on our left. As there was a large gap here we
extended our front for about 400 yards further north.

Enemy movement could be seen on the ridge about 2000 yards
in front, and when our 'planes went across our line, they were
fired on by numerous machine-guns immediately in front of
us, indicating that the enemy was hoping to delay our advance
to the Hindenburg line as long as possible by the lavish use
of machine-guns. The day was fairly quiet, with little shelling, and most of the activity was in the air. At night our
patrols pushed out. The first patrol was from our right post
in Hesbecourt. They went forward along the road for about
250 yards, and saw an enemy patrol of about 12 men advancing towards them. When the enemy was about 20 yards away
they fired. The enemy returned the fire and ran, wounding
No. 3253, Sgt. G. R. Gourlay, the patrol leader. Our party
then returned to our line for a Lewis gun, realising that the
enemy was strongly resisting any attempt at penetration by
patrols. At 2.30 a.m. a patrol went out from the centre of
our front, and had only gone about 100 yards when they were
bombed by a party of the enemy, who were lying up in shellholes. Two of our patrol were wounded and one killed, and
the rest of the patrol returned to our lines, was reinforced,
and went out again, but failed to locate the enemy before
daylight.

At 9 a.m. on the 10th September orders were received from
Brigade that our scouts would move forward at once and locate

the enemy posts. Two scouts from A Company went out 400 yards and were fired on from a post 500 yards east of our lines. Three scouts of C Company also pushed out and were fired on from the same post, which was definitely located just south of the Hargicourt Switch. Four scouts of D Company under Sgt. V. N. Buchanan, also moved forward along the Hargicourt Switch line for 1000 yards, and came back through the enemy outpost line. They located several posts, and reported large numbers of the enemy to be working between Templeux and Hargicourt. The D Company scouts were fired on from a post 700 yards east of Hesbecourt.

During the day there was an increase in the enemy shelling, but most of it fell behind our lines. We were advised that the 10th Brigade would be relieved by the 1st Brigade that night, and during the day several advance parties of the 4th Battalion moved into our line. At 6 p.m. this battalion pushed posts out into the Hargicourt Switch. Their patrols also went out before dark, but were forced by machine-gun fire to come back. At 9 p.m. the relief was complete, and we moved out past Roisel and across country for about 6 miles to Red Wood, just south of Driencourt, where shelters had been erected by the "details" of the battalion, and a hot meal was waiting.

Rain fell all the next day (September 11th), and the day was spent in improving "bivvies." The next day the weather was fine, and remained so for several days, which resulted in the battalion spending one of the pleasantest holidays we had in France. Red Wood was a fine spot, and the weather was glorious. Sports, cricket and football matches, and open-air concerts were held, and never were our spirits so high. It was realised that after a hard spring and summer campaign the result of the war was no longer in doubt, and even the pessimists saw visions of the end. Even the enemy bombing 'planes, which for over a year had been a continual annoyance to us, were brought to a state of inactivity by the use of a new and effective method. These bombing 'planes came over as usual and "laid their eggs" round our area, but the counter-measures surprised them as well as us. Numbers of searchlights had been set up, and when the big Gothas came over, instead of being met with the usual ineffective "Archies," our searchlights concentrated on one, and from above our fighting 'planes, which were waiting somewhere up towards the stars, swooped down like hawks, and sent streams of phosphorescent bullets into the now helpless Gothas. In our vicinity, on the first night of this innovation, no less than three Gothas crashed in flames, and as each one came down loud cheers went up from all the bivouac areas and artillery and transport lines for miles. The next night the enemy had another try, and more Gothas crashed, amid more cheers; and during the remainder of the stay at Red Wood we were not worried by night-bombing.

On the 21st September the commanding officer returned from brigade, and took over command of the battalion again. Sports, cricket, and football were continued, with very little military training, except practice in keeping communications with aeroplanes during an attack, and also attack practices with tanks.

On the 27th September the battalion was ordered to be ready to move at short notice. A muster parade was called during the morning, and the commanding officer, after telling us that we were to take part in the attack on the Hindenburg line, announced that Sgt. P. C. Statton, M.M., had been awarded the Victoria Cross, at which there was great enthusiasm and rejoicing, and the regimental band broke all previous records with their impromptu musical programme. Although there was much gladness among us all, among the older members of the unit there was just an undercurrent of sadness, when the occasion naturally sent our thoughts back a year to the other gallant Victoria Cross winner, Sgt. Lewis McGee, who never came back out of the sodden waste of mud and shell-holes in front of Passchendaele.

Chapter XXVII.

The Attack on the Hindenburg Line, 29th September, 1918.

THE 29th September was the day of the attack by the 4th Army on the Hindenburg Line. The attack was on a frontage of 12 miles, between Holnon and Vendhuille. The Hindenburg Line is described by the Commander-in-Chief as follows:—

" Between St. Quentin and the village of Bantouzelle the principal defences of the Hindenburg Line lie sometimes to the west, but more generally to the east, of the Scheldt Canal. The canal does not appear to have been organised as the enemy's main line of resistance, but rather as an integral part of a deep defensive system, the outstanding characteristic of which was the skill with which it was sited so as to deny us effective artillery positions from which to attack it. The chief *role* of the canal was that of affording cover to resting troops, and to the garrisons of the main defensive trench lines during a bombardment. To this end the canal lent itself admirably, and the fullest use was made by the enemy of its possibilities.

" The general configuration of the ground through which this sector of the canal runs produces deep cuttings of a depth in places of some 60 feet, while between Bellicourt and the neighbourhood of Vendhuille the canal passes through a tunnel for 6000 yards. In the side of the cutting the enemy had constructed numerous tunnelled dugouts and concrete shelters. Along the top of them he had concealed well-sited concrete or armoured machine-gun emplacements. The tunnel itself was used to provide living accommodation for troops, and was connected by shafts with the trenches above.

" On the western side of the canal, south of Bellicourt, two thoroughly organised and extremely heavily wired lines of continuous trench ran roughly parallel to the canal, at average distances from it of 2000 and 1000 yards respectively. Except in the tunnel sector the double line of trenches known as the Hindenburg Line proper lies immediately east of the canal, and is linked up by numerous communication trenches with the trench lines west of it.

" Besides these main features, numerous other trench lines, switch trenches, and communication trenches, for the most part heavily wired, had been constructed at various points to meet local weaknesses, or take advantage of local command of ground. At a distance of 4000 yards behind the most easterly of these trenches lies a second double row of trenches known as the Beaurevoir-Fonsommé Line, very thoroughly wired and holding numerous concrete shelters and machine-gun emplacements. The whole series of defences, with the numerous defended villages contained in it, formed a belt of country varying in depth from 7000 to 10,000 yards, organised by employment of every available means into a most powerful system, well meriting the great reputation attached to it."

On the part of the front which particularly interested the 3rd Australian Division, the intention was for the 27th American Division to attack from the "Brown Line" (see map), and capture the enemy territory up to the "Green Line," which was immediately east of Gouy. The 3rd Australian Division was then to go through the 27th American Division on the "Green Line" and capture the enemy territory as far as the "Red Line," which was immediately east of the village of Beaurevoir. The depth of the American attack was 4500 yards, and the maximum depth of our attack was a similar distance beyond the American objective.

The British 12th Division was to secure the flank of the 3rd Australian Division towards Vendhuille. The 30th American Division was also attacking on the right of the 27th American Division, and the 5th Australian Division was attacking through them on our right. The 3rd Australian Division, assisted by tanks, was attacking with the 10th Brigade on the left, the 11th Brigade on the right, and the 9th Brigade in reserve. The 10th Brigade was attacking with the 38th Battalion on the right, the 39th Battalion in the centre, and the 40th Battalion on the left, with the 37th Battalion in reserve. The 40th Battalion dispositions were the four companies in line, in order of A, B, C, and D Companies from the right, with the exception of two platoons of B Company in battalion reserve.

Tanks were to be employed with each battalion, one tank to operate with A and B Companies and one with C and D Companies. One tank was also to support the other two. A half-section of Australian Light Horse, to act as gallopers and carry messages, was also allotted to the 40th Battalion. One section of the 27th Battery, Australian Field Artillery, was also allotted to the 40th Battalion to engage targets as opportunity offered.

The 40th Battalion was timed to cross the "Brown Line" at a point about 500 yards north-west of Gillemont Farm, at 9 a.m., and to cross the American objective, the "Green Line," at 11 a.m. The advance from the "Green Line" was to be preceded by whippet tanks instead of a barrage. This was the general plan of the attack, but it had to be altered in one important respect, and that alteration was largely responsible for the failure of the 27th American Division. On the 24th September the Americans were to take over the jumping-off line, the "Brown Line." On the right the Australians handed over a good line to the 30th American Division; but on the left, the British 3rd Corps had not succeeded in reaching the "Brown Line," in spite of successive attacks, and the 27th American Division had to take over a line 1000 yards short of the "Brown Line." This was an impossible situation, and the reserve brigade of the American Division was used to make a preliminary attack on the 27th September, to clear up the ground up to the "Brown Line." The operation was a failure. The Americans followed the barrage without difficulty, but entirely failed to mop up after them. The enemy reoccupied the ground and cut off the attacking troops. At the end of the day our line was back where it was at the beginning, with the additional disadvantage that artillery could not be used to support a fresh attack because of the parties of Americans who might still be holding their ground somewhere in front. The only safe course would have been to postpone the attack on the Hindenburg Line, to allow of the ground being cleared up to the "Brown Line." But whole armies were involved, and it was too late to change the general plan. So Fourth Army decided that the Americans should attack from their present position without a barrage at one hour before zero, and try to pick up the barrage at the "Brown Line." It was the only course possible, but probably nobody was very hopeful of its success.

At 7 a.m. the 40th Battalion moved by companies in artillery formation from the bivouac area at Ronssoy to proceed to the "Brown Line." We moved east from Ronssoy to Hussar-road, and then north-east along the Bellicourt-road and the Gillemont-road towards "Z" Copse. About here our troubles began, as we passed through our 18-pdr. batteries, when enemy high explosive and gas began to arrive. The tank with A Company was hit by a shell and put out of action, and another shell wounded 8 men of A Company. The enemy shelling became very heavy, as the enemy had no doubt seen the whole division advancing, and we pushed on quickly past the artillery. We had not gone far when it was realised that all was not well with the Americans, as one officer remarked, " I can hear too many Bosche machine guns." This pessimistic view was confirmed when we reached the top of the ridge about 1200 yards west of the " Brown Line." The first glance indicated disaster, for everywhere the Americans could be seen, wounded and unwounded, streaming back, some falling from enemy fire as they came. The tanks also seemed to have had a rough time, and many were out of action. In one place near Duncan Post there had been an old tank mine. The enemy had marked this with a sign-post stating that it was a mine and better left alone. It seemed a pity that someone had not put up a notice in English for the benefit of the people not conversant with the German language, for about six tanks had formed up on the mine, and it had exploded. Machine-gun fire was very heavy, and caused many casualties. The brigade pushed forward, and the 40th Battalion reached the valley on the left of Gillemont-road, about 700 yards west of Gillemont Farm, at 9 a.m.

The position was rather obscure, and the Americans who were questioned did not seem to know what was happening, except that they had failed. But it appeared as if the enemy were counter-attacking, and the Battalion worked forward into the valley and took up a defensive position, with A Company (Capt. H. L. Foster) in a trench immediately west of Gillemont Farm, with their right flank on the Gillemont-road, and C Company (Capt. Findlay), B Company (Capt. McIntyre), and D Company (Capt. Ruddock), on their left in that order, distributed in depth about 300 yards west of Willow Trench. Battalion Headquarters was established under a bank 500 yards west of Gillemont Farm.

As we were getting into position an enemy aeroplane came over, flying very low, and opened fire with his machine gun on the Battalion. Our Lewis guns opened on him, and he crashed a few hundred yards in front of us. This was about the only cheerful thing that had happened so far.

An enemy smoke barrage was obscuring the position south of Gillemont Farm, but on our front there was now no doubt that the enemy was counter-attacking. Large numbers were seen advancing up the Macquincourt Valley towards us, and the Americans were seen running back to Willow Trench. The commanding officer at 9.30 a.m. sent D Company to Willow Trench, and part of C Company towards " The Knoll " on the left of Willow Trench, to deal with the enemy advancing up the Macquincourt Valley. 2nd Lieut. H. Boden went forward ahead of D Company, and arrived at the junction of Grub-lane and Willow Trench just in time to see a party of the enemy entering Willow Trench from Grub-lane. He had taken several bombs with him, and attacked the enemy single-handed with the bombs, killing and wounding several and driving the remainder back. He signalled to the rest of his platoon to come up, and as he was disposing them in Willow Trench this very gallant officer was severely wounded by an enemy machine gun, and died later during the day.

The enemy machine-gun fire, which was very heavy, seemed to be coming from Lone Tree Trench and Gillemont Crescent, which was about 400 yards in front of us. The American dead and wounded were everywhere, and as small groups of the Americans tried to run back from Willow Trench the machine guns picked them up and wiped them out. The scene in Willow Trench was appalling. Great numbers of wounded and unwounded Americans were huddled in the trench. Their rifles and machine guns lay beside them. They made no attempt to use them, and the enemy were attacking. A wounded man would crawl across the open and drop into the trench on top of the others, and an unwounded man would run back, jump into the trench, and lay there sobbing at the unexpected horror and hopelessness of it all. It was not because they were cowards, for they would have fought if they had known how. They knew nothing beyond what they had been taught in training camps; and just bravery and nothing else is not much use against seasoned soldiers with machine guns. Their fear was the fear of strong men in the grip of a machine stronger than themselves, and of which they knew next to nothing.

Our Lewis gunners put their guns on the parapet of Willow Trench, and opened fire on the enemy in Lone Tree Trench, Gillemont Crescent, and the Macquincourt Valley. Shortly afterwards the enemy made another attack down Grub-lane towards Willow Trench. No. 3276 Cpl. A. J. Barwick took charge of a party of bombers and attacked them, inflicting heavy casualties and driving the enemy back in confusion. A block was made in Grub-lane, about 60 yards up from Willow Trench, and a post established at the block to prevent any further attacks from that direction. A similar attack was also made on the left of Willow Trench, and the enemy were driven out by the prompt action and effective bayonet work of No. 1965 Pte. P. Dransfield, assisted by a few others. The wounded Americans who could walk were pushed out of Willow Trench and told to crawl back to the dead ground in the valley, 200 yards away, and the more severely wounded were attended to by our stretcher-bearers, and were carried out later. The unwounded Americans were placed with our men, and helped to man the posts that we had established the whole length of Willow Trench. Their machine guns were also placed in position. The Americans at once became different men when with others in whom they had confidence. They threw themselves into the work of defence with great energy, and in some cases suggested an immediate attack. They wanted to show us that they could make good, but we understood. The Australians had also bought their experience, and the price had sometimes been heavy.

Meantime, while D Company had advanced to Willow Trench, a platoon of C Company, under Lieut. Frank Lakin, had moved over to the left of D Company to prevent the enemy advancing up the Macquincourt Valley. As they went across a large number of the enemy were seen coming up the valley under cover of their machine-gun fire. On the far slope of the valley the enemy had nearly reached Knoll support trench. Here again the pitiful lack of knowledge of "what to do" on the part of the Americans was apparent. Some of them got out of their trenches and stood up in the open firing their rifles at the advancing enemy, with the inevitable result that they were killed or wounded by the enemy machine guns. This may have been the result of lack of training, or an overdose of cinema war pictures manufactured in U.S.A. The rest of the Americans in Knoll support then ran back to the trenches behind, on the south-west side of "The Knoll," at F. 12 central. By this time Lieut. Lakin had arrived there with his platoon. He collected about 200 Americans, who were absolutely disorganised, put them into posts with his own men, and with their rifles and machine guns started them firing at the enemy. This fire, assisted by our fire from Willow Trench, was quite sufficient to show the enemy that his hope of a successful counter-attack on our front was gone. The attack, which seemed to be developing on a large scale when the 10th Brigade arrived, might easily have had the effect of turning our left flank and cutting off the 3rd Australian Division, as well as forcing the division on our flank to fall back.

Lieut. Lakin's platoon remained with the Americans until 1 o'clock that afternoon, and then came back and took up a position in Willow Trench on the left of D Company.

At 10.30 a.m. a few scouts, under Sergt. E. W. Billing, crawled forward towards Gillemont Crescent. They found a few Americans, wounded and unwounded, in shell-holes in front of Gillemont Farm, waiting to be killed or taken prisoner. They sent them back towards our line, and went on further, but were fired on from the Gillemont Crescent, and got back with casualties.

During the whole morning the Gillemont-road was very heavily bombarded by the enemy, and the pack transport of the Battalion had a very rough time. One pack-mule had been allotted to carry ammunition for each company. Three of these animals were taken some distance from the road, and led up into the valley west of Willow Trench. The other animal was killed near Duncan Post, and the man leading it, No. 688 Pte. J. Shearing, took the ammunition from the dead animal and carried it forward himself, under heavy fire, to the company in Willow Trench for whom it was destined, making two trips to carry it all.

At 1 p.m. scouts, under Sergt. E. W. Billing, again crawled forward toward Gillemont Crescent and Lone Tree Trench. They saw that these trenches were still held by great numbers of the enemy, with numerous machine guns.

They also saw that large numbers of the enemy had concentrated in the sunken road from Gillemont Farm towards Bony. Sergt. Billing sent back for a Lewis gun, and found cover from the enemy in Gillemont Crescent to enable the Lewis gunners to open fire down the road. The Lewis gun swept the road for several hundred yards, and made great havoc in the enemy concentration. This brought fire on to the scouts from the Crescent, and they had to withdraw, two of them being wounded in doing so. In all scouting work of the Battalion the name of Sergt. E. W. Billing is inevitably connected. Scouting parties were seldom complete without him. Cool, resourceful, and fearless, he often brought back information of great value from places into which it was believed impossible to penetrate, and his scouting exploits would fill many chapters. A scout does not get much "limelight," as a rule. He works in the dark, or crawls through the mud and rubbish of the shell-holes by day, lost to the sight of his comrades, and depending on his cleverness to remain invisible to the enemy. His thrilling moments are seen by nobody, but the value of his work is known to the commander, who wants information, and always more information.

The Regimental Medical Officer (Capt. J. S. Reed) and his staff were having a very strenuous time with the wounded.

Capt. Reed had established his aid post in a shell-hole 500 yards west of Gillemont Farm, and he was soon busy with dozens of wounded, chiefly Americans, round him. The Americans did not appear to have any medical details forward. The stretcher-bearers with our companies displayed great gallantry in carrying wounded back to the regimental aid post across the open ground swept by machine-gun fire, and several were killed or wounded while carrying. The stretcher-bearers also rendered first aid to a great number of Americans, whom it was impossible to carry out at the time owing to the shortage of stretchers. The number of stretchers supplied was quite inadequate for the number of wounded, and, to make matters worse, most of the ambulance stretcher-bearing parties working from the regimental aid post towards Ronssoy became casualties from machine gun bullets or shell fire. Too much credit cannot be given to the medical officer, his staff, and the stretcher-bearers, for their ceaseless work during the day under the heaviest fire. That night the situation was relieved somewhat by the arrival of an American medical officer with a number of streacher-bearers and stretchers.

At 2 p.m. we had consolidated a line of defence from Gillemont Farm to Lowland Post, and were in touch with the 39th Battalion on our right. Machine-gun fire was still heavy, and the enemy was still hammering the ruins of Gillemont Farm and the road behind it with his artillery.

At 2.20 p.m. word was received from Brigade that Australian Corps Headquarters reported the Americans on the "Green Line" throughout, and that the 5th Australian Division had gone through the "Green Line" to their objective. It is presumed that this information came from the American Corps, and to us it was obvious that the information was wrong. For the enemy were visibly holding the line of Gillemont Crescent and One Tree Trench, about 300 yards in front of us—a line not appreciably advanced from the "Brown Line," and 4000 yards from the American objective, the "Green Line."

We learned later that on the front of the 30th American Division, on our right, some Americans had actually reached the canal, but the ground they had passed over had been reoccupied by the enemy, so that our 5th Division had to fight their way without a barrage over the same ground. It was just possible that some of the 27th Division had done the same thing on our front, but as in our subsequent advance through the Hindenburg Line no American dead or wounded were found further forward than Lone Tree Trench, it is practically certain that no one (unless perhaps a few scouts) did so on our front. It was noticed, besides, in our advance that the thick wire in front of the Hindenburg Line was almost untouched, and would have been impenetrable against any resolute defence, such as the enemy were putting up on the 29th September.

At 3 p.m., just as our scouts had crawled in front, and companies were about to advance behind them, the order to advance was cancelled, and we again resumed our defensive position, with A Company on the right, in Gillemont Switch, and in touch with the 39th Battalion; B Company on the left of A Company, in the same trench; D Company and Americans holding Willow Trench; and C Company in support of A and B Companies, with the exception of a platoon detached with D Company.

At 6.45 p.m. the enemy again heavily shelled the Gillemont-road, and put down a heavy machine-gun barrage on our front. At the time this gave the impression of the preliminary to another counter-attack, but it was probably to prevent our observation of the enemy withdrawal. The enemy fire slackened at about 10 p.m., and at 11 p.m. practically ceased. Rain set in, with a bitterly cold wind blowing, and made this one of the coldest nights the Battalion ever experienced in the trenches.

The events which led to the enemy withdrawal make a long and complicated story. Briefly it may be said that only on the extreme right did the Australians (5th Division) go straight through to their objective, aided by the brilliant advance of the 46th British Division across the canal still further to the south. From this position of advantage on the right, the attack was turned northward instead of eastward, and pushed along the trenches of the Hindenburg Line by the remainder of the 5th Division and the three brigades of the 3rd Division—battalion after battalion taking up the advance from right to left. The attack pivoted on the 40th Battalion on the extreme left, so that our job during the 29th and 30th was chiefly to hold our ground; but it was a difficult and critical task, because our position made us the obvious target for an enemy counter-attack, which, if successful, would have landed the whole Australian Corps in disaster.

At daylight on the morning of the 30th September three parties of scouts pushed forward to Gillemont Crescent and Lone Tree Trench. They found these trenches had been evacuated by the enemy, who had left several heavy machine guns behind him. Each party had a Lewis gun with them, and they opened fire on the enemy, who could be seen on the road west of Bony in large numbers. A and B Companies at once advanced, and occupied Gillemont Crescent and Lone Tree Trench, in touch with the 39th Battalion on our right, and Lone Tree Trench was occupied by D Company, with English and American troops on the left. C Company remained at Gillemont Farm in support, and Battalion Headquarters was established in Willow Trench. These dispositions were maintained during the day and night.

During the afternoon Capt. W. K. Findlay took two scouts, and, under cover of the embankment on the Gillemont-Bony road, reached the wire that protected the village of Bony. He found a gap the enemy had made in his wire, and through this gap crawled to the outskirts of Bony. He found the village still occupied by the enemy, and located several posts there. One enemy post saw him and his scouts, and opened fire on them, and with great difficulty he managed to withdraw with his scouts, bringing back valuable information.

At 5 p.m. Brigade Headquarters reported that the British Division on our left had entered Vendhuille, and were about to attempt to cross the canal there. Later in the evening all Americans were withdrawn, and we did not see them again. They had failed, and their failure had seriously affected the whole plan and scope of the Australian attack, and for a time had placed the 3rd Australian Division on the defensive. The reason for their failure has been previously stated, but even if they had started at zero hour, with everything going well, their want of training and their inexperience would have made their ultimate success doubtful in such a big operation.

On the morning of 1st October the 37th Battalion moved up on our left flank, and orders were received from brigade that battalions would move forward, and take up a position at the St. Quentin Canal tunnel. Patrols at once went forward from each company and established the fact that we had no resistance to meet except artillery from beyond the canal. The scouts had great difficulty in finding gaps through which the companies could pass, as the wire of the Hindenburg Line was still uncut, and no tanks had reached that far to break it down. The scouts returned and reported that the enemy had evacuated the Hindenburg Line, and was now just east of the canal tunnel, from where they had been fired on by machine guns.

At 11 a.m. companies began to work down R.L. Lane in small parties, and then moved due east through the Hindenburg Line. This advance was under fairly heavy artillery fire. An enemy battery could be seen on the side of the hill north-west of Le Catelet (A. 4 central), firing through open sights at our parties as they advanced. Single guns even followed groups of three and four men with their fire. The Battalion reorganised behind the canal tunnel, opposite the Knob and Bony Point. A platoon of A Company pushed forward about 400 yards, and covered the front of the Battalion. The 37th Battalion were on our left, and the 38th and 39th Battalions in support in the Hindenburg Line.

At 4.30 p.m. orders were received from Brigade that the 37th and 39th Battalions would advance their positions with the 37th Battalion left flank at Knob Wood, and the right flank of the 39th Battalion at Bony Point, while the 38th and 40th Battalions took up a support position in the Hindenburg Line.

Orders were received during the afternoon for the 40th Battalion to ascertain if Macquincourt Farm, south of Vendhuille, was held by the enemy, and Lieut. E. D. Weston, with 6 scouts, carried out a reconnaissance. At 7.30 o'clock that night they approached Macquincourt Farm from Knob Wood, and found the enemy machine guns were firing across the canal from opposite the farm. They went through the farm to the canal bank, and heard the enemy talking in trenches about 150 yards behind the canal, opposite the farm. They also located a machine gun about 200 yards east of the canal, and saw minenwerfer being fired from Le Catelet.

On the night of the 1st October the regimental transport came up through the Hindenburg Line, to within 100 yards of our support position, and delivered a hot meal and a rum ration. The efforts of the transport personnel and the quartermaster and his staff were greatly appreciated by everybody, and during the whole operation their system of supply and initiative in delivering the goods was splendid. One party of the transport, under No. 924 Corpl. D. J. McKenzie, had been to and from the Battalion Headquarters during the three days continuously with food and ammunition on pack animals, suffering casualties among men and animals.

The 2nd October we remained in support in the Hindenburg Line until 6.30 p.m., when we moved back in accordance with brigade orders to the previous bivouac area at Ronssoy. This journey was completed without incident. Our casualties during the whole operation were 1 officer and 14 other ranks killed, and 4 officers and 76 other ranks wounded.

Chapter XXVIII.

Conclusion.

N the 3rd October the Battalion marched back to Aizecourt, and after a day's rest moved to Peronne, and thence by train to Erondelle, where training and reorganisation was commenced and continued during October, with a programme of football and sports meetings.

The Battle of the Hindenburg Line was the last fighting in which the Battalion was engaged, and the end of hostilities was then in sight. The breaking of the Hindenburg Line defences destroyed the last hope the German High Command may have had of staving off disaster. After our victory of the 8th August Ludendorff had seen that all hope of final success was gone, but there was always the chance of rendering the campaign indecisive by a successful defensive on the Western Front. But now the Hindenburg Line had crumbled; the morale of the German Army was gone; Bulgaria and Turkey faced complete defeat; Austria was asking for peace at almost any price. So on the 4th October Germany requested the President of the United States to take in hand the restoration of peace on the basis of his "fourteen points," and also asked for an immediate armistice to avoid further bloodshed.

Fighting continued until the 11th November, with the military position of Germany becoming more and more hopeless, but by the 5th October the whole of the infantry of the Australian Corps had been in action for the last time, and gone into rest areas near Abbeville. With the closing of the campaign as far as the Australian infantry was concerned, there came a tribute to the corps from the Commander of the 4th Army, General Sir Henry Rawlinson, which reads:—

"Since the Australian Corps joined the 4th Army on the 8th April, 1918, they have passed through a period of hard and uniformly successful fighting of which all ranks have every right to feel proud.

"Now that it has been possible to give the Australian Corps a well-earned period of rest, I wish to express to them my gratitude for all that they have done. I have watched with the greatest interest and admiration the various stages through which they have passed, from the hard times at Flers and Pozieres to their culminating victories of Mt. St. Quentin and the great Hindenburg system at Bony, Bellicourt, and Mont-brehain.

"During the summer of 1918 the safety of Amiens has been principally due to their determination, tenacity, and valour.

"The story of what they have accomplished as a fighting army corps, of the diligence, gallantry, and skill which they have exhibited, and of the scientific methods which they have so thoroughly learned and so successfully applied, has gained for all Australians a place of honour amongst nations, and amongst all English-speaking races in particular.

"It has been my privilege to lead the Australian Corps in the 4th Army during the decisive year to a successful conclusion at no distant date. No one realises more than I do the very prominent part they have played, for I have watched from day to day every detail of their fighting, and learned to measure the prowess and determination of all ranks.

"In once more congratulating the corps on a series of successes unsurpassed in this great war, I feel that no mere words of mine can adequately express the renown that they have won for themselves, and the position they have established for the Australian nation not only in France but throughout the world."

There is some excuse for every Australian soldier being proud of this tribute, and it is felt that no apology is necessary for referring to it here. Not for love of praise do we value it, nor do we cherish it as thanks for services rendered. But its value to us lies in the fact that it recognised that Australia now stood among the nations of the world, placed there by the men of Australia in a struggle where only manhood counted.

This tale of "arms and the man" is finished. The remainder of the history of the Battalion is a dull business, and left no impressions but a deep longing for home in most of us, a weariness of everything connected with the army in all of us, and sometimes a moment of deep feeling when the drafts of troops left the dirty little village where we were billeted for the winter, and went down to the sea, bound for England and then to Australia.

The first draft left on the 17th February, 1919, and it was only then that we realised that this brotherhood of men existed no longer as a battalion of infantry. For quite two days before this draft departed there was a feeling of irresponsibility about all of us. We drank in fellowship together, pledged ourselves to meet again in Tasmania, and from a sentiment born of the sadness of farewell, for once felt sorry that the war was over.

Those of us who remained stood in the rain and watched the draft move off as it passed in column before us. Farewells were shouted, mostly facetious farewells with reference to future meetings in favourite **Tasmanian** hostelries. But as the column moved beyond us we stood watching them in silence as they plodded away from us through the mud and rain, till they passed out of sight, and then we returned to billets. The Battalion had broken up.

Epilogue.

A few brief notes may put on record the expiring phases of the 40th Battalion.

From Erondelle we went to Epagne in November, 1918, and then finally settled into our winter billets at Tours-en-Vimeu and the surrounding hamlets, a dozen miles out from Abbeville. It would have been hard to find a more unpromising location. Tours is a somewhat dirty and unattractive village, set in the middle of a large expanse of open cultivation. Billets were scanty and dilapidated, there was no grass-land suitable for games or exercises, and there were no woods handy to supplement the scanty issue of fuel. The villagers, too, were tired of troops, and gave us a cold welcome, so that the usual friendly relations were established but slowly, though of course in the end we became deeply attached to one another, and the final departure of the Battalion was a day of tears.

The problem of the winter was to find occupation. The war was over, and with it the need for military training. Drill was accordingly cut down to the barest minimum for discipline and administration and the care of clothing and equipment, with an occasional route march for exercise. The A.I.F. education scheme came to take the place of military training, and this was the theory of it: some men would go to a special corps school in France and others to a corps workshop for technical training; many more would go to England for training and experience in all manner of commercial and industrial establishments, and at special agricultural schools; and the remainder would be supplied with lectures, teachers, books, and other necessaries for study at their quarters in France. It was a fine scheme, but the staff work was defective. An elaborate inquiry was made into the needs and desires of every man in the unit. The first difficulty was that nearly every man wished to become either a wool-classer or a motor engineer, but with a little persuasion nearly everyone was fitted with some reasonable plan of training for civil life, either in England or with the unit. Then the real hitch occurred. The arrangements for placing them in England hung fire. Instructions would come for fifteen men to get ready to take a farming course in England; the fifteen men were chosen, and got ready, and remained ready until the spring—when they mostly took their places in the drafts returning to Australia rather than wait longer. Those who waited generally got the experience they wanted in the end; but it was too late to help in the problem of winter occupation. The education scheme with the unit was handicapped in various ways. There was no suitable accommodation. Most classes had to be held under very miserable conditions in rough sheds, generally with an earth floor, and often with no windows. Tables and seats were rare, and the cold at most times through a Somme winter made study almost impossible. Further, we got little help from outside the unit. Visiting lecturers were slow to come at all, and then their visits were rare. Worst of all, no material arrived. Books did not begin to come till the winter was half over. It was impossible to get even a text-book for the teacher. Stationery also was so delayed that makeshifts were bought in Abbeville from battalion funds.

It was impossible, then, to supply the teaching required, but if anyone in the Battalion could teach any subject without books he was put on to it, and a class resulted. Some quite good classes were held. Lieut. Downie, with his usual versatility, contrived a long and successful course in farming, relying solely on his memory; and when an old motor was obtained after persistent effort, Lieut. McMillan held a series of classes in motor-engineering which were always crowded. But any subject, however remote from practical utility, might be used. The English banking system was the subject of a course of ten lectures, and Private J. H. B. Walch, with the help of chalk and horribly realistic diagrams, kept a small class interested in physiology.

The total effect educationally of the Battalion's efforts was no doubt negligible, but the main result was attained of keeping a good proportion of all ranks fairly busy during the mornings.

Games were the order in the afternoon, and in spite of the mud and the difficulty of finding grounds, a good deal of football was played. More ambitious were a couple of race meetings, including both gallops and trots, which were successfully carried out in spite of some opposition from the proprietor of the chosen course and an appalling bill for damages. Athletic sports were also held. The great lack was anything of interest in the neighbourhood to draw men naturally out of billets. Even a fair-sized wood, such as are common enough in other parts of the Somme country, would have been a godsend. But flat stretches of bare fenceless and hedgeless fields, plough or stubble, intersected by muddy roads, covered most of the country between one rather mean and squalid village and another.

Fuel rations were barely sufficient for cooking, and the winter cold in Northern France makes fires a necessity. The temptation to make use of stray fence-posts and fragments of derelict buildings was strong, but on the whole the Battalion discipline in this respect was very good. An understanding was come to that each company would be responsible for damage done in and about its own quarters, and the result was excellent. But there was a good deal of private dealing with the villagers for firewood. We found, to our surprise, that every tree, however miserable, and even every stump, had its price, and a tolerably stiff one. Fifty francs produced a very poor specimen of an elm, with the labour of cutting, splitting, and carting all to be done, and very poor fuel in the end. Perhaps the best bargains were ash trees, rotten at the core, and so unfit for timber purposes, and we learned to appreciate the old adage—

"Ash when it's green
Is fire for a queen."

The Battalion was without its commanding officer for most of the winter. Colonel Lord, after temporarily commanding the 10th Brigade, was definitely appointed to the 5th Brigade in January, and left the Somme country for Charleroi. Major Payne commanded till he left for Australia at the end of January, leaving Major Giblin to wind up the estate, with Lieut. E. J. Bertram as adjutant, succeeding Lieut. L. W. Barnett, M.C., who also left in January.

Repatriation was to take place in three drafts, at intervals of about six weeks. Definite principles were laid down giving preference to those with longest service, to those with families, and to those having guaranteed employment in Australia. The application of these principles in detail was left to a committee made up of a representative chosen by the personnel of each company and of Headquarters details. Although a fair sprinkling of officers and men wished to stay on to the very last, there was generally great keenness to get in the first "quota," but there was only one single case of appeal to the C.O. against the decision of the committee.

Beyond the elaborate preparations for the sending off of each quota with records, arms, clothes, and equipment complete for every man, there were two special jobs that occupied the last month or two in France—closing accounts with the villagers and handing in battalion stores to D.A.D O.S.

Claims for damage were a regular feature of every period of billets, but Tours was unique. The village had had many troops billeted there, and we were the last. No doubt many claims for damage, real or imaginary, had been made in the past, and many of them without result. We were the last chance, and we were Australian. Here was a forlorn hope to pay for the war generally, and the claims came pouring in.

The claims divided themselves into three classes—

1. Clear cases of damage or loot, which had to be paid for substantially, though not always to the amount of the claim.

2. Cases where there was damage and we were partly to blame, but the amount of claim was greatly exaggerated.

3. Ridiculous and extravagant claims on the flimsiest of grounds. These included most of the larger claims, running into thousands of francs.

The first class was paid mostly by voluntary contributions of the companies concerned. A substantial claim against one company was proved only as the first quota was marching out, and the contribution of the men in the quota was collected a month later and sent back from England.

The second class was settled chiefly by candles, skilfully handled by Lieut. Garrard and others. The supply of candles had always been short of our needs all through the fighting time right up till the end of 1918. Then mysteriously ample supplies began to appear, and we revelled in candles. As the days lengthened, stocks mounted up, and encumbered the Q.M.'s store, and the Q.M. took thought to refuse further supplies. Then the Q.M. thought again, and he let the stocks go on growing. Candles were scarce and dear in the village shops, and much valued by the villagers. And it was found that a few pounds of candles, with a little tactful speech, settled claims of 40 or 50 francs, with great satisfaction on both sides. So Lieut. Garrard went his rounds with a packful of candles on his back, and the claims of Class 2 mysteriously melted away.

To Class 3 we said " No " firmly, and passed them over, with a brief but forcible expression of our sentiments, to the skilful hands of Mr. Brissenden, the divisional claims officer. Needless to say, we heard no more of them.

The return of battalion stores was a much more solemn affair. Nearly everyone was worried by it to some extent, but the concentrated responsibility fell in the end on the Quartermaster. Everything that had ever been issued to us in France had to be accounted for in some way—either handed in to D.A.D.O.S. or struck off by proper authority before the final ceremony of return to Ordnance. With the gear in actual use there was not as a rule much trouble. The Lewis Gun Officer and the Signalling Officer could be trusted to have not only the stores they ought to have but a great deal more that they ought not to have; and only a little care was needed to see that the surplus was discreetly lost at the proper moment. The Transport men also were equally sure to have all the gear they wanted (and a little more). But in the outfitting of a battalion according to War Office Regulations, an extraordinary number of articles were included—particularly in harness and other transport gear—for which no one had any use. These had been promptly lost in the Flanders mud at the first opportunity. No requisition had ever been put in to replace them, and their existence had been forgotten. Their purpose in life in some cases had never been known. So when the careful Q.M. came back from a visit to D.A.D.O.S., armed with an encyclopædic list of everything that had to be accounted for, the Transport men found themselves called upon to produce an article as to which they had not the faintest idea whether it was a piece of harness, a fitting of a limber, a blacksmith's tool, or an instrument of veterinary science. As the end approached, stories went about of quartermasters and adjutants and commanding officers of expiring units being brought back to France to clear up deficiencies, and a shade of gloom fell across Battalion Headquarters, though the M.O., Captain J. S. Reed, specially organised a jazz-band to combat depression. But the Q.M., Captain Horler, rose to the occasion. There was a way of accounting satisfactorily for every conceivable deficiency, with proper care and forethought. At the cost of a month's very strenuous work, carried out under the principle of believing nothing until you had seen it yourself, Captain Horler passed the ordeal with flying colours, and the Battalion went out with a clean sheet in the matter of stores. Of course, we found afterwards that we had taken rather more trouble than was usual or necessary; but it helped to keep us occupied and to enliven the dreariness of billets at Tours-en-Vimeu.

The first draft for return to Australia (forming part of A.I.F. Quota No. 12) marched out of Tours on 17th February. Their numbers were about 200 of all ranks, under Captain W. C. G. Ruddock. The second draft of 140 (Quota 29) marched out on 4th April, and the remainder of the 10th Brigade then concentrated near our entraining station, Gamaches. We had been cursing Tours heartily for four months, but that did not prevent us leaving it for a much more desirable location under strong protest and with a sense of grievance. But spring came at the same time, and cricket; and we were not inconsolable. By this time a good many of the Battalion had gone to England for civil training—"non-military employment," as it was rather quaintly called—so that there remained only about a hundred for the final draft which entrained at Gamaches early in May on the first stage of the homeward journey. This included the "cadre," composed of about 70 officers and men who had volunteered to stay to the last to do the final cleaning up of stores and transport animals, but were now unexpectedly included in the third draft from the Battalion.

The movements of the three drafts need not be followed in detail. The repatriation plan allowed 40 days between the time a draft began to move in France and the time it finally sailed from England, and this time was generally exceeded on account of scarcity of transports. Men left the drafts in England for non-military employment, and others joined up. On the whole the drafts kept together until reaching Australia, but fifty men were dropped from the first draft for want of room on the transport, and had a rather miserable wait, handed about from one camp to another with no one to look after their interests, before they finally found a passage home.

The itinerary of one draft (the second) may be given as typical:—

    April 4—Quota 29 concentrated at Gamaches.

    ,, 9—Entrained Gamaches.

    ,, 10—Marched in to A.I.B.D. camp at Le Havre, known as the "De-lousing Camp," for hot baths and clean clothes.

April 14—Embarked Le Havre.

" 15—Arrived Southampton, and trained to camp at Codford, about 15 miles out of Salisbury. After a few days to settle down, the whole quota would go on final leave for a fortnight. When it returned—not without a good many A.W.L.'s—there began the lengthy business of outfitting every man for the voyage (including a new uniform), making up pay-books, and preparing many elaborate papers for the quota. After that it waited for a transport, playing cricket and two-up, investigating the downs and beer of Wiltshire, and making fruitless applications for an extra-final leave to attend the funeral of an uncle or the marriage of a cousin. One special item in the second draft's career was :—

" 25—A platoon composed chiefly of the 40th Battalion men took part in the march through London of A.I.F. troops on Anzac Day. The platoon was said to have marched excellently, but another report states that Sergt. J. R. Wilson was the only man in step!

May 27—Embarked at Devonport on the "Rio Pardo," with Lieut.-Col. J. T. McColl, M.C., late 40th Battalion, as O.C. troops.

June 21—Arrived Capetown.

" 23—Sailed from Capetown.

July 17—Arrived Adelaide.

" 21—Arrived Barnes Bay, Tasmania, and went into quarantine.

" 30—Disembarked Hobart, 64 days from leaving Devonport.

All the drafts reported a good homeward voyage. The weather was generally good, except perhaps for a short spell between the Cape and the Leeuwin. The ships were comfortable, and the food was particularly good and plentiful. Work was, of course, very light, but discipline was good, both on the ship and on leave ashore at Capetown and Durban. Goodfellowship prevailed generally, both among the troops and with the officers and crew. Even the last draft, which had included in its quota a large number of unpromising shipmates, the riff-raff of various battalions, including a fair-sized draft straight from gaol, could report a pleasant voyage. With tactful handling by the C.O., Lieut.-Col. Farrell, D.S.O., of the 43rd Battalion, and a good lot of officers, an easy but effective discipline was maintained, and differences adjusted with very little friction; so that when an officer of the repatriation staff boarded the " Wiltshire " at Adelaide and asked generally for " complaints," the prize " tough " of the quota cheerfully offered to throw him overboard; and though the suggestion was not carried out, it seemed to be thought generally to convey the appropriate answer to the question.

Appendix A.

Casualties and Other Statistics.

The total number of men embarked in the A.I.F. was 329,883, of whom about one-fifth were born in the British Isles. The total battle casualties were 226,149, of which the deaths numbered 59,330. The proportion of casualties to enlistments for Australia was rather greater than for the United Kingdom, Canada, or New Zealand.

The casualties in France were about seven times as many as the casualties on Gallipoli, and these were six times the casualties in Palestine. Considering the number of troops engaged, and taking the Gallipoli campaign with rest and reorganisation after it as occupying a year, the intensity of casualties was about the same on the Peninsula and in France, *i.e.*, the number of casualties for the same number of troops engaged for the same time.

The number of casualties, of course, varied greatly in units. The 25th Battalion of Infantry offered the highest chances of a "Blighty"; the field bakeries the lowest of any arms recorded. In France the proportion of casualties per 100 men on the establishment of the principal arms was approximately—

Casualties per 100 of Nominal Strength.

Infantry	244
Machine Gunners	115
Pioneers	107
Artillery	107
Engineers	94
Field Ambulance	75

The above figures probably underestimate the frequency of infantry casualties relative to other arms, as the infantry was more often and more seriously below establishment than the other arms.

Even in the infantry there was great variation in the casualties of different units. The five divisions had approximately the same service in France, except that the Third Division missed the first six months and the heavy Somme fighting in 1916. The totals are approximately—

Casualties in France: Infantry (excluding Pioneers).[*]

Division.	Casualties.
Second	35,700
First	32,100
Fourth	29,800
Fifth	24,800
Third	24,100

[*] These and other figures in this appendix are taken chiefly from "Statistics of Casualties, A.I.F., to 30.6.1919," compiled by the Records Section, A.I.F., London. The totals have been increased to some extent since, but the details are not available, and the additions may be assumed not to affect the comparisons here made.

The casualties in battalions, as might be expected, show greater variations than divisions. As the figures are of general interest, and not readily accessible, a full list of the casualties of infantry battalions in France is given. Gas casualties and prisoners are on somewhat a different footing from the rest, and the most significant figures are those for battle casualties without these two items. These figures are given in the first column, and the battalions arranged in that order, and the total battle casualties given in the second column.

Australian Infantry: Casualties in France.

Battalion.	Killed and Wounded.*	Total Battle Casualties.	Battalion.	Killed and Wounded.*	Total Batt'e Casualties.
25th	3068	3472	47th	2183	2374
26th	2892	3095	49th	2131	2218
18th	2881	3086	15th	2112	2554
20th	2847	2915	6th	2104	2336
28th	2823	2929	14th	2060	2690
12th	2783	2927	7th	2050	2350
21st	2740	3025	**40th**	**2039**	**2155**
3rd	2684	2857	52nd	2033	2095
11th	2605	2840	58th	2031	2153
19th	2599	2999	35th	2028	2232
23rd	2597	2752	53rd	2008	2348
17th	2594	2845	34th	2005	2231
22nd	2592	2926	33rd	1968	2504
1st	2589	2787	31st	1954	2127
24th	2587	3004	60th	1942	2022
10th	2584	2689	32nd	1874	2152
27th	2566	2666	56th	1873	2147
4th	2554	2777	54th	1837	2252
9th	2515	2846	38th	1836	1967
2nd	2495	2682	42nd	1748	2111
48th	2448	2676	37th	1733	1956
8th	2424	2715	29th	1726	1903
51st	2357	2560	41st	1706	2010
45th	2332	2411	57th	1666	1747
59th	2330	2412	39th	1665	1768
46th	2292	2556	44th	1664	1772
13th	2287	2694	55th	1640	1931
50th	2221	2366	36th	1577	1676
5th	2217	2354	30th	1527	1664
16th	2193	2633	43rd	1453	1711

It will be noticed that the battalions of the Second Division are all towards the head of the list, followed by those of the 1st and 3rd Brigades, and then the 12th Brigade. The Third and Fifth Divisions divide the lowest places. The battalion with most killed and wounded in the Second Division is the 25th, which heads the list; in the First Division, the 12th; in the Fourth Division, the 48th; in the Fifth Division, the 59th; and in the Third Division, the 40th. There are 36 battalions having more casualties than the 40th, and 23 with fewer. Considering that the Third Division had six months' less fighting in France than the other divisions, it would appear that the 40th was employed quite as busily as the average Australian battalion. The 40th comes in a group of six battalions having approximately the same number of casualties: the 14th, 7th, 40th, 52nd, 58th, and 35th.

---

* Excluding gassed.

Casualties of 40th Battalion.

The casualties of the 40th Battalion are thus set out in the official statistics up to 30th June, 1919:—

	Officers.	Other Ranks.
Killed in action	9	319
Died of wounds	6	99
Died of disease in France	—	14
Died of other causes	—	1
Total deaths	15	433*
Wounded in action	54	1539
Gassed	—	121
Prisoners of war	—	5
Total battle casualties	69	2098

These figures are not complete, but the full figures are not available. The only correction attempted on the official figures of 1919 is to give the total number of officer deaths as 15, the true number, instead of 13.

On Gallipoli in several battalions the number of killed and died of wounds exceeded the number of wounded who recovered. In France the proportion of killed to wounded in most battalions was between one-half and one-third. It appears to have got less progressively in France. The 40th Battalion was lucky in having one of the lowest proportions of killed to wounded. The proportion depended largely on the possibility of quick removal and treatment of wounded, and many factors combined with the nature of the operations to determine this. The worst conditions in our experience were provided by the bogs of the Ravebeck on October 12, 1917, before Passchendaele, and on that day our proportion of killed to wounded rose from one-quarter to one-half. That our proportion of killed was low compared to that of other battalions in the same brigade is, in part at any rate, a tribute to our medical officers and regimental stretcher-bearers.

Casualties on special occasions and for different periods may be summarised thus:—

	Killed.		Wounded, Gassed, &c.		Total.	
	Os.	O.Rs.	Os.	O.Rs.	Os.	O.Rs.
Messines, 7th June, 1917	0	46	6	297	6	343
Broodseinde, 4th Oct., 1917	1	49	6	198	7	247
Passchendaele, 12th Oct., 1917	2	77	5	164	7	241
Trench warfare, Flanders, 1916-18	5	61	8	409	13	470
Morlancourt, 28th to 30th March, 1918	2	44	10	170	12	214
Hindenburg Line, 29th to 30th Sept., 1918	1	14	4	76	5	90
Somme, March to October, 1918	4	142	15	351	19	493
Total	15	433	54	1665	69	2098

* The latest figures are given by the Defence Department as: Total deaths, 16 officers, 459 other ranks, with the other casualties as in the text. The additional deaths have nearly all taken place after return to Australia. See footnote, p. 212.

The number of killed in the general fighting on the Somme in 1918 is somewhat exaggerated, because it includes a number of "died of wounds" which cannot now be properly distributed to the engagements when the wounds were received. Information as to the subsequent deaths of wounded came to battalions irregularly and incompletely.

SICKNESS AND OTHER STATISTICS.

The full records of sick are not now accessible, but the numbers of evacuated sick are given below, with some other statistics, up to the date of the armistice. It may be noted that the Battalion policy was to do all that was possible to keep cases that were not serious with the Battalion. The mixed convalescent camps in France to which light cases were soon drafted brought our men under the command of Imperial officers and N.C.O.'s, not of the best type, and the results were frequently disastrous. It was no uncommon thing for a man with a perfectly clean sheet in the Battalion to return from a month in one of these camps with two or three entries of No. 1 Field Punishment entered in his pay-book.

Increases and Decreases of Strength to 11th November, 1918.

	Officers.	Other Ranks.
Battle casualties	69	2098
Evacuated sick	28	1436
Total deaths, France and England	16	453
Embarked for Australia	10	402
Rejoined unit	61	1947
Reinforcements	16	1214
Original members with Battalion on 11th November, 1918	7	153

OFFICERS.

The following figures show how the supply of officers was maintained:—

Commissioned in Australia:
Original officers commissioned from C.M.F.	10	
" " " " A. & I. Staff	5	
" " " " Ranks	14	
Reinforcement officers: C.M.F.	1	
" " A. and I. Staff	1	
" " Ranks	14	
		45

Commissioned in the Field:
Direct from the Ranks	41	
Through Cadet Battalions	15	
		56
Total		101

Appendix B.

Decorations and Other Honours.*

VICTORIA CROSS.
456 Sergeant L. McGee.
506 Sergeant P. C. Statton, M.M.

COMPANION OF ST. MICHAEL AND ST. GEORGE.
Lieut.-Col. J. E. C. Lord, D.S.O.

DISTINGUISHED SERVICE ORDER.
Lieut.-Col. J. E. C. Lord.
Major L. H. Payne.
Major L. F. Giblin, M.C.

MILITARY CROSS.

Lieut.	S. I. Suter	Lieut.	M. H. O. Whitaker
Captain	C. L. McVilly	,,	S. G. Stebbins
,,	L. F. Giblin	,,	T. G. Cranswick, D.C.M.
,,	W. I. Clark		
,,	H. J. Dumaresq	,,	S. S. S. McMillan
Lieut.	E. Boyes	T/Captain	G. L. McIntyre
,,	W. L. Garrard	Lieut.	J. S. Rattray
,,	B. J. Jackson	Captain	W. K. Findlay
,,	H. L. Foster	Lieut.	E. D. Weston
2nd Lieut.	A. P. Brown	2nd Lieut.	H. Boden
Captain	F. C. Green	Lieut.	L. W. Barnett
		,,	C. W. Game

DISTINGUISHED CONDUCT MEDAL.

815	Sergt.	T. G. Cranswick	834	Sergt.	W. N. Grey
382	Pte.	W. G. Gale	136	,,	B. A. Beswick, M.M.
1651	,,	J. D. Jeffrey			
2418	Cornl.	W. G. E. Woolley	832	T/R.S.M.	H. Gillam
92	Pte.	F. W. Teniswood	128	Sergt.	E. W. Billing, M.M.
699	Sergt.	H. C. Long			

MILITARY MEDAL.

324	Pte.	J. E. Ackroyd	48	Pte.	P. F. McKinley
460	,,	O. L. E. Molross	799	,,	E. D. Collings
5752	,,	D. L. Pitchford	314	,,	H. Evans
734	,,	E. W. Stevens	518	,,	D. L. Treweek
583	Sergt.	F. Rawson	52	Sergt.	G. M. Young
506	,,	P. C. Statton	231	Pte.	C. Moran
884	Pte.	R. S. McKenzie	218	,,	W. Kelty
57	,,	E. Hilmer	2281	Corpl.	W. Walker
956	Sergt.	S. J. Barrett	556	,,	G. A. Charlesworth
61	Pte.	C. C. Leonard			
288	,,	W. L. Vince	53	L.-Corpl.	F. McDonald
559	,,	E. J. Hart	1850	Pte.	D. C. Francombe
624	,,	H. Elliott	42	L.-Corpl.	C. W. Bell
1649	,,	T. S. Jones	257	Pte.	L. Rogers
818	,,	T. Davidson	987	,,	J. T. Bradley 10th Field Amb. att. 40th Btn.
829	L.-Corpl.	C. T. Fleming			
2156	Sergt.	L. K. Swann			
2562	L.-Corpl.	H. F. Davis	2125	Pte.	D. R. Oates
389	Corpl.	W. J. Gourlay	353	Sergt.	W. T. Burn
587	,,	J. Saddington	2394	T/Corpl.	R. O'C. Swindells
590	,,	R. Smith	2061	Corpl.	E. A. Cook
2146	Corpl.	H. J. Smith	2298	Pte.	J. Boer

* The order of names is that in which awards were gazetted, with rank at the time of the award.

MILITARY MEDAL—continued.

860	Corpl.	A. Jacobson		3544	Pte.		J. D. Lowe
1879	Pte.	B. G. Lane		495	L.-Sergt.		C. W. Shalless
2153	„	E. O. Tang		3016	Pte.		F. D. Brock
2578	L.-Corpl.	E. J. Hicks		2067A	„		J. Cox
207	Drvr.	C. Hearps		7775	„		W. H. Nolan
883	„	C. McIntosh		7478	„		C. E. Dent
1706	„	J. A. Robertson		2604	„		H. Lambert
1964	T/Sergt.	A. H. Richards		3078	„		D. J. New
7438	Pte.	J. D. Brilliant		720	„		F. Mehegan
2771	„	E. Hynds		1965	„		P. Dransfield
128	Sergt.	E. W. Billing		272	„		R. E. J. Smith
3053	Pte.	F. W. Harris		3276	Corpl.		A. J. Barwick
40	„	L. Carroll		2057	Pte.		R. Creswell
3007	„	J. R. Cooper		7527	L.-Corpl.		J. T. Pilkington
980	„	E. Castle		7535	Corpl.		E. V. Reardon
2079	L.-Corpl.	S. E. Dale		3047	L.-Corpl.		E. J. Holmes
2315	Pte.	C. W. Connors		743	Pte.		C. S. Cornes
136	„	B. A. Beswick		1114	„		R. W. Jarvis
2600	„	C. F. Lockwood		1867	„		E. F. Hunter
267A	T/Sergt.	A. H. Purton		85	Sergt.		C. T. Flood

BAR TO MILITARY MEDAL.

2146 Sergt. H. J. Smith

MERITORIOUS SERVICE MEDAL.

26	Sergt.	J. R. Wilson		2158	Sergt.	A. J. Whitney
1807	Corpl.	C. J. Bourke		3	S.-Sergt.	S. G. Taylor
254	L.-Corpl.	A. Rooney		124	Sergt.	R. Ballantyne

COLONIAL FORCES LONG SERVICE MEDAL.

Lieut.-Col. J. E. C. Lord, D.S.O.
Captain J. D. W. Chisholm.

CROIX DE GUERRE (FRENCH).

Lieut.-Col. J. E. C. Lord, D.S.O.

CROIX DE GUERRE (BELGIAN).

Lieut. B. T. Sadler.
1104 C.S.M. H. Boden.
266 C.S.M. E. W. Stevens.
832 T/R.S.M. H. Gillam.

MEDAILLE MILITAIRE (FRENCH).

605 Sergeant R. K. Wilson.

MENTIONED IN DESPATCHES.

	Lt.-Col.	J. E. C. Lord		Lieut.		T. G. Cranswick
	Major	L. H. Payne		Major		L. F. Giblin
370	Sergt.	N. A. M. Findlay		„		L. H. Payne
	Lieut.	L. W. Barnett		Q.M.		T. J. Horler
	Captain	J. D. W. Chisholm		Lt.-Col.		J. E. C. Lord
			547	Sergt.		M. E. Calder
	Lieut.	S. H. Smith	819	Pte.		C. Davie
	„	M. H. O. Whitaker		Lt.-Col. (T/Col.)		J. E. C. Lord
106	Sergt.	S. H. L. Allwright		Lieut.		O. E. Lawrence

OTHER "MENTIONS."

April 20, 1917.—Highly commended by Divisional Commander in connection with attempted enemy raid :—

Captain	H. J. Dumaresq	605 Sergt.	R. K. Wilson
Lieut.	F. C. Green	733 Pte.	J. J. Spellman
2nd Lieut.	T. T. Hoskins	1911 ,,	L. J. Metcalfe

June 21, 1917.—Congratulated by Divisional Commander for rescue of men from a burning ammunition dump at Wulverghem :—

| 2133 Pte. | A. L. Rule | 2542 Pte. | W. R. Cooper |
| 2615 ,, | C. W. V. Matthews | 2158 ,, | A. J. Whitney |

June 28, 1917.—Mentioned in Divisional Orders for gallant conduct at Messines :—

1674 L.-Corpl.	O. W. Sweeney	745 Sergt.	H. S. Winburn
1117 Pte.	J. T. Balmforth	651 ,,	C. Hope
1914 ,,	J. Norquay	2278 Corpl.	J. Braid
85 Corpl.	C. T. Flood	825 Pte.	C. Ellis
360 Pte.	W. C. Clements	945 ,,	W. Tapner
5677 L.-Corpl.	F. J. Cunningham	501 Pte.	C. E. Smith

May 1, 1918.—Highly commended for conduct in repeated raids on enemy post at Ville-sur-Ancre :—

| Lieut. | T. G. Cranswick | 915 L.-Corpl. | R. J. Ratcliffe |
| ,, | A. P. Brown | 92 Pte. | G. Parsissons |

May 21, 1918.—Congratulated by Corps Commander for attempt to save a man from drowning :—

3262 Pte. A. S. L. Hay.

Appendix C.

Roll of the 40th Battalion.

The following roll is the result of a great deal of work on the part of a considerable number of members of the Battalion. It was compiled from the old Battalion nominal roll, and supplemented by a thorough search through the card-index record of Tasmanian enlistments kept at Hobart Military Headquarters, and from this the record of wounds was made almost entirely. Unfortunately this card-index is very inaccurate, particularly in respect to wounds, and complete accuracy could be attained (if at all) only by searching through each man's official papers. This could have been done at the rate of about six names to the hour, and was a job in general beyond our resources; but it was done in all cases where other records were incomplete or obviously in error. Correction has been made in a good many cases also from company and private records. Unfortunately the complete set of Battalion orders, which would have been invaluable for this and many other purposes in this history, was taken from us "temporarily" by Records Section, A.I.F., in London, on demobilisation, and we have never been able to see it since. It cannot, then, be hoped that this roll will be free from errors, particularly in respect to wounds. It is hoped that any reader who notices an error will advise Captain J. D. W. Chisholm, of the Repatriation Department, Hobart. Such cases will then be checked, and a leaflet embodying all consequent corrections will be supplied to purchasers of the present volume.

The roll sets out, in order, regimental number, name, rank on discharge, decorations, date of embarkation, number of wounds; and the date of death, and cause, in the case of those who lost their lives.

It is hoped that no one has been omitted who actually joined up with the Battalion. The roll is not intended to cover those whose connection with the Battalion was only nominal, but some such names have probably been included by inadvertence. In the case of those transferred to or from other units, the information is of necessity more liable to error than in the general run of cases. Deficient information in the case of transferred men is sometimes indicated by the abbreviation "trf."

Finally, apology must be made for the fact that the roll, except in the case of a few of the more important letters, is not strictly alphabetical beyond the first two letters of the name. This was due to a misunderstanding in the first place, and the labour of correcting it no one has been able to undertake.

Nominal Roll of Members of the 40th Battalion, A.I.F.

1781 Abbott, C. N., Pte.—8.8.16
2026 Abelson, C., Pte.—24.10.16
1782 Absolom, D. L. C., Cpl.—8.8.16 (W.; K.I.A., 13.10.17)
323 Ackroyd, C. E., Pte.—1.7.16 (W.2; K.I.A., 8.10.17)
7452 Ackroyd, F., Pte.—9.6.17 (W.)
324 Ackroyd, J. E., L.-Cpl., M.M.—1.7.16 (W.)
325 Adams, A. A., Pte.—1.7.16 (W.)
103 Adams, J. B. P., Pte.—1.7.16
— Adams, S. R., Lieut.—1.7.16
552 Airey, E. M., C.S.M.—1.7.16 (W.2)
2775 Airey, R. J., L.-Cpl.—4.12.16
3609 Airey, T. T., Pte.—10.10.17 (W.)
52244 Aitken, V., Pte.—22.4.18
326 Alexander, B., Pte.—1.7.16 (W.)
327 Alexander, C., Pte.—1.7.16 (W.)
— Alexander, D. D., Lieut.—20.10.14
328 Alexander, E., Pte.—1.7.16 (W.)
1851A Alexander, J., Cpl.—8.1.15 (W.)
2920 Alexander, M. R., L.-Cpl.—4.12.16 (W.)
1784 Alford, S. J., Pte.—8.8.16 (W.3)
— Allan, A. R., Lieut. (trf.)—(D.O.W., 10.1.17)
226 Allan, G. C., Pte.—1.7.16 (W.)
104 Allanby, J. R., Pte.—1.7.16 (W.)
3270 Allen, C. W., Pte.—9.6.17
329 Allen, E., Pte.—1.7.16 (K.I.A., 28.7.17)
766 Allen, E. R., Pte.—1.7.16
108 Allen, P., Pte.—1.7.16 (D.O.W., 3.4.17)
2776 Allen, W., L.-Cpl.—4.12.16
102 Alford, M. R., Pte.—1.7.16
— Allwright, S. H. L., Lieut., M.I.D.—1.7.16 (W.)
2289 Amer, H. G., Pte.—19.10.16 (W.)
330 Amiguet, A. G., Pte.—1.7.16
74 Anderson, Anton, Pte.—1.7.16 (W.)
1697 Anderson, Alex., Pte.—1.7.16 (W.)
331 Anderson, A. D., Pte.—1.7.16 (W.)
2777 Anderson, A. E., Pte.—4.12.16
769 Anderson, A. G., Pte.—1.7.16 (W.3)
— Anderson, A. P., Pte.—23.5.16 (W.)
1940 Anderson, J. D., Pte.—8.8.16
332 Anderson, J. H., Pte.—1.7.16 (W.)
333 Anderson, L. J., Pte.—1.7.16
766 Anderson, O. R., Pte.—1.7.16 (W.)
7451 Anderson, P., Pte.—9.6.17 (W.)
3508 Anderson, S. E., Pte.—10.10.17
2174 Anderson, W., Pte.—17.9.16
2778 Andrews, S. J. P., Pte.—4.12.16 (W.3)
2516 Andrews, T. H., Pte.—24.10.16
7450 Appleby, R. J., Pte.—9.6.17 (W.2)
334 Appleby, W., Pte.—24.10.16 (K.I.A., 4.12.16)
1786 Archer, A., Pte.—8.8.16 (W)
765 Archer, F. S., Pte.—1.7.16
1963 Archie, B. V., Pte.—8.8.16 (K.I.A., 7.6.17)
1612 Armstrong, C. H., Pte.—1.7.16
1611 Armstrong, E. J., Pte.—1.7.16 (W.; K.I.A., 25.4.18)
1712 Armstrong, R., Pte.—1.7.16
105 Armstrong, S. R., Pte.—1.7.16 (W.; K.I.A., 1.9.18)

2518 Arnol, C. B., L.-Sergt.—24.10.16 (W.)
768 Arnol, G. M., Cpl.—1.7.16 (W.2; K.I.A., 12.4.16)
52245 Arnol, M., Pte.—22.4.18
107 Arnold, J. T., Cpl.—1.7.16 (W.)
109 Arnott, L. J. H., Pte.—1.7.16 (K.I.A., 31.8.18)
335 Artis, C. G., Pte.—1.7.16 (W.)
7696 Asley, C. S., Pte.—30.7.17 (W.)
2763 Atkins, A. S., Sergt., 4.12.16 (K.I.A., 4.10.17)
501A Atkins, H., Pte.
3006 Atkins, R. T., Pte.—7.2.17
1091 Atkinson, P. O., Pte.—1.7.16
1788 Atwell, R., Pte.—8.8.16 (K.I.A., 17.2.17)
976 Attfield, Pte.—1.7.16
1790 Austin, E. T., L.-Cpl.—8.8.16 (W 2)
617 Austin, J. W., Pte.—1.7.16 (W.; K.I.A., 13.10.17)
618 Austin, T., Pte.—1.7.16 (W.; K.I.A., 28.11.17)
2517 Avery, V. W., Pte.—24.10.16
2288 Aylett, L., Pte.—17.10.16
7449 Ayres, G. W., Pte.—9.6.17
121 Bacon, J. H., Pte.—1.7.16 (W.2)
7455 Badcock, A. H., Pte.—9.6.17 (W.2)
5656 Badcock, L. M., L.-Cpl.—8.5.16 (W.)
1792 Badkin, S., Pte.—8.8.16 (W.3)
702 Bailey, F. L., Pte.—1.7.16 (W.)
137 Bailey, G. W., Cpl.—1.7.16 (W.)
3271 Bailey, T. J., L.-Cpl.—9.6.17
2523B Bailey, W. T., Pte.—24.10.16
399 Bain, J., Pte.—1.7.16
123 Baker, A. H. B., Sergt.—1.7.16 (W.; K.I.A., 13.10.17)
1793 Baker, A. W., Pte.—8.8.16
123 Baker, B. H., Pte.—1.7.16 (D.O.W., 4.7.18)
5658 Baker, C. D., L.-Cpl.—8.5.16 (W.)
2537 Baker, G. F., Pte.—24.10.16
2536 Baker, N. R., Pte.—24.10.16
3486 Baker, P. H., Pte.—9.6.17
5659 Baker, S. V. G., Pte.—8.5.16 (W.)
7456 Baldock, A. E., Pte.—9.6.17
1794 Baldock, H., Pte.—8.8.16 (W.)
1795 Baldwin, A. T., Cpl.—8.8.16 (W.)
— Baldwin, C. W., Lieut.—1.7.16 (W.2)
2779 Baldwin, G. T., Pte.—4.12.16
3503 Ball, C. H., L.-Cpl.—6.10.17
124 Ballantyne, R. T., Sergt. M.S.M.—1.7.16
1117 Balmforth, J. T., Pte.—1.7.16 (W.2)
2780 Banfield, E. H., Pte.—4.12.16 (W.)
2521 Banks, A., Pte.—24.10.16 (W.)
773 Bannister, A. H., Pte.—1.7.16 (W.3)
2781 Bannister, E. V., Pte.—4.12.16
1093 Bannister, S., Pte.—13.7.15 (W.2)
1621 Bannister, W. T., Pte.—1.7.16 (K.I.A., 3.1.17)
2530 Bantick, A. W., Pte.—24.10.16 (W.)
2538 Bantoft, R. G., Pte.—20.10.16
3272 Barber, H. T., L.-Cpl.—9.6.17
3273 Barber, R., L.-Cpl.—9.6.17 (W.)
43 Barber, R. W., Sergt.—1.7.16 (W.)

	Barclay, H. L., Lieut.—1 7.16	613	Bennett, D. J., Pte.—1.7.16
1614	Barden, W. J., Pte.—1.7.16 (K.I.A., 30.4.17)	127A	Bennett, E. H., Dvr.—1.7.16
		3496	Bennett, F. R., Cpl.—13.10.17 (D., 4.11.18)
1103	Barfoot, R. L., Pte.—1.7.16 (W.)	2588	Bennett, J. C., Pte.—24.10.16
2782	Barker, J. R., Pte.—4.12.16 (K.I.A., 31.8.18)	52250	Bennett, J. E., Pte.—22.4.18
3015A	Barker, T. F., Pte.—3.2.17	75	Bennett, M. R. P., Pte.—1.7.16 (W.)
779	Barling, A. C., Sergt.—1.7.16 (W.)	120	Bennett, R. J., Pte.—1.7.16 (W.)
77	Barnard, G. R. E., L.-Cpl.—1.7.16 (W.)	2372	Bently, J. A., Pte.—19.10.16
781	Barnard, W., Dvr.—1.7.16	2787	Berry, G. A., Pte.—4.12.16 (D.O.W., 6.10.17)
3013	Barnes, C., Pte.—3.2.17	771	Berry, J. J., Pte.—1.7.16 (W.)
2519	Barnes, D., Pte.—24.10.16 (W.)	7700	Berry, L. P., Pte.—30.7.17
1615A	Barnes, E. J., Pte.—1.7.16 (W.2)	782	Berryman, C., Pte.—1.7.16 (W.)
3287	Barnes, J. A., Pte.—9.6.17		Bertram, A., Lieut.—1.7.16 (W.)
2043A	Barnes, J. W.		Bertram, E. J., Lieut.—1.5.16
	Barnett, L. W., Lieut., M.C.—1.7.16	7	Bessell, C. A., Sergt.—1.7.16
2539	Barnett, T. G., Cpl.—24.10.16	610	Bessell, C. E., Pte.—1.7.16 (K.I.A., 5.10.17)
3274	Barrett, E. A., L.-Cpl.—9.6.17	609	Bessell, E. H., Pte.—1.7.16
122	Barrett, E. C., Pte.—1.7.16	612	Bessell, H. L., Sergt.—1.7.16 (W.2)
3509	Barrett, J., Pte.—6.10.17	253	Best, J. R., Pte.—24.10.16
2783	Barrett, M. W., Pte.—4.12.16 (W.)	2525	Best, T. H., Pte.—24.10.16 (W.2)
5660	Barrett, S. D., Pte.—8.5.16 (W.)	136	Beswick, B. A., Pte., D.C.M., M.M.—1.7.16 (W.)
956	Barrett, S. J., Sergt., M.M.—1.7.16 (K.I.A., 12.10.17)	1804	Beswick, D. V., Pte.—8.8.16 (W.)
978	Barrow, J. A., Pte.—1.7.16 (W.2)	1803	Beswick, L., Pte.—8.8.16
2784	Barry, F. C., Pte.—4.12.16	606	Beswick, M. E., L.-Cpl.—1.7.16 (W.; K.I.A., 28.3.18)
2785	Bartels, C., Pte.—4.12.16 (W.)	3129	Bevan, J. E., Pte.—7.2.17 (W.)
1698A	Bartlett, J. F., Pte.—1.7.16 (W.2)	3130	Beven, W. F., Pte.—7.2.17 (W.)
339	Bartlett, S. R., L.-Cpl.—1.7.16 (W.2)	3267	Beveridge, F., Pte.—9.6.17
607	Barton, F. W., Pte.—1.7.16 (W.)	1791	Beveridge, J., Pte.—8.8.16
608	Barton, L. T., Pte.—1.7.16	784B	Bickham, C. H., Cpl.—1.7.16 (K.I.A., 12.10.17)
3276	Barwick, A. J., Sergt., M.M.—9.6.17	783	Bickham, C. W. G., Pte.—1.7.16 (K.I.A., 7.6.17)
1798	Barwick, A. T., L.-Cpl.—1.7.16 (W.)	785	Biggs, E. E., L.-Cpl.—1.7.16 (W.)
1623	Barwick, L., Pte.—1.7.16 (W.2)	38	Biggs, L. W., Pte.—1.7.16
615	Barwick, R. E., Pte.—1.7.16	37	Biggs, R. A., Pte.—1.7.16
340	Barwick, R. J., Pte.—1.7.16	1805	Billing, E. C., Pte.—1.7.16 (W.2)
125	Bassett, C., Pte.—1.7.16	128	Billing, E. W., Sergt., D.C.M., M.M.—1.7.16 (W.)
996	Bassett, E. W., Pte.—1.7.16 (W.)	614A	Billinghurst, H., Pte.—1.7.16
3612	Batchelor, J. A., Pte.—13.10.17	2520	Billinghurst, G., Pte.—24.10.17 (K.I.A., 24.10.17)
2046	Bates, H., Pte.—19.9.16	3510	Bilson, G. R., Pte.—6.10.17
52383	Bayley, C., Pte.—22.4.18	2788	Binns, L. J., Pte.—4.12.16 (W.)
780	Baylis, C. E., L.-Cpl.—1.7.16 (W.)	786	Birchall, N. S.—1.7.16 (W.; K.I.A., 12.10.17)
1799	Beach, G., Pte.—8.8.16 (K.I.A., 7.6.17)	3007	Bird, G. H., Pte.—3.2.17
1800	Beamish, T. J., Pte.—8.8.16 (W.3)		Bisdee, G. S., Capt.—1.7.16
4021	Beams, J. R., Pte.—12.10.15 (W.)	3511	Bjorklund, G. A., Pte.—13.10.17 (W.)
3275	Beard, N. T., Pte.—9.6.17 (W.)	792	Black, A. H., Sergt.—1.7.16 (W.; K.I.A., 13.10.17)
116	Beaton, C. M., L.-Cpl.—1.7.16 (K.I.A., 5.10.17)	3515	Black, J. H., Pte.—13.10.17
3118	Beattie, J. C. A., Pte.—3.2.17	2027	Blake, C. W., Cpl.—17.9.16 (W.2)
10	Beauchamp, R. E. P., Dvr.—1.7.16	2533	Blake, G., Dvr.—24.10.16
1105	Beech, G. W., Pte.—1.7.16 (W.3)	657	Blake, L. W., L.-Cpl.—1.7.16
2535	Beech, S. T., Pte.—24.10.16 (W.1)	3131	Blake, R. A., Pte.—3.2.17 (W.4)
2786	Beechey, W. A., Pte.—4.12.16	343	Blake, W. T., Cpl.—1.7.16 (W.2)
744A	Beecroft, C. N.—1.7.16	2040	Blanch, C. R., Pte.—17.9.16 (W.)
7453	Belbin, F. D. A., Pte.—9.6.17 (K.I.A., 29.5.18)	3514	Blanch, J., Pte.—6.10.17 (W.)
1801	Belbin, P. W., Pte.—8.8.16 (W.)	2789	Bleney, R., Pte.—4.12.16 (W.2)
7474	Belbin, L. J., Pte.—9.6.17	2039	Bligh, F. W., Pte.—17.9.16 (W.1)
42	Bell, C. W., Sergt., M.M.—1.7.16	52234	Blight, J., Sergt.—22.4.18
1802	Dell, G. W., Pte.—8.8.16	344	Blindell, A. W. T., Pte.—1.7.16
140A	Bellenger, C. C., Pte.—1.7.16 (W.3)	2041	Blizzard, E. L., Pte.—17.9.16 (K.I.A., 5.10.17)
341	Bellette, A. S., L.-Cpl.—1.7.16 (W.2)	345	Blizzard, J. L., Pte.—1.7.16 (K.I.A., 5.10.17)
113	Bellinger, P., Pte.—1.7.16 (K.I.A., 7.6.17)	512	Bloom, C. D., Pte.—6.10.17
114	Bender, A. H. T., Sergt.—1.7.16 (D.O.W., 30.3.18)		
3166	Bennett, C. D., Pte.—7.2.17 (W.)		

222

3573 Bloom, J., Pte.—6.10.17
3572 Board, M. A., Pte.—10.10.17 (W.2)
58 Bock, S. H., Pte.—1.7.16
Boden, H., Lieut., M.C., C.D.G. (Belg.)—1.7.16 (W.5; D.O.W., 29.9.18)
2298 Boer, J., Pte., M.M.—19.10.16
775A Bolton, J. L., Pte.—1.7.16 (W.)
1806 Bolton, R., Pte.—8.8.16 (D., 18.10.16)
2522 Bone, J. J. C., Pte.—24.10.16
772 Bonner, C. A., Pte.—1.7.16 (W.)
131 Bonney, R. S., Segt.—1.7.16
2540 Bonser, A., Pte.—24.10.16 (W.2; K.I.A., 28.3.18)
3279 Boote, C. V., Pte.—9.6.17 (W.)
2297 Booth, H. L., L.-Cpl.—24.10.16 (W.)
3573 Boreham, H. N., Pte.—10.10.17 (W.2)
2405B Bosworth, L., Pte.—19.10.16
130 Bottle, F. J., Pte.—1.7.16 (W.2)
3576 Bottreill, F. R., Pte.—10.10.17 (W.)
1618A Boucher, C. H., Pte.—1.7.16 (W.3)
1106 Boucher, J. H., Pte.—1.7.16 (W.)
1807 Bourke, C. J., Sergt., M.S.M.—8.8.16 (W.)
118 Bourke, E. G., Pte.—1.7.16 (D., 16.11.16)
778 Bourke, F. M., Pte.—1.7.16 (W.2)
2526 Bourke, F. R. J., Pte.—24.10.16
3548 Bourke, J. J., Pte.—10.10.17
2122 Bourke, J. T., Pte.—17.9.16 (K.I.A., 5.10.17)
2829 Bouring, H. T., Pte.—4.12.16
1026 Bowen, A. G., Pte.—1.7.16
346 Bowden, W. R., L.-Cpl.—1.7.16 (W.3)
2044 Bowen, C. J., Pte.—17.9.16 (K.I.A., 13.10.17)
2534 Bowerman, J., Pte.—24.10.16
7464 Bowley, E., Pte.—9.6.17 (W.)
7458 Bowley, L. F., Pte.—9.6.17 (W.)
3280 Bowman, J. W., Pte.—9.6.17 (W.)
548 Bowring, J. E. P., Sergt.—1.7.16 (K.I.A., 7.6.17)
378 Boyd, A. H., Pte.—1.7.16
1069 Boyd, J. H., L.-Cpl.—1.7.16 (W.)
52258 Boyd, M., Pte.—22.4.18
Boyes, E., Lieut., M.C.—1.7.16
52249 Boys, G. H., Pte.—22.4.18
52237 Bracey, S. C., Pte.—22.4.18
2666 Bradford, G., Pte.—24.10.16
2295 Bradford, J. P., Lieut.—1.7.16
987 Bradford, S., Pte.—19.10.16
76 Bradley, J. T., Cpl., M.M.—1.7.16
Bradmore, E. H., Pte.—1.7.16 (D.O.W.)
2790 Bradmore, L. N. G., Pte.—4.12.16
2278 Braid, J., Sergt.—1.7.16 (W.)
1838 Bramich, C. A., L.-Cpl.—8.8.16 (W.; D., 6.11.18)
3009 Bramich, C. W., Pte.—3.2.17 (K.I.A., 13.10.17)
1809 Bramich, C. W., Pte.—8.8.16 (W.2)
790A Bramich, C. H., Pte.—1.7.16 (W.)
308 Bramich, H. L., Pte.—3.2.17
2036A Bramich, H. W., Pte.—8.8.16
3282 Bramich, L. F. J., Pte.—9.6.17
1969 Bransden, E. J., Pte.—8.8.16 (W.2)
788 Breen, C. A., Pte.—1.7.16
1613A Breen, J. A., Pte.—1.7.16 (K.I.A., 29.9.18)

139 Brereton, D. A. P., Pte.—1.7.16
1037 Bresnehan, L., Pte.—1.7.16 (W.)
1811 Bresnehan, M. E., Pte.—8.8.16 (W.2; K.I.A., 29.9.18)
949 Brett, A. G., Pte.—1.7.16 (W.2)
350 Breward, G., Pte.—1.7.16 (W.; K.I.A., 12.10.17)
611 Breward, H. A., Pte.—1.7.16
2301 Brewer, E. M., Pte.—19.10.16 (K.I.A., 7.6.17)
2867 Brewer, W. H. P., Pte.—4.12.16
2528 Bricknell, J. W., Pte.—24.10.16
1071 Brickston, J. C., Pte.—1.7.16 (D.O.W., 20.12.16)
622 Briggs, E. L., Pte.—10.2.17 (K.I.A., 28.3.18)
3283 Briggs, H. W., Pte.—9.6.17
7438 Brilliant, J. D., Sergt., M.M.—9.6.17
2524 Brimfield, J., Pte.—24.10.16
3611 Brittain, A., Pte.—13.10.17
1813 Broad, D. A., Pte.—8.8.16 (K.I.A., 10.6.17)
1813 Broad, D. A., Pte.—8.8.16 (K.I.A., 10.6.17)
3010 Broad, T. M., Pte.—3.2.17
2303 Broadby, L. W., Pte.—19.10.16 (W.)
7357 Broadhurst, W., L.-Cpl.—9.6.17 (W.2)
3016 Brock, F. D., Pte., M.M.—3.2.17
3015 Brock, F. W., Pte.—3.2.17 (W.)
7709 Brooker, L. G., Pte.—9.6.17 (W.2)
776 Brooks, A., Pte.—1.7.16
7460 Brooks, A. E., Pte.—9.6.17 (W.)
3012 Brooks, J. B., Pte.—3.2.17
7701 Brooks, J., Pte.—30.7.17 (W.)
787 Broomhall, R., Pte.—1.7.16
703 Brown, A. G., Pte., 1.7.16 (W.)
1815 Brown, A. E., Pte.—8.8.16 (W.)
138 Brown, A. E., L.-Cpl.—1.7.16 (W.; K.I.A., 4.10.17)
2293 Brown, A. J., Pte.—19.10.16 (W.)
Brown, A. P., Lieut., M.C.—1.7.16 (W.)
577 Brown, C. R., Pte.—1.7.16
2028 Brown, O. W., Pte.—17.9.16 (W.2)
3427 Brown, F. W., Pte.—9.6.1. (W.)
2791 Brown, G. E., Pte.—4.12.16
1988 Brown, J., L.-Cpl.—8.8.16
3302 Brown, J. H., Pte.—9.6.17
656 Brown, L. J., Pte.—1.7.16 (W.)
2042 Brown, L. N., Pte.—17.9.16
2291 Brown, M. B. N., Pte.—19.10.16 (D.O.W., 11.6.17)
6546 Brown, P., Pte.—18.10.16
2274 Brown, R. J., Sergt.—19.10.16
21 Brown, S. I., Pte.—1.7.16
2532 Brown, S. S., Pte.—24.10.16
3517 Brown, T. A., Pte.—10.10.17
1816 Brown, W. A., Pte.—8.8.16 (W.2)
1616A Brown, W. D., Sergt.—1.7.16
616 Bruce, W., Pte.—1.7.16
112 Bryan, A., Pte.—1.7.16 (W.2)
1817 Bryan, C. A., Pte.—8.8.16 (W.3)
7703 Bryan, F., Pte.—30.7.17 (W.)
3428 Bryan, F. J., Pte.—9.6.17
2036 Bryden, E. R., Pte.—19.9.16
2524 Brimfield, J., Pte.—24.10.16
979 Buchanan, V. H., Sergt.—1.7.16 (W.3)
2793 Buck, F. J., Pte.—4.12.16 (W.)
5239 Buckley, T. L., Pte.—4.8.15
3284 Bucknell, J. W., Pte.—9.6.17

3626	Buckney, A. J., Pte.—12.9.15 (W.3)		2797	Castles, R. M., Pte.—4.12.16
352	Buckpitt, S. H., Pte.—1.7.16 (W.)		3299	Castle, A., Pte.—9.6.17
2300	Bulmer, B. J., Pte.—19.10.16 (W.)		2796	Carruthers, G., Pte.—4.12.16 (K.I.A., 28.3.18)
6919	Burgess, A. M., Pte.—3.2.17		2550	Carey, J. P., Pte.—24.10.16
2794	Burgess, C., Pte.—4.12.16 (W.)		2548	Caulfield, H. E., Pte.—24.10.16 (K.I.A., 5.10.17)
110	Burgess, C. P., Pte.—1.7.16		141	Casbourne, E. E., Pte.—1.7.16 (K.I.A., 5.5.17)
	Burgess, F. C., Lieut.—1.7.16		2795	Carey, W. P., Pte.—4.12.16
3518	Burgess, H. C., Pte.—6.10.17 (K.I.A., 8.5.18)		3300	Cartledge, G., Pte.—9.6.17
7461	Burgess, J., Pte.—9.6.17 (W.)		1797	Carlile, W., Pte.—8.8.16 (W.2)
135	Burk, W. L., Sergt.—1.7.16		2052	Carthy, P. G., Pte.—19.9.16
3268	Buring, A. G., Cpl.—9.6.17		2041	Carroll, H. J., Pte.—19.9.16
2526	Burke, F. R. J., Pte.—24.10.16 (W.)		1826	Carter, J. M. S., Pte.—8.8.16 (D.O.W., 8.6.17)
	Burn, W. T., Lieut., M.M.—1.7.16		355	Carter, C. W., Pte.—1.7.16
7586	Burnett, T. H., Pte.—9.6.17		1041	Cartledge, R. G., Pte.—1.7.16
7462	Burney, B., Pte.—9.6.17 (K.I.A., 22.4.18)		980	Castle, E., L.-Cpl., M.M.—1.7.16
41	Burns, J. A., Pte.—1.7.16 (W.)		555	Castle, G. E., Pte.—1.7.16
791A	Burns, J. W. E., Pte.—1.7.16 (W.; D.O.W., 22.4.18)		706	Carter, A. C., Pte.—1.7.16
			705	Carr, F. W., Pte.—1.7.16 (W.)
2299	Burns, L. C., Pte.—24.10.16 (W.2)		604	Calder, H. W., L.-Sergt.—1.7.16 (W.)
133	Burr, C. E., Pte.—1.7.16 (D.O.W., 10.10.17)		356	Cartledge, J. S., Pte.—1.7.16
2296	Burrows, H. J., Pte.—19.10.16 (W.2)		158	Carey, N. S., Sergt.—1.7.16 (W.; K.I.A., 28.3.18)
1824	Burrows, J. R., Pte.—8.8.16 (W.)		145	Cairnduff, R. E., L.-Sergt.—1.7.16 (W.)
52253	Burt, A., Pte.—22.4.18			
1823	Burt, W., Pte.—8.8.16 (W.2; K.I.A., 15.6.17)		40	Carroll, L., Pte., M.M.—1.7.16 (W.2)
3285	Burton, J., Pte.—9.6.17		39	Cawthen, J. A., Pte.—1.7.16 (K.I.A., 7.6.17)
3286	Burton, W., Pte.—9.6.17 (K.I.A., 29.9.18)		1070	Chambers, H., Pte.—1.7.16
1818	Bush, C., Pte.—8.8.16		2407	Chambers, O., Pte.—19.10.16 (W.; K.I.A., 30.3.18)
117	Butler, H., Pte.—1.7.16			Champion, N. O., Lieut.—1.6.16
52257	Butler, J. C., Pte.—22.4.18		1630	Cheeseman, W. C.—1.7.16
1617	Butler, S.—1.7.16 (K.I.A., 12.10.17)		3029	Chaplin, T., Pte.—3.2.17 (W.2)
115	Butler, W. J., Pte.—1.7.16 (K.I.A., 28.5.18)		3520	Chatters, H., Pte.—13.10.17
5667	Butterworth, C. O., Pte.—8.8.16 (W.)		2551	Chadwick, H. W., Pte.—24.10.16 (W.2)
111	Button, H. J., Pte.—1.7.16		2547	Childs, H. H., Pte.—24.10.16 (W.)
132	Button, J., Cpl.—1.7.16 (K.I.A., 13.10.17)		2556	Chisholm, C. R., Pte.—24.10.16 (W.; K.I.A., 12.10.17)
134	Button, E. J., Pte.—1.7.16			Chisholm, J. D. W., Capt., M.I.D.—1.7.16 (W.2)
2038	Bye, A. E., Pte.—24.9.16 (W.2)		2052	Childs, A. W., Pte.—17.9.16 (W.)
777	Bye, A. I., Pte.—1.7.16 (W.2)		2054	Charleston, L. L., Pte.—17.9.16 (W.)
129	Bye, W. C., Pte.—1.7.16		155	Chatwin, D., Pte.—1.7.16
3017	Byers, T. E., Pte.—3.2.17 (D.O.W., 28.3.18)		2066A	Chamley, B., Pte.—17.9.16
3018	Byers, W., Pte.—3.2.17		2109	Charleston, J. J., Pte.
354	Bynon, H. L., Pte.—1.7.16 (W.)		2065	Chamley, L., Pte.—17.9.16 (W.)
2316B	Cairns, R., Pte.		5668	Chivers, V. N., Cpl.—8.5.16 (W.)
	Cane, C. H., Lieut.—1.7.16 (W.2)		2373	Chilcott, J., Pte.—19.10.16
2557	Carne, S. J., Pte.—24.10.16 (D.O.D., 5.2.17)		1959	Chalk, R. G., Cpl.—8.8.16 (D.O.W., 13.5.17)
2788A	Carney, F., Pte.—4.12.16		1829	Christensen, C. H., Pte.—8.8.16 (K.I.A., 26.12.16)
3505	Cairns, J. W. R., Pte.—13.10.17			
547	Calder, M. E., C.S.M., M.I.D.—1.7.16 (W.)		1828	Chilcott, L. D., Pte.—8.8.16 (W.2)
3519	Cantrell, C., Pte.—13.10.17		1622	Chilcott, C. H., Pte.—1.7.16
3615	Cantrell, C. E., Pte.—13.10.17 (W.)		310	Chessell, R., Pte.—1.7.16 (K.I.A., 2.4.17)
3443	Carpenter, W. T., Pte.—9.6.17 (W.)			Chamberlain, H., Lieut.—8.8.16 (D.O.W., 30.3.18)
6552	Cawley, J. A., Pte.—18.10.16		1699	Chick, C. W., Pte.—1.7.16 (W.2; K.I.A., 28.3.18)
1825	Cahill, A. R., Pte.—8.8.16 (K.I.A., 13.10.17)		1625	Chaffey, H. W., Pte.—1.7.16 (W.)
2765	Carlisle, G. S., Pte.—4.12.16		816	Churcher, E. D., C.Q.M.S.—1.7.16
1781A	Campbell, C., Pte.—8.8.16		312	Challis, W. A., Pte.—1.7.16 (K.I.A., 24.4.18)
3028	Campbell, T., Pte.—3.2.17 (W.)			
2915	Casey, E. W., Pte.—4.12.16 (K.I.A., 4.10.17)		813	Chugg, C. W., Pte.—1.7.16

707	Charleston, E., Pte.—1.7.16 (K.I.A., 13.1.17)		7476	Cooper, H., Pte.—9.6.17
555	Charlesworth, G. A., Sergt., M.M.—1.7.16 (W.2)		3031	Cooker, L. M., Pte.—3.2.17
			3032	Cooker, H. F., Pte.—3.2.17 (W.)
161	Chapman, H. W., Pte.—1.7.16 (D.O.W., 18.2.17)		3302	Conway, L. H., Pte.—9.6.17
			3304	Cowie, W. H., Pte.—9.6.17 (W.)
154	Charleston, J. A., Pte.—1.7.16 (W.2)		7469	Cooper, A. H., Pte.—9.6.17 (W.)
			3301	Connolly, H. H., Pte.—9.6.17
3614	Clark, N. C., Pte.—13.10.17 (W.)		3007	Cooper, J. R., Pte., M.M.—3.2.17
3616	Clements, P. E. R., Pte.—13.10.17		3036	Colvin, J. P. R., Pte.—3.2.17
593	Clements, A. G., Pte.—1.7.16		627	Collis, T. W., Pte.—1.7.16
	Clark, W. I., Major, M.C.—1.7.16		2043	Cotton, E., Pte.—19.9.16
	Clark, J. P., Lt.-Col., D.S.O.—1.7.16 (W.)		3024	Cole, A. H., Pte.—3.2.17 (W.)
			2315	Connors, C. W., Pte., M.M.—19.10.16 (W.2)
7359	Clayton, L., Sergt.—6.2.17		3134	Cotton, H. K., L.-Cpl.—3.2.17 (W.)
3461	Clark, F. M., L.-Cpl.—9.6.17		2034	Columbine, C. M., Sergt.—17.9.16 (W.3)
7472	Clarke, S. J., L.-Cpl.—9.6.17 (W.)			
7471	Clark, M. A., Pte.—9.6.17 (W.)		311A	Cowan, A., Pte.—1.7.16 (W.)
3133	Clark, W. G., Drvr.—3.2.17		306	Cowen, T., Pte.—1.7.16 (W.)
2549	Clark, A. E., Pte.—24.10.16 (W.2)		307B	Cowen, H., Pte.—1.7.16 (W.)
3132	Clark, L. A., Pte.—3.2.17		366	Cockburn, E. H. C., Pte.—1.7.16
810	Clark, W. C., Pte.—1.7.16		309A	Cox, F. J., Pte.—1.7.16 (W.2)
3030	Clark, T. W., Pte.—3.2.17		3025	Cole, S. J. E., Pte.—3.2.17
308	Clark, D. F., Pte.—1.7.16		3022	Cotterill, G. W.—3.2.17 (W.)
2798	Cleaver, L., Pte.—4.12.16 (W.3)		3020	Cook, T. A., Cpl.—3.2.17 (W.)
358	Cleaver, Lewis, Pte.—1.7.16 (K.I.A., 10.2.18)		557	Cobbett, A. L., Pte.—1.7.16 (K.I.A., 4.7.18)
2306	Clark, Arthur, Pte.—19.10.16 (D.O.W., 7.7.17)		550	Cooper, V. M., Drvr.—1.7.16
			1073	Collins, A. C., Pte.—1.7.16 (K.I.A., 24.7.18)
2304	Clark, Alfred, Pte.—19.10.16 (D.O.W., 7.6.17)		156	Cook, W., Pte.—1.7.16
157	Clayton, C., Pte.—1.7.16 (K.I.A., 7.6.17)		803	Cobern, C. M., Pte.—1.7.16 (K.I.A., 12.10.17)
2055	Clark, C. V., Pte.—19.9.16 (W.)		2559	Cook, C. H. R., Pte.—24.10.16
5670	Clarke, C. E., Pte.—10.5.16 (D.O.W., 19.12.16)		2555	Collins, R. W., Pte.—24.10.16 (W.; K.I.A., 12.10.17)
2154	Clarke, L. W., Pte.—19.9.16		2554	Coward, F., Pte.—24.10.16 (W.)
1832	Clemons, A. J., L.-Cpl.—8.8.16 (D.O.W., 6.2.17)		2546	Coghlan, J., Pte.—24.10.16 (W.2)
			2545	Coghlan, M., Pte.—24.10.16 (D.O.W., 7.7.17)
1830	Clerke, A. G., Sergt.—8.8.16 (K.I.A., 3.1.17)		2544	Cole, W. G., Pte.—24.10.16 (W.)
1810	Clarke, E. A., L.-Cpl.—8.8.16		2543	Columbine, J., Pte.—24.10.16
1085	Clarke, W. J., Cpl.—1.7.16 (W.3; K.I.A., 4.10.17)		2542	Cooper, W. R., Cpl.—24.10.16 (K.I.A., 12.12.17)
997	Clark, C., Cpl.—1.7.16 (D.O.W., 29.3.18)		2311	Cosson, C. S., L.-Cpl.—19.10.16
			2308	Cole, J., Pte.—19.10.16
795	Clifton, L. D., Pte.—1.7.16 (K.I.A., 10.2.18)		2313	Coe, A. V., Pte.—19.10.16
			2016	Cook, C. E. V., Pte.—27.7.15
619	Clayton, F. G., Pte.—1.7.16 (W.)		2049	Cowen, C. W., Pte.—1.9.16 (K.I.A., 23.7.17)
658	Clarke, B. G., Sergt.—1.7.16 (W.; K.I.A., 28.3.18)		2059	Connelly, L. H., L.-Cpl.—17.9.16
360	Clements, W. C., L.-Cpl.—1.7.16		2067A	Cox, J., L.-Cpl., M.M.—17.9.16
2307	Clampett, F. P., Pte.—19.10.16		2061	Cook, E. A., Sergt., M.M.—17.9.16 —(W.4)
809	Claridge, E. G., Pte.—1.7.16 (W.)		2060	Contencin, L. T., Pte.—17.9.16
359	Clements, C. E., Cpl.—1.7.16 (W.2)		2801	Cole, W. E., Pte.—4.12.16
159	Clifford, S. C., Pte.—1.7.16 (W.)		807	Cooper, J., Dvr.—1.7.16
152	Clifford, T. G., Cpl.—1.7.16		2058	Cooper, C. T., Pte.—17.9.16 (W.)
151	Clark, E. A., Pte.—1.7.16 (W.3)		804	Connors, D. J., Pte.—1.7.16 (W.2)
150	Clark, G., Pte.—1.7.16 (W.2)		800	Coxall, C. C., Pte.—1.7.16 (K.I.A., 7.6.17)
19871	Clifton, J. E., Pte.			
20191	Connor, H. F., Pte.		796	Cook, N. J., Pte.—1.7.16 (W.)
4478	Cottrell, H. J., Pte.		5675	Cosgrove, P. L., Pte.—10.5.16 (W.)
21588	Cox, F. E. D., Pte.		5674	Cooper, C. H., Cpl.—8.5.16
20731	Cooper, F., Pte.		5673	Conners, M. L., Pte.—8.5.16 (W.)
20662	Corbett, G. W., Pte.		5672	Cole, J. H. O., Pte.—8.5.16
3499	Cole, S. R., Sergt.—6.10.17 (D.O.W., 13.9.18)		2047	Collins, A. T., Pte.—19.9.16
			1967	Cox, P. F., Cpl.—8.8.16 (W.2)
2553	Cook, A. J., Pte.—24.10.16 (W.1)		1961	Cox, W., Pte.—8.8.16
2305B	Corkindale, Pte.—19.10.16 (W.2)		1837	Coppleman, H. C. J., Pte.—8.8.16 (W.2)
3575	Cocker, A. T., Pte.—10.10.17 (W.)			
3576	Cooper, S. F., Pte.—10.10.17 (K.I.A., 26.5.18)		1624	Cockerill, J. M., Pte.—1.7.16
797	Cox, M. E., L.-Cpl.—1.7.16 (W.2)			

1835	Coombe, M., Pte.—8.8.16 (K.I.A., 4.10.17)		774	Crouch, R. W., Pte.—1.7.16
1833	Cole, H., Cpl.—8.8.16 (W.)		364	Crole, F. C., Sergt.—1.7.16 (K.I.A., 8.5.17)
1819	Colhoun, J. C., Dvr.—8.8.16			Cruickshank, A. La T., Capt.—1.7.16
1701	Cowen, T., Pte.—1.7.16 (W.)			Cruickshank, M. H., Capt.
1700	Cowen, S., Pte.—1.7.16 (W.)		363	Crocker, A. C., Pte.—1.7.16 (W.)
1026	Cormack, G. B., Pte.—1.7.16 (W.3)		3167	Crocker, B. S., Pte.—7.2.17
1010	Cock, J. A., Pte.—1.7.16		80	Crabtree, H. T., Pte.—1.7.16 (W.2)
1678	Collett, A., Pte.—1.7.16		68	Crawford, L. G., Pte.—1.7.16 (W.2)
79B	Conrad, C. J., Dvr.—1.7.16		7963	Cullen, A. V., Pte.—20.7.17
981	Coulson, H. A., Pte.—1.7.16 (W.)		52261	Currier, S. G., Pte.—22.4.18
811	Cole, L. N. M., Pte.—1.7.16		2534	Cush, W. L., Pte.—24.10.16
808	Cole, A. J., L.-Cpl.—1.7.16 (W.)		3497	Cunningham, J., Sergt.—4.11.17
806	Corney, A. C., Pte.—1.7.16		3507	Cullen, I. S., Pte.—13.10.17 (W.)
2309B	Courto, F. J., Pte.—24.10.16 (W.)		7717	Curtis, M. E., Pte.—30.7.17 (D.O.W., 24.8.18)
805	Conrades, C. A., Pte.—1.7.16 (W.)			
802	Corlett, H. R., Pte.—1.7.16		2552	Curtis, A. H., Cpl.—24.10.16 (W.)
801	Cox, C. H., Pte.—1.7.16 (K.I.A., 4.8.17)		3306	Curtin, R., Pte.—9.6.17
799	Collings, E. D., Pte., M.M.—1.7.16 (W., K.I.A. 28.3.18)		3021	Cumming, M. L., Pte.—3.2.17 (W.)
798	Cornish, E. H., Pte.—1.7.16 (W.)		2803	Cure, O., Pte.—4.12.16 (W.)
746	Cornes, C. S., Pte., M.M.—1.7.16		144	Cure, E., Pte.—1.7.16 (W.)
			2802	Cure, A. E., Pte.—4.12.16 (W.2)
704	Cowen, E. J., Pte.—1.7.16 (W.2)		2053	Cullinan, E. J., Pte.—17.9.16 (W.)
362	Copcutt, A. A., Pte.—1.7.16 (W.)			
361	Conacher, K. J., Pte.—1.7.16		2051	Cummins, F., Pte.—17.9.16
3026	Corkery, J. J., Pte.—3.2.17 (W.)		5677	Cunningham, F. J., Cpl.—10.5.16 (W.3; K.I.A., 3.10.17)
153	Cox, O. W. A., Sergt.—1.7.16 (K.I.A., 12.10.17)		2037	Cunningham, D. J., Cpl.—19.9.16 (W.)
149	Collins, V. G., Pte.—1.7.16 (W.2)			
147	Coates, C. H., C.Q.M.S.—1.7.16		1841	Cunningham, D. L., Pte.—8.8.16
148	Conley, L. L., Pte.—1.7.16 (W.)		1840	Cullen, A. R., Sergt.—8.8.16
143	Cornwall, R. H. C., Pte.—1.7.16 (K.I.A., 4.2.17)		1695	Curran, J., Pte.—1.7.16 (W.3)
1834	Collidge, P. T., Pte.—8.8.16		1627	Currier, C. G., Pte.—1.7.16 (W.2)
3023	Connors, J. J., Pte.—3.2.17		1626	Cutler, H., Pte.—1.7.16
142	Colbeck, F., Pte.—1.7.16		812	Cusick, V., L.-Sergt.—1.7.16
93	Colling, G. W., Pte.—1.7.16 (W.)		160	Curran, A., Sergt.—1.7.16 (D.O.W., 6.10.17)
78	Coates, E. T., Dvr.—1.7.16			
26	Collis, C. W., Pte.—1.7.16			Culton, W. J., Lieut.—1.7.16 (W.; K.I.A., 12.2.17)
27	Collis, A. J., Cpl.—1.7.16		7361	Dance, B. J., Pte.—6.2.17 (W.2; D.O.D., 26.5.19)
3574	Croft, S. F., Pte.—13.10.17			
52770	Cross, R., Pte.—22.4.18		6614	Davies, J., Pte.—18.10.16
5676	Cross, A. G., Pte.—8.8.16 (W.)		1112	Daly, J. A., Pte.—1.7.16
52262	Cross, W. J., Pte.—22.4.18		3522	Dandy, C. J., Pte.—6.10.17
3506	Craigie, J. C., Pte.—13.10.17		2322	Davie, M., Pte.—19.10.16
6785	Crace, E. G., Pte.—18.10.16		2804	Davies, W. H. T., Pte.—4.12.16 (K.I.A., 9.6.18)
1110	Crouch, R., Pte.—1.7.16 (K.I.A., 13.10.17)		2079	Dale, S. E., Pte., M.M.—17.9.16 (W.2)
1027	Crosby, G. V., Pte.—1.7.16 (K.I.A., 10.9.18)		2148A	Dale, E. A., Pte.—17.9.16 (W.)
2558	Crosswell, A., Pte.—24.10.16			Dalgleish, A., Lieut.—26.6.15
2312	Crowden, L. L., Pte.—10.10.16 (K.I.A., 7.6.17)		817	Dadson, J. L.-Cpl.—1.7.16 (K.I.A., 4.10.17)
2056	Cresington, E., Pte.—17.9.16		2562	Davis, H. F., Sergt., M.M.—24.10.16 (W.)
2062	Cross, H., Pte.—17.9.16 (W.)			
2057	Cresswell, R., Pte., M.M.—17.9.16 (W.)		1842	Dallas, H. P., Pte.—8.8.16
			3307	Darby, H., Pte.—9.6.17
3521	Creely, J. G., Pte.—6.10.17		5680	Dart, C. S.—10.5.16 (K.I.A., 4.10.17)
1839	Cross, D. O., Pte.—8.8.16 (K.I.A., 31.1.17)		5683	Davis, W. J., Pte.—10.5.16 (W.; D.O.D., 23.10.18)
1629	Crawford, J. H., Pte.—1.7.16 (W.)			
2317B	Crawford, J. W., Pte.—19.10.16 (W.)		622	Davis, S. P., Pte.—1.7.16 (W.)
1628	Crawford, T. J., Cpl.—1.7.16 (W.2)		621	Dart, A. H., Pte.—1.7.16
	Crosby, W. T., Lieut.—1.7.16 (W.2)		708	Dawson, R. S., Pte.—1.7.16 (W.)
			818	Davidson, T., Cpl., M.M.—1.7.16 (W.3)
2050B	Crawford, A. E., Pte.—19.9.16		819	Davie, C., Cpl., M.I.D.—1.7.16 (W.)
	Cranswick, T. G., Lieut., M.C., D.C.M., M.I.D.—1.7.16 (D.O.W., 18.10.20)		181	Darcy, A., Pte.—1.7.16 (W.)
			1035	Dawes, C. C., Pte.—1.7.16 (D.O.W., 6.12.17)
	Cranswick, J. S., Lieut.—20.10.14 (W.; K.I.A., 13.1.17)		69	Dawson, R. H. A., Pte.—1.7.16 (K.I.A., 29.7.17)

998 Dalton, C. J., Pte.—1.7.16
163 Dale, T. W., Pte.—1.7.16 (W.)
1684A Dalgren, C. G., Pte.—1.7.16 (W.)
164 Davis, J. M.—1.7.16 (K.I.A., 3.1.17)
165 Daley, L. F., Pte.—1.7.16 (D.O.W., 15.4.17)
70 Daly, S. W., Dvr.—1.7.16
2276 Dalco, C. S., Cpl.—19.10.16 (W.2; D.O.W., 11.6.18)
505A Davis, A., Pte.—1.7.16
2319 Davis, E. J., Pte.—19.10.16
2325 Dale, R. H., Pte.—19.10.16
2670 Davis, W. C., Pte.—4.10.16
2070 Davis, F. D., L.-Cpl.—17.9.16 (W.)
2323 Davie, G. R., Pte.—19.10.16 (K.I.A., 6.10.17)
52278 Day, C. O. W., Pte.—22.4.18
3523 Davis, W. A., Pte.—6.10.17
2764) Davis, A. H., Pte.—1.7.16 (D.O.W., 29.9.18)
1052)
3501 Davis, E. T., Pte.—16.10.17 (W.)
3052A Davis, H. R., Pte.—15.1.17
2805 Delanty, J. P., Pte.—4.12.16
3309 Dennis, C. E., Pte.—30.3.17 (W.)
7478 Dent, C. E., Pte., M.M.—9.6.17
7479 Derrick, W. J., Pte.—9.6.17 (W.)
7827 Devine, W. H., Pte.—30.7.17
1631 Dell, G. C., Pte.—1.7.16
623 Dennis, G., Pte.—1.7.16
2071 Dent, L. J., Pte.—17.9.16 (W.; K.I.A., 13.10.17)
3033 Denholm, D. A., Pte.—3.2.17
2074 Dennison, J. H., Pte.—19.9.16 (W.2)
820 Dentith, V. G., Pte.—1.7.16
5687 Dennis, H., Pte.—10.5.16 (W.)
5689 Derrick, J. S., Pte.—10.5.16 (W.3)
Dell, H. J., Lieut.—1.7.16 (W.)
662 Dell, E., S'smith—1.7.16
175 Dennis, V. W., Sergt.—1.7.16 (W.)
T1351 Dennis, A. G., Pte.—(D.O.D., 25.6.16)
180 Delaney, W. E., Cpl.—1.7.16 (W.)
365 Denmen, W. H., Pte.—1.7.16 (W.3)
301 Devine, R. L., Pte.—1.7.16 (K.I.A., 12.10.17)
2271 Devenhill, F., Pte.—24.10.16
167 Dennis, M. W., Pte.—1.7.16 (W.)
1821 Dennis, L. C., Pte.—8.8.16 (W.; K.I.A., 28.3.18)
3524 Dillon, T. H., Pte.—10.10.17
170 Dillon, J., Pte.—1.7.16 (D.O.W., 4.5.18)
3577 Dickenson, P., Pte.—10.10.17 (K.I.A., 9.5.18)
3995 Dingle, C. T. R., Pte.—19.10.15
2326 Dicker, D., Tpr.—19.10.16
2321 Dick, A. S., Pte.—19.10.16 (W.)
1843 Dickenson, A. G. J., Pte.—8.8.16 (W.2)
366 Dilger, H. C., Pte.—1.7.16 (K.I.A., 31.1.17)
2069 Dickson, W. G., Pte.—17.9.16 (K.I.A., 29.9.18)
861 Donahoe, P. J., Pte.—1.7.16
52276 Douglas, W. S., Pte.—28.1.18
3036 Donohoe, F., Pte.—20.11.16
3310 Dove, B. S., Pte.—9.6.17 (K.I.A., 9.4.18)
3051 Doak, L., Pte.—30.10.16
3251 Dorum, H. I. V., L.-Cpl.—9.6.17 (W.2)
3525 Dolan, T., Pte.—6.10.17

2066 Dowdy, F. L., Pte.—17.9.16
5691 Dolting, W. J., Pte.—10.5.16 (W.)
3034 Donohue, P., Pte.—3.2.17 (W.2)
3108 Douglas, A. J., Sergt.—3.2.17
2068A Dobson, H. W., Dvr.—17.9.16 (D.O.W., 7.6.17)
Downie, A. A. W., Lieut.—1.7.16 (W.)
5690 Doherty, J., Pte.—8.5.16
2806 Donovan, A. G., Dvr.—4.12.16
2561 Donald, C., Pte.—24.10.16 (W.)
3135 Dove, H. J. V., Pte.—7.2.17 (D.O.D., 11.6.17)
81 Dowie, V. A., Pte.—1.7.16 (W.)
2320 Dolliver, A., Dvr.—19.10.16 (W.)
1630 Donaldson, H. R., Sergt.—1.7.16 (W.)
2067 Dower, T., Pte.—27.6.16
1011 Donald, R. H., Pte.—1.7.16 (W.)
1111 Downie, C. T., Cpl.—14.7.15 (W.)
988 Douglas, R., L.-Cpl.—1.7.16 (W.)
177 Donald, L. C., Pte.—1.7.16 (W.)
661 Down, E., Pte.—1.7.16
176 Doyle, T., Pte.—1.7.16 (W.)
337 Downs, H. A., L.-Cpl.—1.7.16
82 Donoghue, T. E., Cpl.—1.7.16 (W.2)
35 Dobson, L. A., Pte.—1.7.16
162 Doyle, C. D., Pte.—1.7.16 (W.)
176 Down, F., Pte.—1.7.16 (W.5)
2560 Domeney, O. T., Pte.—24.10.16 (W.; 7.6.17)
3526 Douglas, J., Pte.—6.10.17 (W.)
174 Drake, W. W., Pte.—1.7.16
3136 Drew, P., Pte.—7.2.17 (W.)
3570 Drake, A. T., Pte.—13.10.17
1965 Dransfield, P., Pte., M.M.—8.8.16 (W.2)
986 Drew, J., S.-Sergt.—1.7.16
3136 Du Bois, E., Pte.—25.9.16
3527 Duncan, H. E., Pte.—6.10.17
3617 Duke, H., Pte.—13.10.17 (W.)
3312 Dunn, I., Pte.—9.6.17 (W.)
3311 Duggan, J., Pte.—9.6.17
7482 Dunn, C. J., Pte.—9.6.17
7719 Duggan, T., Pte.—30.7.17 (W.2)
1844 Dunlop, M. J., Pte.—8.8.16
2076A Duncan, J., Pte.—10.7.16
Dumaresq, H. J., Capt., M.C.—1.7.16 (W.)
1632 Duggan, L. M., Pte.—1.7.16 (W.)
2068 Dunn, C., Pte.—19.9.16
2324B Dunn, W., Pte.—19.10.16 (W.)
821 Duffy, J. R., Pte.—1.7.16 (W.; K.I.A., 9.4.18)
171 Duffy, K., Pte.—1.7.16 (W.)
172 Duffy, R. T., Pte.—1.7.16 (K.I., 16.4.17)
2073 Duggan, P. M., Pte.—17.9.16 (K.I.A., 12.8.18)
2072 Duggan, F. L., Pte.—17.9.16 (W.)
2280 Duce, W. R., L.-Sergt.—17.9.16 (W.)
52282 Dwyer, J. P., Pte.—24.4.18
179 Dwyer, D. P., Pte.—1.7.16
7727 Dwyer, H. J., Pte.—30.7.17 (W.)
3446 Dwyer, M. M., Pte.—9.6.17
2807 Dyer, F. B., Pte.—4.12.16 (W.2)
5693 Dynan, D., Pte.—8.5.16
822 Dymond, T. W., L.-Cpl.—1.7.16
3035 Dyson, V. C., Pte.—3.2.17 (K.I.A., 5.10.17)
3578 Eastman, L. A. E., Pte.—13.10.17 (W.)

227

3037	Eadie, J. A., Pte.—3.2.17 (W.2)		2086B	Ferguson, M. C., Pte.—19.9.16 (W.)
3313	Eady, J., Pte.—9.6.17		3529	Fenton, C. J., Pte.—10.10.17
46	Eames, A. E., Pte.—1.7.16		3318	Febey, A. G., Pte.—9.6.17 (D.O.W., 16.2.18)
823	Easton, G. J., L.-Cpl.—1.7.16 (W.2)		2811	Ferguson, O. B., Pte.—4.12.16
824	Eberhardt, W., Pte.—1.7.16 (W.)		545	Ferral, H. A., L.-Cpl. (trf.)
52398	Edwards, N. J. H. Pte.—22.4.18		2090	Ferrall, E., Pte.—17.9.16 (W.)
3038	Edwards, T. E., Pte.—3.2.17 (K.I.A., 19.2.18)			Ferguson, C. E. H., Capt., M.C.—1.7.16 (W.)
2809	Edwards, O. H., Pte.—4.1..16		2084	Febey, H. W., Pte.—17.9.16
1028	Edgerton, A., Pte.—1.7.16 (W.3)		2567	Fenner, C. F., Pte.—24.10.16 (D.O.W., 14.1.17)
84	Edgell, D. B., Pte.—1.7.16 (W.2)		1847	Ferguson, R., Sergt.—8.8.16 (W.2)
663	Edwards, B. G., L.-Cpl.—1.7.16 (W.; D.O.W., 12.4.18)		1636	Ferrall, N. W., Pte.—1.7.16
185	Edwards, S. J., Pte.—1.7.16 (W.)		710	Ferguson, I. J., Pte.—1.7.16 (W.)
184	Edwards, B. W., Pte.—1.7.16		709	Featonby, L., Cpl.—1.7.16 (W.2)
183	Edwards, R. W., Pte.—1.7.16 (W.)		626	Ferguson, J., L.-Cpl.—1.7.16 (K.I.A., 30.1.17)
368	Eeles, E., L.-Cpl.—1.7.16 (K.I.A., 28.3.18)		391A	Fitzmaurice, C. C., Pte.—1.7.16 (W.)
5085	Elliott, A. T., Dvr.—23.3.16 (W.3)		2812	Field, C., Pte.—4.12.16
3062	Ellen, W. M., Pte.—3.2.17		3266	Finlayson, W., Pte.—9.6.17
7485	Elphinstone, A. C., Pte.—9.6.17		2566B	Fist, A., Dvr.—24.10.16
7484	Ellis, A. C. M., Pte.—9.6.17 (W.)		7488	Fitzmaurice, C. B., Pte.—9.6.17
2767	Ellis, R. N., Pte.—4.12.16		7489	Fitzmaurice, E. W., Pte.—9.6.17 (W.)
3137	Elliott, R., Pte.—7.2.17 (W.)		7486	Firth, D. M. C., Pte.—9.6.17 (W.)
2563	Ellis, C., Sergt.—24.10.16		2328	Fisher, J. A., Pte.—19.10.16 (D.O.W., 13.10.17)
2327	Ellen, G. T., Pte.—19.10.16 (W.)		3138	Fidler, P. A., Pte.—3.2.17
2080	Ellings, E. T., Pte.—17.9.16 (W.)		2564	Fitzgerald, J. C., Pte.—24.10.16 (W.)
2083	Ellis, H. W., Pte.—17.9.16 (W.2)		2568	Fisher, F. C. D., Pte.—24.10.16 (W.)
826	Eley, F., L.-Cpl.—1.7.16		2129	Fitzallen, C. A., Pte.—17.9.16 (W.2)
825	Ellis, C., Pte.—1.7.16 (W.)		1848	Finney, R. T., Pte.—8.8.16
624	Elliott, H. P., L.-Sergt., M.M.—1.7.16 (W.)		370	Findlay, N. A. M., Sergt., M.I.D.—1.7.16 (W.)
315	Elmer, W., Pte.—1.7.16		190	Fitzgerald, L. E., Pte.—1.7.16
3314	Emms, A. A., Pte.—9.6.17 (W.)			Findlay, W. K., Capt., M.C.—3.2.17
3315	Emerie, A. J., Pte.—9.6.17		6	Fisher, H. G., Sergt. Cook—1.7.16
83	Emery, V. J., Dvr.—1.7.16 (W.)		52290	Fleming, H. D., Pte.—22.4.18
5695	Emmerton, W. J., Pte.—8.5.16 (W.; P.O.W.)		371	Fleming, J., Pte.—1.7.16 (K.I.A., 2.4.17)
5	Emms, H. J., Sergt.—1.7.16 (W.)		52282	Fletcher, I. M., Pte.—22.4.18
3241A	England, R., Pte.—9.6.17 (W.)		3321	Fletcher, W. H., Pte.—9.6.17
1084	Ennis, A. J., Pte.—1.7.16		334	Fletcher, E. T., Pte.—1.7.16
664	Enniss, H. J., Pte.—1.7.16 (W.)		192	Flood, R. C., Cpl.—1.7.16 (K.I.A., 13.10.17)
3528	Espie, J. H. K., Pte.—6.10.17 (W.)		191	Flood, H. C., Pte.—1.7.16 (D.O.D., 28.9.16)
52231	Evans, A., Sergt.—22.4.18		3039	Flint, A. E., Pte.—3.2.17
5718	Evans, J. W., Pte.—10.5.16		2329	Flint, H. W., Pte.—19.10.16
7730	Evans, A. E. S., Pte.—30.7.1, (W.)		2814	Flynn, D. J., Pte.—4.12.16 (W.)
314	Evans, H., Pte., M.M.—1.7.16 (W.3)		2330	Flukes, E. C., Pte.—19.10.16 (D.O.W., 10.6.17)
182	Evans, A. J. E., Pte.—1.7.16 (K.I.A., 4.10.17)		2569	Flanagan, J. E., Pte.—24.10.16 (W.3)
1696	Evans, H. H., Pte.—1.7.16		999	Fletcher, F. E., Sergt.—1.7.16
2081	Evans, W. H., Pte.—17.9.16 (W.)		828	Fletcher, W. E., Pte.—1.7.16 (W.)
5696	Evans, J., Pte.—8.5.16		829	Fleming, C. T., L.-Sergt., M.M.—1.7.16 (W.2)
369	Ewart, H. H., Sergt.—1.7.16 (W.)		85	Flood, C. T., C.S.M., M.M.—1.7.16 (W.2)
827	Farrelly, J. A., Pte.—1.7.16 (D.O.W., 23.7.17)		2065	Fox, E., Pte.—19.9.16 (W.)
3619	Fazackerley, N. C., Pte.—13.10.17 (W.)		7490	Foster, C. H., Pte.—4.12.16
2810	Farnfield, F., Pte.—4.12.16		3322	Fox, A. J. E., Pte.—9.6.17 (W.)
2085	Fagg, H. W., Pte.—17.9.16 (W.)		375	Fox, H. R., Pte.—1.7.16 (W.)
186	Fahey, R., Pte.—1.7.16 (W.2)		2089	Ford, C. R., Pte.—17.9.16
1846	Faulkiner, E. W., Pte.—8.8.16 (W.)		188	Forbes, P., Pte.—1.7.16 (W.3)
1635A	Faulkiner, S., Pte.—1.7.16 (W.)			
1007	Fazackerley, J. T., L.-Cpl.—1.7.16 (W.)			
193	Fahey, J., Pte.—1.7.16 (K.I.A., 13.10.17)			
	Fawcett, C. H., Lieut.			
1824	Farmer, A. G., Pte.—8.8.16			
3618	Farrell, R., Pte.—13.10.17			
31	Feltham, A. A. S., Pte.—1.7.16			
3579	Ferguson, J. S., Pte.—13.10.17 (W.)			

194	Fleming, A. C. M., Pte.—1.7.16 (D.O.W., 17.11.17)		Garrard, W. L., Lieut. M.C.—20.10.14	
3531	Ford, W. J., Pte.—6.10.17	1642B	Garland, H. J., Dvr.—1.7.16 (W.)	
5699	Fox, C. F., Pte.—10.5.16	195	Garland, A. C., Dvr.—1.7.16	
2077	Foubisher, B. S., Pte.—17.9.16	1019	Gardner, J. W., Spr., M.M.—	
	Foster, H. L., Capt., M.C.—1.7.16 (W.)	2333	29.1.17	
2076	Foster, A. E., Pte.—17.9.16 (W.2)	72	Gatenby, L. F., Sergt.—20.10.14 (D.O.W., 14.1.17)	
1633	Fowler, A. G., Pte.—1.7.16	55	Garrett, R. R., Pte.—1.7.16 (W.2)	
830	Fowler, P. L., Pte.—1.7.16 (W.; K.I.A., 13.10.17)	1640	Garlick, L. R., Pte.—1.7.16 (W.2)	
695	Fordham, G. Z., Sergt.—1.7.16 (W.)	3533	Garlick, D., Pte.—6.10.17	
		1641	Garlick, G. C., Pte.—1.7.16 (D.O.W., 19.3.17)	
372	Ford, E. E., L.-Cpl.—1.7.16 (K.I.A., 3.1.17)	3324	Garvin, F. J., L.-Cpl.—9.6.17	
316	Fooks, E. V., Pte.—1.7.16	3325	Gardner, A., Pte.—9.6.17	
189	Forbes, C. A., Pte.—1.7.16	2094	Gardner, J. T., Pte.—17.9.16	
187	Fowler, A. G. W., Pte.—1.7.16 (D.O.W., 6.10.17)	386	Geale, F. F., Pte.—1.7.16 (D.O.W., 13.9.17)	
44	Forslund, F., Pte.—1.7.16	7494	Gale, A. J., Pte.—9.6.17 (K.I.A., 28.3.18)	
627	Fox, W. F., Dvr.—1.7.16 (W.)	3280	Game, P. O., Pte.—9.6.17	
373	Forrest, E. C., Pte.—1.7.16	2030	Galloway, A. O., Pte.—17.9.16	
3620	Freshney, C. T., Pte.—13.10.17	2029	Galloway, J., Cpl.—17.9.16 (D.O.D., 14.1.17)	
43	Fra, F. A. L., Pte.—1.7.16 (W.)			
52238	Franklin, G. C., Pte.—22.4.18	3168	Gerlach, C. A. F., Pte.—7.2.17	
3139	Free, W. T., Pte.—7.2.17 (D.O.D., 17.4.17)	711	Gearing, J., Pte.—1.7.16 (W.2)	
		2571	Gee, H., Pte.—24.10.16 (W.)	
3532	Fry, A. L., Pte.—13.10.17	3622	Geeves, C., Pte.—13.10.17	
3580	Fraser, G., Pte.	2091	George, E. A., L.-Cpl.—19.9.16 (W.)	
378	French, J., Pte.—1.7.16 (P.O.W.)	56541	Geeves, F., Pte.—6.7.18	
831	Frankcombe, E. E., Pte.—1.7.16 (W.)	20251	Gilmour, F. V. V., Pte.	
		653	Genders, H. C., L.-Cpl.—1.7.16 (W.)	
1850	Frankcombe, D. C., Cpl., M.M.—8.8.16		Giblin, L. F., Major, D.S.O., M.C., M.I.D.—1.7.16 (W.3)	
2087A	Freeman, E. W., Pte.—19.9.16 (W.)	52292	Ghananburgh, C. W., Pte.—22.4.18	
1634A	French, A. D., L.-Cpl., M.M.—1.7.16 (W.2)	1120	Giles, A., Pte.—1.7.16	
2088	Frost, F. V., Pte.—17.9.16 (W.)	2083	Gilbert, F. R., Pte.—19.9.16	
2813	Frost, J. H., Pte.—4.12.16	1851	Gillam, A. J., Pte.—8.8.16 (W.)	
665	Freestone, J. A., Corpl.—1.7.16 (W.4)	670	Gill, T. H., Pte.—1.7.16 (W.)	
		2332	Gibson, P. G.—19.10.16 (K.I.A., 5.10.17)	
1637	Freestone, T., Pte.—1.7.16 (W.)	1643	Gilbert, R. E., Pte.—1.7.16 (K.I.A., 31.1.17)	
377	Franks, R., L.-Cpl.—10.9.15 (W.)			
528	French, E. B., Pte.—1.7.16 (W.)	2105	Gill, R. W., Pte.—19.9.16	
376	Franklin, J. R., Pte.—1.7.16 (W.2)	2102	Gill, C., Pte.—19.9.16	
86	French, W. B., Pte.—1.7.16 (W.2)	3117	Gillie, T., Pte.—3.2.17	
56	Frimley, H., Pte.—1.7.16 (W.)	832	Gillam, H., R.S.M., D.C.M., C. de G. (Belg.)—1.7.16 (W.)	
52286	Fulton, J. L., Pte.—22.4.18			
3650	Furmage, L. S., Pte.—13.10.17	2696	Glover, R. W., Pte.—24.10.16	
7491	Fulton, A. J., Pte.—9.4.17	196	Gittus, K. J., Pte.—1.7.16 (K.I.A., 2.4.17)	
2555	Fulton, G. W., Pte.—24.10.16 (W.)			
2570	Fullbrook, G. H., Sergt.—24.10.16 (W.2)	749	Glover, S. W., Sergt.—1.7.16 (W.)	
		667	Gleeson, D., Pte.—1.7.16 (W.2)	
558	Garth, L. G. J., Pte.—1.7.16 (W.)	388	Glover, H. V., Pte.—1.7.16 (W.2)	
203	Gaby, P. F., Sergt.—1.7.16	387	Glasser, H., Pte.—1.7.16 (W.)	
5703	Gardner, P., Pte.—10.5.16 (W.2)	3268	Glover, H. T., L.-Cpl.—9.6.17 (W.)	
834	Gallaher, H., Pte.—1.7.16	3581	Glover, C. E., Pte.—10.10.17 (W.)	
2573	Gall, S. D., Pte.—24.10.16	1092	Goss, F. J., Sergt.—29.6.15 (W.)	
	Game, C. W., Lieut., M.C.—1.7.16 (W.)	2095	Goss, A. J., Pte.—19.9.16 (W.)	
603	Game, S. J., Sergt.—1.7.16 (K.I.A., 7.6.17)	5709	Gowans, A., Cpl.—8.5.16 (W.2)	
		3535	Gower, C. W., Pte.—13.10.17	
385	Gatty, L. F., L.-Cpl.—1.7.16 (W.)	2016	Goninon, P., Pte.—8.8.16	
	Gatenby, J. J., Lieut.—1.7.16 (W.2)	1854	Goss, A. R., Pte.—8.8.16 (W.3; K.I.A., 30.8.18)	
383	Garity, M. H., Pte.—1.7.16	1853	Goninon, J. T., Pte.—8.8.16	
382	Gale, W. G., Pte., D.C.M.—1.7.16		Goodyer, R. J., Lieut.—1.7.16 (W.)	
381	Gale, L. T., Pte.—1.7.16			
198	Garlick, W. W., Pte.—1.7.16 (W.)	669	Goold, A. R., L.-Cpl.—1.7.16 (W.)	
880	Gale, F. L., Pte.—1.7.16 (D.O.W., 30.8.18)	666	Goodwin, H. G., Dvr.—1.7.16 (W.; D.O.W., 12.8.18)	
	Gard, J. H., Capt.—1.7.16 (D.O.W., 31.7.18)	628	Goss, A., Pte.—1.7.16 (W.; D.O.W., 8.10.17)	

389 Gourlay, W. J., Sergt., M.M.—1.7.16 (W.3)
629 Gough, W. J., Pte.—1.7.16 (P.O.W.)
202 Goss, H. H., Pte.—1.7.16 (W.)
199 Goulter, H. L., L.-Cpl.—1.7.16
197 Gorringe, G. A., Pte.—1.7.16 (D.O.W., 15.10.17)
2816 Gower, B., Pte.—4.12.16 (D.O.W., 28.3.17)
87 Goody, W. J., L.-Cpl.—1.7.16 (W.; K.I.A., 31.10.17)
3259 Goldsmith, C. M., Pte.—9.6.17 (K.I.A., 28.3.18)
3534 Goold, F. L., Pte.—6.10.17 (W.)
200 Gordon, F., Pte.—1.7.16 (W.)
2160 Gordon, E., Pte.—17.9.16 (W.)
3389 Gordon, C., Pte.—9.6.17
7496 Goldsworthy, C. T., L.-Cpl.—9.6.17 (W.)
1702A Gordon, R., Pte.—1.7.16
3253 Gourlay, G. R., Sergt.—9.6.17 (W.)
3325 Gossage, R., Pte.—9.6.17 (W.; D.O.W., 2.12.18)
3087 Gordon, J. E., Pte.—3.2.17 (W.)
2815 Gould, D. W., Pte.—4.12.16 (W.)
Green, F. C., Capt., M.C.—1.7.16
2098A Green, C. R., Pte.—17.9.16 (W.2)
2092 Grainger, L. H., Pte.—17.9.16
2097 Groves, C. J. S., Pte.—17.9.16 (W.)
30 Graham, G. G., Pte.—1.7.16
2096 Grundy, E., Pte.—17.9.16 (W.)
5710 Greaves, A., Pte.—10.5.16 (W.2)
2769 Graves, A. M., Pte.—4.12.16 (W.)
2087 Griffin, A. L., Pte.—19.9.16
1639 Gregory, H. P., Pte.—1.7.16 (W.)
838 Groves, P., Pte.—1.7.16 (W.4)
834 Grey, W. N., Sergt., D.C.M.—1.7.16 (W.)
Groom, R. E. D., Lieut.—1.7.16
394 Grundy, J. W., Pte.—1.7.16 (K.I.A., 3.1.17)
Grubb, W. E. K., Lieut.—22.5.15 (K.I.A., 28.3.18)
392 Greenough, L. H., Sergt.—1.7.16 (K.I.A., 16.12.16)
391 Green, R. W., Pte.—1.7.16
390 Green, A. G., Pte.—1.7.16
631 Grimmond, J. T., Pte.—1.7.16 (W.)
551 Grimsey, G. S., Pte.—1.7.16 (W.)
Grimmond, H. L., Lieut.—1.7.16
395 Grundy, T. C., Pte.—1.7.16 (W.; D.O.D., 13.11.18)
393 Grundy, H. T., Pte.—1.7.16 (K.I.A., 3.1.17)
201 Groves, F. W., Sergt.—1.7.16 (W.)
52296 Greatbatch, L. G., Pte.—22.4.18
7495 Griffiths, J., Pte.—9.6.17
3621 Griffiths, R. A.—13.10.17 (K.I.A., 27.7.18)
2085 Graff, F. W., Pte.—17.9.16
3326 Grant, G. D., Pte.—9.6.17
7492 Griffiths, E. R., Pte.—9.6.17 (W.)
2572 Gray, A. E., Pte.—19.10.16 (W.2)
2331 Gregg, J. S., Pte.—19.10.16
2817 Graham, R. D., Pte.—4.12.16 (D.O.W., 30.10.17)
1638 Granger, P. J., Pte.—1.7.16 (K.I.A., 1.4.17)
7577 Groves, T., Pte.—9.6.17 (W.)
2178 Griffiths, R. E. G., Pte.—19.9.16 (W.)

3327 Greenland, P. R.—9.6.17 (K.I.A., 17.7.18)
2818 Grey, C. T., Pte.—4.12.16 (W.)
3042 Green, D. H., Pte.—3.2.17 (W.)
6169 Grant, J. W., Pte.—7.2.17 (W.)
317 Green, E., Pte.—1.7.16 (W.)
3112 Gregg, G. C., Pte.—3.2.17 (W.)
2819 Grey, A. R., L.-Cpl.—4.12.16 (W.)
037 Gurr, G. R., Pte.—1.7.16 (K.I.A., 15.4.17)
836 Gurr, C. H., Pte.—1.7.16 (W.)
3041 Guest, J. J., Pte.—3.2.17 (W.)
671 Gunton, P. T., Pte.—1.7.16 (W.2)
52295 Gurr, E. P., Pte.—22.4.18
205 Haas, T. J., Pte.—1.7.16 (K.I.A., 13.12.16)
845 Hadfield, L. A., Pte.—1.7.16
7505 Haig, J., Pte.—9.6.17
2342 Haig, H., Pte.—19.10.16 (W.)
2826 Haigh, J. E., Pte.—4.12.16
52259 Hales, W. M., Pte.—22.4.18
3051 Hall, A. J., Pte.—3.2.17
2591 Hall, C. A., Pte.—19.10.16 (W.)
1068 Hall, E. C., Cpl.—1.7.16 (W.)
840 Hall, E. V., Pte.—1.7.16 (D.O.W., 13.2.17)
842 Hall, F. G., Pte.—1.7.16 (W.; K.I.A., 13.10.17)
2923 Hall, H., Pte.—4.12.16
2346 Hall, J., Pte.—19.10.16 (K.I.A., 13.10.17)
396 Hall, J. J., Pte.—1.7.16
6490 Hall, J. J., Pte.—27.9.16
397 Hall, K. C., Cpl.—1.7.16
7504 Hall, R. H., Pte.—9.6.17
398 Hall, T. G., Pte.—1.7.16
2335 Hall, W. E., Pte.—19.10.16 (W.2)
2534 Hamer, C. E. G., Pte.—19.10.16
3046 Hamilton, C. T., Pte.—3.2.17 (D.O.W., 7.10.17)
52300 Hampton, D. A., Pte.—22.4.18
99 Hancock, A. J., Pte.—1.7.16
2031 Hancock, R., Pte.—17.9.16
843 Hanigan, C., Pte.—1.7.16 (W.)
6044 Hand, F. C., Pte.—3.2.17
2583 Hanigan, E. L., Pte.—24.10.16 (W.2)
400 Hanks, F. H., Pte.—1.7.16
2574 Hannigan, P. J., Pte.—24.10.16 (W.)
401 Hanlon, P. B., Pte.—1.7.16
402 Hanslow, G. A., Pte.—1.7.16
844 Hansson, O. H., Cpl.—1.7.16 (W.)
27 Hansen, H., Pte.—1.7.16 (W.)
846 Harding, A. J., L.-Cpl.—1.7.16 (W.2)
3145 Harding, W. H., Pte.—7.2.17
634 Hardman, B., Pte.—10.2.17 (D.O.W., 3.2.18)
5714 Hardstaff, N. J., Pte.—10.5.16 (W.)
5715 Hardwick, W. J. J., Pte.—8.8.16 (W.2)
7251 Hardy, H. H., Pte.—19.2.17
3329 Harington, R. J. P., Pte.—9.6.17
3140 Harman, A., Pte.—3.2.17 (W.; D.O.W., 5.9.19)
3052 Harper, E., Pte.—3.2.17 (K.I.A., 13.10.17)
403 Harper, J. R., 1.7.16 (W.)
2347 Harper, H. A., Pte.—19.10.16 (W.)
675 Harper, R. B., Pte.—1.7.16 (D.O.W., 12.2.17)
839 Harrington, G. P., Pte.—1.7.16

2345	Harris, A. E., Pte.—19.10.16 (W.)	3331	Hepburn, C. L., Pte.—9.6.17
1059	Harris, A. E. O., Pte.—1.7.16	2590	Heriot, A., Pte.—24.10.16 (W.)
2770	Harris, A. J., Cpl.—4.12.16 (W.; K.I.A., 9.4.18)	408	Hern, J., Pte.—1.7.16
2100	Harris, B. E., Pte.—19.9.16 (W.)	850	Heron, F. J., L.-Cpl.—1.7.16 (P.O.W., 31.8.18)
3536	Harris, C. N., Pte.—13.10.17	3606	Herron, A. T., Pte.—10.10.17
3053	Harris, F. W., L.-Cpl., M.M.—3.2.17 (W.2)	7590	Hervey, H., Pte.—9.6.17 (W.)
3605	Harris, G. D., L.-Cpl.—10.10.17	1863	Hetherington, V. V., Pte.—8.8.16 (D.O.W., 14.6.17)
2593	Harris, H. J., Pte.—24.10.16 (K.I.A., 7.6.17)	3264	Hey, C. D., L.-Cpl.—9.6.17
2827	Harris, H. N., Pte.—4.12.16 (D.O.W., 9.9.18)	851	Hickey, J. D., Sergt.—1.7.16 (W.2)
5716	Harris, T. T., Pte.—8.8.16	206	Hickman, E. H., Pte.—1.7.16
2581	Harris, T. W. F., Sergt.—24.10.16	409	Hickman, P. G., Pte.—1.7.16 (W.)
2828	Harris, W. N., Pte.—4.12.16 (K.I.A., 17.2.18)	3607	Hickman, V. V., Cpl.—13.10.17
		2578	Hicks, E. J., L.-Cpl., M.M.—24.10.16 (W.2)
2829	Harrison, C. J., Pte.—4.12.16	852	Higgins, S. L., Pte.—1.7.16
404	Harrison, H. A., Pte.—1.7.16	3332	Higgins, W., Pte.—9.6.17 (K.I.A., 28.3.18)
559	Hart, E. J., Pte., M.M.—1.7.16 (W.)	713	Hill, A. R., Pte.—1.7.16 (K.I.A., 7.6.17)
674	Hartley, B., Pte.—1.7.16	2577	Hill, E. J., Pte.—24.10.16
841	Harvey, A. A., Pte.—1.7.16 (K.I.A., 17.1.17)	2337	Hill, G., Pte.—19.10.16
		2576	Hill, G. H., Pte.—24.10.16
3043	Harvey, J. B., Pte.—3.2.17 (K.I.A., 29.9.18)	2467	Hills, G. T., Pte.—9.7.15 (W.2)
		2348	Hills, L. F., Pte.—19.10.16 (W.; D.O.W., 12.10.17)
405	Harvey, J. W., Pte.—1.7.16 (W.)	410	Hilliard, F., Pte.—1.7.16
1029	Harvey, L. W., Pte.—1.7.16 (K.I.A., 7.6.17)	3141	Hillier, H., Pte.—3.2.17
406	Harvey, V. P., Pte.—1.7.16 (W.2)	3142	Hillier, W. G., Pte.—3.2.17 (W.)
2580	Harwood, J. W., Pte.—24.10.16	57	Hilmer, E., Cpl., M.M.—1.7.16
3432	Hasking, A. G., Pte.—9.6.17	3433	Hind, H., Pte.—9.6.17
847	Hastie, A., Sergt.—1.7.16 (K.I.A., 13.10.17)	7501	Hinds, J. R. C., Pte.—9.6.17
		2579	Hinds, W. A., Pte.—24.10.16
712	Hastie, H. W., Pte.—1.7.16 (W.)	853	Hingston, E. S., Pte.—1.7.16 (K.I.A., 14.5.17)
1860	Hathaway, W. J., Pte.—8.8.16 (W.; K.I.A., 13.10.17)	1475A	Hirst, J. H., Pte.—11.5.17 (W.)
		411B	Hite, J., Pte.—1.7.16 (W.)
2830	Hawes, H. H., Pte.—4.12.16	412	Hobson, A. P., Pte.—1.7.16 (W.)
22	Hawkins, A., L.-Cpl.—1.7.16	3049	Hocking, A., Pte.—3.2.17
984	Hawkins, R. G., Pte.—1.7.16 (W.)	673	Hodge, C. J., Pte.—1.7.16 (D.O.W., 13.12.16)
3262	Hay, A. S. L., Cpl.—9.6.17		
672	Hay, C. I., Pte.—1.7.16 (W.2)	2098	Hodges, N. T., Pte.—(W.; D.O.W., 28.3.18)
52301	Hay, R. T. D., Pte.—22.4.18	413	Hodgetts, C., Cpl.—1.7.16
7503	Hayes, A. E., L.-Cpl.—9.6.17	7580	Hodgetts, H. L., Pte.—9.6.17 (D.O.W., 13.8.18)
1861	Hayes, E. H. R., Pte.—8.8.16 (W.; K.I.A., 12.2.17)	632	Hodgetts, M., Pte.—1.7.16 (P.O.W., D.P.W., 6.5.17)
3583	Hayes, J., Pte.—13.10.17	45	Hoggett, C. J., Spr.—1.7.16
1831	Hayes, T. T., Pte.—8.8.16 (W.; D.O.W., 30.3.18)	3624	Holden, R. J., Pte.—13.10.17 (W.)
56550	Hayes, W. M., Pte.—6.7.18	2101	Holford, S. J., Pte.—17.9.16 (W.)
2175	Haynes, C. G., Pte.—17.9.16 (W.)	208	Hollingworth, B. G., L.-Cpl.—1.7.16 (D.O.W., 16.6.17)
52308	Hayward, A. N., Pte.—22.4.18		
1644	Hayter, B., Pte.—1.7.16 (W.)	3047	Holmes, E. J., L.-Cpl., M.M.—3.2.17
2092	Hayton, B., Pte.—19.9.16		
2587	Hazell, F. A., Pte.—24.10.16 (K.I.A., 30.9.17)	2589	Holmstrom, A. H., Pte.—24.10.16 (W.)
3537	Hazlewood, G. E., Pte.—6.10.17	2344	Hoole, C. J., Pte.—19.10.16 (K.I.A., 13.10.17)
2339	Healey, J. M., Pte.—19.10.16 (W.2)		
2575	Hean, C. T., Pte.—24.10.16 (W.3)	2823	Hooper, E. W., Pte.—4.12.16 (W.)
207	Hearps, C., Pte., M.M.—1.7.16	3045	Hooper, T., Pte.—3.2.17 (W.)
848	Healey, J. L., Pte.—1.7.16	7248	Honey, P., Pte.—19.2.17 (W.)
2670	Heazlewood, G. E., Pte.—6.10.17	2594	Honner, S. J., Pte.—24.10.16 (W.)
3330	Heazlewood, W. G., Pte.—9.6.17 (K.I.A., 31.8.18)	651	Hope, C., Sergt.—20.10.14 (W.3)
2290	Heeney, W. J., Pte.—19.10.16 (W.3)	2584	Hope, W., Pte.—24.10.16
2338	Hedge, E., Pte.—19.10.16 (W.)		Horler, T. J., Capt., M.I.D.—1.7.16
849	Henderson, R., Pte.—1.7.16 (W.; D.O.W., 8.3.17)	415	Horne, A., Cpl.—1.7.16 (W.)
1703	Henley, G. H., Sergt.—1.7.16 (W.2)	2336	Horne, E. G., Pte.—19.10.16
3444	Henri, L., Pte.—9.6.17 (W.)	2294	Horne, H. H., Pte.—19.10.16 (W.; K.I.A., 22.4.18)
2821	Henry, H. L., L.-Cpl.—4.12.16 (K.I.A., 4.10.17)	416	Hoskin, F. J., Pte.—1.7.16

231

	Hoskins, T. T., Lieut.—1.7.16 (W.2)
2824	Hosking, J. J., Pte.—4.12.16 (W.2)
855	Howard, A., Pte.—1.7.16 (W.)
3050	Howard, A. C., Pte.—3.2.17 (W.)
3048	Howard, B., Pte.—3.2.17
7683	Howard, H. H., Cpl.—9.6.17 (W.)
1647	How, D. R., Pte.—1.7.16 (W.; D.O.W., 24.4.18)
418	Howe, F. A., Pte.—1.7.16 (W.)
2099	Howell, A. J., Pte.—19.9.16
854	Howell, D. R. S., Pte.—1.7.6 (W.2; K.I.A., 22.4.18)
560	Howell, E., Pte.—1.7.16 (W.; K.I.A., 4.10.17)
419	Howell, E. C., Pte.—1.7.16 (K.I.A., 4.10.17)
318	Howell, L. A., Cpl.—1.7.16 (D.O.W., 16.6.17)
836	Howells, W. J. V., L.-Cpl.—1.7.16 (W.4)
	Howes, W., Chaplain—1.7.16
1113	Hudson, A. D., L.-Cpl.—1.7.16 (W.4)
1866	Hudson, A. E., Pte.—8.8.16 (W.)
3571	Hudson, E. H., Pte.—13.10.17 (W.)
2585	Hudson, W. T. J., Pte.—24.10.16
1067	Hughes, F., Pte.—1.7.16
420	Hume, W. J., Pte.—1.7.16 (D.O.W., 1.2.17)
204	Hunn, A. W., Pte.—1.7.16
561	Hunt, R., Pte.—1.7.16 (W.2)
1197	Hunt, W., Pte.—20.12.14 (W.)
7825	Hunt, W. J., Pte.—30.7.17
1867	Hunter, E. F., Pte., M.M.—8.8.16 (W.)
1645A	Hunter, W. R., Pte.—1.7.16 (K.I.A., 6.5.17)
421	Hurd, C. H., Pte.—1.7.16
5722	Hurst, R. H., Pte.—8.8.16
2825	Hutcheson, F. W., Pte.—1.7.16 (W.; D.O.W., 24.4.18)
422	Hutchins, D., Pte.—1.7.16
857	Hutchinson, E. A., C.S.M.—1.7.16 (W.2)
2919	Hutchison, A. M., Pte.—1.7.16 (W.)
3333	Hutton, H., Pte.—9.6.17
5723	Huxley, C. H. A., Pte.—10.5.16 (W.; K.I.A., 8.6.17)
3625	Huxtable, A. S., Pte.—13.10.17
5724	Hyde, C., Pte.—8.5.16
858	Hyland, G. F., Pte.—1.7.16
5686	Hyland, H. J., Pte.—8.8.16
1646	Hyland, L. W., Pte.—1.7.16 (W.2; D.O.W., 16.12.17)
2592	Hyland, M. F., Pte.—24.10.16 (K.I.A., 12.10.17)
2771	Hynds, E., Pte., M.M.—4.12.16
2582	Hynes, S., Pte.—24.10.16
2831	Ibbott, M. A., Pte.—4.12.16
2107	Ikin, A. L., Pte.—17.9.16 (W.)
1962A	Illslow, J., Pte.—8.8.16
2832	Illingworth, O. J., Cpl.—4.12.16 (W.)
423	Imlach, J., L.-Cpl.—1.7.16 (W.)
2833	Ingram, J. H., Pte.—4.12.16
562	Innis, A. R., L.-Cpl.—1.7.16
424	Ion, J. W., Cpl.—1.7.16 (W.2)
859	Ireland, H. L., Pte.—1.7.16
2103	Ivey, W. J. P., Pte.—17.9.16 (K.I.A., 7.6.17)
1869	Ivory, B. J., Pte.—8.8.16 (W.)
319	Izard, A. E., L.-Cpl.—1.7.16

3626	Isaacs, L. E., Cpl.—13.10.17
1070	Jackman, T. T., Pte.—1.7.16
52314	Jamieson, F. D., Pte.—22.4.18
3539	James, H., Pte.—6.10.17 (W.)
425	Jackson, B., Cpl.—1.7.16 (W.)
3538	Jackson, J. V., Pte.—6.10.17
426	Jackson, G. E., Pte.—1.7.16 (W.)
3585	Jacques, A. H., Pte.—13.10.17
7750	James, E. W. R., Pte.—30.7.17
7507	Jackson, H., Pte.—9.6.17 (W.2)
10486	James, A. L. F., Pte.
2032	James, H. O., Cpl.—19.9.16 (D.O.W., 14.10.17)
2835	James, A., Pte.—4.12.16 (W.2)
2350	Jackson, C. C., Pte.—19.10.16 (W.2)
2104	Jacobs, W. G., Pte.—17.9.16 (W.2)
212	James, A. E., Pte.—1.7.16 (W.2)
860	Jacobson, A., Sergt., M.M.—1.7.16 (W.2)
427	Jacobsen, A. E., Pte.—1.7.16 (W.)
1870	James, W. A., Pte.—8.8.16
1872	Jaffray, W., Pte.—8.8.16 (K.I.A., 13.10.17)
1114	Jarvis, R. W., Pte., M.M.—1.7.16 (W.)
919A	Jackson, W. J., Pte.
428	Jago, G. H., Pte.—6.10.17 (D.O.W., 7.6.17)
2284	Jago, A., L.-Cpl.—19.10.16 (D.O.W., 7.10.17)
211	James, H. T., Pte.—1.7.16
59	Jack, A. E., Pte.—1.7.16 (W.)
2834	Jack, C. L., Pte.—4.12.16 (W.)
	Jackson, B. J., Lieut., M.C.—1.7.16 (W.)
1871	Jarritt, C. W., Pte.—8.8.16
52311	Jeffrey, A. E., Pte.—22.4.18
3540	Jensen, L. H., Pte.—6.10.17 (W.)
6584	Jeffs, E. A., Pte.—13.10.17 (K.I.A., 5.7.18)
2925	Jenkins, R. A., Pte.—4.12.16 (W.)
5728	Jetson, W. T., Pte.—10.5.16 (W.)
209	Jessup, W. W., Pte.—1.7.16 (D.O.D., 23.10.16)
3334	Jenkins, H., Pte.—9.6.17 (W.)
3445	Jenkins, W. R. S., Pte.—9.6.17 (W.2)
2352	Jeffrey, D., Pte.—17.10.16 (W.; K.I.A., 4.8.17)
2105	Jesser, T. L., Pte.—17.9.16 (W.)
1651	Jeffrey, J. D., Cpl., D.C.M.—1.7.16 (W.4)
861	Jenkins, A. B., Cpl.—1.7.16 (W.2)
751	Jenkins, F. W., Pte.—1.7.16 (W.)
3541	Jones, G., Pte.—13.10.17
3337	Jones, M. G., Pte.—9.6.17
3339	Jones, W. J., Pte.—9.6.17
377	Jones, J. A., L.-Cpl.—4.8.16
737	Jackson, L. W. S., Pte.—1.7.16 (D.O.D., 11.9.16)
3336	Jones, D. L., Pte.—9.6.17
3338	Jones, W. G., Pte.—9.6.17 (W.)
3627	Johnson, C. A. G., Pte.—13.10.17 (W.)
7508	Johnson, A. J., Pte.—9.6.17
6360	Johnson, H. W., Pte.—9.6.17
3341	Johnson, H. J., Pte.—9.6.17 (D.O.W., 18.7.18)
3342	Jordan, A. B., Pte.—9.6.17 (W.3)
432	Jordan, E. T., Pte.—1.7.16 (W.)
3340	Johnson, E. H., Pte.—9.6.17 (W.)
3243	Jones, P. L., Sergt.—9.6.17
2351	Johnson, H., Pte.—19.10.16 (W.)

3242	Jones, F. G., Pte.—7.2.17 (W.)		2353	Kelly, W. E. J., Pte.—19.10.16 (W.)
1000	Jones, J. A. E., Pte.—1.7 16 (W.)			
3054	Jones, R. R., Dvr.—3.2.17 (W.)		868	Kelb, W., Pte.—1.7.16 (K.I.A., 17.7.17)
2177	Johnson, G. D., Pte.—17.9.16			
3504	Joyce, T. P., Pte.—10.10.17		5736	Kiddle, R., L.-Cpl.—10.5.16 (W.; K.I.A., 28.3.18)
430	Jones, W. T., Pte.—1.7.16 (K.I.A., 12.7.17)			
2349	Jones, A. A., Pte.—17.10.16 (K.I.A., 7.6.17)		3345	King, A. E., Pte.—9.6.17
		1652	King, J. O., Pte.—1.7.16
2596	Jones, G. E., Pte.—24.10.16 (W.)		437	Kingston, G. E. H., Pte.—1.7.16 (W.2)
2595	Jones, B J. H., Pte.—24.10.16 (W.2)		3586	Kirfoot, B. H., Pte.—10.10.17
		3059	Kippax, K. M., Pte.—2.3.17
2063	Johnstone, A. J., Pte.—17.9.16		3434	Kimberley, J. F., Pte.—10.10.17
2106	Johnstone, E. E., Pte.—17.9.16		216	Kilpatrick, H. R., Pte.—1.7.16
3335	Jolly, J., Pte.—9.6.17		3346	Kirkwood, S., L.-Cpl.—9.6.17
2837	Jones, E. J., Pte.—4.12.16		3143	Kircaldy, W. I. N., Pte.—7.2.17
5730	Jones, D. W., Pte.—8.5.16 (W.)		3061	King, J. R., Pte.—3.2.17 (W.)
5729	Johnson, W. C., Pte.—8.5.16 (W.3)		2969	King, O. H., Pte.—4.12.16
1874	Jones, A. R., Pte.—8.8.16		2840	Knight, H., Pte.—4.12.16 (W.2)
1873	Jones, H. H., Pte.—8.8.16 (W.)		1036	Knight, W. J., Pte.—1.7.16
1121	Jones, T. S., Sergt., M.M.—1.7.16 (W.2)		869	Knight, N., Pte.—1.7.16
		678	Knight, T. G.—1.7.16 (W.; K.I.A., 13.1.17)
1650	Jones, F. P., Pte.—1.7.16 (W.3)			
1086	Jones, A. J., L.-Cpl.—1.7.16 (W.)		23	Knight, C. I., Pte.—1.7.16 (W.)
866	Johnson, E. J. E. H., Pte.—1.7.16 (W.)		2841	Knight, J. W., Pte.—4.12.16 (W.)
		3113	Knights, P. J. G., Pte.—3.2.17
865	Johnson, A. P., Pte.—1.7.16 (W.2)		2839	Knight, A., Pte.—4.12.16
864	Johnson, R. F. L., Pte.—1.7.16 (W.)		3058	Knight, H. A., Pte.—3.2.17 (K.I.A., 4.10.17)
862	Johnson, L., Pte.—1.7.16 (K.I.A., 31.8.18)		56563	Knight, B., Pte.—6.7.18
		2598	Knight, L. T., Pte.—24.10.16 (W.2)
863	Johnson, C. R., L.-Cpl.—1.7.16 (W.2)		954	Knowles, T., Pte.—1.7.16
		438	Koppleman, W., Sergt.—1.7.16
677	Jones, W. H., Cpl.—1.7.16 (D.O.W., 7.5.17)		2109	Koty, G. H., Pte.—8.8.16
		2842	Kupech, F. W., Pte.—4.12.16 (W.3)
633	Jones, E. S., Dvr.—1.7.16 (W.)			
429	Jones, T., Pte.—1.7.16 (D.O.W., 1.2.17)		3628	Kubank, V. E., Pte.—13.10.17 (D.O.D., 16.1.18)
431	Jones, W. H., Pte.—1.7.16 (W.2)		219	Lakin, N. E., Lieut.—4.12.16
210	Jones, T. O., Pte.—1.7.16 (W.)			Lade, F. G., Pte.—1.7.16 (W.)
46	Jordan, H. W., Pte.—1.7.16		2602A	Lacey, J. V., Cpl.—19.10.16 (W.)
3542	Jupp, J., Pte.—6.10.17		565	Lapthorne, C. G., Sergt.—1.7.16 (W.2)
1855	Kane, F. B., Pte.—8.8.16 (W.)			
433	Kavanagh, J., Pte.—1.7.16		221	Lapham, M., Pte.—1.7.16 (K.I.A., 13.10.17)
1875	Kaye, P. G. L., Pte.—8.8.16			
2354	Kettle, L. J., Pte.—19.10.16 (W.2)		220	Laredo, A. J., Pte.—1.7.16
5734	Kelleher, J., Dvr.—10.5.16		222	Lawler, H. W., Sergt.—1.7.16 (W.)
2838	Keogh, L., Pte.—4.12.16		3632	Lavell, A. E., Pte.—13.10.17
2599	Kelly, A. J., Pte.—24.10.16		3347	Lavell, E. A., Pte.—9.6.17
435	Keeley, S. V., Pte.—1.7.16 (W3)		223	Lawrence, A., Sergt.—1.7.16
2590	Kennedy, P. F., Pte.—24.10.16		871	Lampkin, P. J., Cpl.—1.7.16
52318	Kerrison, G., Pte.—22.4.18		679	Lawes, W. G., Pte.—1.7.16 (W.)
213	Kerrison, F., Pte.—1.7.16 (W.; D.O.W., 20.10.17)		2115	Lambert, H. L., Pte.—17.9.16 (D.O.W., 8.5.18)
7512	Kean, H. H., Pte.—9.6.17 (W.)		680	Lancaster, L. O., Pte.—1.7.16 (K.I.A., 7.6.17)
4518	Kean, A. E., Pte.—9.6.17 (W.2)			
1878	Kerrison, M., Sergt.—8.8.16 (W.)		7514	Lamfrey, W. A., Pte.—9.6.17 (W.)
	Kerrison, J., Lieut.—8.8.16 (W.)		7513	Large, R. J., Pte.—9.6.17 (W.)
1876	Keats, J. E., Pte.—8.8.16 (W.2)		440	Larsen, A. V., Pte.—1.7.16 (W.; K.I.A., 28.5.18)
1658	Kelly, T. W., Pte.—1.7.16 (W.)			
3343	Kelly, W., Pte.—9.6.17		3588	Landsell, C. E., Pte.—10.10.17
715	Kelly, J. W., L.-Cpl.—1.7.16 (W.)		20888	Lawton, W. P., Pte.
563	Kettle, A., Pte.—1.7.16 (W.2)		3631	Lamont, A. J., Pte.—13.10.17
434	Keeley, G. D., Pte.—1.7.16 (W.)		1875	Lawford, R. S., Pte.—8.8.16
218	Kelty, W., Pte., M.M.—1.7.16 (W.2)		52240	Larsen, L. J., Pte.—22.4.18
3144	Keelan, J., Pte.—7.2.17			Latta, D. M., Lieut.—1.7.16 (W.)
217	Kelty, G. E., Pte.—1.7.16 (K.I.A., 7.6.17)		872A	Larcombe, S., Pte.—1.7.16
			Lakin, F. L., Lieut.—2.3.18
215	Kearney, G. P., Pte.—1.7.16 (W)		2416	Lawrence, V., Pte.—24.10.16 (W.)
214	Kelly, J., Pte.—1.7.16 (W.)		2604	Lambert, H., L.-Cpl., M.M.—24.10.16 (W.)
436	Kestle, L., Pte.—1.7.16 (W.2)			
3252	Keen, C. H., Sergt.—9.6.17 (W.)			Lawrence, O. E., Lieut., M.I.D.—2.3.18
108	Kelty, M. W., Pte.—1.7.16 (W.2; K.I.A., 28.3.18)			

2033	Langdon, W. R. C., Pte.—8.8.16 (W.)		2607	Lord, A., Pte.—24.10.16
89	Lawler, S. H., Cpl.—1.7.16 (W.2)		446	Locke, C. A., Pte.—1.7.16 (W.)
3245	Last, J. A., Pte.—3.2.17 (W.)		444	Linton, T., Pte.—1.7.16 (D.O.W., 31.3.17)
1879	Lane, B. G., Pte., M.M.—8.8.16 (W.2)		1887	Lockhart, J., Pte.—8.8.16 (K.I.A., 5.10.17)
2643	Lane, W. E., Pte.—24.10.16		870	Lord, H., Pte.—1.7.16 (W.; D.O.W., 1.7.17)
1881	Langdon, N. A., Pte.—8.8.16			
2112	Langley, T., Pte.—17.9.16 (W.2)		2600	Lockwood, C. F., Pte., M.M.—24.10.16
1883	Laurie, W. J., C.Q.M.S.—8.8.16 (W.2)			Loane, R. J. D., Lieut.—1.7.16
3065	Lawrenceson, E., Pte.—3.2.17		3063	Loveless, W. A., Pte.—3.2.17 (W.)
566	Lewis, W., L.-Cpl.—1.7.16 (W.)			Lovett, T. W., Lieut.—17.9.16
441	Leitch, R. W., Pte.—1.7.16 (K.I.A., 31.5.17)		3064	Lockley, H. T., Pte.—3.2.17 (K.I.A., 5.10.17)
442	Lewis, F. W., Sergt.—1.7.16 (D.O.W., 31.1.17)		2108	Locke, F. J., Pte.—17.9.16
			2605	Locket, R. C., Pte.—24.10.16
3144	Lee, H. R., Pte.—3.2.17 (W.)		2844	Locke, N., Pte.—4.12.16
7110	Lea, E., Pte.		1889	Loane, C. H., Pte.—8.8.16
2359B	Leary, J. C., Pte.—19.10.16		2113	Loane, J. H., Pte.—17.9.16 (W.; K.I.A., 30.8.18)
70	Leslie, J., Pte.—1.7.16			
52321	Levy, F., Pte.—22.4.18		3546	Ludby, K., Pte.—6.10.17 (W.)
2356	Lewis, L., Pte.—19.10.16 (K.I.A., 5.10.17)		3547	Luttrell, W., Pte.—6.10.17 (W.)
			3587	Luttrell, T. G., Pte.—10.10.17 (W.2)
3348	Lewis, C. J., Pte.—9.6.17			
1884	Lewis, L. W., L.-Cpl.—8.8.16 (W.2)		3354	Lucas, E. J. F., Pte.—9.6.17
2601	Leaman, A. W., Pte.—24.10.16		2606	Lucas, E. T., Pte.—24.10.16
2357	Lewis, R. N., Cpl.—19.10.16 (K.I.A., 12.8.18)		447	Lucas, A. K., Sergt.—1.7.16 (D.O.W., 8.11.17)
2111A	Lewis, F., Pte.—17.9.16 (W.2)		448	Lyne, R. B., Pte.—1.7.16 (W.2)
5739	Lee, M. R., Pte.—8.5.16		52323	Lyons, F. A., Pte.—22.4.18
3066	Le Grand, B., Pte.—3.2.17		2110	Lynch, O. A., Pte.—17.9.16
875	Lee, F. C., L.-Cpl.—1.7.16		2114	Lyall, H. H., Pte.—17.9.16 (W.)
61	Leonard, C. C., Pte., M.M.—1.7.16		271	Lyell, P. S., Pte.—1.7.16
985	Lee, R. E., Pte.—1.7.16 (W.2)			Mackinnon, A. D., Capt.—1.7.16 (W.2)
2355B	Lethborg, M., Pte.—19.10.16 (W.)			
71	Lindsay, W. A., L.-Cpl.—1.7.16 (W.)		1894	Marvell, W. C., Pte.—8.8.16 (W.2; K.I.A., 13.10.17)
667	Liddall, E. E., L.-Cpl.—1.7.16 (D.O.D., 11.12.18)		236	Machen, J. C., Pte.—1.7.16
1654	Livingstone, H. W. J., Pte.—1.7.16 (W.2)		1895	Mason, L. S., Pte.—8.8.16
			1896	Masters, H. H., Pte.—1.7.16 (W.2)
443	Linnell, J. E., Cpl.—1.7.16 (W.)			Marshall, C. W., Lieut.—1.7.16 (W.)
2026	Lincey, J. A., Sergt.—17.9.16 (K.I.A., 28.11.17)		451	Manefield, A. J., Pte.—1.7.16 (W.)
3062	Little, C. A., Pte.—3.2.17		1897	Masters, J. T., Pte.—8.8.16 (K.I.A., 3.1.17)
1051	Little, A., Pte., M.M.—1.7.16		242	Marsden, L. W., Cpl.—1.7.16
2603	Linton, S., Pte.—24.10.16		1898	Maxfield, F. J., Pte.—8.8.16 (W.)
20101	Lilley, H. J., Pte.		452	Marshall, S. A. G., Pte.—1.7.16 (K.I.A., 13.10.17)
445	Lisbey, A. R., Cpl.—1.7.16 (W.)			
717	Ling, W. G., Pte.—1.7.16 (W.2)		1899	Maxfield, W. G., Pte.—8.8.16 (W.)
718	Ling, C. R., L.-Cpl.—1.7.16 (W.)		453	Mason, R. J., Pte.—1.7.16 (W.3)
748	Ling, C. H., Pte.—1.7.16 (W.)		454	Mason, W. H., Pte.—1.7.16 (W.2)
2114	Livingstone, A. G., Pte.—17.9.16		455	Maxfield, J. P., Pte.—1.7.16 (W.2)
873	Lillico, H. D., Pte.—1.7.16		2119	Marks, E., Pte.—17.9.16
6006	Llewellyn, R., Pte.		723	Marsh, G., Cpl.—1.7.16 (W.)
3349	Lobban, G. M., Pte.—9.6.17		2848	Marsh, F. H., Pte.—4.12.16 (W.)
	Lord, J. E. C., Lt.-Col., C.M.G., D.S.O., C. de G. (F.), 3 M.I.D.—1.7.16		2045	Martyn, J. T., Pte.—17.9.16 (W.)
			5742	Marquis, D. C., Pte.—10.5.16 (W.)
654	Love, A. F., C.Q.M.S.—1.7.16 (W.)		683	Mathers, H. C., Pte.—1.7.16 (W.3)
699	Long, H. C., Sergt., D.C.M.—1.7.16 (W.; K.I.A., 28.3.18)		876	Machin, W., Pte.—1.7.16 (K.I.A., 13.10.17)
3352	Lowe, W. J., Pte.—9.6.17 (K.I.A., 31.8.18)			Mahoney, T., Lieut.—30.11.14 (W.; K.I.A., 29.8.18)
3545	Lockhart, V., Pte.—6.10.17 (W.)		2116	Martyn, W., Pte.—17.9.16
1888	Lonergan, F. C., Pte.—8.8.16 (W.)		5743	Marriott, D., Pte.—10.5.16 (K.I.A., 7.6.17)
88	Lovell, Pte.—1.7.16			
3447	Lockwood, A., Pte.—6.10.17		3077	Martyn, H., Pte.—3.2.17
3258	Lowe, G. T., L.-Cpl.—9.6.17 (W.)		2117	Marshall, W. C., Pte.—17.9.16
3353	Lowry, J., Pte.—9.6.17 (W.)		2615	Matthews, C. W. W., Pte.—19.10.16 (W.2)
3544	Lowe, J. D., Pte., M.M.—6.10.17			
3543	Lockwood, W. G., Pte.—6.10.17		2360	Martin, P., Pte.—19.10.16 (W.)
599A	Long, L. E., Pte.—1.7.16 (W.)		2611	Mason, G. B., Pte.—24.10.16 (D.O.W., 6.10.17)
20217	Low, L. R., Pte.			

2610 Marston, E., Pte.—24.10.16 (W.; K.I.A., 13.10.17)
232 Mayne, H., Pte.—1.7.16
 Mackenzie, E. S., Lieut.—19.10.16 (W.)
2613 Matson, H. S., Pte.—24.10.16 (W.2)
2623 Martin, A. V., Pte.—24.10.16 (W.2)
2672 Maddox, C. A., Pte.—24.10.16 (W.)
5744 Mason, I. S., Pte.—8.5.16 (W.)
3608 Masterman, K. C., Cpl.—10.10.17 (P.O.W., 31.8.18)
3549 Manson, T., Pte.—13.10.17
2234 Manson, R. H., Pte.—1.7.16 (W.)
3550 Marsden, H., Pte.—13.10.17 (W.)
91 Marshall, D. B., Cpl.—1.7.16 (W.2)
752 Marshall, L., Pte.—1.7.16
895A Marchant, C. H., Dvr.—1.7.16
877 Maingay, L. C., Pte.—1.7.16 (W.)
878 Maingay, B. S., Pte.—1.7.16 (W.)
1892 Mallot, J., Cpl.—8.8.16 (W.)
1893 Marvell, C. R., Pte.—8.8.16 (K.I.A., 22.6.17)
449 Mackey, J., Pte.—1.7.16 (W.2)
— Maher, B. H., Pte.—(W.)
450 Maher, E. A., Pte.—1.7.16
2847 Maher, H. A., Pte.—4.12.16
7595 Mayson, A., Pte.—9.6.17
3633 Martin, E. J., Pte.—13.10.17
5136 Madders, D. G., Pte.—26.1.16
2849 Maxfield, W. E., Pte.—4.12.16 (W.)
2845 Mackey, A. C., Pte.—4.12.16
3073 Madden, J., Pte.—3.2.17
3068 Marshall, E., Pte.—3.2.17 (D.O.W., 30.9.17)
3070 Mazey, L. W., Pte.—3.2.17 (K.I.A., 13.10.17)
3147 Mackey, F. J., Pte.—7.2.17 (K.I.A., 5.10.17)
698 Mantach, E. J. A., Sergt.—1.7.16 (K.I.A., 12.10.17)
5462 MacLaren, L., R.Q.M.S.
7445 Martin, J., Pte.—9.6.17 (K.I.A., 24.8.18)
52335 Marshall, W. E., Pte.—22.4.18
7516 Mason, R. C., Pte.—9.6.17
635 Matthews, C., Pte.—10.2.17 (W.; D.O.D., 26.10.18)
3355 Mansell, M., Pte.—9.6.17 (D.O.D., 1.11.18)
3356 Mansell, W. H., Pte.—9.6.17
2335 Marshall, J. T., Pte.—19.10.16
3358 Martin, E., Pte.— 9.6.17 (D.O.W., 1.4.18)
— Matheson, J. F., Pte.—26.10.16
3359 Martin, J. H., Pte.—9.6.17 (K.I.A., 30.8.18)
91 Matheson, F. H., Pte.—1.7.16
 McColl, J. T., Lieut.-Col., M.C., O.B.E.
 McInnes, S. A., Lieut.—1.7.16 (K.I.A., 1.2.17)
 McVilly, C. L., Capt., M.C., M.I.D.—1.7.16 ((W.2)
 McIntyre, G. L., Capt., M.C.—1.7.16 (W.)
11 McConnell, D. J., Dvr.—1.7.16 (W.)
 McMillan, S. S. S., Lieut., M.C.—4.12.16 (W.)
1903 McGiveron, C. G., Pte.—8.8.16 (K.I.A., 13.10.17)
1904 McIver, E. A., Pte.—8.8.16
459 McVan, A., Pte.—1.7.16 (K.I.A., 31.8.16)
1906 McLeod, J. N., Sergt.—8.8.16 (W.)

2851 McKenna, W., Pte.—4.12.16 (W.; D.O.W., 29.11.17)
2618 McBean, W. L., Cpl.—24.10.16
3260 McQuitty, J. McC., Pte.—9.6.17
1907 McLoughlin, E. A., Pte.—8.8.16 (W.3)
7520 McArthur, J. B., Pte.—9.6.17 (D.O.W., 3.8.18)
2123 McKay, A. J., Pte.—17.9.16
2366 McEnnulty, H. J., Pte.—19.10.16 (W.)
2364 McKenna, S. P., Pte.—19.10.16 (W.)
2120 McKenna, W. W., Pte.—17.9.16 (W.)
2363B McKenna, J. T., Pte.—19.10.16 (W.)
3634 McPhillips, W. J., Pte.—13.10.17 (W.)
1908 McPherson, J., Pte.—8.8.16 (W.)
3367 McCarthy, C. J., Pte—9.6.17 (W.)
1244 McPherson, S. G., Pte.—1.7.16
52327 McDonald, D. C., Pte.—22.4.18
19466 McLennan, K., Pte.—30.1.17
52334 McQueeney, M. C., Pte.—22.4.18
52242 McNamara, J. T., Pte.—22.4.18
52330 McLaren, H. H., Pte.—22.4.18
52338 McCoy, A. T., Pte.—22.4.18
2614 McShane, E. P. J., Pte.—24.10.16
3589 McCormack, L. J., Pte.—13.10.17 (W.)
228 McGuinness, W. A., Pte.—1.7.16 (W.2)
2365 McMahon, J. A., Pte.—19.10.16 (W.2; K.I.A., 2.10.17)
7764 McCauley, E. N., Pte.—30.7.17 (W.)
2617 McGuinness, A. E., L.-Cpl.—24.10.16 (W.4)
1116 McKenzie, L., Pte.—1.7.16 (W.3)
7770 McNally, C. C., Pte.—30.7.17
7772 McBain, J., Pte.—30.7.17
1902 McCoy, J., Pte.—8.8.16 (W.4)
2362 McKenzie, R. H., Pte.—19.10.16
700 McFarlin, J. H., Cpl.—1.7.16
48 McKinley, P. F., L.-Cpl., M.M.—1.7.16 (W.2)
719 McDermott, F. J., Pte.—1.7.16 (D.O.W., 3.2.17)
53 McDonald, F., Cpl., M.M.—1.7.16
3071 McDougall, W. J., Pte.—3.2.17 (W.3)
883 McIntosh, C., Dvr., M.M.—1.7.16
224 McHugh, W. G., Pte.—1.7.16 (W.2)
2850 McGree, T. M., Pte.—4.12.16 (W.; K.I.A., 30.4.18)
682 McDougall, W. G., Pte.—1.7.16 (K.I.A., 7.6.17)
882 McGuire, A. H., Pte.—1.7.16 (K.I.A., 29.11.17)
90 McInroy, H., Sergt.—1.7.16 (W.3)
1904 McIvor, E. A., Pte.—8.8.16
3072 McDougall, F. R., Pte.—3.2.17
884 McKenzie, R. S., Cpl., M.M.—1.7.16 (K.I.A., 4.10.17)
3074 McKenzie, J. G., Pte.—3.2.17 (W.)
227 McBain, W. J., Pte.—1.7.16
2337 McBain, H., Pte.—22.4.18
3075 McDougall, J. H. G., Pte.—3.2.17 (K.I.A., 13.10.17)
886 McGuinness, F. F., Pte.—1.7.16 (K.I.A., 7.6.17)
457 McGuinness, O. J., Pte.—1.7.16
229 McPhee, P. J. W., Pte.—1.7.16 (W.)

2279 McKibben, K. G., Pte.—19.10.16 (W.)
3110 McGree, W. F., Pte.—3.2.17 (W.)
887 McArthur, J., Jun., Pte.—1.7.16 (W.)
456 McGee, L., Sergt., V.C.—1.7.16 (K.I.A., 13.10.17)
458 McNiece, W. L., L.-Cpl.—1.7.16
888 McGough, W. H., L.-Cpl.—1.7.16
571 McDonald, G. H. T., L.-Cpl.—1.7.16 (W.)
459 McVan, A., Pte.—1.7.16 (W.3; K.I.A., 31.8.18)
397 McFarlane, H. S., Pte.—1.7.16 (W.2)
572 McDowall, J. D., Pte.—5.4.16 (W.)
3260 McWhitty, J. Mc., Pte.—9.6.17
10452 McGillivray, M., Pte.
McBean, H. W., Lieut.—24.10.16 (K.I.A., 9.5.18)
924 McKenzie, D. J., Cpl.—1.7.16
2361B McKenzie, A. A., Pte.—19.10.16 (W.)
681 McHugh, J., Pte.—1.7.16
3149 McCormick, G. J., Pte.—7.2.17
1001 McDonald, W., Cpl.—1.7.16
2118 McElwee, G. E., Pte.—8.8.16 (W.)
4 McNally, J., Sergt.—1.7.16 (K.I.A., 28.3.18)
885 McLeod, D. M., Pte.—1.7.16
3076 McGuire, E. G., Pte.—5.2.17 (W.)
3363 McGuire, H., Pte.—9.6.17
880 Mead, W. H., Cpl.—1.7.16 (W.2)
1911 Metcalf, L. J., Pte.—8.8.16 (W.; K.I.A., 7.6.17)
2121 Meers, A. F., Pte.—17.9.16 (W.2)
Meagher, N. R. J., Lieut.—1.7.16 (K.I.A., 4.10.17)
747 Mennie, L. S., Pte.—1.7.16 (W.; D.O.D., 31.8.19)
879 Meaney, T. J., Pte.—1.7.16 (W.)
3083 Medwin, P. R. E., Pte.—3.2.17 (K.I.A., 1.10.18)
720 Mehegan, F., Pte., M.M.—1.7.16
3067A Menhitz, W. F., Pte.—3.2.17 (W.)
7583 Merrick, J. S., Pte.—9.6.17 (W.)
Mills, A. E., Lieut.—19.10.16 (W.)
235 Mitchell, A. F., Pte.—1.7.16 (K.I.A., 14.3.17)
881 Mitchell, H. J., L.-Cpl.—1.7.16 (W.2)
Mikkleson, W., Lieut.—1.7.16
3148 Milbourne, S., Pte.—3.2.17
1909 Milbourne, H. L., L.-Cpl.—8.8.16 (W.2; K.I.A., 28.3.18)
5734A Millington, O. A., L.-Cpl.—10.5.16
722 Michelson, R., Pte.—1.7.16
2119A Mills, H., Pte.—17.9.16 (W.2)
1655A Mills, K. D., Pte.—1.7.16 (K.I.A., 10.4.18)
321 Mitchell, H. J., Pte.—1.7.16 (W.)
1659 Mitchell, W. A., Pte.—1.7.16 (W.)
3636 Milne, L. C., Pte.—13.10.17
36 Mirrlees, W. M., Pte.—1.7.16 (W.)
724 Miller, A. H., C.S.M.—1.7.16 (W.)
2852 Miller, T. J., Pte.—4.12.16
1031 Millington, J. H., Pte.—1.7.16 (K.I.A., 30.1.17)
63 Miller, W. J., Pte.—1.7.16
2612B Miller, C. A. J., Pte.—24.10.16 (W.)
2804A Milne, W. S., Pte.—4.12.16
1656 Milne, T., Dvr.—1.7.16

3255 Miller, W. T., L.-Cpl.—9 6.17
7513 Miller, W. C., Pte.—9.6.17
890 Morrison, A. F., Cpl.—1.7.16
892 Mortyn, T. P. M., Pte.—1.7.16
Moon, W. A., Lieut.—1.7.16 (W.)
460 Mollross, O. L. E., Pte., M.M.—1.7.16 (W.)
463 Morris, G., L.-Cpl.—1.7.16 (K.I.A., 3.1.17)
461 Monks, W. J., Pte.—1.7.16 (K.I.A., 1.4.17)
462 Moore, A. R., Pte.—1.7.16 (D.O.W., 1.4.17)
570 Morton, G. S., Dvr.—1.7.16
721 Moses, J. E., Pte.—1.7.16
1912 Molloy, W., Pte.—8.8.16 (W.)
Moon, G. E. H., Lieut.—1.12.15
889 Moran, C. F., Pte.—1.7.16 (K.I.A., 7.6.17)
5747 Morey, W. S., Pte.—10.5.16 (K.I.A., 7.6.17)
7517 Mollison, R. J., Pte.—9.6.17 (W.)
1032 Mollross, R. H., Pte.—1.7.16
1042 Montgomery, R., C.Q.M.S.—1.7.16 (W.)
230 Moran, C. E., Sergt.—1.7.16
1115 Moran, D. J., L.-Cpl.—1.7.16 (K.I.A., 12.10.17)
231 Moran, C., Pte., M.M.—1.7.16 (W.2)
3590 Morgan, M., L.-Cpl.—13.10.17 (W.)
3651 Morgan, L. H., Pte.—15.10.17 (W.)
1657 Morgan, W., Pte.—1.7.16 (W.2)
Moore, S., Lieut.—1.7.16 (W.)
3655 Morrison, W. J., Pte.—13.10.17
3530 Morris, W. C., Pte.—13.10.17
3253 Moore-Robinson, J., Pte.—9.6.17
52329 Morgan, H. J., Pte.—22.4.18
891 Montgomery, M., Pte.—1.7.16 (D.O.D., 27.1.17)
52331 Morgan, W., Pte.—22.4.18
52332 Mousley, W. E., Pte.—22.4.18
2853 Montressor, C. A., L.-Cpl.—4.12.16 (W.2)
3364 Morris, A. B., Pte.—9.6.17 (D.O.W., 18.7.18)
3435 Moore, A. C., Pte.—9.6.17 (W.)
3369 Monaghan, J. W., Cpl.—9.6.17 (W.)
3436 Moore, S. E., Pte.—9.6.17 (W.)
725 Moore, G. J., Pte.—1.7.16
569 Munro, D. C., Pte.—1.7.16 (W.)
2854 Murfit, C. W., Pte.—4.12.16 (W.)
2128 Murray, R., Pte.—17.9.16
3069 Murray, F., Pte.—3.2.17 (W.)
2609 Mudge, B., Pte.—24.10.16 (W.2)
2616 Murfet, L. J., Pte.—24.10.16
233 Murray, T., Pte.—1.7.16
3637 Murray, H. J., Pte.—13.10.17
52313 Muir, W. M., Pte.—22.4.18
3106 Murphy, G.—3.2.17
7518 Mudge, W. L., Pte.—9.6.17
894 Murphy, F., Pte.—1.7.16 (K.I.A., 7.6.17)
56571 Monson, C. A., Pte.—6.7.18
3146A Munday, A. B., Pte.—7.2.17
893 Murphy, W. J., Pte.—1.7.16
3115 Murray, W. H., Cpl.—3.2.17
2093 Nance, C., Pte.—17.9.16 (W.)
7522 Nation, C., Pte.—9.6.17 (W.)
3256 Naden, N. C., Cpl.—9.6.17 (K.I.A., 9.5.18)

2150	Naylor, F. A., Pte.—7.2.17 (K.I.A. 28.3.18)	2861	O'Keefe, A. H., Pte.—4.12.16 (W.2)
726	Nash, E. T., Pte.—1.7.16 (W.4)	2047	O'Keefe, R., Pte.—17.9.16
898	Nas, B. W., Cpl.—1.7.16 (W.3)	3120	Oliver, M. H., Pte.—3.2.17
2619	Newcombe, A. J., Pte.—24.10.16	3161	Olding, J. S., Pte.—3.2.17 (W.)
3639	Neuteboom, P., Pte.—13.10.17 (K.I.A., 29.7.18)	7777	Olsen, F. K., Pte.—30.7.17
		200	Oliver, J. D., Pte.—1.7.16
2855	Newman, C. R., Pte.—4.12.16		Oliver, J. D., Lieut. (trf.)—(K.I.A.)
3078	New, D. J., Pte., M.M.—3.2.17 (W.2)	470	Olding, C. A., Pte.—1.7.16 (W.2)
1647	Nevinson, J. R., Pte. (trf.)—(W.)	246	Oliver, H. M., Pte.—1.7.16
3592	Newman, A. H., Pte.—10.10.17 (W.)	3374	O'Neal, A. E., Pte.—9.6.17 (W.)
		754	Oliver, N. O., Pte.—1.7.16 (K.I.A., 11.4.17)
3370	Newnham, C. A., Pte.—9.6.17	6588	O'Rourke, E. F., Pte.—18.10.16 (K.I.A., 4.10.17)
52342	Newman, G. E., Pte.—22.4.18		
3079	Neilson, J. W., Pte.—3.2.17 (W.2)	2862	O'Shannessy, E., Pte.—4.12.16 (W.; K.I.A., 5.10.17)
573	Nelson, J. J., Pte.—1.7.16 (W.)		
1662	Newman, H., Pte.—1.7.16 (W.2; K.I.A., 25.5.18)	1663	O'Rourke, J. D., Pte.—1.7.16 (K.I.A., 5.4.17)
1913	Neal, A. H., Pte.—8.8.16	1704	O'Rourke, A. J., Cpl.—1.7.16
244	Neil, E., Pte.—1.7.16 (W.)	728	O'Reilly, O., Pte.—1.7.16
2367	Nichols, J. J., Pte.—19.10.16	727	Orchard, W. A., Pte.—1.7.16 (W.; D.O.W., 11.4.18)
2856	Nichols, R. V., Pte.—4.12.16		
243	Nichols, E. G., Pte.—1.7.16	2176	O'Sullivan, E. J., Pte.—17.9.16
	Nichols, W., Lieut.—1.7.16	2032	Osborne, J. H., Pte.—17.9.16
574	Nibbs, C. L., Pte.—1.7.16 (W.; K.I.A., 12.10.17)	2126	Osborne, R., Pte.—19.9.16
		3569	Osmond, A. E. Pte.—6.10.17
5741	Nicholls, T., Pte.—10.5.16		O'Sullivan, T. J., Lieut.—1.7.16 (W.)
245	Nibbs, W. F. D., Pte.—1.7.16 (W.)		
1661	Nibbs, L. R., L.-Cpl.—1.7.16	2420	Oswald, B., Pte.—19.10.16 (W.)
465	Nicholas, N, Pte.—1.7.16 (W.2)	2368	O'Toole, H., Pte.—19.10.16
3372	Norman, S., Pte.—9.6.17	472	O'Toole, C. J., Pte.—1.7.16 (W.)
3371	Nordquist, F. A., Pte.—9.6.17	578	Owen, S. J., Pte.—1.7.16
7775	Nolan, W. H., Pte., M.M.—30.7.17 (W.)	52344	Owen, R. V., Pte.—22.4.18
		902	Oxley, E. A., Pte.—1.7.16 (W.; D.O.W., 12.10.17)
3151	Norman, M., Pte.—7.2.17 (W.3)		
2286	Norton, H. O., Pte.—19.10.16 (W.)		Payne, L. J. W., Lieut., M.C.—1.7.16 (D.O.W., 30.5.18)
52340	Norman, W. J., Pte.—22.4.18		
1039	Norris, J., Pte.—1.7.16		Payne, L. H., Major, D.S.O., 2 M.I.D.—1.7.16 (W.2)
3152	Norris, T. H., Pte.—7.2.17 (K.I.A., 13.10.17)		
1914	Norquay, W. J., Cpl.—8.8.16 (K.I.A., 13.10.17)	992	Payne, P. J., Pte.—1.7.16 (W.)
		32	Patton, J. A., Pte.—1.7.16
3591	Nunn, E. A., Pte.—13.10.17	473	Parry, R. B., Sergt.—1.7.16 (W.)
2857	Nunn, R. C., Pte.—4.12.16	904	Palmer, P., L.-Sergt.—1.7.16 (W.2)
753	Nunn, J. E., Pte.—1.7.16 (W.3)	97	Parsissons, J. S. J., Dvr.—1.7.16 (W.; K.I.A., 11.8.18)
1660	Nunn, E. H., Dvr.—1.7.16		
2620	Oakley, R., Pte.—24.10.16 (W.2)	2064	Palmer, A., Pte.—17.9.16 (W.; K.I.A., 22.4.18)
2125	Oates, D. R., Pte., M.M.—17.9.16 (W.2)		
		1864	Parsonage, J., Pte.—8.8.16 (D.O.W., 4.1.17)
2369B	Oates, E. J., Pte.—19.10.16		
2124	Oates, A. T., Pte.—17.9.16	903	Palmer, J., Pte.—1.7.16 (W.)
468	Oates, C., Pte.—1.7.16 (W.2)	2623	Page, S. G., Pte.—24.10.16 (W.)
1916	Oakley, J. W., Pte.—8.8.16 (W.)	578	Partridge, L. T., Sergt.—1.7.16 (W.)
2859	O'Brien, E., Pte.—4.12.16 (W.)		
1917	O'Brien, M. J., Pte.—8.8.16	2370	Parkes, A. L., Pte.—19.10.16 (W.4; D.O.W., 5.2.19)
901	O'Brien, H., Pte.—1.7.16 (W.; K.I.A., 10.4.17)		
		2631	Page, C. W., Pte.—24.10.16 (W.)
755	O'Bierne, J. B., Pte.—1.7.16 (W.)	3080	Palmer, S. H., Pte.—3.2.17 (W.)
94	O'Brien, B. G. H., L.-Cpl.—1.7.16 (K.I.A., 7.6.17)	579	Palmer, L. R., Pte.—1.7.16 (W.2)
		3081	Palmer, L., Pte.—3.2.17 (W.)
2858	O'Brien, G. G., Pte.—4.12.16	6780	Partridge, A. H., Pte.—28.9.16 (W.)
247	O'Brien, S. G., Pte.—1.7.16 (K.I.A., 30.3.18)		
		580	Palmer, R. A., Pte.—1.7.16 (W.)
575	O'Connor, F. R., Pte.—1.7.16 (W.2)	3082	Palmer, E., Pte.—3.2.17 (W.)
900	O'Connor, W. N., Pte.—1.7.16 (W.2)	2626	Patterson, A., Pte.—24.10.16 (W.2)
		2864	Paul, E. L., Pte.—4.12.16 (W.3)
5750	O'Donnell, J.—10.5.16 (W.; K.I.A., 5.10.17)	2916	Partridge, W. J., Pte.—4.12.16 (W.)
469	O'Garey, R. A., Pte.—1.7.16 (W.)	2630	Parish, J. H., Pte.—24.10.16 (W.)
92	Ohlson, Q. E., Pte.—1.7.16 (W.; D.O.W., 26.2.17)	639	Parish, C. H., Pte.—1.7.16
		2128A	Parsons, F. C., Pte.—17.9.16 (K.I.A., 9.5.17)
7525	O'Keefe, J. M., Pte.—9.6.17		

3118	Patterson, A. M., Pte.—3.2.17	7527	Pilkington, J. T., Pte., M.M.—9.6.17 (W.)
20424	Pakvis, A., Pte.		
	Parry, L. L., Lieut.—20.10.14 (W.)	3378	Pitt, J. M., Pte.—9.6.17
2624	Partridge, W. T., Pte.—24.10.16 (W.)	3553	Power, D., Pte.—10.10.17
		3552	Pickett, F. W., Pte.—6.10.17 (W.)
52352	Page, J. L. J., Pte.—22.4.18	3377	Pitt, I., Pte.—9.6.17 (W.)
2863	Page, V. J., Pte.—4.12.16	3594	Pitman, T. H., Pte.—10.10.17 (K.I.A., 29.9.18)
3641	Parry, W., Pte.—13.10.17 (W.)		
7526	Parsell, G. H., Pte., M.M.—9.6.17	910	Plummer, J. W., Sergt.—1.7.16 (W.)
2632	Patman, C. G., Pte.—24.10.16	2772	Playsted, E. H., Cpl.—24.10.16
3551	Parker, B., Pte.—6.10.17	2625	Plunkett, E. W. D., Pte.—24.10.16 (K.I.A., 7.6.17)
1666	Parker, H., Pte.—1.7.16 (W.)		
5231	Paul, M., Pte. (trf.)	7529	Plummer, B. O., Pte.—9.6.17
52353	Page, R. H. J., Pte.—22.4.18	248	Powers, W. C., Pte.—1.7.16
475	Pearton, A. J., Pte.—1.7.16 (W.)	5692	Porter, E. H., Pte.—10.5.16 (W.)
908	Peterson, A. J., Pte.—1.7.16 (W.)	56589	Poulton, M. R., Pte.—6.7.18
1119	Peter, C. C., Pte.—1.7.16 (W.2)	2123A	Powlett, H. V., Pte.—17.9.16 (W.2)
684	Peebles, G., Pte.—1.7.16 (D.O.W., 1.2.17)		
		252	Powe, H. J., Pte.—1.7.16
13	Pearce, R. H., Dvr.—1.7.16 (W.)	2627	Poynton, J. F., Pte.—24.10.16 (W.2)
1919	Pearson, F. A., Pte.—8.8.16 (W.2)		
250	Pettit, J. T., Pte.—1.7.16	3084	Powell, T. W., Pte.—3.2.17 (W.)
	Penny, B. B., Lieut.—1.7.16 (W.)	2870	Popowske, J. P., Pte.—4.12.16 (W.)
906	Pedder, B. J., Pte.—1.7.16 (W.)	2371	Powell, S. J., Pte.—19.10.16 (K.I.A., 8.10.17)
2629	Perry, C. H., Pte.—24.10.16 (W.)		
909	Pedder, F. E., Pte.—1.7.16 (K.I.A., 7.6.17)	363	Porter, C. J., Pte.—1.7.16
		757	Porter, G. H., Pte.—1.7.16 (W.4)
251	Perry, J. G., L.-Cpl.—1.7.16 (W.; K.I.A., 12.10.17)	3379	Pollington, L. V., Pte.—9.6.17 (W.)
		3373	Powell, W. D., Pte.—9.6.17 (W.)
2167	Peebles, A., Pte.—17.9.16 (W.)	3380	Poole, L. F., Pte.—9.6.17 (W.)
477	Peck, L. R., Cpl.—1.7.16 (W.2)	481	Porter, R. E., Pte.—1.7.16
907	Petrie, D. J., Pte.—1.7.16 (D.O.W., 9.6.17)	911	Price, A., Pte.—1.7.16 (K.I.A., 7.6.17)
3376	Peebles, A. H., Pte.—9.6.17 (K.I.A., 28.3.18)	905	Price, A. W., Pte.—1.7.16 (W.)
		549	Propsting, F., Cpl.—1.7.16
2271	Pepper, H., Pte.—19.10.16	652	Pretyman, E. E., Sergt.—1.7.16 (W.)
6848	Peddle, F. J., Pte.—(W.)		
5771	Pennington, W., Pte.—10.5.16 (W.)	3555	Pregnell, S. G., Pte.—10.10.17 (D.O.W., 2.9.18)
1401	Pettigrew, J. J., Pte. (trf.)—(W.)		
638	Pearce, A. H. A., Pte.—1.7.16 (K.I.A., 7.1.17)	2869	Prout, H. V., Pte.—4.12.16 (W.)
		912	Pritchard, J., Pte.—1.7.16
476	Peck, C. S., Pte.—1.7.16 (D.O.W., 28.10.18)	52351	Price, H., Pte.—22.4.18
		2867	Prewer, W. H. P., Pte.—4.12.16 (W.2)
2865	Pegler, W., Pte.—4.12.16 (W.; K.I.A., 4.10.17)	2866	Pratchett, F. W., Pte.—4.12.16 (K.I.A., 28.3.18)
52346	Perkins, A., Pte.—22.4.18		
2130	Pennington, W., Pte.—19.9.16 (W.)	482	Price, A. V., Pte.—1.7.16 (W.)
2138	Pennington, F., Pte.—19.9.16	3556	Prismall, W. J., Pte.—10.10.17 (W.)
2628	Peddle, G., Pte.—24.10.16 (W.)		
3375	Pearce, A. A., Pte.—9.6.17 (W.2)	3554	Pregnell, J., Pte.—10.10.17 (W.)
7576	Peirce, L., Pte.—9.6.17	7530	Priest, A. V., L.-Cpl.—9.6.17 (W.)
7321	Perry, G. D., Pte.—6.2.17	2868	Priest, C. T., Pte.—4.12.16
3440	Peebles, D., Pte.—9.6.17 (W.)	7779	Pritchard, M., Pte.—30.7.17 (W.)
7317	Philpott, J. V. G., Pte.—6.2.17 (W.; K.I.A., 24.8.18)		Purvis, J. S., Lieut.—1.7.16 (W.2)
		1924	Purcell, E., Pte.—8.8.16
729	Phillips, V. A. R., Pte., M.M.—1.7.16 (W.)	1088	Pursell, R., Pte.—1.7.16 (W.)
		484	Pursell, K., Pte.—1.7.16 (W.)
478	Philipson, T. F., Pte.—1.7.16	1923	Purcell, C. M., Pte.—8.8.16 (K.I.A., 31.1.17)
1665	Pinkard, F. S., Pte.—1.7.16		
480	Pinkard, E. D., C.Q.M.S.—1.7.16	483	Pugh, W. A., Pte.—1.7.16
2761	Piesse, J. S., a/Sergt.—4.12.16 (K.I.A., 13.10.17)	253	Pugh, J., Sergt.—1.7.16 (K.I.A., 28.1.17)
989	Piercey, S. R., Cpl.—1.7.16	7782	Pursell, D., Pte.—30.7.17 (W.)
5752	Pitchford, D. L., Cpl. M.M.—10.5.16 (W.)	267A	Purton, A. H., L.-Sergt., M.M.—20.10.14 (W.4)
3085	Pickett, H. W., Pte.—3.2.17 (W.)	3382	Punshon, H. J. D., Pte.—9.6.17
20281	Pitt, R., Pte.	913	Pyke, T. A., Pte.—1.7.16 (W.)
249	Pitham, J. A., Pte.—1.7.16 (K.I.A., 10.6.17)	7531	Pye, P., Pte.—9.6.17
		3693	Purton, L. C., Pte.—10.10.17
7528	Piper, E., Pte.—9.6.17 (K.I.A., 25.8.18)	577	Purton, R. S., Pte.—1.7.16
		96A	Purdon, R., Pte.—1.7.16

2376 Pyne, J., Pte.—19.10.16
983 Quinn, J. L., Pte.—1.7.16 (W.; K.I.A., 13.6.18)
2131 Quinn, H. R., Pte.—17.9.16 (D.O.W., 30.3.18)
3086 Quintal, R. E., Pte.—3.2.17 (K.I.A., 5.10.17)
54 Quinn, F. F., Pte.—1.7.16
914 Quinn, G. H., Pte.—1.7.16 (W.2)
7790 Rathbone, P. R., Pte.—30.7.17 (D.O.W., 14.4.18)
7793 Ransley, V. S., Pte.—30.7.17 (W.)
3595 Rainbow, O. D., Pte.—10.10.17 (W.)
2374 Radford, S., Pte.—19.10.16 (W.)
3154 Radford, R. C., Pte.—3.2.17 (K.I.A., 28.3.18)
993 Randall, J., Pte.—1.7.16 (W.2)
3092 Rattray, W. B., Pte.—3.2.17
3088 Radford, A., Pte.—3.2.17
3153 Radford, A., Pte.—7.2.17
793A Raynor, J. A., Pte.—1.7.16
2639 Raymond, C. E., Pte.—24.10.16 (W.; K.I.A., 5.10.17)
2380 Rasmussen, G. R., Pte.—19.10.16 (W.)
Rattray, J. S., Lieut., M.C.—1.7.16
2377B Ray, W., Pte.—19.10.16 (W.)
255 Ray, L. W., Pte.—1.7.16 (W.)
486 Ray, E., Pte.—1.7.16 (W.)
582 Rapley, L. M., Pte.—1.7.16 (K.I.A., 12.2.17)
915 Ratcliffe, R. J., Cpl.—1.7.16 (W.2)
583 Rawson, F., Sergt., M.M.—1.7.16 (K.I.A., 5.10.17)
7535 Reardon, E. V., L.-Sergt., M.M.—9.6.17
7537 Reed, M. W., Pte.—9.6.17
2139 Reid, W. C., Pte.—17.9.16
2634 Reed, H., Pte.—24.10.16 (W.)
3557 Reed, A., Pte.—10.10.17
2638 Ready, T. P., Pte.—24.10.16 (W.)
2871 Ready, M. M., Pte.—4.12.16
2872 Reid, W., Pte.—4.12.16 (W.)
2340 Reynolds, C. T., Pte.—19.10.16 (W.2)
2633 Reardon, L. C., Pte.—24.10.16 (W.2)
2375 Riley, T., Pte.—19.10.16
2135 Reilly, F. W., Pte.—17.9.16 (W.2)
3596 Riley, J. M., Pte.—10.10.17
1926 Reid, C. F., Pte.—8.8.16 (W.2)
2132 Reynolds, W. H., Pte.—(W.)
2132 Reynolds, W. S., Pte.—17.9.16
258 Revell, R. L., Pte.—1.7.16 (W.3)
52356 Reader, A. E. C., Pte.—22.4.18
1669 Rector, F., Cpl.—1.7.16 (W.2)
Reed, J. S., Major, R.A.M.C.
1671 Rhodes, A. W., Pte.—1.7.16 (K.I.A., 30.8.18)
916 Rhodes, J. E., Cpl.—1.7.16
7539 Ricketts, L. B., Pte.—9.6.17
52355 Richardson, A. G., Pte.—22.4.18
1694 Rigby, A. J., Pte.—1.7.16 (K.I.A., 2.4.17)
2874 Richards, A., Pte.—4.12.16 (W.2)
1670 Ricketts, A., Pte.—1.7.16 (W.2)
3093 Richards, G. A., Pte., 3.2.17 (W.)
49 Richards, H. J., L.-Cpl.—1.7.16
2873 Richardson, G. C., Pte.—4.12.16 (K.I.A., 2.10.17)
2768 Ring, N. E., Pte.—4.12.16 (W.2)

2136 Richardson, R. W., L.-Sergt.—19.9.16 (W.)
6593 Riggs, R. W., Pte.—18.10.16 (K.I.A., 5.5.17-8.5.17)
1927 Ringrose, A. J., Pte.—8.8.16 (W.)
2637 Richards, C., Pte.—24.10.16
2140 Richards, J., Pte.—17.9.16
2636 Richardson, C. W., Pte.—24.10.16 (D.O.W., 3.8.17)
730 Richards, G. F., L.-Cpl.—1.7.16 (W.; K.I.A., 28.3.18)
917 Richardson, E. I., Pte.—1.7.16 (Died, 10.11.18)
487 Rice, F., Pte.—1.7.16
1964 Richards, A. K., Cpl., M.M.—8.8.16 (D.O.W., 18.7.18)
50 Rivett-Carnac, C. W., Pte.—1.7.16
3385 Rodd, H. C., Pte.—9.6.17
920 Roach, W. W., Pte.—1.7.16 (W.2)
488 Roach, C. J., Pte.—1.7.16 (Died, 17.8.16)
3582 Roughley, A. R., Pte.—10.10.16 (W.)
7541 Robertson, A. E., L.-Cpl.—9.6.17 (W.2)
2137 Rodman, C. D., Pte.—19.9.16
3384 Roughley, J. T., Pte.—9.6.17 (K.I.A., 28.3.18)
7540 Round, A., Pte.—9.6.17
3091 Rogers, J. R., Pte.—3.2.17 (K.I.A., 9.12.17)
3089 Rometch, A. S., Pte.—3.2.17 (K.I.A., 13.10.17)
2383 Rock, A., Pte.—19.10.16 (W.2)
2134 Robertson, A. G., Pte.—17.9.16 (D.O.W., 8.6.17)
2635 Rowbottam, R. A., Pte.—24.10.16 (W.2)
5760 Roberts, R. R., Pte.—10.5.16 (K.I.A., 29.9.18)
2378 Roach, M., Pte.—19.10.16
5757 Roach, C. A., Pte.—8.5.16 (W.)
1667A Roche, W., Pte.—1.7.16
5759 Roberts, H. E., Pte.—8.5.16 (W.)
1706 Robertson, J. A., Dvr., M.M.—1.7.16
641 Rose, G. W. P., Pte.—1.7.16 (W.)
2379B Rowe. A., Pte.—19.10.16
982 Roughley, G. A., Pte.—1.7.16 (W.3; Died. 2.11.18)
686 Rose, F., Pte.—1.7.16 (K.I.A., 17.7.18)
919 Rollins, V. E., Pte.—1.7.16 (W.; K.I.A., 5.10.17)
921 Rootes, W. A., Pte.—1.7.16
257 Rogers, L., Pte., M.M.—1.7.16
640 Rossington, G. M., Pte.—1.7.16 (K.I.A., 11.4.17)
489 Roberts, J. H., Cpl.—1.7.16 (W.)
492 Rollins, L. V., Pte.—1.7.16 (W.2)
491 Rollins, J. C., Pte.—1.7.16 (W.)
302 Roles, L. H., Pte.—1.7.16 (W.; K.I.A., 15.4.17)
685 Robinson, R., Pte.—1.7.16
918 Rowberry W. G., Pte.—1.7.16 (W.)
99 Rose, F. A., Sergt.—1.7.16
256 Robertson, C., Pte.—1.7.16 (W.)
56497 Ross, J., Pte.—6.7.18
490 Rogers. C. J., Pte.—1.7.16 (W.2)
3090 Robertson, E. T., Pte.—3.2.17 (K.I.A., 5.10.17)
254 Rooney, A., Cpl., M.S.M.—1.7.16 (W.2)

239

Ruddock, W. C. G., Capt.—1.7.16 (W.4)
Rock, C. W., Lieut.—1.7.16 (W.)
7542 Rutherford, E., L.-Cpl.—(W.)
1088 Russell, R., Pte.—1.7.16
2899 Ruston, C. R., Pte.—4.12.16
3094 Russell, W., Cpl.—3.2.17
2283 Russell, E. W., L.-Cpl.—19.10.16 (W.)
2875 Russell, M. E., Pte.—4.12.16 (W.)
2133 Rule, A. L., Pte.—19.9.16 (W.)
922 Rust, T., Pte.—1.7.16 (Died, 29.10.16)
923 Russell, C. E., Pte.—1.7.16
1002 Rushton, E. G., Pte.—1.7.16
1928 Russell, H. McD., 8.8.16 (W.; K.I.A., 31.5.17)
98 Rutter, J. C., Sergt.—1.7.16 (W.)
5762 Ryan, A., Pte.—10.5.16 (W.2)
2381 Ryan, J. J., Pte.—19.10.16 (K.I.A., 7.6.17)
493 Ryan, M. P., Dvr.—1.7.16 (D.O.W., 11.8.18)
Sadler, B. T., Lieut., C. de G. (Belg.)—1.7.16
2878 Saunders, T. S., Cpl.—4.12.16
15 Saunders, D. W., Dvr.—1.7.16
2877 Saunders, A. F., Pte.—4.12.16 (K.I.A., 13.10.17)
1107 Saunders, R. E. A., Pte.—1.7.16 (K.I.A., 28.2.17)
494 Salter, R. E., Pte.—1.7.16 (W.)
587 Saddington, J., Cpl., M.M.—1.7.16 (K.I.A., 21.2.18)
2389 Saltmarsh, H. E., Pte.—19.10.16 (W.; D.O.W., 5.10.17)
2142 Saunders, M., Pte.—17.9.16
2150 Saunders, H. J. L., Pte.—17.9.16 (K.I.A., 2.10.17)
2645 Salmon, C. G., Pte.—24.10.16 (K.I.A., 28.3.18)
2393 Sayer, K. H. W., Pte.—19.10.16
2876 Sainty, J. T., Pte.—4.12.16 (W.2)
2648 Sainty, H., Pte.—24.10.16
3387 Saggers, E., Pte.—9.6.17
7545 Saunders, L. J., Pte.—9.6.17 (K.I.A., 8.2.18)
7544 Saward, A. G., Pte.—9.6.17 (W.)
7543 Saward, H. H., Pte.—9.6.17
64 Scales, W. A., Pte.—1.7.16
279A Sams, N. K., Pte.—1.7.16
2385 Scully, W. J., Pte.—19.10.16 (K.I.A., 20.9.17)
2880 Scull, W., Pte.—4.12.16 (W.; D.O.W., 14.7.18)
65 Scolyer, R. C., Pte.—1.7.16 (W.)
280 Schultz, M. C., Sergt.—1.7.16
283 Scott, J. A., L.-Cpl.—1.7.16
14 Scott, J., Dvr.—1.7.16
929 Scolyer, M. W., L.-Cpl.—1.7.16 (W.5)
2082 Scanlon, M., Pte.—17.9.16 (W.2)
5763 Scott, J. H., Pte.—8.8.16
6466 Scott-Holland, E. S., Sergt.—18.10.16
2388 Scott, C., Pte.—19.10.16 (W.2)
2643 Scott, W. G., Pte.—24.10.16
3389 Scott, C., Pte.—9.6.17
Selwyn, T., Lieut.—20.10.4 (W.)
1709 Sellers, H. T., Pte.—1.7.16
591 Senior, J., Dvr.—1.7.16
2271 Seager, A. E., Sergt.—19.10.16 (W.)
7804 Seward, F., Pte.—30.7.17

2147 Sharp, A. V., Pte.—17.9.16 (W.)
927 Shearing, T. E., Pte.—1.7.16 (W.; D.O.W., 26.11.19)
497 Sheppard, F., Pte.—1.7.16 (D.O.D., 22.2.19)
1932 Shires, T. C., Pte.—8.8.16 (W.)
496 Sheppard, J. D., Pte.—1.7.16 (K.I.A., 15.4.17)
Sharland, C. F., Lieut.—17.9.16 (K.I.A., 12.10.17)
1929 Shaw, L. L., Pte.—8.8.16
495 Shalless, C. W., Cpl., M.M.—1.7.16 (W.3)
1930 Shepherd, M. E., Pte.—8.8.16 (D.O.W., 3.10.17)
275 Shadwick, F., Pte.—1.7.16
276 Sherrin, G., Pte.—1.7.16 (W.2)
12 Shepperd, H. E., Dvr.—1.7.16
735 Shearing F., Cpl.—1.7.16 (W.; D.O.W., 26.11.16)
739 Shepherd, F. C., L.-Cpl.—1.7.16 (W.)
925 Sharp, F. H., Pte.—1.7.16 (W.; K.I.A., 13.10.17)
926 Sherrin, E. C., L.-Cpl.—1.7.16 (D.O.W., 6.5.17)
586 Sherrin, C. R., L.-Sergt.—1.7.16 (W.)
588 Shepperd, E. V., Pte.—1.7.16 (K.I.A., 2.1.17)
5766 Shipley, J., Pte.—10.5.16 (W.2)
1054 Shaw, A., Pte.—1.7.16 (K.I.A., 13.5.17)
2764 Shoobridge, R. O., Cpl.—4.12.16 (W.)
2149 Shea, G., Pte.—17.9.16 (W.)
2391 Shires, A. A., Pte.—9.6.17 (D.O.W., 1.9.18)
2398 Sheedy, D. J., Pte.—19.10.16
2642 Shadwick, E., Pte.—24.10.16 (D.O.D., 1.2.17)
3439 Shea, A. E., Pte.—9.6.17 (W.)
3592A Shelton, W., Cpl.—15.9.15 (W.)
3502 Sharp, C. S., Pte.—10.10.17
688 Shearing, J., Pte.—1.7.16
19925 Shedden, S. A., Pte.
2143 Singline, G. T., Pte.—17.9.16 (W.2)
499 Singline, K. K., Pte.—1.7.16
2145 Simmonds, F. E., Pte.—17.9.16
498A Simmonds, W. J., Pte.—1.7.16
2881 Singline, L., Pte.—4.12.16 (W.2)
20788 Simes, C. W., Pte. (trf.)
2287 Simpkins, G. D., L.-Cpl.—19.10.16
19926 Skan, J., Pte. (trf.)
1672A Sims, A. R., Cpl.—1.7.16
928 Skeggs, W. O., L.-Cpl.—1.7.16 (W.2)
3392 Skjottrup, A. W., Pte.—9.6.17 (W.2)
24 Slade, R. J., Pte.—1.7.16
3699 Slade, L. R., Pte.—10.10.17 (D.O.W., 26.5.18)
500B Slatter, H. C., Dvr.—1.7.16 (W.)
932 Smith, W. A., L.-Cpl., M.M.—1.7.16
Smith, V. C., Lieut.—1.7.16
270 Smith, B. H., Pte., M.M.—1.7.16
Smith, R. H., Lieut.—1.7.16
273 Smith, E., Pte.—1.7.16 (W., K.I.A., 12.10.17)
1619 Smythe, A. E. E., Pte.—1.7.16
1092 Smith, G., Pte.—1.7.16 (W.3)
2141 Smith, M. C., Pte.—17.9.16 (W.3)
1118 Smith, H. J., Pte.—1.7.16 (W.2)

933	Smith, L. L., Cpl.—1.7.16 (W.2)		2391	Spaulding, D. E., L.-Cpl.—19.10.16 (W.)
501	Smith, C. E., L.-Cpl.—1.7.16 (W.; K.I.A., 12.10.17)		2644	Spillane, T. F., Pte.—24.10.16 (W.2)
502	Smith, J. F., Pte.—1.7.16 (W.)		7550	Spinks, T., Pte.—9.6.17 (W.)
731	Smith, P., L.-Cpl.—1.7.16 (W.; K.I.A., 28.3.18)		3141	Spurrell, C. H., Pte.—3.2.17
1934	Smith, G. K., Pte.—8.8.16 (W.2)		7799	Squires, D. B., Cpl.—30.7.17
268	Smart, L. W., Pte.—1.7.16 (W.2)		2392	Stock, T. W., Pte.—19.10.16
5156	Smith, P. J., Pte.—7.2.17		2641	Stokes, A. G., Pte.—24.10.16 (W.2)
272	Smith, R. E. J., Pte., M.M.—1.7.16		938	Stephens, W. H., Pte.—1.7.16 (K.I.A., 7.1.17)
66	Smith, G. H., Pte.—1.7.16 (W.)		936	Stops, F. E., L.-Cpl.—1.7.16 (W.)
67	Smith, F., Pte.—1.7.16		3095	Stansfield, G. C., Pte.—3.2.17
8	Smith, J., R.S.M.—1.7.16 (W.)		957	Stuart, R. S., Pte.—1.7.16 (W.)
589	Smith, C. A., Pte.—1.7.16 (K.I.A., 9.4.17)			Stuart, H., Lieut.—1.7.16 (D.O.D., 13.3.17)
590	Smith, R., Pte., M.M.—1.7.16 (W.3)		505	Stanton, W. E., Pte.—1.7.16 (D.O.W., 12.7.17)
931	Smith, A. E., Pte.—1.7.16 (K.I.A., 7.6.17)		506	Statton, P. C., Sergt., V.C., M.M.—1.7.16 (W.)
2077B	Smith, J. J., Pte.—17.9.16		266	Stevens, E. W., C.S.M., C. de G. (Belg.)—1.7.16
636	Smith, H. L., Pte.—1.7.16		1675	Stearnes, A. G., Pte.—1.7.16
2146	Smith, H. J., Sergt., M.M. & Bar—17.9.16		584	Stubbs, P. J., Pte.—1.7.16
1710	Smith, J. H., Pte.—1.7.16		2399	Stevens, J. H. H., Pte.—19.10.16
2127	Smith, W. T., Pte.—17.9.16 (W.2)		2397B	Stephens, H. E., Pte.—19.10.16 (K.I.A., 25.8.18)
5767	Smart, B. F., L.-Sergt.—10.5.16 (W.2; K.I.A., 30.4.18)		2282	Stirling, R. F., Cpl.—19.10.16 (K.I.A., 13.10.17)
5770	Smith, E. W., Pte.—10.5.16		939	Sturzaker, L., Pte.—1.7.16 (W.)
5772	Smith, J. D., Pte.—10.5.16 (W.2)		1648	Stubbings, F. E., L.-Cpl.—1.7.16 (W.)
2395	Smith, T. L., Pte.—19.10.16			
	Smith, S. H., Lieut., M.I.D.—8.8.16		282	Stone, R. J., Pte.—1.7.16 (W.)
2148	Smith, M.—17.9.16		940	Stephens, H. J., Sergt.—1.7.16
1960	Smith, G. T. J., Pte.—8.8.16 (W.)		734	Stevens, E. W., Cpl., M.M.—1.7.16 (W.2; K.I.A., 28.3.18)
2396	Smith, W. S. H., Pte.—19.10.16 (W.2)		736	Stacey, T. A., Pte.—1.7.16 (W.2)
3098	Smith, W. H., Pte.—3.2.17 (K.I.A., 5.10.17)		3116	Sturzaker, G. H., Cpl.—3.2.17
2646	Smith, A. L., Pte.—24.10.16 (K.I.A., 4.10.17)		687	Stewart, C. J., Pte.—1.7.16 (K.I.A., 7.6.17)
2917	Smart, F. A., Pte.—4.12.16 (W.)		701	Stebbins, S. G., Lieut., M.C.—1.7.16 (W.)
2882	Smith, G. W. T., Pte.—4.12.16 (W.)		3600	Stebbings, S., Pte.—10.10.17
2147A	Smith, S., Pte.—17.9.16		2341	Stantan, H. J., Pte.—19.10.16 (W.)
7548	Smallbon, J., Pte.—9.6.17 (W.)		2310	Stanton, W. A., Pte.—19.10.16 (W.)
1004A	Smith, B., L.-Cpl.—1.7.16			
16652	Smith, L. H., Pte.		2384	Stott, R., Pte.—19.10.16
4007	Smith, E. A., Pte.		265	Stehens, E., Pte.—1.7.16 (W.2)
7549	Smith, J. V., Pte.—9.6.17		5774	Stephens, R., Pte.—10.5.16
7801	Smith, G. C., Pte.—30.7.17		5775	Stott, A. A., Pte.—10.5.16 (W.2)
3644	Smith, A. C., Pte.—13.10.17 (D.O.W., 15.8.18)		5777	Stott, H. V., Pte.—10.5.16 (W.2)
3558	Smith, M. J., Pte.—13.10.17		5778	Sturzaker, N.—10.5.16 (W.2)
6615	Smith, W. W., Pte.—18.10.16		281	Stewart, R., Pte.—1.7.16
52366	Smith, T. J., Pte.—22.4.18		5789	Stacey, E. J., Pte.—10.5.16 (W.3; K.I.A., 10.9.18)
20202	Smith, C., Pte.		1939	Stewart, C. M., Pte.—8.8.16 (W.)
52367	Smith, W. J. R., Pte.—22.4.18		3126	Stevenson, L. M., Cpl.—7.2.17 (K.I.A., 28.1.18)
930	Smith, H. A. H., Pte.—1.7.16 (W.4)		2386	Stott, L., Pte.—19.10.16 (K.I.A., 13.10.17)
274	Smyth, P. N., Pte.—1.7.16		2173	Steele, F. W., Lieut.—17.9.16
	Suter, S. I., Capt., M.C.—1.7.16		2465	Stanley, W. H. M., Pte.—19.10.16 (W.2)
732	Snare, G. McK., Pte.—1.7.16 (W.2)			
3109	Snowden, R. C., Sergt.—3.2.17		2884	Stewart, J. J., Pte.—4.12.16
2390	Sproule, E. F., Pte.—19.10.16 (W.; D.O.W., 5.10.17)		507	Steers, H. R., Pte.—1.7.16 (W.)
935	Spradon, M. A., Cpl.—1.7.16 (W.3; K.I.A., 1.10.18)		1676	Steers, D. R., Pte.—1.7.16 (W.)
261	Spinks, K., Pte.—1.7.16 (W.)		3157	Stanfield, D. S., Dvr.—7.2.17 (W.)
733	Spellman, J. J., L.-Sergt.—1.7.16 (K.I.A., 29.9.18)		3096	Stansell, C. W., Pte.—3.2.17 (W.; K.I.A., 10.9.18)
738	Spinks, C. L., Pte.—1.7.16 (W.2)			
2883	Spurr, T. H., Pte.—4.12.16		7806	Stops, A. F., Pte.—30.7.17
5773	Stephens, L. J., Pte.—10.5.16 (W.3)		3265	Stephens, L. A., Pte.—9.6.17 (W.)
1936	Speed, E. J., Pte.—8.8.16		5114	Stockdale, G. E., L.-Cpl.—3.2.17 (W.)
1937	Speed, G., L.-Sergt.—8.8.16 (W.2; K.I.A., 17.4.18)		1972	Stafford, T. J., Pte.—8.8.16

2387	Stone, G. F., Pte.—19.10.16 (W.)	3	Taylor, S. G., S.-Sergt., M.S.M.—1.7.16
3394	Steel, N. P., Pte.—9.6.17 (K.I.A., 28.3.18)	545	Tatham, E., C.Q.M.S.—1.7.16
7553	Steele, R. A., Pte.—9.6.17	943	Tate, J. A., Pte.—1.7.16
3397	Stokes, W. F., Pte.—9.6.17 (W.)	946	Tapner, F., Dvr.—1.7.16 (W.)
2649	Stephens, L., Pte.—24.10.16	945	Tapner, W., Pte.—1.7.16 (W.; K.I.A., 4.10.17)
3395	Stephens, W. G., Pte.—9.6.17	740	Tarr, R. H., Pte.—1.7.16
1677	Stubbs, C. H., Pte.—1.7.16 (W.)	944	Taylor, A. J. W., Pte.—1.7.16 (K.I.A., 17.7.17)
7551	Steadwell, M. A. J., Pte.—9.6.17 (D.O.W., 16.6.18)	1000A	Talbot, N. R., Pte.—1.7.16
3396	Stokes, J. J., Pte.—9.6.17 (D.O.W., 3.7.17)	2402	Taylor, T., Pte.—19.10.16 (W.3)
262	Styles, Leslie, Pte.—1.7.16 (K.I.A., 12.8.18)	994	Taylor, F. H., Pte.—1.7.16 (W.; D.O.W., 31.3.18)
3642	Stephens, C. H., Pte.—13.10.17	1901	Taber, A. C., Pte.—8.8.16 (W.; K.I.A., 4.10.17)
3643	Stephens, T. B., Pte.—13.10.17 (W.)		
3645	Strong, T. H., Pte.—13.10.17	2275	Taylor, A. A., L.-Sergt.—19.10.16 (K.I.A., 13.10.17)
3149	Stanley, J. C., Pte.—3.2.17		
990	Stubbings, O. G., Pte.—1.7.16	92	Teniswood, F. W., Sergt., D.C.M.—21.10.14
3598	Stacey, A. J., Pte.—13.10.17		
3099	Sullivan, J. E., Pte.—3.2.17 (W.)	2152	Terry, L. M., Pte.—17.9.16 (K.I.A., 13.10.17)
3426	Sutton, A. E., Pte.—9.6.17 (W.)		
3398	Stuart, A. J., Pte.—9.6.17	2653	Templeton, C., Pte.—24.10.16 (W.2)
7554	Sundquist, C. H., Pte.—9.6.17 (K.I.A., 31.8.18)		
		2888	Terry, H., Pte.—4.12.16 (W.)
2151	Suckling, J., Pte.—17.9.16 (K.I.A., 5.10.17)	2887	Terry, T., Pte.—4.12.16 (K.I.A., 4.10.17)
1940	Sumpter, H., L.-Cpl.—8.8.16 (W.)	2886	Terry, W., Pte.—4.12.16 (W.2)
2144	Sutton, A. J., Pte.—17.9.16 (W.2)		Thurstan, A. C., Lieut.—9.6.17 (K.I.A., 5.4.18)
1941	Sutcliffe, W. H., Pte.—8.8.16 (W.3)		
	Sutcliffe, C. S., 2/Lieut.—9.6.17	7808	Thompson, H. L., Pte.—30.7.17 (W.2; D.O.D., 16.11.18)
585	Summers, C. H., Pte.—1.7.16 (W.)		
267	Summers, T. J., Pte.—1.7.16 (W.2)	2654	Thompson, J., Pte.—24.10.16 (W.)
1707	Sutton, E. H., L.-Cpl.—1.7.16 (K.I.A., 5.10.17)	2400	Thornton, C. W., Pte.—19.10.16 (W.2)
509	Sullivan, L. D., Pte.—1.7.16 (W.2)	1679	Thompson, A. A., L.-Cpl.—1.7.16 (W.)
747	Sullivan, T. C., Pte.—1.7.16		
942	Swan, A., Pte.—1.7.16 (W.)	109	Thomas, E. A., Pte.—1.7.16
	Swan, R. A., Lieut.—7.2.17 (W.)	950	Thompson, C. R., Pte.—1.7.16
2394	Swindells, R. O., Cpl., M.M.—19.10.16 (W.2)	949	Thompson, F., Pte.—1.7.16
		517	Thorne, J. F., Pte.—1.7.16
	Swann, L. K., Lieut., M.M.—19.9.16 (K.I.A., 10.11.18)	951	Thomson, H. M. D., Sergt.—1.7.16
1942	Sweeney, E. S., Pte.—8.8.16 (W.)	515	Thompson, W. L., L.-Cpl.—1.7.16 (D.O.W., 15.1.17)
941	Swain, R., Pte.—1.7.16 (K.I.A., 8.1.17)		
		517	Thow, J. F., Pte.—1.7.16 (W.)
512	Swan, W. N., Pte.—1.7.16 (W.)	1680	Thorne, E., Pte.—1.7.16 (W.)
263	Swinton, H., Sergt.—1.7.16 (W.)	516	Thorne, R. E., Pte.—1.7.16 (W.)
	Swinton, C. H., Lieut.—1.7.16	948	Thorpe, T. R., Pte.—1.7.16
511	Swan, W. J., Pte.—1.7.16	643	Thomas, K., Pte.—1.7.16 (W.3)
510	Swan, A. G., Pte.—1.7.16	7578	Thunder, P., Pte.—9.6.17
1674	Sweeny, O. W., Cpl.—1.7.16 (W.)	3402	Thorne, L. W., Pte.—9.6.17
3146	Swan, D. C., Pte.—3.2.17	7559	Thomas, A. E., Pte.—9.6.17 (W.)
2885	Symes, E., Pte.—4.12.16 (W.)	3400	Thompson, R. C., Pte.—9.6.17
513	Sylvester, T. G., Pte.—1.7.16 (W.)	3401	Thompson, W., Pte.—9.6.17
584	Stubbs, P. J., Pte.—1.7.16	1034	Thompson, C. T., Cpl.—1.7.16 (W.)
3097	Sturman, C. J., Pte.—3.2.17	592	Thompson, G., S.-Smith.—1.7.16
1708	Sutcliffe, C. E., Pte.—1.7.16	60	Tilley, L. W. M., Pte.—1.7.16 (W.)
1673A	Sweetman, R., Pte.—1.7.16 (W.)	2918	Thompson, T. W., Pte.—4.12.16
52241	Swift, L. R. W., Pte.	1089	Tippet, A. S., Pte.—1.7.16 (W.2)
644	Targett, R. H., Pte.—1.7.16 (K.I.A., 25.1.17)	2650	Tilyard, H. C., Pte.—24.10.16 (W.; K.I.A., 28.3.18)
52387	Taylor, H., Pte.—22.4.18	3560	Townsend, W. D., Pte.—6.10.17
284	Taylor, E. A., Pte.—1.7.16	9	Totham, R., Dvr.—1.7.16
20008	Taylor, B., Pte.	3561	Townsend, C. B., Pte.—6.10.17
1681	Taylor, J. W., Pte.—1.7.16	2652	Tomlin, W. J., Pte.—24.10.16 (W.)
2889	Taylor, A. E., Pte.—4.12.16 (W.; K.I.A., 17.7.18)	16	Tolson, T. E., Dvr.—1.7.16
		2890	Tolman, H. O., Pte.—4.12.16 (W.)
2153	Tang, E. O., Pte., M.M.—4.12.16 (W.; K.I.A., 12.8.18)	1108	Townsend, T., Pte.—1.7.16
		3403	Townsend, F. H. G., Pte.—9.6.17 (K.I.A., 24.8.18)
5779	Talbot, D., Pte.—8.5.16 (W.)		
2157	Talbot, T. W., Pte.—19.9.16	3158	Triffett, L. G., Pte.—7.2.17 (W.)

	Tracey, T. J., Lieut. (see T. J. O'Sullivan)—1.7.16 (W.)	527	Voss, O., Cpl.—1.7.16 (W.)
	Trethewie, H. R., Lieut.—1.7.16 (W.2)	3407	Voss, S. J., Pte.—9.6.17
		7351	Waller, S. M., Pte.—6.2.17 (D.O.D., 12.11.18)
640	Treager, A. F., L.-Cpl.—1.7.16 (W.)	3110	Ward, J. K., L.-Cpl.—3.2.17 (W.)
2154	Trotter, W., Pte.—17.9.16	965	Walker, A. F., C.Q.M.S.—23.10.14
519	Trotter, D., L.-Sergt.—1.7.16 (W.)	647	Waters, J., Pte.—1.7.16 (W.)
519	Trotter, D., S.-Sergt.—1.7.16 (W.)	101	Walker, A. E., Pte.—1.7.16 (W.; D.O.W., 1.9.18)
3442	Triffett, V. Cpl.—9.6.17 (K.I.A., 3.10.18)	961	Warring, W. H., Pte.—1.7.16 (W.)
518	Treweek, D. L., Pte., M.M.—1.7.16 (W.)	690	Walker, A. G., Cpl.—1.7.16 (K.I.A., 12.10.17)
2892	Tregena, H. E., Pte.—4.12.16 (W.)	1946	Warring, T. R., Pte.—8.8.16
1943	Triffitt, A. C., Pte.—8.8.16 (W.2)	963	Walker, W. C., Pte.—1.7.16 (W.3)
2891	Tregenna, P. A., Pte.—4.12.16 (W.)	529	Waller, G. H., Sergt.—1.7.16
2655	Tribolet, J. W., Cpl.—1.7.16		Walters, R. C., Lieut.—1.7.16 (W.3)
3500	Traynor, M. J., Sergt.—6.10.17 (W.)	18	Waldon, E., L.-Sergt.—1.7.16
2974	Turner, E. C., Pte., M.M.—6.10.17 (W.)	294	Wade, F. H., Pte.—1.7.16
		17	Walker, L. J., L.-Cpl.—1.7.16
953	Turnbull, S. G., L.-Cpl.—1.7.16 (W.2)	295	Wainwright, G. A., Pte.—1.7.16
524	Turvey, H. W., Pte.—1.7.16	696	Wallace, G., Pte.—1.7.16 (W.)
520	Tuck, F. G., Sergt.—1.7.16 (K.I.A., 31.1.17)	973	Warburton, C. G., L.-Sergt.—1.7.16 (W.)
1944	Turner, J., Pte.—8.8.16 (W.2)	1690	Warren, W. H., Pte.—1.7.16
955	Turner, L. R., Cpl.—1.7.16 (W.)	1918	Walker, W. T., Cpl.—8.8.16 (W.2)
952	Turner, J. C., Cpl.—1.7.16 (W.)	2162	Walker, R. E., Pte.—19.9.16
521	Turner, H., Pte.—1.7.16 (K.I.A., 31.1.17)	959	Watson, G., Pte.—1.7.16 (D.O.W., 24.11.16)
285	Turner, C. H., L.-Cpl.	5783	Wallace, R. A. T., Pte.—10.5.16 (W.2)
642	Tubbs, C. G., Cpl.—1.7.16 (K.I.A., 8.12.16)	1948	Watson, W., Cpl.—8.8.16 (W.)
523	Turner, W., Pte.—1.7.16 (W.)	2161	Wakeling, F. J., Pte.—17.9.16 (W.)
3601	Turner, J. F. H., Pte.—13.10.17		
4398	Turner, O. H., Pte.	5410	Watson, W. J. D., Pte.—9.6.17
954	Turnbull, J. C., Pte.—1.7.16 (W.3)	2415	Watkins, H. T., Pte.—19.10.16
	Turner, B. W., Lieut.—19.10.16	2898	Wakefield, W. B., Pte.—4.12.16 (W.; D.O.D., 7.11.18)
2155	Turnbull, G. A., Sergt.—17.9.16 (K.I.A., 28.3.18)	2281	Walker, W., Sergt., M.M.—17.9.16
522	Turner, L., Pte.—1.7.16 (W.3)	2985	Watt, Roy, Pte.—4.12.16
2893	Turner, A., Pte.—4.12.16	962	Washington, A., Sergt.—1.7.16 (K.I.A., 5.10.17)
2401B	Tuthill, V. J., Pte.—19.10.16 (W.)	2899	Walker, W. P., Pte.—4.12.16 (W.)
3159	Turner, C. J., Pte.—7.2.17 (W.)	2897	Walker, H. G., Pte.—4.12.16 (W.)
2457A	Turner, F. C., Pte.—19.10.16	624	Watts, E., Pte.—1.7.16
947	Turner, D., Pte.—1.7.16 (W.)	3408	Warden, L., Pte.—9.6.17
52373	Twining, G. A., Pte.—22.4.18	3102	Walker, L., Pte.—3.2.17
2651	Tyler, E. A., Pte.—24.10.16 (W.)	3562	Warren, T. S., Pte.—6.11.17 (K.I.A., 15.6.18)
2894	Tyson, G. A., Pte.—4.12.16	3153	Wakefield, T. V., Pte.—3.2.17
	Tyrrell, J. T., Capt.—24.5.15 (K.I.A., 10.1.17)	3563	Warren, D., Pte.—7.5.17
957	Upchurch, W. J. W., Cpl.—1.7.16 (W.2)	3254	Warner, R. H., Sergt.—9.6.17
		3409	Watkins, W. H., Pte.—9.6.17
286	Utteridge, A., Pte.—1.7.16 (K.I.A., 26.2.17)	3155	Warnecke, J. H., Pte.—3.2.17
3160	Valentine, C. H., Sergt.—7.2.17	642	Watts, E., Pte.—21.5.17 (W.2)
958	Vaughan, W. M., Pte.—1.7.16 (W.2)	7563	Warren, R., Pte.—9.6.17 (W.2)
		62	Wallace, S. E., Pte.—1.7.16 (W.)
1642A	Vaughan, A. E., Pte.—1.7.16 (W.)	2653	Watson, V. J., Pte.—24.10.16
2269	Verrall, F., Pte.—19.10.16	52376	Watchorn, A., Pte.—22.4.18
2895	Vertigan, A. C., Pte.—4.12.16 (W.)	52339	Walch, J. H. B., Pte.—22.4.18
287	Vertigan, O., Pte.—1.7.16 (K.I.A., 16.1.17)	2903	Webb, T. H., Pte.—4.12.16 (W.)
2285	Verren, E. J., Cpl.—19.10.16	3647	Weaver, G. V., Pte.—13.10.17
5782	Viney, C. T., Pte.—10.5.16 (W.3)	4926	Webster, E. D., Pte.
2403B	Viney, C. L., Pte.—19.10.16 (W.)	2663	Weeks, S. S., Pte.—24.10.16 (W.2)
19064	Vincent, R. C., Pte.	2659	Webb, W. H., Pte.—24.10.16 (K.I.A., 8.12.17)
2896	Vince, W. C., Pte.—4.12.16 (W.2)	1686	Westbrook, L. J., Pte.—1.7.16 (W.)
25	Viney, L. G., Pte.—1.7.16	741	Westbrook, V. G., Pte.—1.7.16 (D.O.W., 18.6.17)
2656	Viney, W. T., Pte.—24.10.16	1685	Webber, T., Pte.—1.7.16 (W.)
288	Vince, W. L., Pte., M.M.—1.7.16 (W.)	648	Webb, E. E., Sergt.—1.7.16 (W.2)
526	Vince, O. H., Pte.—1.7.16 (W.)	744	Westwood, R. T., Cpl.—1.7.16 (W.)

534 Wells, W. R., Pte.—1.7.16 (K.I.A., 3.1.17)
532 Webb, W. E., Pte.—1.7.16 (K.I.A., 30.1.17)
693 Weldon, C., Pte.—1.7.16 (K.I.A., 7.6.17)
649 Westcott, F. D., Pte.—1.7.16 (W.)
1950 Webb, J. H. W., Pte.—8.8.16 (W.)
290 West, B., Cpl.—1.7.16 (W.2)
2159 Webster, D. S., Pte.—17.9.16
2406 Webb, F. C., Pte.—19.10.16 (W.2)
2413 Webster, E. L., Pte.—19.10.16 (W.2)
531 Webb, L. G., Pte.—1.7.16 (W.)
2166 Wells, W. A. D., Pte.—17.9.16 (W.)
1938 Wells, W. J., Pte.—8.8.16 (W.3)
2901 Wells, A. W., Pte.—4.12.16
2657 Webb, H. J., Pte.—24.10.16 (W.3)
964 Webster, H. C., Pte.—1.7.16
2902 Wells, G. A., Pte.—4.12.16
2900 Wells, J., Pte.—4.12.16 (K.I.A., 30.3.18)
2754 Wellard, L. W., Pte.—4.12.16
600 Wells, J. C., Dvr.—1.7.16
3411 Websdale, E. G., Pte.—9.6.17
 Weston, E. D., Lieut., M.C.—24.8.15
3648 Webb, J. L., Pte.—13.10.17
32233 Welling, W. J., Sergt.
52396 Wells, J. B., Pte.—22.4.18
2417 Whelean, J., Cpl.—19.10.16
2411 White, F. D. D., Pte.—24.10.16
966 White, F. J., Cpl.—1.7.16 (W.)
965 Whiting, D., Pte.—1.7.16 (W.2)
2904 Whittingham, L. W., Pte.—4.12.16 (D.O.D., 14.5.17)
5697 Whyman, L. P., Pte.—10.5.16 (K.I.A., 5.10.17)
1688 Whitcombe, J. F., Pte.—1.7.16 (W.2)
594 Whitelaw, F. H., Pte.—1.7.16
 Whittle, B. H., Lieut.—1.7.16 (W.3)
 Whitaker, M. H. O., Lieut., M.C., M.I.D.—1.7.16 (W.4)
1952 Whelean, J. J., Pte.—8.8.16
1953 White, J. J. H., Pte.—8.8.16 (W.2)
2108 Whitney, A. J., Sergt., M.S.M.—19.9.16
2048 Whitney, J., Pte.—19.9.16
1090 Wheatley, E. D. B., Pte.—1.7.16 (W.)
1692A Wheat, A., Pte.—1.7.16
1937A White, C. T., Pte.—8.8.16
799A White, A., Pte.—1.7.16
3412 White, S. E., Pte.—9.6.17
7565 Whittle, E. A., Pte.—9.6.17 (K.I.A., 31.8.18)
3564 Whittaker, W. L. C., Pte.—13.10.17
3418 Williams, S. H., Pte.—9.6.17 (W.)
3103 Wicks, A. L., Pte.—3.2.17
3101 Williams, R. V., Pte.—3.2.17 (W.)
2412 Wheatley, A. V., Pte.—19.10.16 (D.O.D., 11.2.17)
23 Williams, W. A., Pte.—1.7.16 (W.2; K.I.A., 5.10.17)
2404 Wing, R. A., Pte.—19.10.16
2164 Wilson, C., Pte.—19.9.16 (W.)
5717 Williams, H. J., Pte.—10.5.16 (W.)
1956 Wilson, S., Pte.—8.8.16 (W.)
1023 Williams, W. A., Pte.—1.7.16
535 Wickham, A. H., Pte.—1.7.15

3107 Wickham, E. J., Pte.—3.2.17
745 Winburn, H. S., Sergt.—1.7.16 (W.; K.I.A., 13.10.17)
539 Williams, W. L., Pte.—1.7.16 (W.)
742A Williams, J. A., Pte., M.M.—1.7.16
536 Wilcox, W., Pte.—1.7.16 (W.; K.I.A., 5.10.17)
605 Wilson, R. K., C.S.M., Medaille Militaire (Fr.)—1.7.16 (W.3; K.I.A., 12.10.17)
537 Wilkins, P. A., L.-Sergt.—1.7.16 (D.O.W., 3.1.17)
297 Williams, G. D., L.-Cpl.—1.7.16 (K.I.A., 2.5.18)
293 Winburn, F. G., Pte.—1.7.16 (W.)
28 Williams, R., Cpl.—1.7.16
19 Williams, A. L., Dvr.—1.7.16
29 Williams, J. J., Pte.—1.7.16
26 Wilson, J. R., Sergt., M.S.M.—1.7.16
597 Williams, G., Pte.—1.7.16 (W.)
598 Williams, P. S. F., Pte.—1.7.16 (W.; D.O.W., 1.12.17)
1683 Wiggins, V. T., Pte.—1.7.16 (K.I.A., 20.11.16)
967 Williams, W. J., Sergt.—1.7.16 (W.)
3448 Williams, F. J., Pte.—9.6.17
968A Wilby, G., Pte.—1.7.16 (W.)
970 Wise, H. A. C., Pte.—1.7.16 (W.)
969 Wilson, G. T., Pte.—1.7.16 (W.)
991 Williams, R. C., Pte.—1.7.16
995 Wilson-Lowe, G. H., Pte.—1.7.16
1687 Williams, A. B., Pte.—1.7.16
5791 Williams, K. E., Pte.—10.5.16 W.)
5792 Willis, V. E., Pte.—10.5.16 (W.2)
291 Wilson, J. M., Sergt.—1.7.16
2163 Williams, D. E., Pte.—17.9.16
2165 Wise, L. C., Pte.—17.9.16
2408 Wing, A. J. J., Pte.—19.10.16 (K.I.A., 13.10.17)
2661 Wilson, H. E., Pte.—24.10.16 (W.2)
2664B Wilson, E. C. S., Pte.—24.10.16 (W.2)
2171 Wilson, F. H., Pte.—17.9.16 (K.I.A., 7.6.17)
2169 Wilson, J. E., Pte.—17.9.16 (W.2)
2660 Wilson, V. R., Pte.—24.10.16
7568 Williams, J., Pte.—9.6.17
2909 Williams, J. C. A., Pte.—4.12.16
2907 Williams, W. A., Pte.—4.12.16
2662B Wilson, A. E., Pte.—24.10.16 (K.I.A., 23.4.18)
2773 Wilson, W., Pte.—24.10.16
2170 Williams, W. H. H., Pte.—17.9.16 (W.)
2905 Wilson, E. R., Pte.—4.12.16 (W.)
2906 Williams, J. J., Pte.—4.12.16 (W.)
1955 Wilson, G., Pte.—8.8.16
5905 Williams, J. J., Pte.—29.5.16 (K.I.A., 29.8.18)
2409 Williams, A., Pte.—19.10.16 (W.)
3106 Wilson, W., Pte.—3.2.17
3646 Widdicombe, H. D., Pte.—13.10.17
7579 Williams, A. E., Pte.—9.6.17 (W.)
7570 Wilson, E. R., Pte.—9.6.17 (W.)
3421 Withers, D., Pte.—5.10.17
7566 Wiedemann, E. A., Pte.—9.6.17
3602 Williams, A., Pte.—6.10.17
7819 Williams, L., Pte.—9.6.17
1711 Williams, T. M., Pte.—1.7.16 (W.)
3415 Williams, H. J., Pte.—9.6.17 (W.)
3565 Williams, W., Pte.—6.10.17

3566 Wilkins, R. T., Pte.—6.10.17
7569 Williamson, C. F., Pte.—(W.; K.I.A., 23.3.18)
51 Woolcock, B. F., Pte.—1.7.16 (D.O.D., 28.8.16)
3603 Williams, H. A., Pte.—6.10.17
3649 Williams, H. J., Pte., M.M.—13.10.17
52378 Williams, A., Pte.—24.4.18
Williams, F. M., Lieut.—2.3.18
3604 Wood, C. P., Pte.—13.10.17
2911 Woolley, K. H., Pte.—4.12.16 (W)
3257 Woods, C. A. H., Cpl.—9.6.17
5794 Wootton, G. C., Pte.—10.5.16 (W.)
2418 Woolley, W. G. E., Sergt., D.C.M. 19.10.16 (W.; K.I.A., 21.2.18)
595 Woods, E., Pte.—1.7.16 (W.; K.I.A., 12.10.17)
542 Wood, W. E., Pte.—1.7.16
1006 Woods, A. W., Pte.—1.7.16
292 Wood, C. C., Pte.—1.7.16 (W.)
692 Wood, B. E.—1.7.16 (K.I.A., 13.10.17)
689 Woolley, F. W., Pte.—1.7.16 (W.3)
2810 Wood, K. R. J. H., Cpl.—4.12.16
2658 Wood, G. A., Pte.—24.10.16 (K.I.A., 26.4.18)
2912 Woodward, W., Pte.—4.12.16 (W.; K.I.A., 31.8.18)
2914 Wood, J., Pte.—4.12.16
2913 Wood, S., Pte.—4.12.16
2358 Woolley, R. W., Pte.—19.10.16 (W.)
971A Woodgate, A., Pte.—1.7.16 (W.)
3567 Wolfe, R. J., Pte.—6.10.17
3568 Worbey, H. R., Pte.—6.10.17
1005 Woods, S. W., Pte.—1.7.16 (D.O.W., 16.10.17)
299 Wood, L. A., Cpl.—1.7.16
599 Wright, W. S., Dvr.—1.7.16

300 Wright, G. C. A., Cpl.—1.7.16 (W.3)
289 Wright, C. G., Pte.—1.7.16 (W.)
109 Wright, R., Pte.—1.7.16 (W.)
646 Wright, B. A., Pte.—1.7.16 (K.I.A., 31.1.17)
2162 Wright, A. D., Pte.—17.9.16 (W.)
2766 Wright, C. N., Pte.—4.12.16 (D.O.W., 5.10.17)
3104 Wright, G. T., Pte.—3.2.17
7573 Wright, W. L., Pte.—9.6.17
7571 Wright, G. S., Pte.—9.6.17 (K.I.A., 28.3.18)
3448 Wright, W. J., Pte.—9.6.17 (W.)
1957 Wrigley, J. T., Pte.—8.8.16 (D.O.D., 7.9.16)
7572 Wright, L., Pte.—9.6.17
2277 Wright, J., Cpl.—19.10.16 (K.I.A., 6.10.17)
2168 Wyett, V. L., Pte.—17.9.16 (K.I.A., 4.10.17)
2157 Wyatt, L. H., Pte.—17.9.16 (D.O.W., 9.6.17)
975 Yates, A. W., Sergt.—1.7.16
3424 Young, H. G., Pte.—9.6.17 (W.)
2168A Young, R. C., L.-Cpl.—17.9.16 (W.3)
3425 Young, F. H., Pte.—9.6.17
2665 Young, C. R., Pte.—24.10.16 (W.2; K.I.A., 13.10.17)
52 Young, G. M., Sergt., M.M.—1.7.16 (W.)
20 Young, A. H., Sergt.—1.7.16
1958 Young, A. M., Cpl.—8.8.16 (W.)
2075 Young, J. A., Pte.—17.9.16 (W.; K.I.A., 4.10.17)
3125 York, J. W., Pte.—7.2.17 (K.I.A., 9.4.18)
543 Young, C., Pte.—1.7.16 (K.I.A., 11.4.17)
1693 Yaxley, L. L., Pte.—1.7.16

Index to Names of Persons and Places Mentioned in Narrative.

Abbé Wood, 135, 138, 142.
Abbeville, 201.
Accroche Wood, 149.
Ackroyd, J., 23.
Acquaire Wood, 146.
Aizecourt, 201.
Albert, 124.
Allan A. R., 24.
Amiens, 120, 157.
Amiens, Battle of, 148, 157.
Amiens-St. Quentin Road, 151.
Ancre, 114, 115, 124, 125, 127, 130, 133.
Armentières, 8, 23, 27, 41, 43, 106.
Aubigny, 145.
Aubigny Line, 135.
Auchonvillers, 114.
Augustus Wood, 79, 86, 88, 89, 91.

Bailleul, 6, 68.
Baldwin, C. W., 57, 86, 88.
Balmforth, J. T., 65.
Barclay, H. L., 25, 29, 30.
Barker, J. R., 96, 137.
Barnett, L. W., 52, 53.
Barrett, S. J., 62, 78.
Barwick, A. J., 194.
Baupaume, Battle of, 160, 184.
Bean, C. E. W., 105.
Beard, N. T., 156.
Beaumont-sur-Ancre, 114.
Beaurevoir, 190.
Beaurevoir-Fonsomme Line, 191.
Bécourt, 68, 72, 95.
Beecham Farm, 79, 86.
Belbin, L. J., 137.
Bellevue Spur, 76, 88, 93.
Bellicourt, 190.
Berlin Wood, 87, 178, 186.
"Berrima" Transport, 3.
Bertram, A., 118.
Bertram, E. J., 114.
Bethleem Farm, 57, 64.
Billing, E. W., 155, 156, 164, 196.
Binns, L. J., 137.
Birdwood, Sir William, 105, 110, 136.
Bisdee, G. S., 104, 108, 116, 124, 127, 145, 153.
Black, H., 88.
Blangy-Tronville, 134, 142.
Blequin, 68.
Boden, H., 78, 194.
Bois-Grenier, 27, 28, 37.
Bony, 196, 199.
Bony Point, 200.
Bordeaux Farm, 75, 86.
Bouchavesnes, 179, 182.
Boyes, E., 76, 136.
Braid, J., 65.
Bray, 116, 159, 160, 165, 166.
Bray-Cappy Road, 166.
Bray-Corbie Road, 115, 116, 117, 118, 121, 160.
Bremen Redoubt, 74, 86.
Brilliant, J. D., 129.
Brock, F. D., 179.
Broodseinde, 73, 75, 82, 84.

Brown, A. P., 96, 101, 111, 119, 130.
Brown, G. S., 49.
Brune Gaye, 50, 54.
Buchanan, V. H., 162, 174, 188.
Bucquoy, 114.
Buire, 127, 129, 132.
Buire Wood, 186.
Bunhill Row, 43, 58.
Burnt Farm, 36.

Cambridge Avenue, 22.
Campagne, 112, 113.
Canadian Tunnellers, 49.
Cane, C. H., 116, 124, 127, 145, 153.
Cape Town, 3.
Cappy, 165.
Catacombs, 45, 108.
Cell Trench, 24.
Cemetery Wood, 168.
Chamberlain, H., 88, 104, 118.
Chapelle D'Armentières, 37, 38.
Chard's Farm, 37.
Chipilly, 148.
Chisholm, J. D. W., 10, 29, 41, 57, 61, 86, 88, 116, 138.
Claremont Camp, Tasmania, 1.
Clark, J. P., 51, 68.
Clark, W. I., 58, 82, 120, 124, 136.
Clements, W. C., 65.
Clery, 169, 170, 172, 177, 178.
Clery Copse, 170, 173, 174, 176.
Connaught Road, 66.
Conners, C. W., 174.
Cook, T. A., 161.
Cooper, W. R., 66.
Cossom, O. S., 96.
Cowgate, 33.
Cox, J., 171.
Cranswick, T. G., 62, 63, 109, 130, 145, 161, 162, 173, 174, 175.
Cranswick, J. S., 25.
Crest Farm, 90.
Crosby, W. T., 61, 81, 140, 142, 153.
Cruickshank, A., 41, 121.
Culton, W. J., 36, 37.
Cunningham, F. J., 65.
Curlu, 167, 168.

Dab Trench, 77, 86, 87, 91.
Dagger Trench, 77.
Dakar, 3.
Dale, S. E., 172.
Davidson, J., 62.
Davies, B. L., 179.
Dead Cow Farm, 36.
Dent, C. E., 173.
Dernancourt, 124, 130.
Dèsvres, 68.
Dignopré, 68.
Doherty, J., 152.
Dolting, W. J., 152.
Donnington Hall, 58.
Downie, A. A., 62.
Downs, H. A., 137.
Douve Farm, 46, 67.
Douve River, 46, 47, 49, 56, 57, 58, 97.

Douve Walk, 98, 100.
Dragoon Farm, 85.
Dransfield, P., 194.
Driencourt, 188.
Du Biez Farm, 29, 34, 37.
Dumaresq, H. J., 29, 41, 43, 48, 73, 76, 77, 81.

Eblinghem, 112.
Edmeads' Farm, 10, 22, 42.
Eel Pie Forts, 44.
Ellis, C., 65.
Ellis, G., 167.
Emms, H., 64, 144.
Erondelle, 201.
Erquinghem, 39.
Evans, H., 45.

Fargny Mill, 168.
Fenton, C. H., 137.
Feuillaucourt, 182.
"Fighting Fortieth," 2.
Findlay, N. A. M., 33.
Findlay, W. K., 138, 145, 193, 199.
Fleiter, E., 29, 30.
Flint, A. E., 96.
Flood, C. T., 65.
Fletcher, F. A., 111, 133, 136.
Foster, H. L., 57, 64, 101, 104, 124, 127, 139, 145, 193.
Franvillers, 115.
Frechencourt, 134, 143.
Freestone, J. A., 77.
Friesland Copse, 79, 90.

Game, C. W., 155, 161, 172, 178, 180.
Gard, J. H., 46.
Garrard, W. L., 86.
Garrett, R., 36, 119.
Garth, L. G., 96.
Gatenby, J. J., 76.
Gellibrand, Major-General, 136.
Giblin, L. F., 10, 29, 41, 43, 57, 62, 86, 90, 108, 120, 138, 139, 152, 161, 162, 186.
Gill, R. W., 96.
Gillam, H., 90.
Gillemont Crescent, 194, 196, 198, 199.
Gillemont Farm, 192, 193, 196, 197, 199.
Glisy, 138, 143.
Glover, H., 179.
Godley, Sir A., 70.
Goldsworthy, C. T., 137.
Goodyer, R. J., 63, 96.
Gourlay, G. R., 187.
Gouy, 191.
Grant, A. R., 77, 88, 92.
Gravenstafel Switch, 75.
Gressaire Wood, 160.
Grey, W. N., 90, 174, 175, 178.
Grimmond, H. L., 107.
Grondona, L., 29, 30.
Grubb Lane, 194.
Grubb, W. E. K., 111, 117.

Haarlem, 81, 90.
Haig, Sir Douglas, 72.
Hallue River, 134.
Hamburg Redoubt, 76, 77.
Hamel, 144, 145.
Hargicourt Switch, 187, 188.
Haut Wood, 186.
Hearps, C., 118.
Hebuterne, 114.

Heilly, 115, 120, 123, 125.
Hem, 169, 184.
Heron, F. J., 174, 175.
Hesbecourt, 186, 187.
Hill "63," 45, 46, 59, 100, 107.
Hilmer, E., 36.
Hindenburg Line, 178, 187, et seq.
Hobbs' Farm, 12, 23, 42.
Holnon, 190.
Hope, C., 65, 88.
Horler, T. J., 10.
Hoskins, T. T., 43, 140.
Houplines, 10, 13, 41.
Howitzer Wood, 169.
Huns' Walk, 57.
Hunter's Avenue, 44.
Hussar Farm, 85, 93.
Hutchinson, E. A., 174.
Hyde Park Corner, 45, 58, 59, 97, 108, 110.

Imlach, J., 137.
Irish Avenue, 22.

Jackson, B., 91, 92, 133, 180, 181.
Jeffrey, J. D., 33.
Jess, C. H., 112.
Johnson, A. H., 137.
Jones, T. S., 62.

"K" Track, 85, 86, 87, 92.
Kelty, W., 53.
Kemmel Hill, 67.
Knob, The, 200.
Knob Wood, 200.
Knoll, The, 193, 195.
Koppleman, W., 137.
Kruistraathoek, 94.

La Basse Ville, 68, 97, 108.
La Grenouillere, 186.
La Motte, 97.
La Potterie Farm, 62.
Laambeek, 90.
La Flaque, 150, 152, 153, 157.
Lakin, F., 195.
Lakin, N. E., 163.
Lambert, H., 137.
Lancaster House, 44.
Langdon, W. R., 75.
Langemarck, 84.
Lark Hill, 4.
Launceston, 2.
Lawler, S. H., 45.
Lawrence, O. E., 168, 173, 175.
L'Epinette, 10.
Le Catalet, 199.
Le Havre, 5, 7.
L'Hallobeau, 29.
Lincey, J., 96.
Lille Gate, 94.
Lille Post, 29, 34, 37.
Linnell, J. E., 24.
Loane, R. J. D., 62, 63.
Lone Tree Trench, 194, 196, 197, 199.
Long, H. C., 42, 102.
Lord, J. E. C., 1, 2, 46, 90, 103, 110, 174.
Lowland Post, 197.
Lowndes Avenue, 48.
Lumbres, 110, 111, 112.
Lynde, 35.
Lys, River, 9, 10, 27, 42.

Mackenzie, R. S., 146.
Macquincourt Farm, 200.
Macquincourt Valley, 193, 194.
Mahony, T., 170, 173, 174, 175.
Marett Wood, 116, 125, 126.
Marshall, C. W., 118.
Masterman, K. C., 174, 175.
Mathers, C. W. V., 66.
Matto Wood, 157.
Maurepas, 169.
McColl, J. T., 110, 120, 125, 136.
McCoy, J., 137.
McGee, L., 76, 77, 88, 189.
McIntosh, C., 118.
McIntyre, G. L., 104, 108, 138, 139, 161, 170, 180, 193.
McKenzie, D. J., 200.
McKinnon, A. D., 37.
McMillan, S. S. S., 132, 133, 134, 155, 164, 172, 183.
McNicol, W. R., 69, 112.
McVilly, C. L., 24, 48, 52, 57, 63, 73, 76, 107.
Meagher, N. R., 52, 61, 73, 76, 77.
Menin Gate, 94.
Menin Road, 94.
Mericourt L'Abbé, 115, 124, 126.
Merris, ?.
Messines, 45, 46, 52, 56, 60, 67, 73.
Metcalfe, L. F., 43.
Mills, A. E., 67, 127, 153.
Monacu, 169.
Monash, Major-General, 41, 69, 70, 136
Mondicourt, 113, 114.
Moon, E., 101.
Moon, W. A., 62.
Mont de Lille, 39.
Mont St. Quentin, 159, 179.
Morbecque, 51, 72, 84.
Moriarty, J. J., 137.
Morlancourt, 116, 118, 120, 121, 147.
Mud Lane, 45, 58, 59.

Neuve Eglise, 66, 67, 68, 105, 106.
Neuville-les-Bray, 161.
Newman, H., 137.
Nieppe, 64, 66.
Norquay, N., 65.

Oates, D. R., 170.
Observation Wood, 169.
Oliver, J. D., 49.
Oosthove Farm, 50, 51.
Orchard Post, 29, 37.
O'Sullivan, T. J., 36, 37.

Paradise Alley, 37.
Parry, L., 154.
Parry, R. O., 137.
Parsissons, G., 131.
Parsissons, J., 137.
Partridge, L. T., 96.
Pas, 114.
Passchendaele, 79, 80, 83, 84, 86, 93.
Payne, L. H., 10, 23, 29, 41, 68, 110, 116, 117, 120, 134, 159, 186.
Penny, R. B., 89.
Pepper, H., 163.
Peronne, 159, 201.
Peters, C. H., 29, 31.
Petit Sec Bois, 39.
Pilkington, J. T., 137.
Pitchford, D. L., 42, 43.

Ploegsteert Wood, 43, 44, 48 58, 107, 109.
Ploegsteert-Messines Road, 44, 45, 58, 64.
Plumer, Sir Herbert, 40.
Plymouth, 3.
Polygon Wood, 72, 73.
Pont Ballot, 29.
Potijze, 73, 85.
Pregnall, J., 137.
Prowse Point, 52, 97, 101.
Proyart, 150, 153, 154, 155, 157.
Pugh J., 31.
Purton, A. H., 162.

Querrieu, 143, 144.

Ransley, J., 137.
Ratcliffe, R. J., 131.
Rattray, J. S., 171, 178, 180, 181.
Raveoeck, 86, 88, 89, 92.
Rawlinson, Sir Henry, 201.
Reardon, E. V., 170.
Red Lodge, 100, 107.
Red Wood, 188.
Reed, J. S., 134, 147, 196.
Regina Camp, 51, 54.
Reginald Wood, 150, 151, 157, 158.
Remilly Werquin, 72.
Rhodes, J. E., 175.
Ribemont, 121, 122, 123, 124, 126, 129, 130.
Richards, A. H., 129, 146.
Richmond Wood, 151.
Rifle House, 44.
Robert Wood, 155.
Robinson, J. A., 118.
Rock, C. W., 153, 154, 155, 163.
Rogers, L., 90, 92.
Roisel, 186, 187.
Romarin, 51, 54, 97, 110.
Ronssoy, 192, 200.
Rooney, A., 183.
Ruddock, W. C. G., 48, 73 76, 104, 108, 124, 125, 139, 153, 193.
Rue du Bois Salient, 35 36.
Rule, A. L., 66.

Saddington, J., 109.
Sadler, B. T., 10.
Sailly Laurette, 159, 160.
Salisbury Plains, 4.
Schnitzel Farm, 46, 57.
Seaforth Farm, 48, 52, 58, 64.
Seninghem, 110, 112.
Sercus, 72.
Shankhill Camp, 105.
Sharland, C. F., 88.
Shalless, C. W., 137.
Shearing, J., 196.
Smith, C. E., 65.
Smith, H. A. H., 107, 158.
Smith, H. J., 107.
Smith, R. H., 36.
Smith, V. C., 177.
Somme River, 114, 115, 125, 135 143, 148, 150, 159, 160, 161, 163, 164, 168, 184, 186.
Spellman, J., 43.
Spinks, T., 137.
Springfield, 75.
Spur Wood, 168.
St. Omer, 6, 41, 113.
St. Quentin Canal, 199.
St. Yves, 45, 107.
Statton, P. C., 155, 156, 189.
Stebbins, S. G., 129.

Steenje, 39.
Steenvoorde, 72.
Steenwerck, 41.
Stevens, E. W., 42, 43.
Stott, A. A., 96.
Styles, L., 156.
Sutcliffe, W. H., 137.
Suter, S. I., 25, 29, 30, 31.
Sutton, A. J., 174.
Suzanne, 164, 165, 167.
Swan, L. K., 161.
Swan, R. A., 101, 102, 118.
Sweeney, O. W., 65.

Tankadrome, 68.
Tapner, W., 65.
Tatinghem, 40, 41.
Teniswood, F. W., 92.
Terdeghem, 72.
Thompson, C. T., 137.
Thompson, H. L., 137.
Thurstans, A. C., 125.
Tincourt, 186.
Tir Anglais, 97.
Touquet Berthe, 44, 58.
Traynor, M. J., 137.
Treux, 126, 129.
Trois Marquets, 68.
Turner, L. E., 174.
Tyrell, J. T., 10, 24.

Ulna Trenches, 46, 56, 61, 64.
Ulrica Trench, 52.
Ungodly Avenue, 57.
Upchurch, W. J., 156.

Van Isacker's Farm, 74, 86.
Vaudringhem, 68.
Vaux Wood, 167, 168.

Vendhuille, 190, 199.
Vieux Berquin, 97.
Ville-sur-Ancre, 129, 131, 132, 134.
Villers Bretonneux, 135, 136, 138, 139, 142.
Vlamertinghe, 72, 73, 82, 84.

Walker, A. E., 137.
Walters, R. C., 52, 88, 163, 166, 171.
Warfusée Abancourt, 150.
Warneton, 68, 97, 98, 100, 107.
Warneton Tower, 98.
Warneton Track, 101.
Waterfields, 88, 89, 90.
Waterlands Camp, 97.
Wellington Avenue, 35.
Wellington Dump, 36.
Weston, E. D., 77, 200.
Wez Macquart, 29, 34.
Whitaker, M. H. O., 88, 111, 116, 136, 161, 178.
Whitney, A. J., 66.
Whittle, E. A., 137, 166.
Williams, H. A., 137.
Willow Trench, 193, 194, 195, 199.
Wilson, R. K., 43, 88.
Winburn, H. S., 65.
Winnezeele, 72.
Wizernes, 68.
Woolley, W. G. E., 109.
Wulverghem, 66.

Yakko Copse, 166, 167.
Ypres, 56, 72, 73, 74, 84, 94, 112.

Zombo Trench, 179, 180.
Zonnebeke Creek, 74, 84, 85, 95.
Zonnebeke Road, 92, 94.

John Vail, Government Printer, Tasmania.

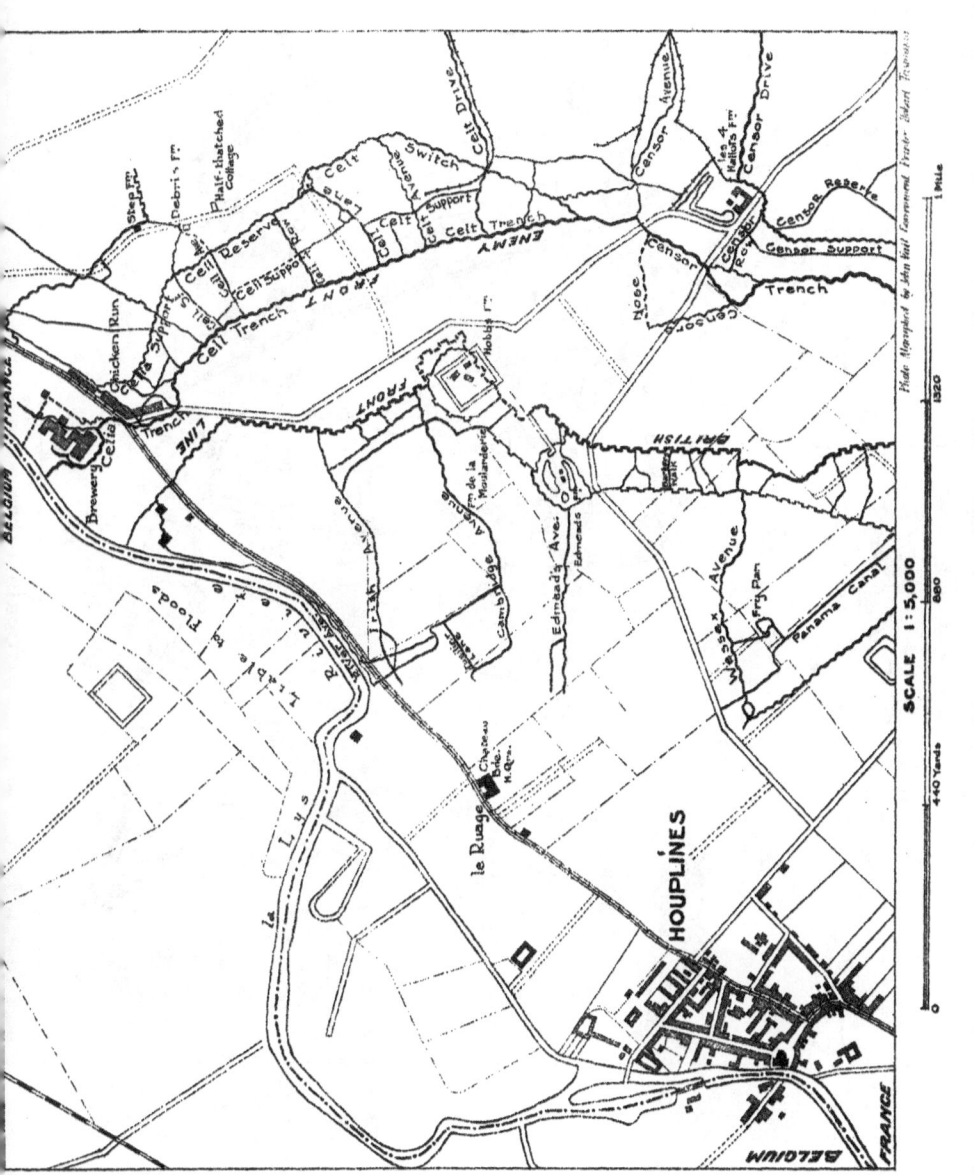

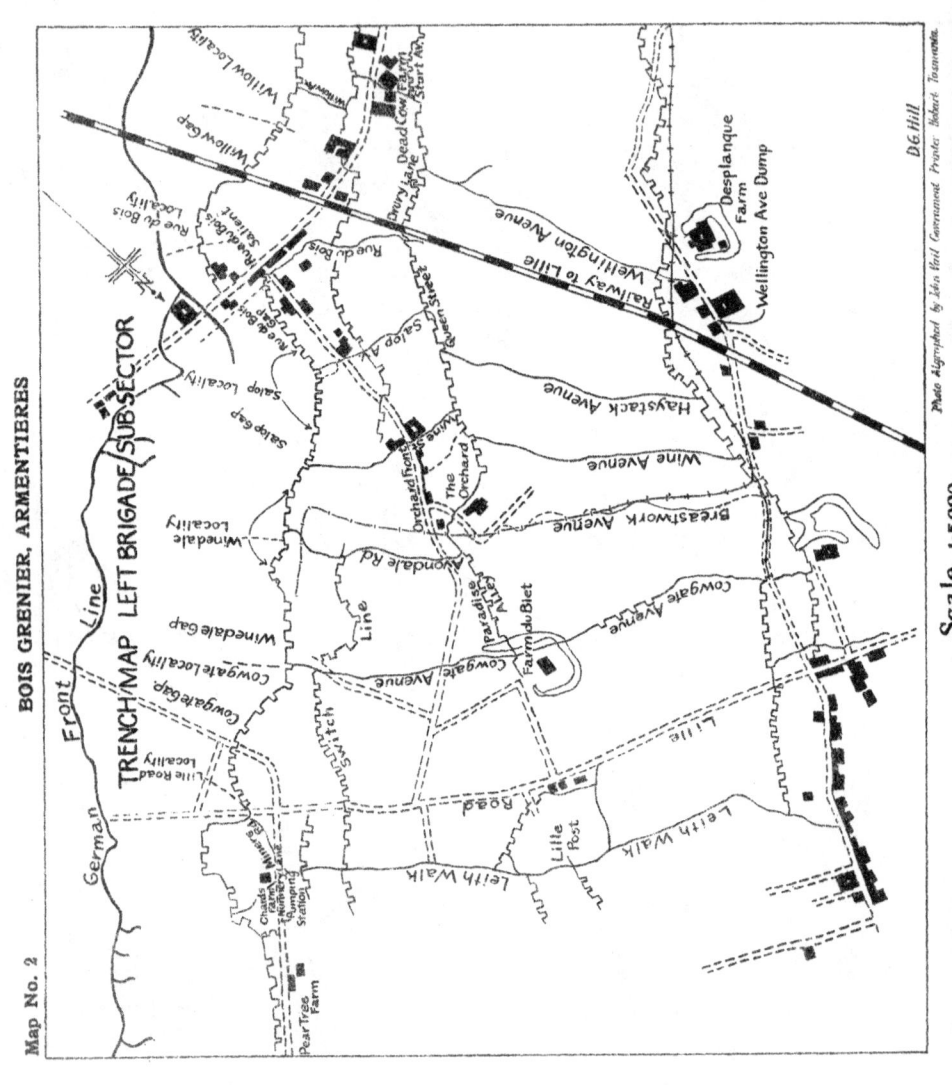

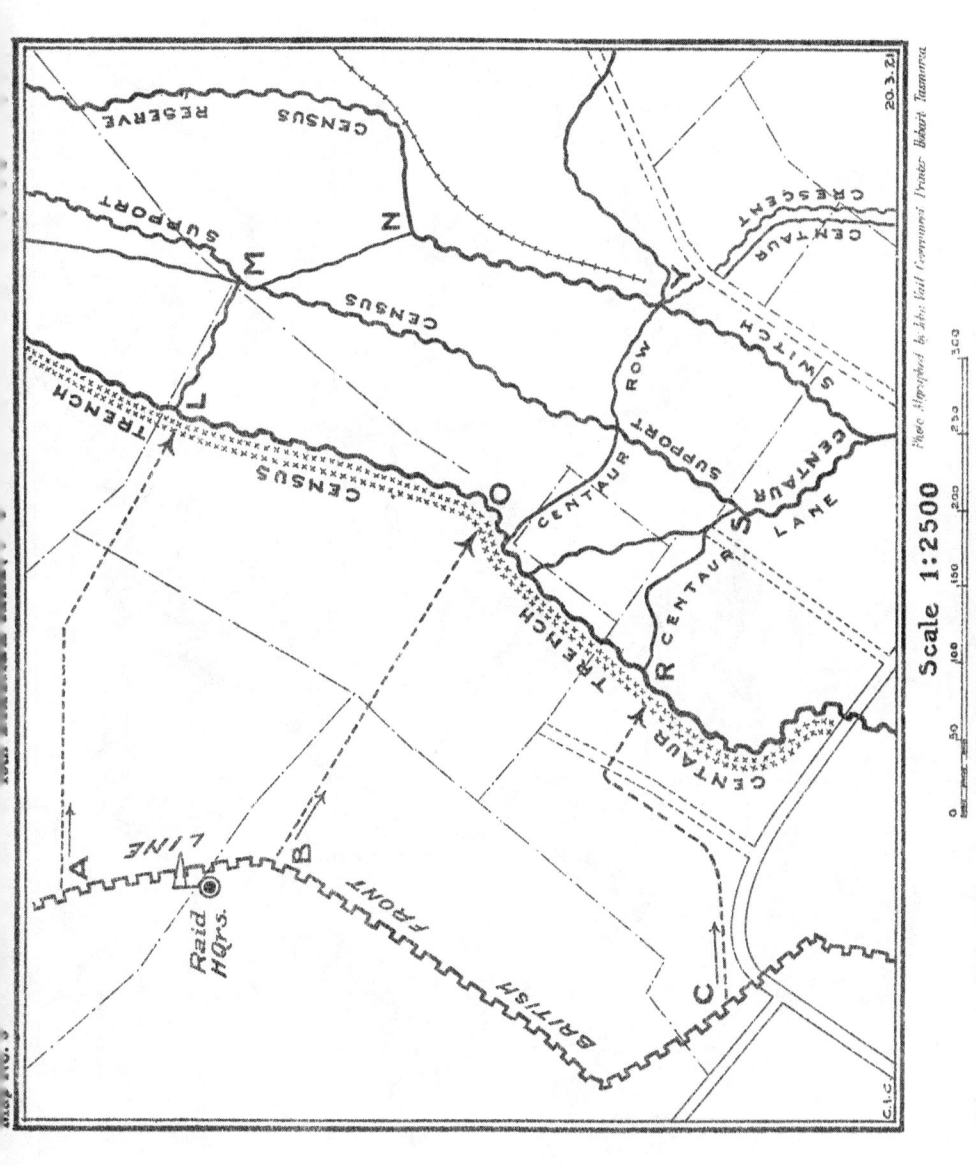

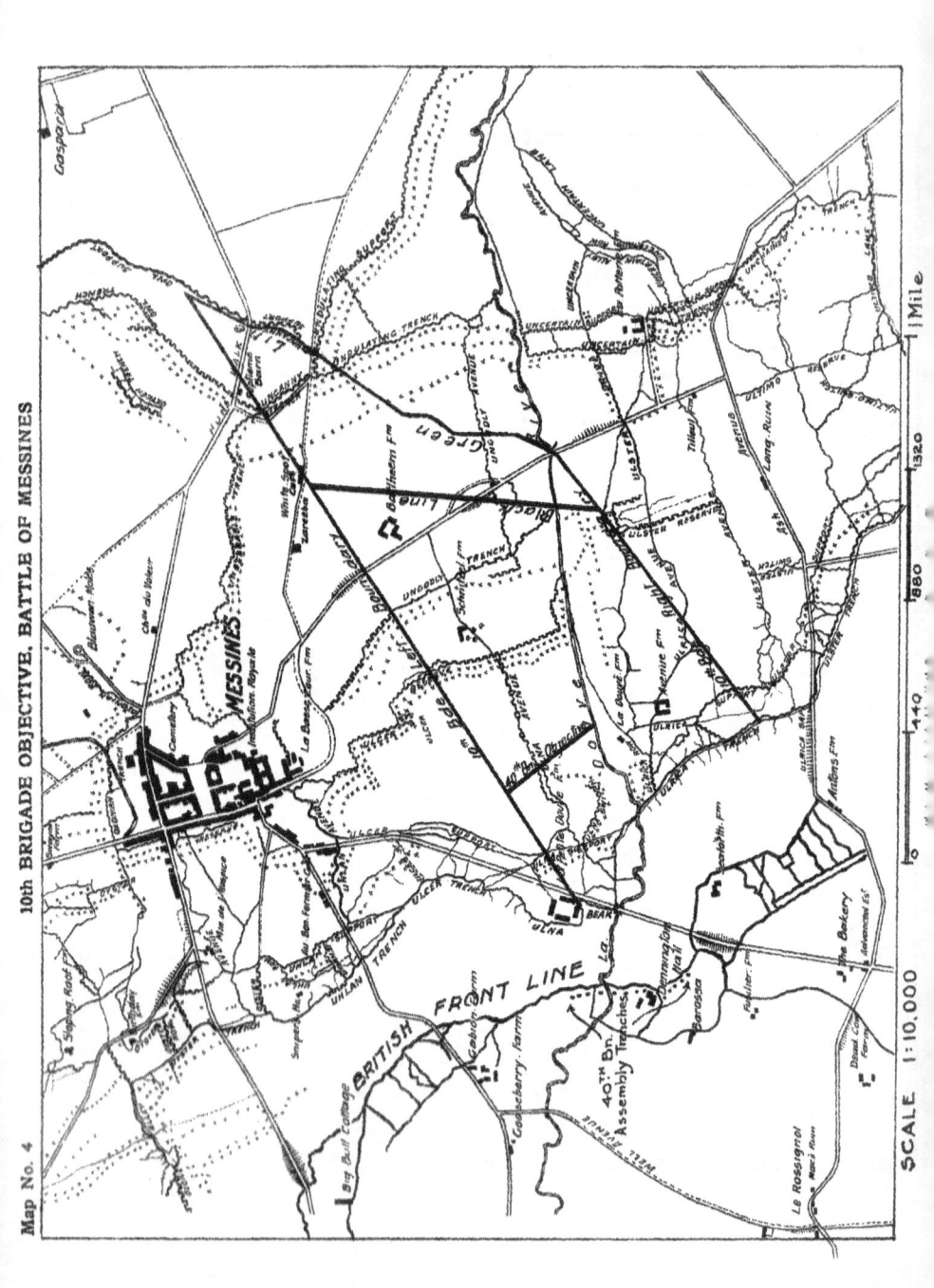

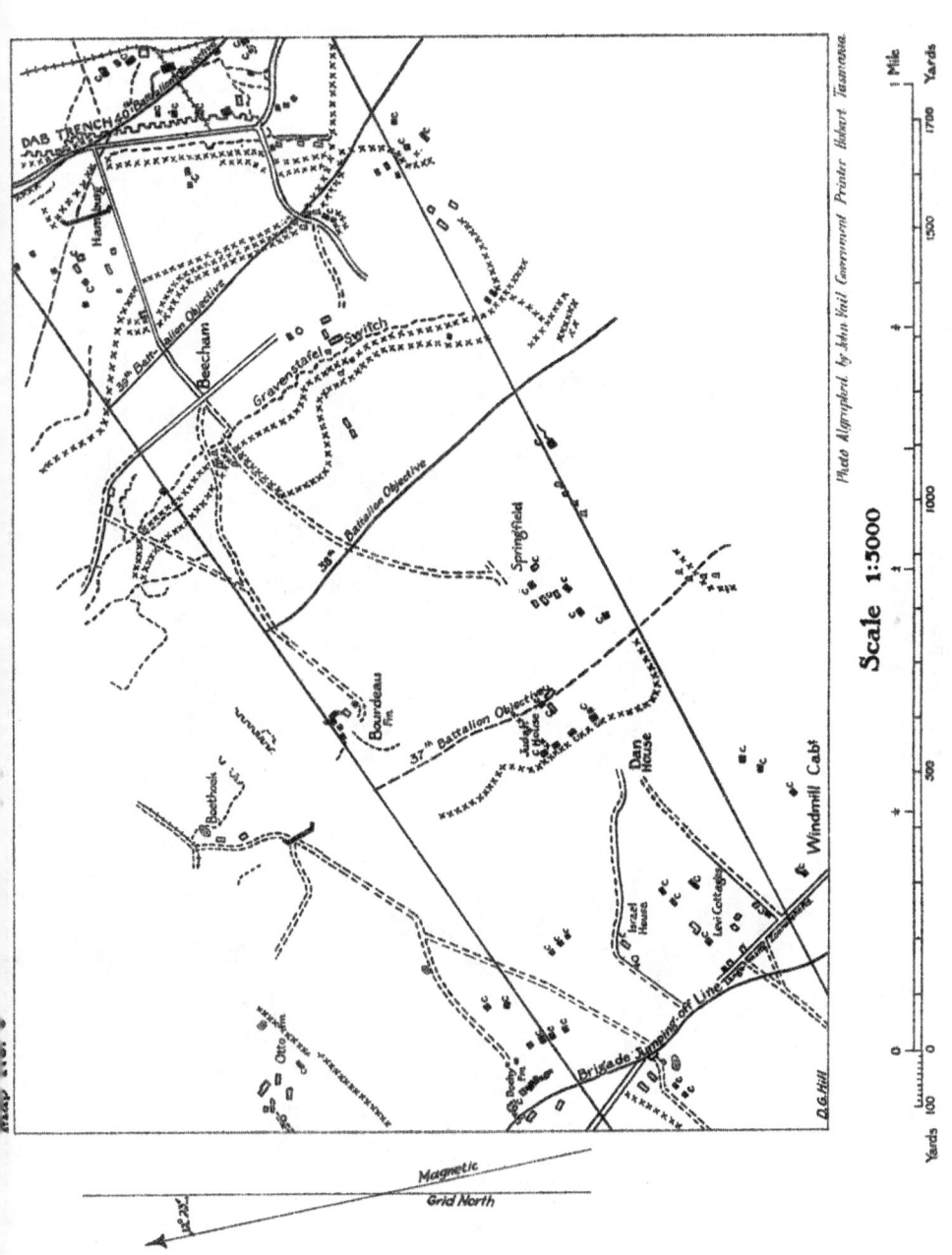

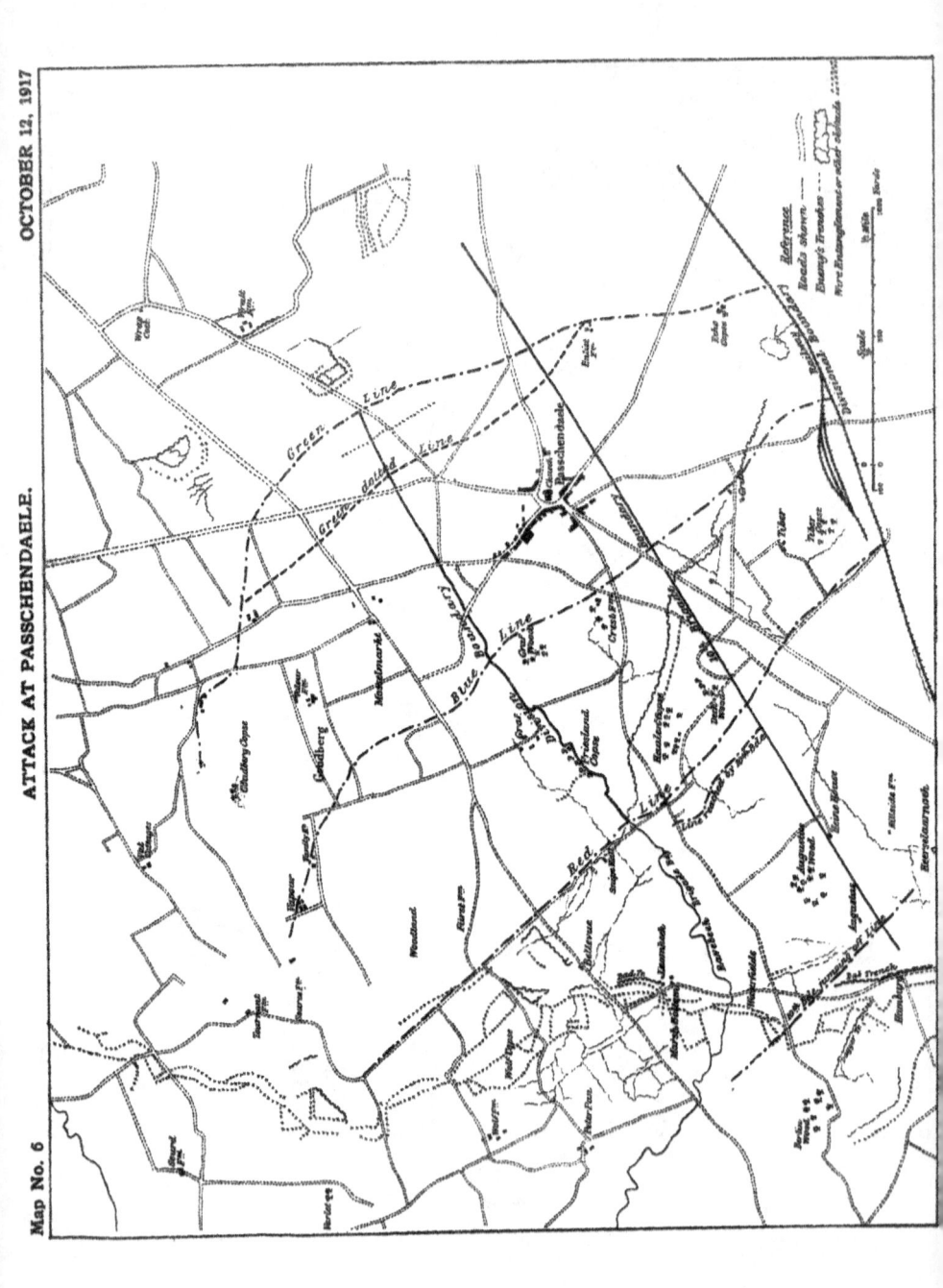

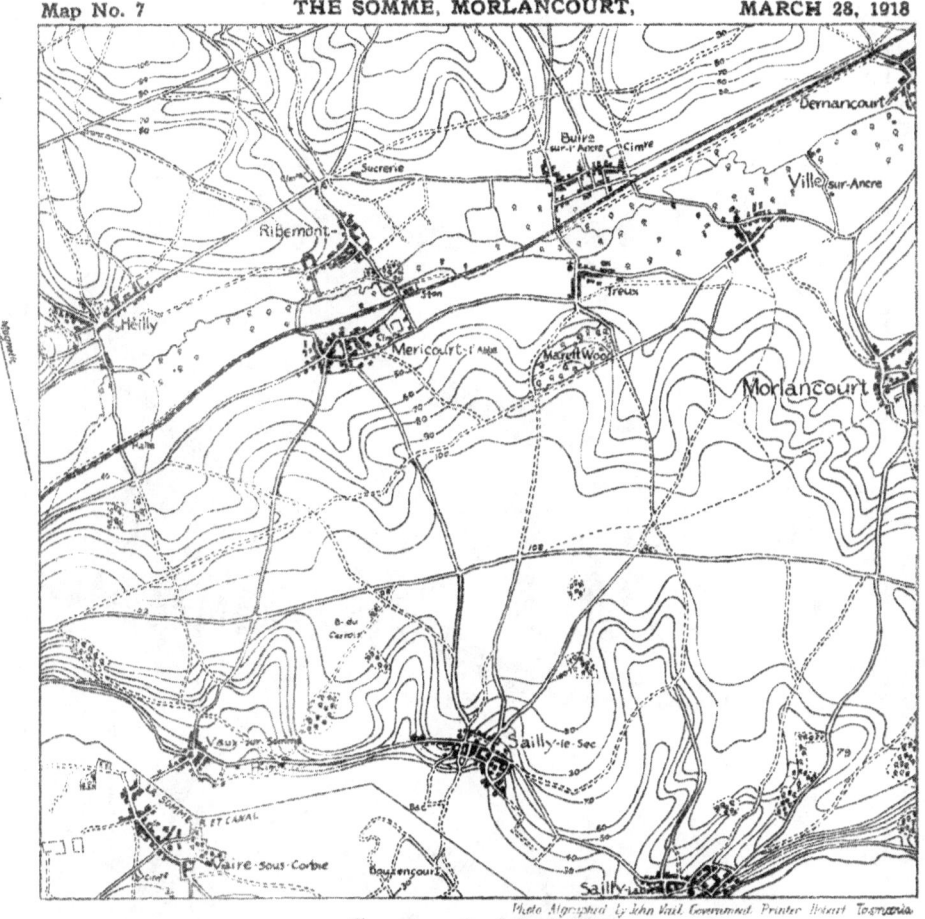

Map No. 7 THE SOMME, MORLANCOURT, MARCH 28, 1918

Scale 1:40,000

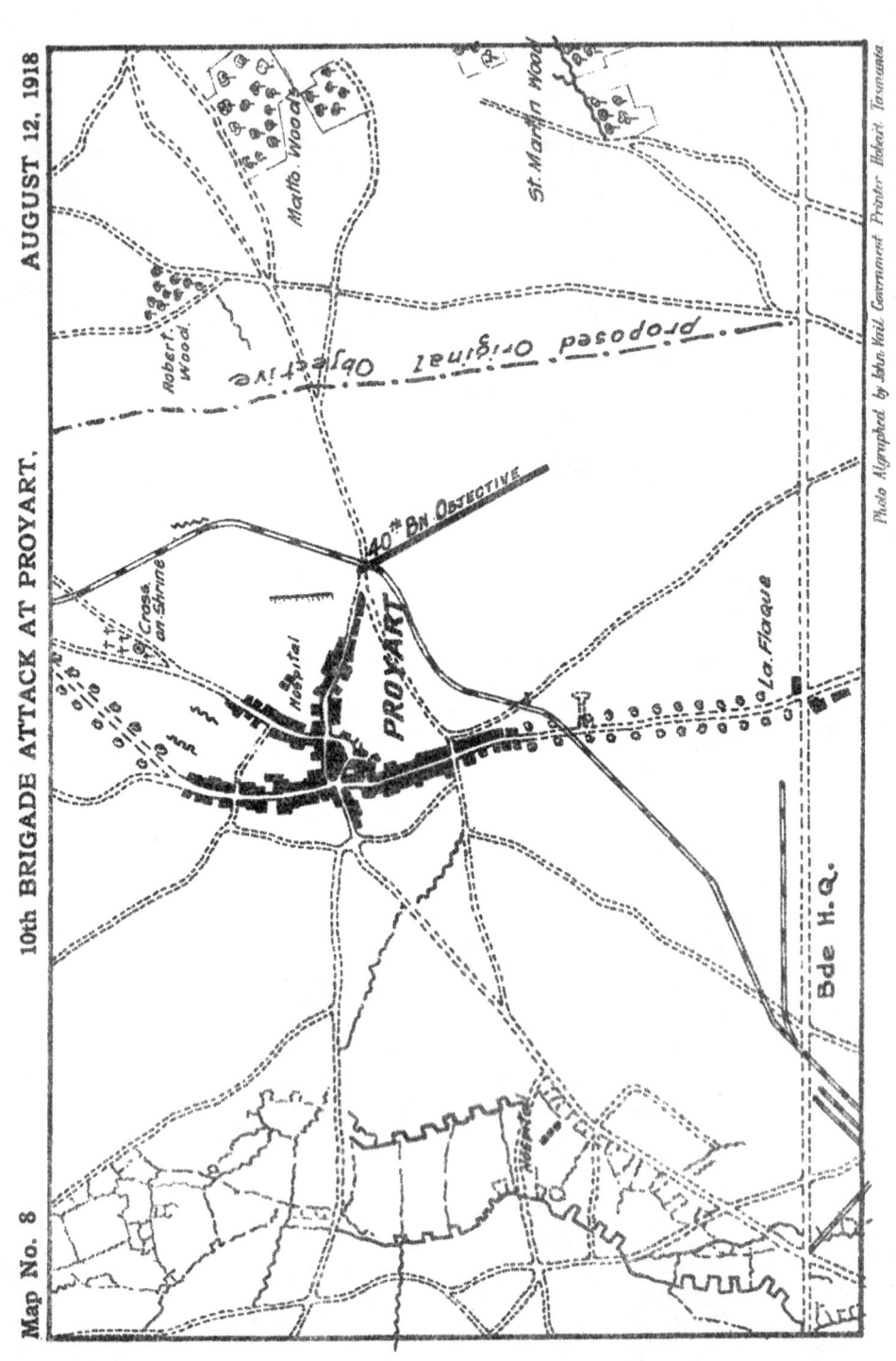

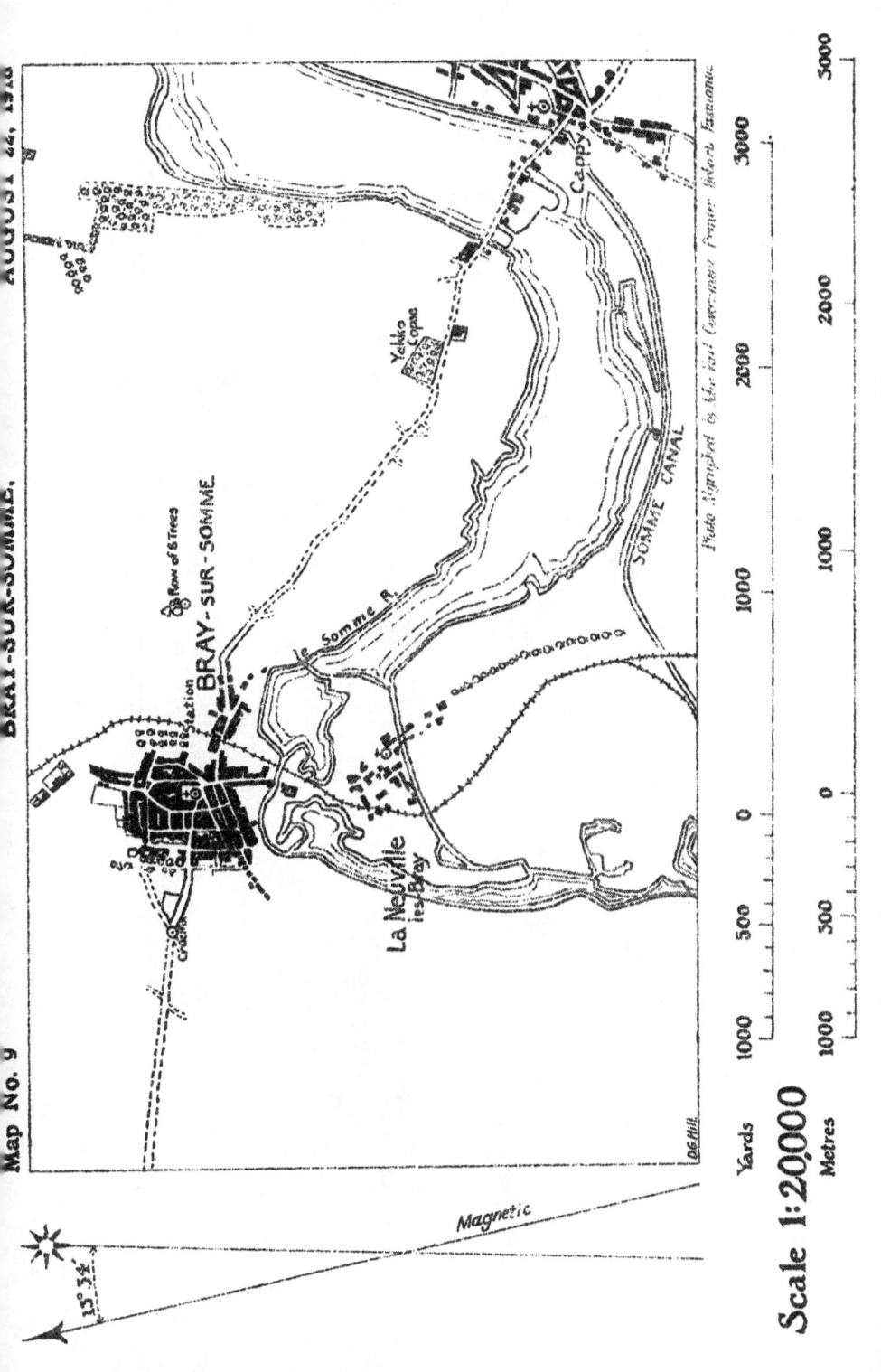

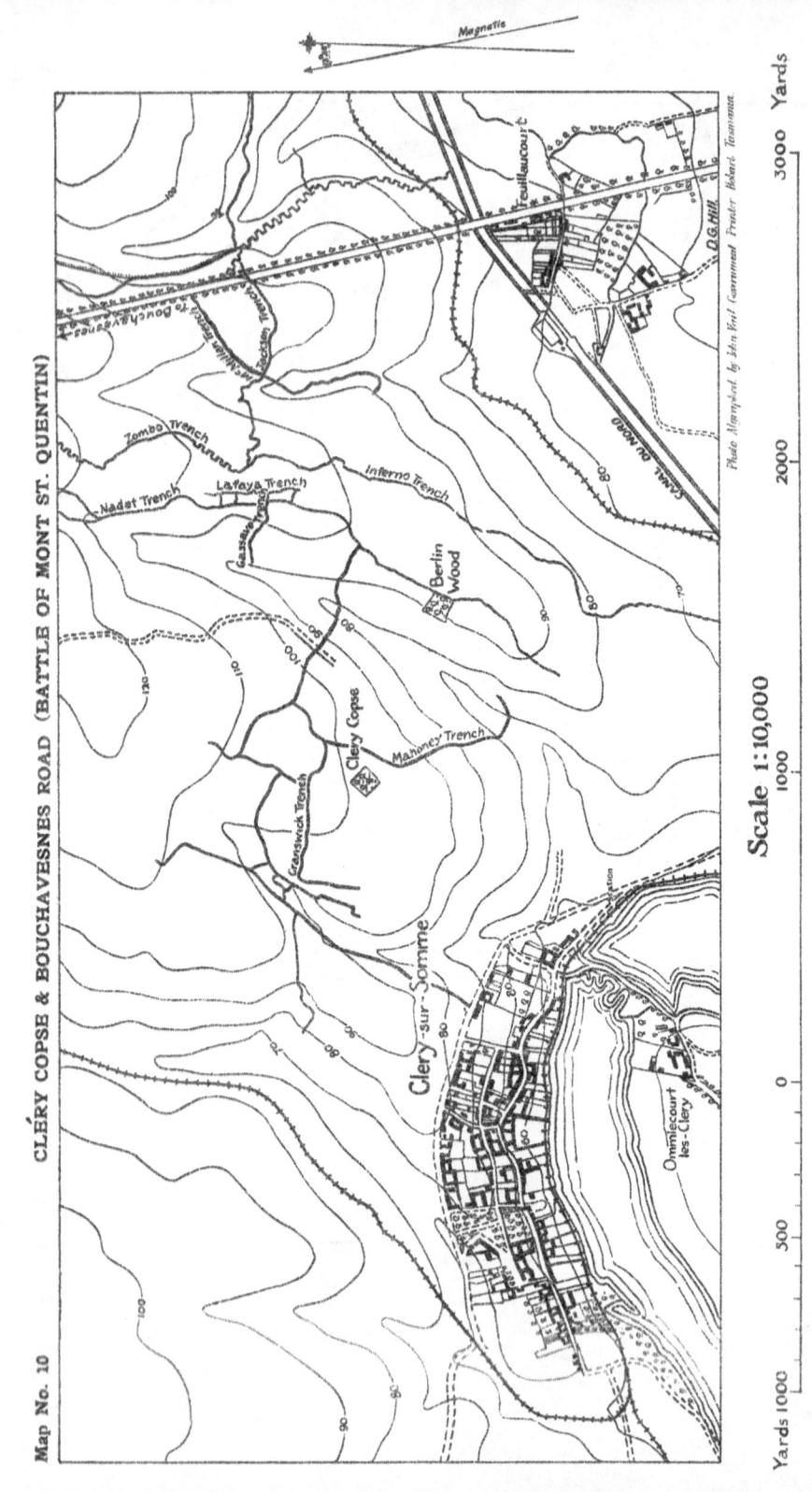

Map No. 10a SKETCH SHEWING POINTS REFERRED TO
BY CORPORAL MASTERMAN (page 175)

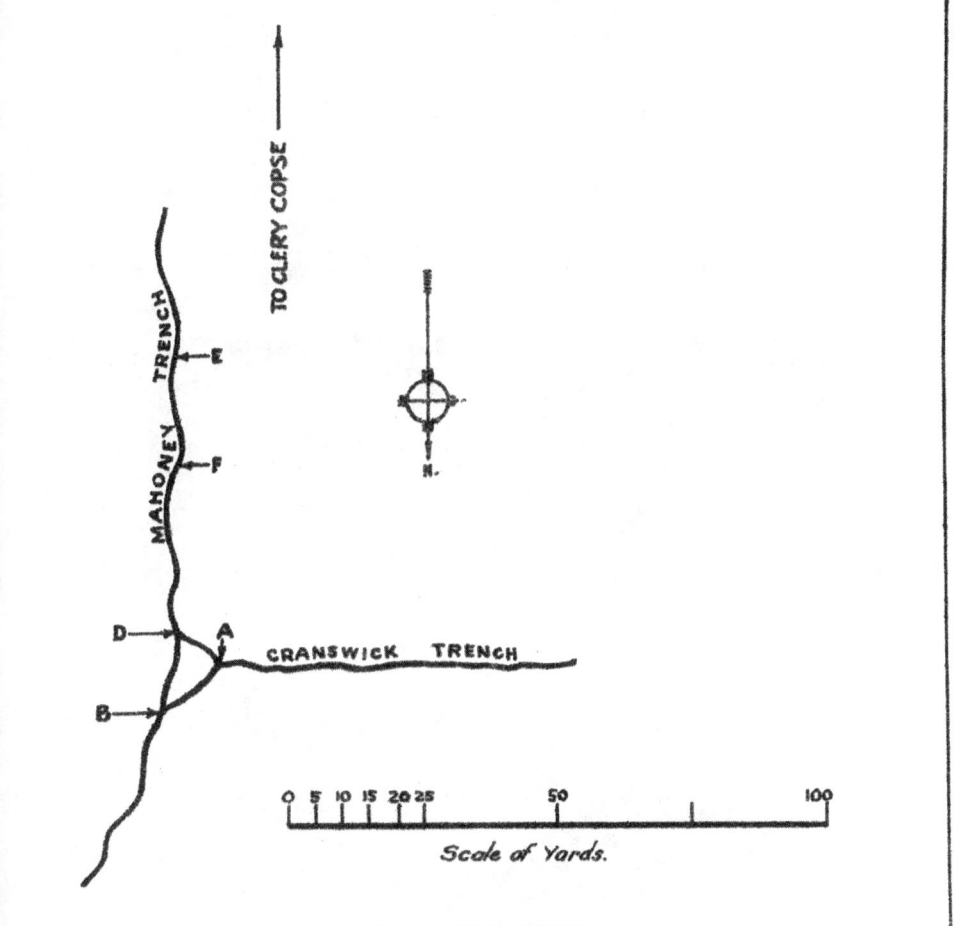

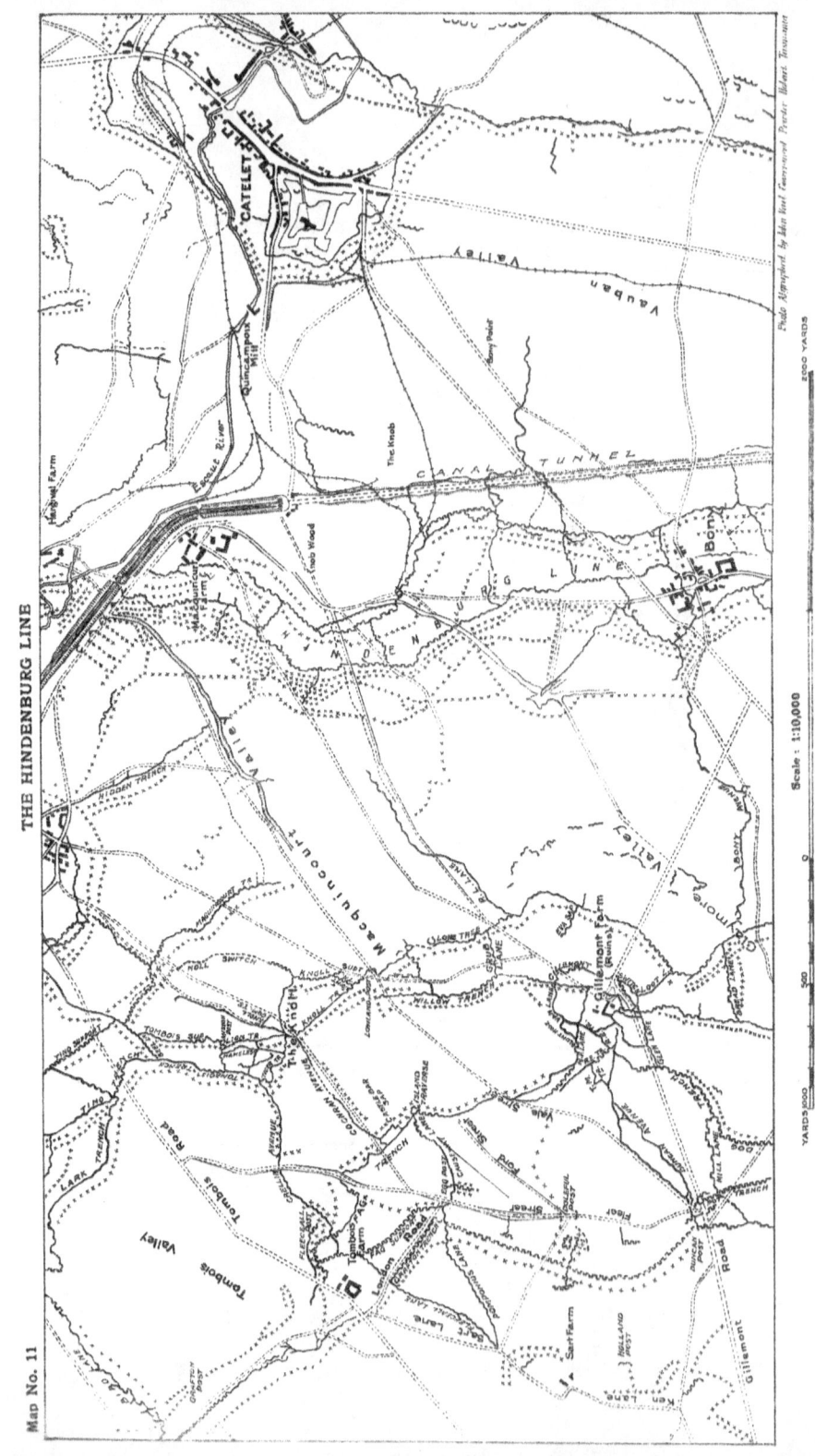

www.ingramcontent.com/pod-product-compliance
Lightning Source LLC
Chambersburg PA
CBHW021837220426
43663CB00005B/282